Injia on Sentencing in Papua New Guinea and the Pacific

Salamo Injia

University of Papua New Guinea Press and Bookshop, 2013

Injia on Sentencing in Papua New Guinea and the Pacific

ISBN: 978-9980-87-900-4

PUBLISHED BY:

The University of Papua New Guinea Press and Bookshop
PO Box 413
University PO, NCD
Papua New Guinea
Email: upngpress@gmail.com

FOREWORD

This textbook is one of six (6) textbooks written under my hand and supervision:

'Injia on Criminal Offences in Papua New Guinea and the Pacific'

'Injia on Criminal Practice and Procedure in Papua New Guinea and the Pacific'

'Injia on Sentencing in Papua New Guinea and the Pacific'

'Injia on Statutory Interpretation in Papua New Guinea and the Pacific'

'Injia on Coronial Proceedings in Papua New Guinea and the Pacific'

'Injia on Investigatory Practice in Papua New Guinea and the Pacific'

Each of those textbooks is an effort to offer to Judicial officers, legal practitioners and students of law a comprehensive set of principles and practical guidelines on criminal law and practice in Papua New Guinea and the Pacific. The work undertaken under the auspices of AusAID through the PNG-Australia Law and Justice Partnership Project is an extension of a similar project undertaken previously in writing the textbook *Criminal Law and Practice in Papua New Guinea* co-authored by myself, Professor Don Chalmers, Dr Weisbrot and Justice Andrew.

The textbooks will be of great benefit to the criminal justice system in Papua New Guinea and the Pacific and specifically will assist judges, magistrates, lawyers, law students and police officers in the performance of their duties.

The assistance of AusAID and its development practitioner Mr Errol Gibson who provided research and spent countless hours in the production of these textbooks is acknowledged.

Sir Salamo Injia, Kt

Chief Justice of Papua New Guinea

7th June 2013

TABLE OF CONTENTS

TABLE OF CONTENTS

TABLE OF CONTENTS

TABLE OF CONTENTS

TABLE OF CONTENTS

TABLE OF CONTENTS

TABLE OF CONTENTS

TABLE OF CONTENTS

TABLE OF CONTENTS

TABLE OF CONTENTS

TABLE OF CONTENTS

TABLE OF CONTENTS

TABLE OF CONTENTS

TABLE OF CONTENTS

Page

APPEALS AGAINST SENTENCE

INTRODUCTION TO SENTENCING

[1.0] CONSTITUTIONAL PROVISIONS

The starting point in relation to sentencing must be section 37(2) of the *Constitution of the Independent State of Papua New Guinea* that states:

> 'Except, subject to any Act of the Parliament[1] to the contrary, in the case of the offence commonly known as contempt of court[2], nobody may be convicted of an offence that is not defined by, and the penalty for which is not prescribed by, a written law'.[3]

Furthermore, section 42 of that Constitution states (in part):

> '(1) No person shall be deprived of his personal liberty except –
>
> (b) in the execution of the sentence or order of a court in respect of an offence of which he has been found guilty, or in the execution of the order of a court of record punishing him for contempt of itself or another court or tribunal'.

[2.0] INTERPRETATION ACT

Section 14 of the *Interpretation Act* (Ch. 2) states:

> 'Where a statutory provision specifies a penalty for an offence[4] against the provision, the penalty is the maximum penalty that may be imposed for that offence'.

---

[1] The term 'Act of the Parliament' means a law (other than a Constitutional Law) made by the Parliament, and includes a subordinate legislative enactment made under any such law, see section 8 and Schedule 1.1.2 of the *Constitution of the Independent State of Papua New Guinea*.

[2] Refer also to the chapter titled 'Contempt Of Court' in the text titled 'Injia on Criminal Practice and Procedure in Papua New Guinea and the Pacific'.

[3] See *Acting Public Prosecutor v Uname Aumane and others* [1980] PNGLR 510.

[4] The term 'offence' in relation to a law is defined in section 3(1) of the *Interpretation Act* (Ch. 2) as including:
'a breach or contravention of, or a failure to comply with, the law'.

The term 'law' is also defined in section 3(1) as meaning:
'a law of Papua New Guinea, and includes –
(a) the underlying law; and
(b) subordinate enactments'.

A 'subordinate enactment' is an instrument (whether of a legislative nature or not) made under an Act such as a regulation, see also section 3(1).

Section 15 states:

'(1) The penalty, pecuniary or other, set out –

(a) at the foot of a section of a statutory provision; or

(b) at the foot of a subsection of a section of a statutory provision, but not at the foot of the section,

means that a contravention of the section or the subsection, as the case may be, whether by act or omission, is an offence against the provision punishable on conviction by a penalty not exceeding the penalty mentioned.

(2) Where the penalty is expressed to apply to a part only of the section or subsection, it applies to that part only'.

Section 16 states:

'(1) Where in, or at the foot of, any section or part of a section of a statutory provision the expression "Default penalty" appears, it indicates that a person who is convicted of an offence against that provision in relation to that section or part –

(a) is guilty of a further offence against that provision if the offence continues after he is so convicted; and

(b) is liable to an additional penalty, for each day during which the offence so continues, of not more than the amount expressed in the section or part as the amount of the default penalty.

(2) Where an offence is committed by a person by reason of his failure to comply with a section or part of a statutory provision referred to in Subsection (1) by or under which he is required or directed to do anything within a particular period, the offence shall be deemed, for the purposes of that subsection, to continue for so long as the thing required or directed to be done by him remains undone, notwithstanding that the period has elapsed'.

Section 17 states:

'Where under a statutory provision imprisonment may be awarded for an offence, it may be awarded with or without hard labour'.

INTRODUCTION TO SENTENCING

[3.0] CRIMINAL CODE ACT[5]

[3.1] SAVING OF POWERS OF COURTS UNDER OTHER ACTS

Section 6 of the *Criminal Code Act* (Ch. 262) states:

> 'This Act does not limit or affect in any way any provision of any other Act conferring on a court a power to pass a sentence or impose a punishment or make an order in addition to or instead of a sentence or punishment prescribed by the Code, or otherwise to deal with an accused person'.

[3.2] TYPES OF PUNISHMENT

The following statutory provisions only apply to those offences as provided for by the *Criminal Code* (Ch. 262).[6]

Section 18 of the *Criminal Code* (Ch. 262) states:

> 'The punishments that may be inflicted under this Code are –
>
> (a) death; or
>
> (b) imprisonment with hard labour; or
>
> (c) imprisonment without hard labour; or

---

[5] The power of disposition of accused persons dealt with under the *Criminal Code* (Ch. 262) is exclusively and exhaustively provided for therein, see *SCR No. 2 of 1981; Re s19(1)(f) Criminal Code (Ch. 262)* [1982] PNGLR 150, [1982] PGSC 18.

[6] Section 2 of the *Criminal Code Act* (Ch. 262) states:

> 'The provisions contained in Schedule 1 are the law of Papua New Guinea with respect to the matters dealt with in that Schedule'.

Section 6 of that Act states:

> 'This Act does not limit or affect in any way any provision of any other Act conferring on a court a power to pass a sentence or impose a punishment or make an order in addition to or instead of a sentence or punishment prescribed by the Code, or otherwise to deal with an offender'.

As regards the law in relation to 'Acts in pari materia', refer to the section titled 'Extrinsic Aids' in the chapter titled 'Aids To Interpretation' in the text titled 'Injia on Statutory Interpretation in Papua New Guinea and the Pacific'.

(d) detention in an institution as defined in –

(i) the *Child Welfare Act 1961*; or

(ii) the *Juvenile Courts Act 1991*[7];

(e) fine; or

(f) finding security to keep the peace and be of good behaviour; or

(g) restriction of movement'.

[3.3] SENTENCING DISCRETION

Section 19 of the *Criminal Code* (Ch. 262)[8] states:

> 'In the construction of this Code, it is to be taken that, except when it is otherwise expressly provided –
>
> (aa) a person liable to death[9] may be sentenced to imprisonment[10] for life or for any shorter term; and
>
> (a) a person liable to imprisonment for life or for any other period, may be sentenced to imprisonment for any shorter term; and
>
> (b) a person liable to imprisonment may be sentenced to pay a fine[11] not exceeding K2,000.00 in addition to, or instead of, imprisonment; and

---

7 See section 30 of the *Juvenile Courts Act 1991* ['Powers Of Court To Make Orders'].

Therefore, the punishments as provided for by section 30 apply to the offences as specified in the *Criminal Code* (Ch. 262).

8 The National Court does not have the discretion not to record a conviction before proceeding to determine the appropriate sentence as provided for by section 19 of the *Criminal Code* (Ch. 262), see *Public Prosecutor v Arthur Jawodimbari and Monty Derari* (2006) SC891, [2006] PGSC 28.

9 Refer also to the section titled 'Sentence Of Death' in the chapter titled 'Sentencing Options'.

10 Refer also to the section titled 'Imprisonment' in the chapter titled 'Sentencing Options'.

11 Refer also to the section titled 'Fine' in the chapter titled 'Sentencing Options'.

(c) a person sentenced on conviction on indictment[12] to pay a fine may be sentenced –

(i) to be imprisoned until the fine is paid, in addition to any other punishment to which he is sentenced; and

(ii) instead of being sentenced to be imprisoned until the fine is paid – to be imprisoned for a term (not exceeding the term provided for in Subparagraph (i)) if the fine is not paid within a specified period (which period may be extended as the court thinks fit); and

(d) a person convicted on indictment of an offence not punishable with death may –

(i) instead of, or in addition to, any punishment to which he is liable – be ordered to enter into his own recognizance, with or without sureties, in such amount as the court thinks proper, to keep the peace and be of good behaviour for a time fixed by the court; and

(ii) comply with such other conditions as the court may, in its discretion, impose[13]; and

(e) a person convicted of any offence on summary conviction[14] may, instead of being sentenced to any punishment to which he is liable, be discharged on his entering into his own recognizances, with or without sureties, in such amount as the court thinks proper, to keep the peace and be of good behaviour for a term not exceeding one year[15]; and

---

[12] The term 'indictment' is defined in section 1(1) of the *Criminal Code* (Ch. 262) as meaning:

> 'a written charge preferred against an accused person in order to his trial before some court other than a court of summary jurisdiction'.

The term 'court of summary jurisdiction' is defined in section 3(1) of the *Interpretation Act* (Ch. 2) as meaning:

> 'a District Court'.

[13] Refer also to the section titled 'Good Behaviour Bond in the chapter titled 'Sentencing Options'.

[14] The term 'summary conviction' is defined in section 1(1) of the *Criminal Code* (Ch. 262) as meaning:

> 'conviction by a court of summary jurisdiction'.

The term 'court of summary jurisdiction' is defined in section 3(1) of the *Interpretation Act* (Ch. 2) as meaning:

> 'a District Court'.

[15] Refer also to the section titled 'Good Behaviour Bond' in the chapter titled 'Sentencing Options'.

(f) when a person is convicted of an offence not punishable with death, the court may instead of passing sentence, discharge the accused person on his entering into his own recognizance, with or without sureties, in such sum as the court thinks proper, conditioned that –

(i) he shall appear and receive judgement at some future sittings of the court or when called on within a period specified by the court; and

(ii) if the court thinks fit, he shall in the meantime keep the peace and be of good behaviour and comply with such other conditions as the court, in its discretion, imposes[16].

(2) Imprisonment in accordance with Subsection (1)(c)(i), for non-payment of the fine –

(a) shall not extend for a term longer than two years; and

(b) shall not together with the fixed term of imprisonment (if any) extend for a term longer than the longest term for which he might be sentenced to be imprisoned without fine.

(3) In a case to which Subsection (1)(c) applies, the court may give such directions as it thinks proper as to the enforcement of the sentence of imprisonment, including a direction that the person sentenced appear at some future sittings of the court or when called on, by notice in the prescribed form, to show cause why the sentence of imprisonment should not be executed because of the non-payment of the fine within the specified period or any extension of that period.

(4) If under Subsection (3) a person directed to appear, or called on by notice in the prescribed form, to show cause why the sentence of imprisonment should not be executed because of the non-payment of the fine within the specified period, or any extension of that period, does not appear at the required time and place, a Judge[17] may issue a warrant to arrest him and to bring him before a Judge.

---

[16] Refer also to the section titled 'Good Behaviour Bond' in the chapter titled 'Sentencing Options'.

[17] The term 'Judge is defined in section 3(1) of the *Interpretation Act* (Ch. 2) as meaning:
'a Judge of the Supreme Court or of the National Court'.

(5) Imprisonment under Subsection (1)(d) for not entering into a recognizance –

(a) shall not extend for a term longer than one year; and

(b) shall not together with the fixed term of imprisonment (if any) extend for a term longer than the longest term for which he might be sentenced to be imprisoned without fine.

(6) When a court sentences any person convicted under Subsection (1)(d) to a term of imprisonment, it may further order that –

(a) the accused person be imprisoned for such portion of that term as it thinks proper; and

(b) the execution of the sentence for the remaining portion of the sentence be suspended[18] on his entering into a recognizance, with sureties if so directed, in accordance with Subsection (1)(d) but further conditioned that, if called on, he shall appear and receive judgement in respect of his service of the portion of the sentence.

(7) A Judge may, on being satisfied that the accused person has committed a breach of any of the conditions of a recognizance under Subsection (6), forfeit the recognizance and commit him to prison to undergo the suspended portion of his sentence or any part of it.

(8) [Repealed.]

(9) Notwithstanding that restriction of movement is not specified as a punishment for an offence, a court may, in addition to any other punishment or punishments imposed, also impose restriction of movement in accordance with Section 600.[19]

(10) When a court is considering the punishment or punishments to be imposed in any case it shall also consider whether, in the circumstances of the case, restriction of movement is an appropriate punishment'.

---

[18] Refer also to the subsection titled 'Suspended Sentence' in the section titled 'Imprisonment' in the chapter titled 'Sentencing Options'.

[19] Refer also to the section titled 'Restriction Of Movement Order' in the chapter titled 'Sentencing Options'.

[3.4] ADMINISTRATION OF ALLOCATUS

Section 593 of the *Criminal Code* (Ch. 262)[20] states:

> 'Where an accused person –
>
> (a) pleads that he is guilty of an offence[21]; or
>
> (b) on trial, is convicted of any offence,
>
> the proper officer shall ask him whether he has anything to say why sentence should not be passed on him, but an omission to do so does not invalidate the judgement'.

[3.5] PASSING SENTENCE

Section 596 of the *Criminal Code* (Ch. 262)[22] states:

> '(1) If a motion to arrest the judgement is not made or is dismissed[23], the court may –

---

[20] This statutory provision only applies in the National Court in relation to offences under the Code.

[21] Section 2 of the *Criminal Code* (Ch. 262) states:

> 'An act or omission that makes the person doing or making it liable to punishment is called an offence'.

However, this statutory provision only applies to offences contained in the *Criminal Code* (Ch. 262), see section 2 of the *Criminal Code Act* (Ch. 262).

Refer also to the subsection titled 'Acts in pari materia' in the section titled 'Extrinsic Aids' in the chapter titled 'Aids To Interpretation' in the text titled 'Injia on Statutory Interpretation in Papua New Guinea and the Pacific'.

See also:

- sections 3(1) and 15(1) of the *Interpretation Act* (Ch. 2); and
- *Public Employees Association of Papua New Guinea v Public Services Commission* [1983] PNGLR 206, [1983] PGSC 18; *SCR No. 1 of 1981; Re Inter-Group Fighting Act 1977* [1981] PNGLR 151 at 154 and *SCR No. 2 of 1989; Re Village Courts Act* (Ch. 44) [1988-89] PNGLR 491, [1988] PGSC 30.

[22] This statutory provision only applies in the National Court in relation to offences under the Code.

[23] Refer also to section 594 of the *Criminal Code* (Ch. 262) ['Arrest Of Judgement'].

As regards the law in relation to 'Wording Of Charges', refer to the chapter titled 'Charges' in the text titled 'Injia on Criminal Practice and Procedure in Papua New Guinea and the Pacific'.

(a) pass sentence on the accused person immediately; or

(b) discharge him on his recognizance, as provided for in this Code, conditioned that he shall appear and receive judgement –

(i) at some future sittings of the court; or

(ii) when called on by notice in the prescribed form.[24]

(2) If sentence is not passed immediately, a Judge[25] may at any subsequent sitting of the court at which the accused person is present pass sentence on him.

(3) If an accused person (including an accused person called on by notice in the prescribed form to appear and receive judgement in respect of a portion of his sentence suspended under any provision of this Code) does not appear at the required time and place, a Judge –

(a) may forfeit the accused person's recognizance and the recognizance of his sureties (if any); and

(b) may issue a warrant to arrest the accused person and to bring him before a Judge,

and such accused person may be arrested and brought before the court accordingly.

(4) Before passing sentence, the court may receive such evidence as it thinks proper in order to inform itself as to the proper sentence to be passed'.

---

[24] See *The State v Eric Papen (No. 1)* (2009) N3638, [2009] PGNC 57 and *The State v Elizabeth Teka (No. 2)* (2009) N3604, [2009] PGNC 46.

As regards a breach of such a recognizance, Order 3, Division 5 of the *Criminal Practice Rules 1989* states:

> '17. Upon proof by affidavit or otherwise that a convicted person who entered into a recognizance as ordered by the Court is in breach of the conditions of the recognizance, the Court may issue a warrant for his arrest.
>
> 18. A person arrested upon warrant issued under Rule 17 shall --
> (a) be brought before the Court or a Judge as soon as possible; or
> (b) if compliance with sub-rule (*a*) is not possible, then the person arrested shall be brought before a Magistrate to be dealt with according to law.
>
> 19. A warrant under Rule 17 shall be in accordance with Form 8'.

[25] The term 'Judge is defined in section 3(1) of the *Interpretation Act* (Ch. 2) as meaning:

> 'a Judge of the Supreme Court or of the National Court'.

[4.0] JUVENILE COURTS ACT

The scheme of the *Juvenile Courts Act 1991* is essentially to:

- protect;
- promote; and
- foster

the welfare and interest of children who violate the criminal law.[26]

One of the objects of this legislation is to provide a regulatory guideline and procedure in sentencing[27] of juvenile[28] offenders.[29]

The Juvenile Court has no jurisdiction to deal with:

- a person over 18 years of age[30]; or
- a juvenile charged with homicide, rape or other offence punishable by death[31].

Upon committal by the Juvenile Court to the National Court, the procedure is the same as that applied by the Juvenile Court.[32]

---

26 See *The State v Henry David* (2010) N4544, [2010] PGNC 210 and *The State v Desmond Gobe* (2011) N4547, [2011] PGNC 205.

27 As regards sentences imposed in the Juvenile Court, see Part VII of the *Juvenile Courts Act 1991*.

28 The term 'juvenile' is defined in section 2 of the *Juvenile Courts Act 1991* as meaning:
'a person aged not less than seven years and less than 18 years'.

29 See *The State v Henry David* (2010) N4544, [2010] PGNC 210 and *The State v Desmond Gobe* (2011) N4547, [2011] PGNC 205.

30 See section 16(1) of the *Juvenile Courts Act 1991* ['Limitation On Jurisdiction'].

31 See section 15(b) of the *Juvenile Courts Act 1991* ['General Jurisdiction'].

32 See section 18(2)(a) of the *Juvenile Courts Act 1991* ['Exercise Of Jurisdiction By National Court'].

INTRODUCTION TO SENTENCING

Section 24 of the *Juvenile Courts Act 1991* states (in part):

> 'A Court[33] –
>
> (a) shall permit a Juvenile Court Officer[34] to be present at any stage during its sitting; and
>
> (b) unless it is impracticable to secure the presence of a Juvenile Court Officer, may not pass sentence under Section 30'.

Section 30 states:

> '(1) Where the Court is satisfied that an offence has been proven, or where the juvenile admits the facts constituting the offence, the Court shall, after considering the pre-sentence report[35] and any other relevant matters before it, make any one or more of the orders specified under Subsection (2).

---

[33] The term 'Court' is defined in section 2 of the *Juvenile Courts Act 1991* as meaning:
'(a) a Juvenile Court; or
(b) a court of summary jurisdiction or the National Court, exercising the jurisdiction of a Juvenile Court under this Act'.

The term 'Juvenile Court' is also defined in section 2 as meaning:
'a Juvenile Court established under Section 5'.

The term 'court of summary jurisdiction' is defined in section 3(1) of the *Interpretation Act* (Ch. 2) as meaning:
'a District Court'.

The term 'the National Court' is also defined in section 3(1) as meaning:
'the National Court of Justice established by Section 163 (*establishment of the National Court*) of the *Constitution*'.

[34] The term 'Juvenile Court Officer' is defined in section 2 of the *Juvenile Courts Act 1991* as meaning:
'a Juvenile Court Officer appointed to the Juvenile Court Service under Section 9'.

[35] The term 'pre-sentencing report' is defined in section 2 of the *Juvenile Courts Act 1991* as meaning:
'a report prepared under Section 29'.

(2) Subject to this section, the Court may, in addition to any other powers under this Act[36] or any other law[37] –

(a) where it considers that the appearance of the juvenile before it has served the purposes of this Act – order the discharge of the juvenile without conviction; or

(b) enter a conviction but impose no further order and discharge the juvenile; or

(c) enter a conviction and order any one or more of the following:–

(i) having regard to the ability of the juvenile to pay, order him to pay a fine of an amount not exceeding K200.00[38];

(ii) having regard to the ability of the juvenile to pay, order him to pay damages of an amount not exceeding K200.00 to a person named in the order[39];

(iii) subject to Section 32[40], order that the juvenile be placed on probation in accordance with the *Probation Act 1979* for a period of not less than six months but not more than three years[41];

---

[36] The term 'this Act' is defined in section 2 of the *Juvenile Courts Act 1991* as including:
'the Regulations'.

[37] The term 'law' is defined in section 3(1) of the *Interpretation Act* (Ch. 2) as meaning:
'a law of Papua New Guinea, and includes –
(a) the underlying law; and
(b) subordinate enactments'.

Refer also to the section titled 'Underlying Law' in the chapter titled 'Sources Of Law' in the text titled 'Injia on Criminal Practice and Procedure in Papua New Guinea and the Pacific'.

A 'subordinate enactment' is an instrument (whether of a legislative nature or not) made under an Act such as a regulation, see also section 3(1).

[38] Refer also to the section titled 'Fine' in the chapter titled 'Sentencing Options'.

[39] Refer also to the section titled 'Compensation Order' in the chapter titled 'Sentencing Options'.

[40] The Heading to that section is 'Conditions Relating To Probation'.

[41] Refer also to the section titled 'Probation Order' in the chapter titled 'Sentencing Options'.

(iv) order that the juvenile be made a ward[42] of the Director of Child Welfare[43];

(v) after taking into account the factors specified in Section 31[44], order that the juvenile be made a ward and committed to the care of the Director[45], with a directive that the ward be committed to custody in a juvenile institution selected by the Director;

(vi) after taking into account the factors specified in Section 31, and subject to Subsection (5), sentence the juvenile to a term of imprisonment in the juvenile section of a corrective institution[46].[47]

(3) The total of time periods specified in any combination of orders under Subsection (2), with the exception of an order of wardship under Subsection (2)(c)(iv), shall not exceed three years.

(4) A sentence of custody in a juvenile institution[48] under Subsection (2)(c)(v) –

---

[42] The term 'ward' is defined in section 2 of the *Juvenile Courts Act 1991* as meaning:
'a juvenile –
(a) committed under this Act to the care of the Director; or
(b) made a ward of the Director in accordance with an order of a Court'.

[43] The term 'Director of Child Welfare' is defined in section 2 of the *Juvenile Courts Act 1991* as meaning:
'the person appointed as such under the *Child Welfare Act 1961*'.

[44] The Heading to section 31 is 'Factors To Be Taken Into Account In Committal To Imprisonment Or Custody'.

[45] The term 'Director' is defined in section 2 of the *Juvenile Courts Act 1991* as meaning:
'the Director of the Juvenile Courts Service'.

[46] The term 'corrective institution' is defined in section 3(1) of the *Interpretation Act* (Ch. 2) as meaning:
'premises declared to be a corrective institution under the *Correctional Service Act 1995*'.

[47] Refer also to the section titled 'Imprisonment' in the chapter titled 'Sentencing Options'.

[48] The term 'juvenile institution' is defined in section 2 of the *Juvenile Courts Act 1991* as meaning:
'a juvenile institution approved under Section 47'.

(a) shall not be made unless the Magistrate[49] is satisfied that the Superintendent[50] of the institution is capable of accepting the juvenile; and

(b) shall not be for any definite period, but shall be subject to a review in accordance with Part VIII[51] at intervals not exceeding six months or such lesser period as the Court orders; and

(c) in any case shall determine when the juvenile attains the age of 18 years, at which time he shall be released.

(5) A term of imprisonment under Subsection (2)(c)(vi) –

(a) shall not be made unless the magistrate is satisfied that the corrective institution has the appropriate facilities for the imprisonment of the juvenile according to Section 48[52]; and

(b) shall not include hard labour or exceed 18 months cumulatively; and

(c) shall be subject to a custody review in accordance with Part VIII at intervals not exceeding six months or such lesser period as the Court orders.

(6) Where a Court orders a term of imprisonment under this section, the Court may –

(a) in addition, make some other order under Subsection (2); and

(b) order the suspension of the term of imprisonment and place the juvenile on probation with the condition that the other order is complied with.

---

49 The term 'magistrate' is defined in section 2 of the *Juvenile Courts Act 1991* as meaning:

- a Juvenile Court Magistrate.

  The term 'Juvenile Court Magistrate' is defined in section 2 of the *Juvenile Courts Act 1991* as meaning a Magistrate appointed as such under Section 6; or

- a Magistrate of a court of summary jurisdiction exercising jurisdiction in accordance with Section 17 [The Heading to that section is 'Exercise Of Jurisdiction By Courts Of Summary Jurisdiction'].

  The term 'court of summary jurisdiction' is defined in section 3(1) of the *Interpretation Act* (Ch. 2) as meaning a District Court.

50 The term 'Superintendent' is defined in section 2 of the *Juvenile Courts Act 1991* as meaning: 'the person in charge of a juvenile institution or remand centre'.

51 The Heading to Part VIII is 'Review And Variation Of Orders'.

52 The Heading to section 48 is 'Juvenile Section Of A Corrective Institution'.

(7) Where the other order referred to in Subsection (6) is not carried out, the term of imprisonment originally imposed shall take effect.

(8) Where an order is made under Subsection (2)(c)(iii), (iv) or (v), the Court may order that the juvenile is detained in a remand centre until the Director, the Director of Child Welfare or a probation officer[53], as the case may be, is able to accept responsibility for the juvenile as ordered'.

[5.0] GENERAL PRINCIPLES

It is the responsibility of the National Parliament and the House of Representatives of the Autonomous Region of Bougainville to determine:

- what behaviour constitutes an offence[54]; and
- what penalties may apply for committing an offence.[55]

---

[53] The term 'probation officer' is defined in section 2 of the *Juvenile Courts Act 1991* as meaning:
'a probation officer appointed under the *Probation Act 1979*'.

[54] See:
- sections 3(1) and 15(1) of the *Interpretation Act* (Ch. 2) and section 2 of the *Criminal Code* (Ch. 262) [However, this statutory provision only applies to offences contained in the *Criminal Code* (Ch. 262), see section 2 of the *Criminal Code Act* (Ch. 262) and the subsection titled 'Acts in pari materia' in the section titled 'Extrinsic Aids' in the chapter titled 'Aids To Interpretation' in the text titled 'Injia on Statutory Interpretation in Papua New Guinea and the Pacific']; and
- *Public Employees Association of Papua New Guinea v Public Services Commission* [1983] PNGLR 206, [1983] PGSC 18; *SCR No. 1 of 1981; Re Inter-Group Fighting Act 1977* [1981] PNGLR 151 at 154 and *SCR No. 2 of 1989; Re Village Courts Act* (Ch. 44) [1988-89] PNGLR 491, [1988] PGSC 30.

[55] See *Re Poning* (1982) SC224, per Kearney DepCJ and *SCR No. 2 of 1981; Re s19(1)(f) Criminal Code (Ch. 262)* [1982] PNGLR 150, per Kearney DepCJ at 158, [1982] PGSC 18.

See also: *Deaton v The Attorney-General and The Revenue Commissioners* [1963] IR 170, per Ó Dálaigh CJ at 181.

As regards 'General Law-Making Powers', refer to the text titled 'Injia on Statutory Interpretation in Papua New Guinea and the Pacific'.

INTRODUCTION TO SENTENCING

A conviction is a precondition for imposing a sentence for an offence under the *Criminal Code* (Ch. 262).[56]

What is sentencing? There exists a general consensus as to the etymology of the expression 'sentence' – from the Latin '*sententia*', meaning literally 'feeling' or 'opinion'.[57]

Sentencing is an important part of the process of criminal justice. As Sir James Stephen once said:

> 'The sentence ... is to the trial what the bullet is to the powder'.[58]

Sentencing has been described as:

- the act of a criminal court imposing punishment on an individual found guilty of an offence[59];
- the sharp edge of the criminal justice system.[60]

  That moment when a Court determines:

  - what degree of punishment or rehabilitation constitutes justice in a particular case; and
  - how consistent that justice will be[61]; and

---

[56] See *SCR No. 2 of 1981; Re s19(1)(f) Criminal Code (Ch. 262)* [1982] PNGLR 150, [1982] PGSC 18 and *Public Prosecutor v Arthur Jawodimbari and Monty Derari* (2006) SC891, [2006] PGSC 28.

[57] See The Law Reform Commission of Ireland, 1993, 'Consultation Paper on Sentencing', paragraph 1.1.

[58] See *Agoara Kebo and Karunai Uraki v The State* (1981) SC198.

[59] See The Law Reform Commission of Ireland, 1993, 'Consultation Paper on Sentencing', paragraph 1.4.

[60] See *The State v Iori Veraga* (2005) N2921, [2005] PGNC 43.

[61] See *The State v Iori Veraga* (2005) N2921, [2005] PGNC 43.

- the punch line of the criminal justice system.[62]

  It is at this point that the law is seen to have its impact.[63]

The sentence imposed is not only determined by the conduct of the accused person, but also by the consequences of that conduct.[64]

However, an accused person should only be sentenced for an offence for which he or she:

- has been convicted[65], whether by:
  - pleading guilty[66]; or
  - being found guilty[67].

---

[62] See The Law Reform Commission of Ireland, 1993, 'Consultation Paper on Sentencing', paragraph 2.21.

[63] See The Law Reform Commission of Ireland, 1993, 'Consultation Paper on Sentencing', paragraph 2.21.

[64] See *The State v John Telape* (2009) N3815, [2009] PGNC 181.

[65] See *R v De Simoni* (1981) 147 CLR 383, [1981] HCA 31 and *Walsh v R* (1996) 6 Tas R 70 at 76 and 93, [1996] TASSC 59.

[66] See *Toiona v Bryant* [1969-70] PNGLR 201, [1969] PGSC 41.

See also: *R v Clutterham* (1982) 4 Cr App R (S) 40; *R v Booker* (1982) 4 Cr App R (S) 53; *R v Ayensu and Ayensu* (1982) 4 Cr App R (S) 248; *R v Fisher* (1981) 3 Cr App R (S) 313; *Kidd* [1998] 1 WLR 604 and *Clark* [1996] 2 Cr App R (S) 351, per Henry LJ at 356.

Refer also to:
- the section titled 'Plea Of Guilty' in the chapter titled 'Mitigating Factors'; and
- the subsection titled 'Plea Of Guilty' in the section titled 'Taking Of A Plea' in the chapter titled 'Court Procedure' in the text titled 'Injia on Criminal Practice and Procedure in Papua New Guina and the Pacific'.

[67] See *Acting Public Prosecutor v Uname Aumane and others* [1980] PNGLR 510.

See also: *Kidd* [1998] 1 WLR 604 and *Clark* [1996] 2 Cr App R (S) 351, per Henry LJ at 356.

This sentencing principle is expressed in the ancient maxim 'nulla poena sine lege', i.e. no one is to be punished on a charge for which they have not been tried and found guilty, see The Law Reform Commission of Ireland, 1993, 'Consultation Paper on Sentencing', paragraph 1.41.

Where an accused person has pleaded not guilty to a criminal charge and has been convicted after a trial, the facts implicit in the verdict of guilty cannot be controverted during the sentencing process. The Court must sentence according to those facts. Usually, the facts implied by the verdict will be clear[68]; or

- has requested to be taken into consideration as provided for by section 603 of the *Criminal Code* (Ch. 262)[69].[70]

The task of sentencing is however a very difficult one because a Court is dealing with a life of a human being who has broken the law.[71]

A law usually:

- sets down the maximum sentence for an offence[72]; and

- gives the Court very wide powers to impose the appropriate punishment for the particular accused person.[73]

---

[68] See *R v Storey* [1998] 1 VR 359 at 366 and *Bennett v The State of Western Australia* [2012] WASCA 70.

[69] Refer also to the chapter titled 'Outstanding Charges'.

[70] See *DPP v Anderson* (1978) 76 Cr App R 185, [1978] AC 964; *R v Canavan* [1998] 1 Cr App R (S) 243, [1997] EWCA Crim 1773, per Bingham LCJ; *R v De Simoni* (1981) 147 CLR 383, [1981] HCA 31; *Walsh v R* (1996) 6 Tas R 70 at 76 and 93, [1996] TASSC 59 and *R v Smith and Tovey* [2005] EWCA Crim 530.

[71] See *Uname Aumane and others v The State* [1980] PNGLR 510, per Kapi J (as he then was) at 537.

[72] See section 14 of the *Interpretation Act* (Ch. 2) ['Penalties Prescribed To Be Maximum Penalties'].

In relation to the Supreme and National Courts the offence of 'Contempt of Court' is an exception to the requirement under section 37(2) of the *Constitution of the Independent State of Papua New Guinea* that a criminal offence must be defined and the penalty prescribed by a written law. It is now established that contempt of court is a matter of the underlying law, see *R v Rooney* [1979] PNGLR 448 and *The Attorney General, Michael Gene and others v Dr Pirouz Hamidian-Rad* (1999) SC618, [1999] PGSC 29.

Refer also to:

- the chapter titled 'Contempt Of Court' in the text titled 'Injia on Criminal Practice and Procedure in Papua New Guinea and the Pacific';
- the section titled 'Underlying Law' in the chapter titled 'Sources Of Law' in the text titled 'Injia on Criminal Practice and Procedure in Papua New Guinea and the Pacific'; and
- the chapter titled 'Maximum Sentence'.

[73] See *Uname Aumane and others v The State* [1980] PNGLR 510, per Kapi J (as he then was) at 537.

INTRODUCTION TO SENTENCING

The task of sentencing, though coming at the end of the trial process in the criminal justice system:

- is no less important than the other earlier stages of the process[74]; and
- has just as much significance for the accused person as the process by which guilt was determined[75].

Therefore, the importance of the sentencing stage can hardly be overstated.[76]

Sentencing may be considered as the following process:

- **Stage One**

  The first stage involves choosing the correct principle or approach to adopt in the instant case according to the particular characteristics of the accused person and offence.[77]

  This is decided by reference to the traditional 'objectives' or 'purposes' of sentencing.[78]

- **Stage Two**

  The second stage involves choosing the particular penalty or measure appropriate to the accused person by reference to the approach adopted in the first stage.[79]

It is the duty of the Court to balance often incommensurable factors and to arrive at a sentence that is just in all of the circumstances.[80]

---

[74] See *The State v Iori Veraga* (2005) N2921, [2005] PGNC 43.

[75] See *R v Olbrich* (1999) 199 CLR 270 at 274, [1999] HCA 54.

[76] See The Law Reform Commission of Ireland, 1993, 'Consultation Paper on Sentencing', paragraph 2.21.

[77] See The Law Reform Commission of Ireland, 1993, 'Consultation Paper on Sentencing', paragraph 1.44.

[78] Refer also to the chapter titled 'Objectives And Purposes Of Sentencing'.

[79] See The Law Reform Commission of Ireland, 1993, 'Consultation Paper on Sentencing', paragraph 1.44.

[80] See *Elias v R; Issa v R* [2013] HCA 31.

INTRODUCTION TO SENTENCING

The administration of the criminal law involves individualised justice, the attainment of which is acknowledged to involve the exercise of a wide sentencing discretion.[81]

A Court should instinctively synthesise[82] by:

- identifying all of the various competing factors relevant to the sentence[83];
- discussing their significance; and
- then making a value judgement as to what is the appropriate sentence[84],

but should not identify a prima facie sentence and then adjust up or down that sentence according to the influence of particular factors[85].[86]

Sentencing principles must be applied irrespective of the racial, cultural or ethnic background of an accused person.[87]

Whilst the sentencing principles remain uniform, their application may require weight to be given to local factors.[88]

---

[81] See *House v R* (1936) 55 CLR 499, per Starke J at 503, [1936] HCA 40; *Engert* (1995) 84 A Crim R 67, per Gleeson CJ at 68; *Ryan v R* (2001) 206 CLR 267, per McHugh J at 283-284; *Wong v R* (2001) 207 CLR 584, per Gaudron, Gummow and Hayne JJ at 612, and *Elias v R; Issa v R* [2013] HCA 31.

[82] As regards the 'instinctive synthesis' approach, see also: *Wong and Leung v R* (2001) 207 CLR 584, (2001) 76 ALJR 79, [2001] HCA 64; *Cameron v R* (2002) 209 CLR 339, (2002) 76 ALJR 382, [2002] HCA 6; *R v AM; AM v R* [2010] NZCA 114 and *R v Williscroft* [1975] VR 292, [1975] Vic Rp 27.

[83] See *Ryan v R* (2001) 206 CLR 267, (2001) 75 ALJR 815, (2001) 179 ALR 193, [2001] HCA 21, per Hayne J.

[84] See *Muldrock v R* (2011) 85 ALJR 1154, [2011] HCA 39 and *Markarian v R* (2005) 215 ALR 213, (2005) 228 CLR 357 at 377-378, [2005] HCA 25.

[85] See *The State v Tovita Mann* (2009) N4028.

See also: *AB v R* (1999) 198 CLR 111, [1999] HCA 46, per McHugh J.

[86] See *Veen v R (No. 2)* (1988) 164 CLR 465 at 476-477, (1988) 33 A Crim R 230, [1988] HCA 14 and *AB v R* (1999) 198 CLR 111 at 121-122, [1999] HCA 46.

[87] See *Neal v R* (1982) 149 CLR 305, per Brennan J at 326.

[88] See *Leeth v Commonwealth* (1992) 174 CLR 455, per Brennan J at 476.

INTRODUCTION TO SENTENCING

In determining an appropriate sentence a Court may display mercy.[89] The whole history of criminal justice has shown that severity of punishment begets the need of a capacity for mercy.[90] However, in deciding whether to show mercy a Court may consider whether the accused person had shown any mercy in the commission of the offence.[91]

A Court should not:

- take into account facts and circumstances that constitute a different or more serious offence from that with which the accused person has been charged with[92] when imposing a sentence;
- impose a sentence on the basis of an opinion that the accused person is actually guilty of an offence with which he or she has not been charged[93];
- impose a sentence based on the evidence of a charge for which the accused person has been acquitted[94];
- take into account an act, omission, matter or circumstance if it would then establish:
  - a separate offence which consisted of, or included, conduct that do not form part of the offence to which the accused person to be sentenced has been convicted; or

---

[89] See *Porewa Wani v The State* [1979] PNGLR 593, [1979] PGSC 30; *The State v Ure Hane* (1983) N442, [1983] PGNC 10 and *The State v Donald Robin* (1980) N230, [1980] PGNC 8.

See also: *R v M (CA)* [1996] 1 SCR 500, per Lamer CJ; *R v Wihapi* [1976] 1 NZLR 22, per McCarthy P at 424; *MacGregor v Police* (1995) 66 SASR 269 at 272-273; *R v Miceli* [1998] 4 VR 588, per Tadgell JA at 592 and Charles JA at 594; *R v Osenkowski* (1982) 30 SASR 212; *DPP v Carteri* [1998] 1 VR 601; *R v Holland* (2002) 134 A Crim R 451, per Eames JA at 453-454 and *Moyse v R* (1988) 38 A Crim R 169, per Jacobs J at 172-173.

[90] As observed by Windeyer J in *Cobiac v Liddy* (1969) 43 ALJR 257 at 269.

[91] See *The State v Donald Poni* [2004] PNGLR 17.

[92] See *Saperus Yalibakut v The State* (2006) SC890, [2006] PGSC 27; *The State v Issau Parao* (2009) N3625, [2009] PGNC 38 and *The State v Marcus Pitmete* (2007) N3229, [2007] PGNC 105.

See also: *Dediya v The Republic of Nauru* [1969-1982] NLR 57, [1976] NRSC 8; *R v De Simone* (1981) 147 CLR 383, per Gibbs J at 389, [1981] HCA 31; *Savvas v R* (1995) 183 CLR 1 at 5; *R v Boney; ex parte Attorney-General* [1986] 1 Qd R 190 and *R v D* [1996] 1 Qd R 363, (1995) 80 A Crim R 50.

[93] See *R v Connor* (1981) 3 Cr App R (S) 225 and *The People (DPP) v O'Leary* 3 Frewen 163.

[94] See *R v Ajit Singh* [1981] Crim LR 724, (1981) 3 Cr App R (S) 180; *R v Hudson* (1979) 1 Cr App R (S) 130 and *R v Hazelwood* (1984) 6 Cr App R (S) 52.

- a more serious offence than the offence to which the accused person to be sentenced has been convicted[95]

when imposing a sentence;

- indicate what sentence would be imposed if a plea of guilty[96] was entered[97];
- postpone sentencing in order to allow an accused person to assist police in recovering property[98];
- postpone sentencing in order to allow an accused person to pay back money that had been unlawfully obtained[99];
- impose a sentence for an offence for which an accused person has not been convicted, subject to the provisions of section 603 of the *Criminal Code* (Ch. 262)[100];

---

[95] See *John Baipu v The State* (2005) SC796, [2005] PGSC 19; *The State v Issau Parao* (2009) N3625, [2009] PGNC 38 and *The State v Marcus Pitmete* (2007) N3229, [2007] PGNC 105.

[96] Refer also to:
- the section titled 'Plea Of Guilty' in the chapter titled 'Mitigating Factors'; and
- the subsection titled 'Plea Of Guilty' in the section titled Taking Of A Plea' in the chapter titled 'Court Procedure' in the text titled 'Injia on Criminal Practice and Procedure in Papua New Guinea and the Pacific'.

[97] See *R v Turner* (1970) 54 Cr App R 352, [1970] 2 QB 321.

See also: *R v Plimmer* (1975) 61 Cr App R 264; *R v Grice* (1978) 66 Cr App R 167 and *R v Ryan* (1978) 67 Cr App R 177.

See however: *R v Goodyear* [2005] EWCA Crim 888.

[98] See *R v Collins* (1969) 53 Cr App R 385.

See also: *The State v Singh* [2007] FJCA 35.

[99] See *West v R* (1959) 43 Cr App R 109.

See also: *The State v Singh* [2007] FJCA 35.

[100] See *DPP v Anderson* (1978) 76 Cr App R 185, [1978] AC 964; *Ketner v The Republic of Nauru* [1969-1982] NLR 67, [1978] NRSC 8; *R v D* [1996] 1 Qd R 363, (1995) 80 A Crim R 50; *R v Cooksley* [1982] 1 Qd R 417 and *R v Jobson* [1989] 2 Qd R 464 at 466 and 471.

Refer also to the chapter titled 'Outstanding Charges'.

- withhold any degree of leniency for which an accused person might be entitled, thereby imposing a sentence disproportionate to the offence in question[101];

- take into consideration the possibility of a parole application[102].

  Parole refers to the existence and exercise of a discretionary power about the timing and conditions of an inmate's release.[103]

  The basic theory of the parole system is that, notwithstanding that a sentence of imprisonment is the appropriate punishment for the particular offence in all the circumstances of a case, considerations of mitigation or rehabilitation may make it unnecessary, or even undesirable, that the whole of that sentence should actually be served in custody.[104]

  Parole, in theory, in based on the following rationales:

  - it allows the State to satisfy calls for severe court-imposed sentences while at the same time mitigating the social and fiscal costs of those sentences by releasing offenders at an earlier date; and

---

[101] See *Ibbs v R; Baumer v R* (1988) 188 CLR 51 at 57, (1988) 83 ALR 8, [1988] HCA 67.

Refer also to:
- the chapter titled 'Equality In Sentencing'; and
- the section titled 'Disparity In Sentencing' in the chapter titled 'Appeals Against Sentence'.

[102] See *R v Black* [1971] Crim LR 109.

Section 17(1) of the *Parole Act 1991* states:
'Subject to this Act, a detainee who –
(a) having been sentenced to a term of imprisonment of less than three years–has served not less than one year; or
(b) having been sentenced to a term of imprisonment of three years or more–has served not less than one third of the sentence; or
(c) having been sentenced to life imprisonment or detention during Her Majesty's pleasure–has served not less than 10 years,
is eligible for parole'.

[103] See New Zealand Law Commission, 2006, 'Reforms to the Sentencing and Parole Structure: Consultative Draft', Preliminary Paper 1, page 50.

[104] See *R v Shrestha* (1990-1991) 173 CLR 48 at 67.

  - it is a tool for managing the recidivism risk of former inmates.[105]

The intention that underpins legislation as to parole eligibility is the mitigation of punishment in favour of rehabilitation through conditional release[106];

- gather documentary information in the determination of an appropriate sentence itself if that information is adverse to an accused person[107];
- allow political statements to be made during the course of sentencing[108]; and
- take into consideration that the prosecution could have selected a less serious offence[109].

[105] See New Zealand Law Commission, 2006, 'Reforms to the Sentencing and Parole Structure: Consultative Draft', Preliminary Paper 1, page 50.

[106] See *Deakin v R* (1984) 58 ALJR 367, [1984] HCA 31 and *Power v R* (1974) 131 CLR 623 at 629, [1974] HCA 26.

[107] See *R v Wise* [2000] VR 287.

[108] See *R v King and Simpkins* (1973) 57 Cr App R 696, [1973] Crim LR 380.

[109] See *Elias v R; Issa v R* [2013] HCA 31.

INTRODUCTION TO SENTENCING

An accused person is entitled to an opportunity to be heard[110] on sentence by administering the allocutus[111], otherwise it is a denial of 'natural justice'[112] thereby rendering the sentence pronounced a nullity.[113]

The minimum requirement of 'natural justice' is:

> The duty to act fairly and, in principle, to be seen to act fairly.[114]

---

[110] See *Saperus Yalibakut v The State* (2006) SC890 and *Peter Man v John Korul* (1996) N1434.

Refer also to the section titled 'Right To Be Present' in the chapter titled 'Rights Of Accused Person' in the text titled 'Injia on Criminal Practice and Procedure in Papua New Guinea and the Pacific'.

[111] Section 593 of the *Criminal Code* (Ch. 262) states:

> 'Where an accused person –
> (a) pleads that he is guilty of an offence; or
> (b) on trial, is convicted of any offence,
> the proper officer shall ask him whether he has anything to say why sentence should not be passed on him, but an omission to do so does not invalidate the judgement'.

As regards the administering of the allocutus in the District Court, see *Leonard Sabadi v Police* (2002) N2164; *Moses Aikaba v Tami* [1971-72] PNGLR 155 at 157 and *Peter Man v John Korul* (1996) N1434.

[112] Section 59(1) of the *Constitution of the Independent State of Papua New Guinea* states:

> 'Subject to this Constitution and to any statute, the principles of natural justice are the rules of the underlying law known by that name developed for control of judicial and administrative proceedings.

See also: *Tom Longman Yaul v The State* (2005) SC803, [2005] PGSC 29 and *Gipe v The State* (2001) SC661.

The principles of 'natural justice' are part of the underlying law [see *Tindiwi, for and on behalf of Members of the Suspended Enga Provincial Government v Nilkare, Minister for Provincial Affairs, and The State* [1984] PNGLR 191, [1984] PGSC 18; *Premdas v The State* [1979] PNGLR 329 and *Lambakey Okuk v Fallscheer* [1980] PNGLR 274], but do not have a constitutional status [see *Parakas v The State* [1985] PNGLR 224, [1985] PGSC 16].

See also: *Lloyd v McMahon* [1987] AC 625, per Lord Bridge at 702 and *R v Commission of Racial Equality; ex parte Cottrell and Rothon* [1980] 3 All ER 265, per Lord Lane at 271.

[113] See *Moses Aikaba and others v Tami* [1971-72] PNGLR 155, [1971] PGSC 2; *Agiru Aieni and twelve others v Paul T Tahain* [1978] PNGLR 37; *Michael Gende v The State* (1999) SC626, [1999] PGSC 25; *Tom Longman Yaul v The State* (2005) SC803, [2005] PGSC 29 and *The State v Aaron Lahu* (2005) N2798, [2005] PGNC 161.

[114] See section 59(2) of the *Constitution of the Independent State of Papua New Guinea*.

See also: *The State v Aaron Lahu* (2005) N2798, [2005] PGNC 161.

INTRODUCTION TO SENTENCING

A Court should advise an accused person what factors and circumstances it took into consideration in determining the appropriate sentence.[115]

However, an accused person may be sentenced in absentia.[116]

All outstanding charges should be dealt with at the same time, if possible.[117]

An accused person who takes advantage of his or her liberty on parole to commit further offences and thereby breaches[118] the conditions[119] of his or her parole should:

- suffer the revocation of his or her parole[120];
- suffer the consequent need to serve out the balance of the original sentence[121]; and
- suffer a significant punishment for the later offence to mark the gravity of his or her conduct in thus abusing his or her parole.[122]

---

[115] See *Public Prosecutor v Atis Willie* [2004] VUCA 4.

[116] See:
- section 571 of the *Criminal Code* (Ch. 262) ['Presence Of Accused']; and
- *Thomas Kavali v Thomas Hoihoi* [1986] PNGLR 329; *The State v Frank Johnston (No. 2)* (2004) N2586; *John Konobo v The State* (2004) N2500; *The State v Justin Komboli* (2005) N2891 and *The State v Peter Wirundi* (2010) N3994, [2010] PGNC 34.

[117] See *The Acting Public Prosecutor v Andrew Amona Yongga* [1981] PNGLR 314.

See also: *Bennett* [1980] 2 Cr App R (S) 96 and *Smith* (1921) 15 Cr App R 172.

Refer also to the chapter titled 'Oustanding Charges'.

[118] See section 26 of the *Parole Act 1991* ['Breach Of Parole'].

[119] See section 24 of the *Parole Act 1991* ['Conditions Of Parole'].

[120] See section 27(1)(a) of the *Parole Act 1991* ['Decision Of Board In Relation To Breach'].

[121] See section 26(6) of the *Parole Act 1991* ['Breach Of Parole'].

[122] See *R v Moffitt* (1990) 20 NSWLR 114, per Badgery-Parker J at 128.

See also: *Power v R* (1974) 131 CLR 623, [1974] HCA 26; *Deakin v R* (1984) 58 ALJR 367, [1984] HCA 31; *Bugmy v R* (1990) 169 CLR 525; *R v Miller* (2000) 76 SASR 151, [2000] SASC 16 and *R v Beauregard-Smith* (2001) 79 SASR 408, [2001] SASC 69.

INTRODUCTION TO SENTENCING

Once the Court has pronounced its sentence, the presiding judge or magistrate becomes *functus officio.*[123]

In other words, the sentencing judge or magistrate has completed his or her duty and there is nothing left for him or her to do.[124]

The only exception would be in a case in which an Act of Parliament allows for a deferment of decision on sentence as in the case of section 19(1)(f)(i) of the *Criminal Code* (Ch. 262). Save only for such an exception, after a sentence has been pronounced and the prisoner starts serving his or her term of imprisonment, there is no power in a Court except, on appeal, to revisit the decision on sentence.[125]

[6.0] SENTENCING CONSIDERATIONS

A Court in determining an appropriate sentence should take into consideration the following:

The Relevant Objective/s and Purpose/s Of Sentencing

The Court should:

- evaluate different 'objectives' or 'purposes' ('principles') of sentencing; and
- decide which of those 'objectives' or 'purposes' should be achieved in the particular case at hand.[126]

The Relevant Facts

A Court should determine the facts relevant for sentence consistent with the establishment of the essential legal ingredients of the offence; whether by way of:

---

[123] See *Daniel Ronald Walus v The State* (2007) SC882, [2007] PGSC 4.

[124] See *Daniel Ronald Walus v The State* (2007) SC882, [2007] PGSC 4.

[125] See *Daniel Ronald Walus v The State* (2007) SC882, [2007] PGSC 4.

Refer also to the chapter titled 'Objectives And Purposes Of Sentencing'.

[126] See *Uname Aumane and others v The State* [1980] PNGLR 510, per Kapi J (as he then was) at 537-538.

- an admission on the plea of guilty[127]; or
- pursuant to a verdict of guilty.[128]

Maximum Sentence

The Court should take into consideration the maximum sentence that may be imposed for the offence/s whilst taking into consideration any circumstance of aggravation[129] as alleged in the charge/s.[130]

Minimum Sentence

The Court should take into consideration the minimum sentence that may be imposed.[131]

Plea Bargain

The Court should take into consideration whether the charge been selected as a consequence of a plea bargain.[132]

---

[127] Refer also to the chapter titled 'Sentencing Proceedings'.

[128] See *Veen v R (No. 1)* (1979) 143 CLR 458, per Stephen J at 466 (1979) 53 ALJR 305, [1979] HCA 7; *Kingswell v R* (1985) 159 CLR 264, per Mason J at 283, [1985] HCA 72; *Maher v R* (1987) 163 CLR 221, per Mason, Wilson and Toohey JJ at 228, [1987] HCA 31; *R v Martin* (1981) 1 NSWLR 640, per Hope JA at 643; *R v The Accused* (1988) 1 NZLR 422 at 426-427 and *Saffron (No. 3)* (1988-1989) 39 A Crim R 123 at 125.

[129] Refer also to:
- the section titled 'General Principles' in this chapter; and
- the section titled 'Circumstance Of Aggravation' in the chapter titled 'Aggravating Factors'.

[130] Refer also to the chapter titled 'Maximum Sentence'.

[131] Refer also to the chapter titled 'Minimum Sentence'.

[132] Refer also to the chapter titled 'Plea Bargain'.

Co-accused

The Court should take into consideration the sentence/s imposed on any co-accused.[133]

Aggravating Factors

A Court should take into consideration the 'aggravating factors'[134] that make the offence as committed by an accused person so serious.[135]

If a 'circumstance of aggravation'[136] is to be taken into account for the purpose of increasing the maximum sentence above what it would otherwise be, then it must be:

- specified or particularised in the charge and proven 'beyond reasonable doubt[137]' as an element of the offence[138]; or

---

[133] Refer also to:
- the chapter titled 'Equality In Sentencing'; and
- the section titled 'Disparity In Sentencing' in the chapter titled 'Appeals Against Sentence'.

[134] Refer also to the chapter 'Aggravating Factors'.

[135] See *The State v Micky John Lausi* (2001) N2073.

However, each of those factors will not necessarily be given the same 'weight', see *The State v Jeffery Wangi* (2006) N3016, [2006] PGNC 48.

[136] The term 'circumstances of aggravation' is defined in section 1(1) of the *Criminal Code* (Ch. 262) as including:

> 'any circumstances by reason of which an offender is liable to a greater punishment than that to which he would be liable if the offence were committed without the existence of that circumstance'.

As regards the law in relation to 'Wording Of Charges', refer to the chapter titled 'Charges' in the text titled 'Injia on Criminal Practice and Procedure in Papua New Guinea and the Pacific'.

[137] Refer also to the chapter titled 'Proof Of Issues' in the text titled 'Injia on Criminal Practice and Procedure in Papua New Guinea and the Pacific'.

[138] See *Paul Palma v The State* (2008) SC1214, [2008] PGSC 56; *The State v Marcus Yame* (2010) N4131; *The State v Dibol Petrus Kopal* (2004) N2778 and *The State v James Yali* (2006) N2989, [2006] PGNC 26.

See also: *R v Bright* [1916] 2 KB 441 and *R v De Simoni* (1981)147 CLR 383, per Gibbs CJ at 389.

- admitted on a plea of guilty upon the Court accepting the plea and entering a conviction[139] or otherwise found guilty 'beyond reasonable doubt[140,141].

If a 'circumstance of aggravation' is not specified or particularised in a charge, it may nonetheless be taken into account as an 'aggravating factor' when deciding on a sentence within the allowable range.[142]

However, a 'circumstance of aggravation' must not be taken into account that:

- itself constitutes a separate offence with which the accused person has not been convicted[143]; or
- does not form part of the offence with which the accused person:
  - has been convicted; or

---

[139] See *SCR No. 2 of 1981; Re s19(1)(f) Criminal Code (Ch. 262)* [1982] PNGLR 150, per Kearney J at 156, [1982] PGSC 18; *R v Ebulya* [1964] PNGLR 200, per Smithers J at 231 and *The State v Binga Thomas* (2005) N2828, [2005] PGNC 189.

[140] Refer also to the chapter titled 'Proof Of Issues' in the text titled 'Injia on Criminal Practice and Procedure in Papua New Guinea and the Pacific'.

[141] See *Jack Mari v The State* (2007) SC 1147, [2007] PGSC 49; *The State v Michael Butemo Jiregari* [1984] PNGLR 62; *The State v Dibol Petrus Kopal* (2004) N2778; *The State v Binga Thomas* (2005) N2828; *The State v James Yali* (2006) N2989 and *The State v Jeffery Wangi* (2006) N3016.

See also: sections 528 ['Form Of Indictment'] and 538 ['Offences Involving Circumstances Of Aggravation'] of the *Criminal Code* (Ch. 262).

Refer also to the chapter titled 'Proof Of Issues' in the text titled 'Injia on Criminal Practice and Procedure in Papua New Guinea and the Pacific'.

[142] See *The State v Marcus Yame* (2010) N4131 and *The State v Mark Samuel Haupas* (2007) N3186, [2007] PGNC 81.

[143] See *R v De Simoni* (1981) 147 CLR 383 at 389, [1981] HCA 31 and *R v Olbrich* (1999) 199 CLR 270, [1999] HCA 54.

- has not asked to be taken into consideration in accordance with the procedure set out in section 603 of the *Criminal Code* (Ch. 262)[144];

Mitigating Factors

A Court should take into consideration the 'mitigating factors'[145] that are unrelated to the circumstances of the offence that mitigate and call for leniency.[146]

A Court cannot reject facts asserted in mitigation without giving an accused person an opportunity to support his or her version on oath. However, it is at the discretion of an accused person as to whether he or she will give evidence.[147]

In sentencing the general practice is to consider all 'mitigating factors' in arriving at an appropriate sentence.[148]

---

144 See *John Baipu v The State* (2005) SC796, [2005] PGSC 19 and *Ben Wafia and others v The State* (2006) SC851, [2006] PGSC 19.

See also: *Lane v Auckland City Council* [1975] 1 NZLR 353 and *R v Pattison* (2002) 19 CRNZ 407.

Refer also to the chapter titled 'Outstanding Charges'.

145 Refer also to the chapter titled 'Mitigating Factors'.

146 See *Steven Loke Ume, Charles Patrick Kaona and Greg Wawa Kavoa v The State* (2006) SC836, [2006] PGSC 9.

See also: *The State v Micky John Lausi* (2001) N2073.

However, each of those factors will not necessarily be given the same 'weight', see *The State v Jeffery Wangi* (2006) N3016, [2006] PGNC 48.

147 See *R v Vagi* [1973] PNGLR 30, [1973] PGSC 51.

Refer also to the chapter titled 'Sentencing Proceedings'.

148 See *Babai v The State* [1995] PNGLR 179, [1995] PGSC 10 and *Acting Public Prosecutor v Nitak Mangilonde Taganis of Tambitanis* [1982] PNGLR 299, [1982] PGSC 6.

See however: *R v Taueki* [2005] 3 NZLR 372.

Although emphasis is sometimes given to certain 'mitigating factors' no actual period should be allowed for any particular one.[149]

If a Court does not expressly refer to all of the 'mitigating factors' in sentencing it is not to be necessarily inferred that the Court did not take such factors into account[150].

The distinction between 'aggravating factors[151]' and 'mitigating factors', for sentencing purposes may sometimes be unclear or even, and on occasions, ambiguous.[152]

Extenuating Circumstances

A Court should take into consideration the 'extenuating circumstances'[153] that relate to:

> The circumstances of the commission of the offence itself that reduce or diminish the gravity of the offence.[154]

'Extenuating circumstances', as distinct from 'mitigating factors', of the offence must be considered.[155]

A Court cannot reject facts asserted in mitigation without giving an accused person an opportunity to support his or her version on oath. However, it is at the discretion of an accused person as to whether he or she will give evidence.[156]

---

149 See *Babai v The State* [1995] PNGLR 179, [1995] PGSC 10 and *Acting Public Prosecutor v Nitak Mangilonde Taganis of Tambitanis* [1982] PNGLR 299, [1982] PGSC 6.

See however: *R v Taueki* [2005] 3 NZLR 372.

150 See *Avia Aihi v The State (No. 3)* [1982] PNGLR 92, [1982] PGSC 9.

151 Refer also to the chapter titled 'Aggravating Factors'.

152 See *R v Storey* [1998] 1 VR 359.

153 Refer also to the chapter titled 'Extenuating Circumstances'.

154 See *Steven Loke Ume, Charles Patrick Kaona and Greg Wawa Kavoa v The State* (2006) SC836, [2006] PGSC 9.

155 See *Manu Kovi v The State* (2005) SC789, [2005] PGSC 34.

156 See *R v Vagi* [1973] PNGLR 30, [1973] PGSC 51.

Refer also to the chapter titled 'Sentencing Proceedings'.

INTRODUCTION TO SENTENCING

In sentencing the general practice is to consider all 'extenuating circumstances' in arriving at an appropriate sentence.

Although emphasis is sometimes given to certain 'extenuating circumstances' no actual period should be allowed for any particular one.

If a Court does not expressly refer to all of the 'extenuating circumstances' in sentencing it is not to be necessarily inferred that the Court did not take such circumstances into account.

Pre-sentence Report

A Court should consider a well-balanced pre-sentence report that has been obtained.[157]

Sentencing Alternatives

A Court should take into consideration all sentencing alternatives.[158]

Sentencing Trends

The Court should take into consideration the range of sentences that have been imposed for the offence/s based on previous cases.[159]

While the provision of statistical information on sentencing patterns may be useful in discerning the range of sentences that have thus far been imposed for a particular offence it should be used with care.[160]

---

[157] Refer also to the chapter titled 'Pre-sentence Report'.

[158] See *The State v Abel Airi* (2000) N2007.

Refer also to the chapter titled 'Sentencing Options'.

[159] See *The State v Abel Airi* (2000) N2007.

Refer also to the chapter titled 'Comparative Sentences'.

[160] See *Robertson v R* [2007] NSWCCA 270, see Rothman J.

Sentencing statistics are, at their highest, of limited guidance only.[161]

The sentencing range in any case must extend to the maximum penalty.[162]

Sentencing statistics of their nature do not reflect the range which the legislature had intended by the maximum penalties.[163]

Sentencing Tariffs And Guidelines[164]

A Court should take into consideration sentencing tariffs and guidelines.[165]

---

[161] See *Bombardieri v R* [2010] NSWCCA 161 and *R v AEM Snr; R v KEM; R v MM* [2002] NSWCCA 58.

[162] See *Ma and Pham v R* [2007] NSWCCA 240.

[163] See *Williams v R* [2010] NSWCCA 15; *Clinton v R* [2009] NSWCCA 276 and *England v R, Phanith v R* [2009] NSWCCA 274.

[164] Notwithstanding their limitations [see New Zealand Law Commission, 2005, 'Criminal Pre-Trial Processes: Justice Through Efficiency', Report 89, page 93], tariff or guideline judgements are used as a tool for directing judicial discretion:

- in the United Kingdom.

  The United Kingdom Sentencing Guidelines Council has published a compendium of guideline judgements which can be viewed at http://www.sentencing-guidelines.gov.uk/index.html;

- to a lesser extent in Australia.

  See for example *R v Jurisic* (1998) 45 NSWLR 209; *R v Henry* (1999) 46 NSWLR 346; *R v Wong and Leung* (1999) 48 NWSWLR 340; *R v Thomson* (2000) 49 NSWLR 383 and *R v Ponfield* (1999) 48 NSWLR 327; and

- in New Zealand.

  See *R v Taueki* [2005] 3 NZLR 372.

See also: New Zealand Law Commission, 2006, 'Reforms to the Sentencing and Parole Structure: Consultative Draft', Preliminary Paper 1, page 20.

[165] See *Richard Liri v The State* (2007) SC883, [2007] PGSC 3; *Joe Giamur v The State* (2007) SC884, [2007] PGSC 7; *James Pangnan and Patrick Ponat v The State* (2006) SCRA Nos. 39 and 54 of 2004 and *The State v Dobi Ao (No. 2)* (2002) N2247.

As regards the disadvantages of the tariff system, see *Griffiths v R* (1977) 137 CLR 293, (1977) 51 ALJR 749 at 765, [1977] HCA 44.

INTRODUCTION TO SENTENCING

Sentencing tariffs give a sentencing Court detailed guidance in relation to a particular type of offence by:

- specifying the starting point and sentence range for the offence or for various categories of an offence; and

- outlining the aggravating and mitigating factors that should determine the point within the range at which a sentence should fall.[166]

Sentencing tariffs must be considered in determining sentences in future cases if subsequent sentences are to have any relevance to the interest of society to appropriately deal with accused persons.[167]

There is some evidence that the absence of comprehensive guidance from appellate courts, particularly at the lower end of sentencing, results in inconsistency in sentencing.[168]

The Supreme Court may fix guidelines for sentences in respect of different categories of the same offence, but without fixing actual sentences in those categories.[169]

Where the Supreme Court provides some guidelines as to how a power vested in the National Court can be exercised, such guidelines should be followed, unless there is a good reason that is sound in law that warrants a departure.[170]

---

[166] See New Zealand Law Commission, 2006, 'Reforms to the Sentencing and Parole Structure: Consultative Draft', Preliminary Paper 1, page 20.

[167] See *The State v Dobi Ao (No. 2)* (2002) N2247.

[168] See:
- New Zealand Law Commission, 2006, 'Reforms to the Sentencing and Parole Structure: Consultative Draft', Preliminary Paper 1, page 22; and
- Report of the Canadian Sentencing Commission, 1987, 'Sentencing Reform: A Canadian Approach', Canadian Government Publishing Centre.

[169] See *Lialu v The State* [1990] PNGLR 487, [1990] PGSC 16.

[170] See *Richard Liri v The State* (2007) SC883, [2007] PGSC 3 and *Joe Giamur v The State* (2007) SC884, [2007] PGSC 7.

[7.0] JUDICIAL DISCRETION

Sentencing is the exercise of a judicial discretion[171] having regard to the particular circumstances of the case whilst noting that each case has to be determined on its own facts[172].[173]

In exercising the sentencing discretion, the Court must act in accordance with statutory and any applicable common law principles and in a manner that is consonant with reasonable consistency.[174]

Whilst all discretionary decision-making carries with it the probability of some degree of inconsistency like cases should be treated in like manner. The administration of criminal justice should be systematically fair, and that involves, amongst other things, reasonable consistency.[175]

The judicial task is:

> To pass a sentence as is appropriate in all the circumstances of the case[176] having regard to the body of sentencing principles[177], including:

---

[171] See *Wesley Nobudi, John Evoa and Frank Yalikiti v The State* (2009) SC999, [2009] PGSC 20 and *The State v Jeffery Wangi* (2006) N3016, [2006] PGNC 48.

See also: *Skinner v R* (1913) 16 CLR 336; *House v R* (1936) 55 CLR 499; *Cranssen v R* (1936) 55 CLR 509, [1936] HCA 42 and *R v Storey* [1998] 1 VR 359 at 366.

[172] See *Lawrence Simbe v The State* [1994] PNGLR 38; *The State v Relvie Joe* (2005) N2832, [2005] PGNC 127; *The State v Philip Peter* (2010) N4011 and *The State v Sou Mesak and others* (2009) N3907.

[173] See *Avia Aihi v The State (No. 3)* [1982] PNGLR 92 at 105, [1982] PGSC 9; *Ian Napoleon Setep v The State* (2001) SC666, [2001] PGSC 14; *The State v Kennedy Arus* (2001) N2081; *The State v Ian Bob Wali* (2004) N2580; *The State v Abel Airi* (2000) N2007 and *The State v Robert Kawin* (2001) N2167.

[174] See *Elias v R; Issa v R* [2013] HCA 31.

[175] See *Hili v R* (2010) 242 CLR 520 at 535, [2010] HCA 45 and *Wong v R* (2001) 207 CLR 584 at 591, [2001] HCA 64.

[176] See *R v Waisopo; ex parte Secretary for Law* [1974] PNGLR 41, [1974] PGSC 40 and *Rakatani v The State* [1979] PNGLR 556, [1979] PGSC 21.

See also: *R v Young* [1990] VR 951 at 954.

[177] See *Pearce v R* (1998) 194 CLR 610 at 624 and *Ryan v R* (2001) 206 CLR 267, (2001) 75 ALJR 815, (2001) 179 ALR 193, [2001] HCA 21, per McHugh J.

- proportionality[178];
- parity[179];
- totality[180]; and
- the avoidance of double punishment[181].

The discretion which the law commits to a Court is of vital importance in the administration of criminal justice.[182]

The judicial power that is exercised by the Courts belongs to the people.[183]

---

178 Refer also to:
- the chapter titled 'Equality In Sentencing'; and
- the section titled 'Disparity In Sentencing' in the chapter titled 'Appeals Against Sentence'.

179 See *Elias v R; Issa v R* [2013] HCA 31.

Refer also to:
- the chapter titled 'Equality In Sentencing'; and
- the section titled 'Disparity In Sentencing' in the chapter titled 'Appeals Against Sentence'.

180 Refer also to the subsection titled 'Totality Principle' in the section titled 'Imprisonment' in the chapter titled 'Sentencing Options'.

181 Refer also to the chapter titled 'Double Jeopardy' in the text titled 'Injia on Criminal Practice and Procedure in Papua New Guinea and the Pacific'.

182 See *Lowndes v R* (1999) 195 CLR 665, [1999] HCA 29.

Refer also to the chapter titled 'Minimum Sentence'.

183 See *Avia Aihi v The State* [1981] PNGLR 81, [1981] PGSC 9 and *SCR No. 4 of 1980; Re: Petition of Michael T Somare* [1981] PNGLR 265.

Section 158(1) of the *Constitution of the Independent State of Papua New Guinea* states:

> 'Subject to this Constitution, the judicial authority of the People is vested in the National Judicial System'.

INTRODUCTION TO SENTENCING

There can be no argument that:

- sentencing is a community responsibility[184]; and
- community involvement in the punishment of accused persons should be considered[185].

However, whilst the attitude of the community is a factor to be taken into consideration in formulating sentencing policy, it should not be given undue importance.[186]

The Courts do not have to reflect public opinion, but on the other hand Courts must not disregard it.[187]

It is the responsibility of the Courts to determine as to what is the appropriate punishment to be imposed for each individual case[188].

Whilst sentencing is not an exact science[189] or a purely logical exercise[190], it has been described as a 'nuanced art'[191].

---

[184] See *The State v Dobi Ao (No. 2)* (2002) N2247.

As regards the involvement of the community in relation to suspended sentences, refer also to the section titled 'Imprisonment' in the chapter titled 'Sentencing Options'.

[185] See *Public Prosecutor v Don Hale* (1998) SC564.

[186] See *The Public Prosecutor v Etape; Public Prosecutor v Tapo; Public Prosecutor v Mombi* [1977] PNGLR 416, [1977] PGSC 14.

[187] As observed by Lawston LJ in *R v Sargeant* (1975) 60 Cr App R 74 at 77.

[188] See *Gerea and others v DPP* [1984] SILR 161 at 174-175 and *Deaton v The Attorney-General and The Revenue Commissioners* [1963] IR 170 at 181.

[189] See *Jerry Wasu v The State* (2002) SC697, [2002] PGSC 16; *Acting Public Prosecutor v Nitak Mangilonde Taganis of Tambitanis* [1982] PNGLR 299 at 303, [1982] PGSC 6; *The State v Iori Veraga* (2005) N2921, [2005] PGNC 43 and *The State v Jeffery Wangi* (2006) N3016, [2006] PGNC 48.

[190] See *Veen v R (No. 2)* (1988) 164 CLR 465 at 476-477, (1988) 33 A Crim R 230, [1988] HCA 14.

[191] See *Boesaleana v Public Prosecutor* [2011] VUCA 33.

INTRODUCTION TO SENTENCING

The view that sentencing is an art derives from the belief that it demands the intuitive balancing of a myriad of factors that will vary substantially from case to case.[192]

Sentencing is a very difficult task.[193]

It must recognise and reconcile contrasting, even contending, public and private values or interests.[194]

Sentencing requires consideration and balancing of many different and often conflicting matters[195], including:

- matters relevant to the offence[196]; and
- matters relevant to the accused person[197].

The exercise of a Court's discretion is not a matter of mathematics.[198]

Recognition that the court is sentencing *the* offender for *the* offence does not mean that the Court is engaged in a mechanical exercise with a predetermined range of outcomes.[199]

---

192 See New Zealand Law Commission, 2006, 'Reforms to the Sentencing and Parole Structure: Consultative Draft', Preliminary Paper 1, page 18.

193 See *Investment Promotion Authority v Niugini Scrap Corporation Pty Ltd; Investment Promotion Authority v James Sinton Spence* (2001) N2104.

See also: *Weininger v R* (2003) 212 CLR 629, [2003] HCA 14, per Kirby J.

194 See New Zealand Law Commission, 2001, 'Proof of Disputed Facts on Sentence', Report 76, page 1.

195 See *Ryan v R* (2001) 206 CLR 267, (2001) 75 ALJR 815, (2001) 179 ALR 193, [2001] HCA 21, per Hayne J.

196 See *R v Stuckless* (1998) 17 CR (5th) 330, per Abella JA at 339.

197 See *R v Stuckless* (1998) 17 CR (5th) 330, per Abella JA at 339.

198 See *R v Storey* [1998] 1 VR 359 at 366.

199 See *Weininger v R* (2003) 212 CLR 629 at 638, [2003] HCA 14; *Engert* (1995) 84 A Crim R 67, per Gleeson CJ at 68 and *Elias v R; Issa v R* [2013] HCA 31.

INTRODUCTION TO SENTENCING

The Court should avoid taking a mathematical approach, as this would depart from principle because it does not take into account that there are many conflicting and contradictory elements that bear upon sentencing an accused person.[200]

Sentencing is not a process that leads to a single correct answer arrived at by some process admitting of mathematical precision[201], and nor is it a mechanical, numerical, arithmetical or rigid activity in which one starts from the maximum sentence[202] fixed by Parliament and works down in mathematical steps[203].

The sentencing process is not so scientific.[204]

Metaphorical references to 'credit', 'discount', or the like, must therefore not be taken literally.[205]

There is no single correct sentence[206], unless it is lawfully fixed by Parliament.[207]

---

[200] See *Markarian v R* (2005) 228 CLR 357, (2005) 215 ALR 213, [2005] HCA 25.

[201] See *Jerry Wasu v The State* (2002) SC697, [2002] PGSC 16; *Acting Public Prosecutor v Nitak Mangilonde Taganis of Tambitanis* [1982] PNGLR 299 at 303, [1982] PGSC 6 and *The State v David Carol* (2009) N3762, [2009] PGNC 143.

See also: *Markarian v R* (2005) 228 CLR 357, (2005) 215 ALR 213, [2005] HCA 25; *House v R* (1936) 55 CLR 499; *Weininger v R* (2003) 212 CLR 629, [2003] HCA 14, per Kirby J; *Pearce v R* (1998) 194 CLR 610 at 624 and *Ryan v R* (2001) 75 ALJR 815 at 821, (2001) 179 ALR 193 at 201, (2001) 206 CLR 267, [2001] HCA 21.

[202] Refer also to the chapter titled 'Maximum Sentence'.

[203] See *AB v R* (1999) 198 CLR 111 at 121-122, [1999] HCA 46; *Wong and Leung v R* (2001) 207 CLR 584 at 611-612, (2001) 76 ALJR 79, [2001] HCA 64 and *R v Whyte* (2002) 55 NSWLR 252 at 278, [2002] NSWCCA 343.

[204] See *Markarian v R* (2005) 228 CLR 357, per Kirby J at 405, (2005) 215 ALR 213, [2005] HCA 25.

[205] See *Ryan v R* (2001) 206 CLR 267, (2001) 75 ALJR 815, (2001) 179 ALR 193, [2001] HCA 21, per Hayne J.

[206] See *House v R* (1936) 55 CLR 499; *Lowndes v R* (1999) 195 CLR 665, [1999] HCA 29; *Markarian v R* (2005) 228 CLR 357, (2005) 215 ALR 213, [2005] HCA 25 and *R v Storey* [1998] 1 VR 359 at 366.

Refer also to the chapter titled 'Sentencing Options'.

[207] See *Markarian v R* (2005) 228 CLR 357, per Kirby J at 405-406, (2005) 215 ALR 213, [2005] HCA 25.

Refer also to the chapter titled 'Minimum Sentence'.

No particular opinion will be uniquely right[208] and there will be differences of opinion which, within a given range, are legitimate and reasonable[209].

However, a Court is not bound by concessions made by the Public Prosecutor on behalf of the State.[210]

[8.0] APPROPRIATE SENTENCE

Whilst a Court has a wide discretion as to the sentence to be imposed[211], a Court:

- can only impose a sentence that is prescribed by law[212]; and
- has no power to impose any other form of punishment, including customary punishment[213].

It is part of the judicial function to determine:

- the nature; and
- the extent

[208] See *Lowe v R* (1984) 154 CLR 606, per Mason J at 612, [1984] HCA 46.

[209] See *Boughey v R* (1986) 161 CLR 513 at 518; *DPP v McMaster* [2008] VSCA 102 and *Young, Dickensen and West v R* (1989) 45 A Crim R 147 at 151.

[210] See *GAS v R* (2004) 217 CLR 198, [2004] HCA 22 and *Wood v R* (2002) 130 A Crim R 518, [2002] WASCA 95.

[211] See *Ben Wafia and others v The State* (2006) SC851, [2006] PGSC 19.

[212] See *John Foe Leslie Leslie v The State* (1998) SC560, [1998] PGSC 22; *Kembu v Mason* [1971-72] PNGLR 407, [1971] PGSC 28; *Acting Public Prosecutor v Uname Aumane and others* [1980] PNGLR 510; *Public Prosecutor v Arthur Jawodimbari and Monty Derari* (2006) SC891, [2006] PGSC 28 and *The State v Michael Waragu and Anton Marko (No. 3)* (2007) N3282, [2007] PGNC 139.

Section 37(2) of the *Constitution of the Independent State of Papua New Guinea* states:

> 'Except, subject to any Act of the Parliament to the contrary, in the case of the offence commonly known as contempt of court, nobody may be convicted of an offence that is not defined by, and the penalty for which is not prescribed by, a written law'.

[213] See *Uname Aumane and others v The State* [1980] PNGLR 510 and *The State v Michael Waragu and Anton Marko (No. 3)* (2007) N3282, [2007] PGNC 139.

of the sentence whenever the general rule laid down by statute or common law gives a range of choice.[214]

However, it is a fundamental assumption of sentencing jurisprudence that in no case will only one sentence be correct.[215]

When determining the appropriate sentence to be imposed a Court should:

- proceed cautiously and with a tight rein on emotions; and
- endeavour to sift the wheat from the chaff and proceed rationally and logically.[216]

A sentence should not only be determined by:

- the conduct of an accused person; and
- the consequences of that conduct[217],

but also bear a relationship to the intrinsic nature and gravity of the offence.[218]

When exercising its discretion there may be differences in the sentence imposed by the Courts for similar offences depending on the nature and circumstances in which the offence was committed[219].[220]

---

[214] See *The People (DPP) v Cahill* [1980] IR 8, per Henchy J at 11.

[215] See *Foster v R* [2011] NSWCCA 285.

[216] See *Paia Lifi v Phillip Dege* (1981) N291(M).

[217] See *The State v John Telape* (2009) N3815.

[218] See *R v Ward* [1976] 1 NZLR 588 at 590.

[219] Different minds will attribute different weight to various facts in arriving at the 'instinctive synthesis' which takes account of the various purposes for which sentences are imposed, see *R v Storey* [1998] 1 VR 359 at 366.

[220] See *The State v Kennedy Arus* (2001) N2081; *The State v Ian Bob Wali* (2004) N2580; *The State v Abel Airi* (2000) N2007; *The State v Robert Kawin* (2001) N2167 and *The State v Keputong Nagong* (1980) N225.

INTRODUCTION TO SENTENCING

There are a multitude of factors to be taken into account, many of them pulling successively in opposite directions, the evaluation, in terms of imprisonment, quantity of fine or other sanctions, is necessarily imprecise.[221]

But not one factor usually influences a Court's exercise of its discretionary power of sentencing.[222]

A Court should pass an appropriate sentence whilst having regard to all the circumstances relating to:

- the offence; and

- the accused person.[223]

The severity of the sentence imposed must be strictly proportionate to:

- the seriousness and gravity of the offence[224].

  The maximum penalty is one of many factors that bear on the ultimate discretionary determination of the sentence for the offence.[225]

---

[221] See *Weininger v R* (2003) 212 CLR 629 at 645, [2003] HCA 14.

[222] See *Michael Kamane Wai v The State* (1983) SC263.

See also: *Ryan v R* (2001) 206 CLR 267, (2001) 75 ALJR 815 at 821, (2001) 179 ALR 193, [2001] HCA 21, per McHugh J.

[223] See *R v Roche* [1999] 2 Cr App R (S) 105, per Bingham LCJ at 109; *The People (DPP) v Tiernan* [1988] IR 250 at 254, [1989] ILRM 149 and *Elias v R; Issa v R* [2013] HCA 31.

[224] See *Goli Golu v The State* [1979] PNGLR 653, [1979] PGSC 9 and *The State v Tom Keroi Gurua and others* (2002) N2312, [2002] PGNC 41.

See also:

- *Veen v R (No. 1)* (1979) 143 CLR 458, (1979) 53 ALJR 305, [1979] HCA 7; and
- New Zealand Law Commission, 2001, 'Proof of Disputed Facts on Sentence', Report 76, page 1.

The 'just deserts' principle of sentencing requires the severity of the sentence to be in proportion to the seriousness of the offending behaviour, although it is based on the harm caused or risked by the offending conduct and the culpability of the accused person in committing the crime, see The Law Reform Commission of Ireland, 1993, 'Consultation Paper on Sentencing', paragraph 4.75.

Refer also to the section titled 'Seriousness Of An Offence Generally' in the section titled 'Aggravating Factors'.

[225] See *Elias v R; Issa v R* [2013] HCA 31.

Irrespective of the theory of punishment applied the sentence must be a 'fit' sentence proportionate to the seriousness of the offence, thereby enabling the public to:

- be satisfied that the accused person 'deserved' the punishment that he or she received; and
- feel confidence in the fairness and rationality of the criminal justice system[226]; and

- the degree of culpability of the accused person[227].

  In determining the appropriate sentence the assessment must start with the nature and culpability of the offence.[228]

  Culpability refers to the factors of intent, motive and circumstance that determine how much the accused person should be held responsible for his or her actions.[229]

Each case:

- has its own facts and circumstances; and
- has to be decided on its own merits.[230]

---

[226] See *Re BC Motor Vehicle Act* [1985] 2 SCR 486, per Wilson J at 533.

[227] See:

- *R v Wilmott* (1966) 58 DLR (2d) 33; *R v Solowan* 2008 SCC 62, [2008] 3 SCR 309 and *R v Nasogaluak* 2010 SCC 6, [2010] 1 SCR 206; and
- New Zealand Law Commission, 2001, 'Proof of Disputed Facts on Sentence', Report 76, page 1.

Refer also to

- the section titled 'Role Played In The Commission Of An Offence' in the chapter titled 'Extenuating Circumstances'; and
- the section titled 'Member Of A Gang' in the chapter titled 'Aggravating Factors'.

[228] See *R v Lepupa* (1997) 15 CRNZ 262 and *R v Horton* [1991] 3 NZLR 549 at 552.

[229] See The Law Reform Commission of Ireland, 1993, 'Consultation Paper on Sentencing', paragraph 4.79.

[230] See *The State v Philip Soni and Tony Ilong* (2008) N3694, [2008] PGNC 237.

OBJECTIVES OR PURPOSES OF SENTENCING

[1.0] INTRODUCTION

Sentencing is an agonising task that involves:

- the evaluation of different 'objectives' or 'purposes' ('principles') of sentencing, including deterrence, separation (incapacitation), rehabilitation (reformation) and retribution; and

- deciding which of those 'objectives' or 'purposes' should be achieved in the particular case at hand.[231]

The 'objectives' or 'purposes' of sentencing vary:

- from accused person to accused person; and

- from offence to offence.[232]

The troublesome nature of the sentencing discretion arises in large measure from unavoidable difficulty in giving weight to each of the 'objectives' or 'purposes' of sentencing.[233]

The 'objectives' or 'purposes' of sentencing overlap[234], and sometimes are in conflict[235].

None of the 'objectives' or 'purposes' of sentencing should be considered in isolation when making a determination as to what is an appropriate sentence in a particular case.[236]

Whilst the 'objectives' or 'purposes' of sentencing are guideposts to the appropriate sentence, sometimes they point in different directions.[237]

---

[231] See *Uname Aumane and others v The State* [1980] PNGLR 510, per Kapi J (as he then was) at 537-538.

[232] See *R v Kane* [1974] VR 759 at 764-766; *R v Williscroft* [1975] VR 292 at 299, [1975] Vic Rp 27; *R v Holder and Johnston* [1983] 3 NSWLR 245 at 270, (1983) 13 A Crim R 375 and *R v Young* [1990] VR 951 at 955.

[233] See *Veen v R (No. 2)* (1988) 164 CLR 465 at 476-477, (1988) 33 A Crim R 230, [1988] HCA 14.

[234] See *Veen v R (No. 2)* (1988) 164 CLR 465 at 476-477, (1988) 33 A Crim R 230, [1988] HCA 14.

[235] See *Veen v R (No. 2)* (1988) 164 CLR 465 at 476-477, (1988) 33 A Crim R 230, [1988] HCA 14.

[236] See *Veen v R (No. 2)* (1988) 164 CLR 465 at 476-477, (1988) 33 A Crim R 230, [1988] HCA 14.

[237] See *Veen v R (No. 2)* (1988) 164 CLR 465 at 476-477, (1988) 33 A Crim R 230, [1988] HCA 14.

OBJECTIVES OR PURPOSES OF SENTENCING

Such 'objectives' or 'purposes' of sentencing include:

- The public interest;
- The need for education;
- The need for incapacitation;
- The need for restorative justice;
- The need for retribution;
- The need for deterrence;
- The need for justice for the victim;
- The need for prevention; and
- The need for reformation or rehabilitation.

The agonising task for a Court is to evaluate which of these theories of sentencing should be achieved in the particular case that it is dealing with. A Court may be faced with a dilemma because if it chooses one theory of sentencing it is likely to frustrate the other theories. In some cases, a Court will need to give a balanced consideration to all the theories of sentencing. In others, a Court will want to emphasise or achieve one theory of sentencing more than others in certain classes of offences.[238]

In the exercise of the sentencing discretion, any combination of the foregoing purposes may be opted for in appropriate circumstances.[239]

---

[238] As commented by Kapi J (as he then was) in *Uname Aumane and others v The State* [1980] PNGLR 510.

[239] See *The State v Iori Veraga* (2005) N2921, [2005] PGNC 43.

However, when several conflicting principles are pursued simultaneously, the resulting sentence may frustrate them all. The sentence may rely too much on rehabilitation to satisfy retributive factors, yet it may not use deterrent factors enough to have any use as a preventive strategy. When the principles of sentencing are in conflict, as they are, following a little of each may achieve no purpose at all.[240]

Irrespective, what must be borne in mind in sentencing is the function and the purpose of criminal law. The purpose of criminal law, like the purpose of customary law in the village, is for the protection of society. The society is made up of individual members. In achieving the purpose of criminal law, regard must be given to the protection of the individual. The individual has constitutional rights which must be protected. However, a Court should not be so preoccupied with the rights of the accused person that it forgets the rights of the innocent members of our villages, tribes, cities and the country who are entitled to protection against criminal behaviour. Therefore, all these considerations must be carefully balanced.[241]

Whatever sentence the Court decides to impose must reflect the purposes of the criminal justice system that should balance out between the offence or accused person and the effect it may have on the community.[242]

It is obvious from all this that there is no easy solution to the task of sentencing.[243]

[2.0] THE PUBLIC INTEREST

The first consideration in determining a sentence is the 'public interest[244]' which is served:

- not merely by:
    - punishing the accused person; and

---

[240] See The Law Reform Commission of Ireland, 1993, 'Consultation Paper on Sentencing', paragraph 2.17.

[241] As commented by Kapi J (as he then was) in *Uname Aumane and others v The State* [1980] PNGLR 510.

[242] See *The State v Douglas Mareva* (2012) N4805, [2012] PGNC 222.

[243] As commented by Kapi J (as he then was) in *Uname Aumane and others v The State* [1980] PNGLR 510.

[244] See *The State v Iori Veraga* (2005) N2921, [2005] PGNC 43.

See also: *R v Ball* (1951) 35 Cr App R 164, per Hilbery J at 165-166.

  - showing a deterrent to others;

- but also by affording:

  - a compelling inducement; and

  - an opportunity

  to the accused person to reform.[245]

The Courts have a constitutional duty to:

- seriously take into consideration the wishes of the community in relation to the kind of sentence an accused person should receive; and

- ensure that the sentence is reflective of the wishes of the community.[246]

[3.0] THE NEED FOR EDUCATION

The need for education involves:

> Education of the community continually in the proper standards of conduct which have to be observed if a decent life is to be possible for everybody.[247]

[4.0] THE NEED FOR PREVENTION

The need for prevention involves:

> Threatening punishment on conviction.[248]

---

245 As stated by Gannon J in *The State (Stanbridge) v Mahon* [1979] IR 214.

246 See *The State v Irox Winston* (2003) N2347.

See also: *Paia Lifi v Phillip Dege* (1981) N291(M) and *Investment Promotion Authority v Niugini Scrap Corporation Pty Ltd; Investment Promotion Authority v James Sinton Spence* (2001) N2104.

247 See *The State v Iori Veraga* (2005) N2921, [2005] PGNC 43.

248 See *The State v Iori Veraga* (2005) N2921, [2005] PGNC 43.

[5.0] THE NEED FOR INCAPACITATION

The need for incapacitation[249] refers to:

> The need to protect the community by separating the accused person from the community[250], the so-called 'reductive' justification for prison sentences.[251]

This theory of sentencing is considered appropriate in relation to offences that involve a grave risk to the personal peace and safety of the members of the community, such as murder, robbery, rape, etc.[252]

Emphasis is placed on the protection of the community, rather than the accused person.[253]

It is obvious that incapacitation is an immediate and direct effect of custodial sentences since society at large is protected from the possibility of repeat offences so long as the accused person is detained.[254]

---

[249] See The Law Reform Commission of Ireland, 1996, 'Report on Sentencing', paragraph 2.44.

[250] See *The State v Sukope Tova* (1997) N1522; *The State v Iori Veraga* (2005) N2921, [2005] PGNC 43 and the comments of Kapi J (as he then was) in *Uname Aumane and others v The State* [1980] PNGLR 510.

See also: *Veen v R (No. 2)* (1988) 164 CLR 465 at 476-477, (1988) 33 A Crim R 230, [1988] HCA 14; *R v Storey* [1998] 1 VR 359 at 366; *R v Cuthbert* (1976) 86 WN (Pt. 1) NSW 272, per Herron CJ at 274 and *Webb v O'Sullivan* [1952] SASR 65, per Napier CJ at 66.

[251] See *Ryan v R* (2001) 206 CLR 267, (2001) 75 ALJR 815, (2001) 179 ALR 193, [2001] HCA 21, per McHugh J.

[252] As commented by Kapi J (as he then was) in *Uname Aumane and others v The State* [1980] PNGLR 510.

Refer also to the section titled 'Seriousness Of An Offence Generally' in the chapter titled 'Aggravating Factors'.

[253] See *Uname Aumane and others v The State* [1980] PNGLR 510, per Kapi J (as he then was) at 537-538.

[254] See The Law Reform Commission of Ireland, 1993, 'Consultation Paper on Sentencing', paragraph 4.45.

However, a fundamental precept of the criminal law is that a sentence should not be increased beyond that which is proportionate to the offence in order to extend the period of protection of the community[255]. The distinction between:

- extending a sentence to protect society; and
- taking into account society's protection in determining the appropriate sentence

may not always be easy to draw[256].[257]

A Court may make a prediction as to the future dangerousness of an accused person to society at the time of sentencing that will often be many years before possible release.[258]

[6.0] THE NEED FOR RESTORATIVE JUSTICE

Restorative justice has been described as 'a generic term for all those approaches to wrongdoing that seek to move beyond condemnation and punishment to address both the causes and the consequences – personal, relational and societal – of offending in ways that promote accountability.[259]

Restorative justice:

- emphasises the acceptance of guilt and responsibility;
- is based on reparation which encompasses actions which attempt to repair the damage caused by crime, either materially or symbolically; and

---

[255] See *Veen v R (No. 2)* (1988) 164 CLR 465 at 476-477, (1988) 33 A Crim R 230, [1988] HCA 14 and *Ibbs v R; Baumer v R* (1988) 188 CLR 51, per Mason CJ and Wilson, Deane, Dawson and Gaudron JJ at 57-58, (1988) 83 ALR 8, [1988] HCA 67.

Refer also to:
- the chapter titled 'Equality In Sentencing'; and
- the section titled 'Disparity In Sentencing' in the chapter titled 'Appeals Against Sentence'.

[256] See *Veen v R (No. 2)* (1988) 164 CLR 465 at 476-477, (1988) 33 A Crim R 230, [1988] HCA 14.

[257] See *Muldrock v R* (2011) 85 ALJR 1154, [2011] HCA 39.

[258] As observed by Gleeson CJ in *Fardon v Attorney General for the State of Queensland* (2004) 223 CLR 575, [2004] HCA 46.

[259] See New Zealand Law Commission, 2004, 'Delivering Justice For All: A Vision for New Zealand Courts and Tribunals', Report 85, page 77.

- involves the victim, the offender and the community.[260]

The aim of restorative justice is:

> To reconcile the parties so that previous good relations between them are restored.[261]

[7.0] THE NEED FOR RETRIBUTION

The need for retribution[262] refers to:

> The need for an accused person to be punished for committing an offence.[263]

This involves punishing an accused person to the extent that is just and fair in all the circumstances[264], justified by the fact that the accused person:

- has done wrong; and
- deserves to be punished.[265]

---

[260] See New Zealand Law Commission, 1997, 'Criminal Prosecution – A Discussion Paper', Preliminary Paper 28, page 92.

[261] See *The State v Inge Gotama* (2006) N3156, [2006] PGNC 135.

[262] See *Uname Aumane and others v The State* [1980] PNGLR 510, per Kapi J (as he then was) at 537-538 and *Investment Promotion Authority v Niugini Scrap Corporation Pty Ltd; Investment Promotion Authority v James Sinton Spence* (2001) N2104.

See also: *Veen v R (No. 2)* (1988) 164 CLR 465 at 476-477, (1988) 33 A Crim R 230, [1988] HCA 14 and *R v Radich* [1954] NZLR 86 at 87.

[263] See The Law Reform Commission of Ireland, 1993, 'Consultation Paper on Sentencing', paragraph 1.45.

[264] See *Paia Lifi v Phillip Dege* (1981) N291(M) and *The State v Dobi Ao (No. 2)* (2002) N2247.

See also: *R v Storey* [1998] 1 VR 359 at 366.

[265] See *The State v Iori Veraga* (2005) N2921, [2005] PGNC 43.

See also: The Law Reform Commission of Ireland, 1996, 'Report of Sentencing', paragraph 2.1.

OBJECTIVES OR PURPOSES OF SENTENCING

Colloquially put:

> 'Do the crime, do the time'.[266]

This theory of sentencing may be referred to as 'vengeance'. This conveys the notion that the person who commits a crime must 'pay' for it, or 'deserves' it. This purpose of sentence is not foreign to the cultures of the people of this country. This is what is normally referred to as 'payback'. This notion grew out of many years of tradition in the village. A person who broke the rules or customs of the village deserved punishment.[267]

This purpose explains why there are varying punishments that are prescribed for offences, depending on the seriousness or heinousness of the offence[268].[269]

Notwithstanding the enlightened approach that is now made to sentencing compared to earlier days, the concept of punishment, ie., coercive action, is fundamental to correctional treatment in society.[270]

A retributive response to wrongdoing is a strong expression of denunciation[271] of the offence.[272]

The place of retribution in the sentencing process is a natural phenomenon – a response to an offence that fails to condemn the offender scarcely seems morally adequate. To leave an act unpunished is close to condoning it since punishment:

- acts as a re-assertion that the law has been broken; and
- expresses the moral indignation of the community.[273]

---

[266] See *The State v Iori Veraga* (2005) N2921, [2005] PGNC 43.

[267] As commented by Kapi J (as he then was) in *Uname Aumane and others v The State* [1980] PNGLR 510.

[268] Refer also to the section titled 'Seriousness Of An Offence Generally' in the chapter titled 'Aggravating Factors'.

[269] See *The State v Iori Veraga* (2005) N2921, [2005] PGNC 43.

[270] See *R v Williscroft* [1975] VR 292 at 299, [1975] Vic Rp 27.

[271] See *R v Storey* [1998] 1 VR 359 at 366.

[272] See The Law Reform Commission of Ireland, 1993, 'Consultation Paper on Sentencing', paragraph 4.14.

However, as regards the sentencing of children[274] retribution is, in most cases, of lesser significance then when sentencing an adult for the same offence.[275] But the significant public interest in deterring antisocial behaviour cannot be completely ignored.[276]

Furthermore, retribution is an important issue when a child commits a serious offence.[277]

[8.0] THE NEED FOR REFORMATION OR REHABILITATION

The emphasis in this theory is on the accused person.[278]

The need for reformation[279] or rehabilitation[280] refers to:

---

[273] See The Law Reform Commission of Ireland, 1993, 'Consultation Paper on Sentencing', paragraph 4.14.

[274] Refer also to:

- the section titled 'Juvenile Courts Act' in the chapter titled 'Introduction To Sentencing'; and
- the section titled 'Youthfulness' in the chapter titled 'Mitigating Factors'.

[275] See *KT v R* (2008) 182 A Crim R 571, [2008] NSWCCA 51; *R v GDP* (1991) 53 A Crim R 112 at 115-116; *R v E (a child)* (1993) 66 A Crim R 14 at 28 and *R v Adamson* (2002) 132 A Crim R 511, [2002] NSWCCA 349.

[276] See *R v Pham and Ly* (1991) 55 A Crim R 128, per Lee CJ at CL at 135.

[277] See *R v Williscroft* [1975] VR 292 at 299, [1975] Vic Rp 27.

[278] As commented by Kapi J (as he then was) in *Uname Aumane and others v The State* [1980] PNGLR 510.

Refer also to the section titled 'Seriousness Of An Offence Generally' in the chapter titled 'Aggravating Factors'.

[279] See *Veen v R (No. 2)* (1988) 164 CLR 465 at 476-477, (1988) 33 A Crim R 230, [1988] HCA 14 and *R v Radich* [1954] NZLR 86 at 87.

[280] See *Uname Aumane and others v The State* [1980] PNGLR 510, per Kapi J (as he then was) at 537-538; *The State v Obert Poesan Pokanas* (2004) N2702 and *Investment Promotion Authority v Niugini Scrap Corporation Pty Ltd; Investment Promotion Authority v James Sinton Spence* (2001) N2104.

See also: *R v Storey* [1998] 1 VR 359 at 366; *The People (Attorney-General) v O'Driscoll* (1972) 1 Frewen 351 at 359 and *The People (DPP) v Conroy (No. 2)* [1989] IR 160 at 165.

> The need for an accused person to be given an opportunity to reform by mending his or her ways and becoming a better law-abiding citizen.[281]

The theory behind rehabilitation is that the accused person should receive correctional treatment so that when he or she completes his or her sentence he or she becomes a useful member of the community, that is, he or she will obey the law rather than disobey it.[282]

An accused person learns from his or her punishment the folly of his or her way.[283]

The rehabilitative ideal assumes that:

- criminal behaviour is the product of antecedent causes which may be identified and controlled; and
- measures may be employed to treat the convicted accused person so as to effect changes in his or her behaviour for:
    - his or her own good; and
    - the good of society.[284]

In other words 'crime' is viewed as a disease capable of treatment and cure. This utilitarian theory of rehabilitation of accused persons is by no means a new one; it is at least as old as Plato.[285]

---

[281] See *The State v Dobi Ao (No. 2)* (2002) N2247.

See also: The Law Reform Commission of Ireland, 1996, 'Report of Sentencing', paragraph 2.42 and The Law Reform Commission of Ireland, 1993, 'Consultation Paper on Sentencing', paragraph 1.45.

[282] As commented by Kapi J (as he then was) in *Uname Aumane and others v The State* [1980] PNGLR 510.

Refer also to the section titled 'Seriousness Of An Offence Generally' in the chapter titled 'Aggravating Factors'.

[283] See *The State v Iori Veraga* (2005) N2921, [2005] PGNC 43 and *The State v Dobi Ao (No. 2)* (2002) N2247.

[284] See The Law Reform Commission of Ireland, 1993, 'Consultation Paper on Sentencing', paragraph 4.19.

[285] See The Law Reform Commission of Ireland, 1993, 'Consultation Paper on Sentencing', paragraph 4.19.

Accused persons found guilty after trial should not be automatically deprived of a finding of good prospects of rehabilitation, unless they acknowledge their guilt.[286]

It is in the interest of the community to rehabilitate accused persons so as to ensure that they do not re-offend, where possible, in order to achieve the main objective of keeping the community free of accused persons.[287]

When determining an appropriate sentence whilst considering the need for rehabilitation a Court should not consider the:

- ‘aggravating factors[288]’;
- ‘mitigating factors[289]’; and
- ‘extenuating circumstances[290]’

because these types of sentence are based on the likelihood of the accused person or others re-offending, rather than on the gravity of the offence.[291]

The evidence of likelihood of rehabilitation is not a factor in mitigation, but rather a ground for supposing that there was a reasonable chance that the accused person could be rehabilitated, provided that he or she was induced by the length of his or her sentence to have an expectation of eventually returning to society.[292]

However, rehabilitation remains necessarily subsidiary to the need to protect the public in relation to serious offences.[293]

---

[286] See *Alseedi v R* [2009] NSWCCA 185.

[287] See *The State v Sul Kora* (2001) N2092, [2001] PGNC 93.

[288] Refer also to the chapter titled ‘Aggravating Factors’.

[289] Refer also to the chapter titled ‘Mitigating Factors’.

[290] Refer also to the chapter titled ‘Extenuating Circumstances’.

[291] See The Law Reform Commission of Ireland, 1996, ‘Report of Sentencing’, paragraph 3.9.

[292] As stated by Finlay CJ in *The People (DPP) v Conroy (No. 2)* [1989] IR 160 at 165.

[293] See *Acting Public Prosecutor v Andrew Lalaina and Angelo Ume* (1981) SC201 and *John Elipa Kalabus v The State* [1988-89] PNGLR 193.

Rehabilitative considerations commonly lead a Court to impose a reduced sentence. However, since a rehabilitative approach involves an attempt by the Court to find a sentence that is most likely to induce reform, a rehabilitative sentence may sometimes appear to be more severe than a sentence imposed following some other approach.[294]

The imposition of a non-custodial sentence in appropriate cases can assist to achieve rehabilitation.[295]

The emphasis given to rehabilitation, rather than general deterrence and retribution when sentencing young accused persons[296], may be moderated when a young person has:

- conducted himself or herself in the way an adult might conduct himself or herself; and
- committed a crime of violence or considerable gravity.[297]

Rehabilitation remains necessarily subsidiary to:

- the need for a sentence to act as a deterrent to the public[298]; and
- the need to protect the public in relation to serious offences.[299]

---

[294] See The Law Reform Commission of Ireland, 1993, 'Consultation Paper on Sentencing', paragraph 1.54.

[295] See *The State v Salle Sorowi* (2007) N3467.

As regards the law in relation to a suspended sentence, refer also to the section titled 'Imprisonment' in the chapter titled 'Sentencing Options'.

[296] Refer also to:
- the section titled 'Juvenile Courts Act' in the chapter titled 'Introduction To Sentencing'; and
- the section titled 'Youthfulness' in the chapter titled 'Mitigating Factors'.

[297] See *KT v R* (2008) 182 A Crim R 571, [2008] NSWCCA 51; *R v Tran* [1999] NSWCCA 109; *R v TJP* [1999] NSWCCA 408; *R v LC* [2001] NSWCCA 175; *R v AEM Snr; R v KEM; R v MM* [2002] NSWCCA 58; *R v Adamson* (2002) 132 A Crim R 511, [2002] NSWCCA 349 and *R v Voss* [2003] NSWCCA 182.

[298] See *R v Gordon* (1994) 71 A Crim R 459, per Hunt CJ at CL at 469.

[299] See *Acting Public Prosecutor v Andrew Lalaina and Angelo Ume* (1981) SC201 and *John Elipa Kalabus v The State* [1988-89] PNGLR 193.

OBJECTIVES OR PURPOSES OF SENTENCING

[9.0] THE NEED FOR JUSTICE FOR THE VICTIM

'Justice is a two edge sword', as the saying goes, so when a Court is considering justice for the accused person, it must also consider justice for the victim[300] which may include the payment of compensation.[301]

[10.0] THE NEED FOR DETERENCE

Deterrence is one of the most frequently used purposes in sentencing.[302]

---

300 See *Ian Napoleon Setep v The State* (2001) SC666, [2001] PGSC 14.

See also: *The State v Iori Veraga* (2005) N2921, [2005] PGNC 43 and *The State v Charlie Pupuka* (2007) N3184, [2007] PGNC 168.

301 See also: 'Consultation Paper on Sentencing', The Law Reform Commission of Ireland, 1993, paragraph 4.61.

Refer also to the section titled 'Compensation Order' in the chapter titled 'Sentencing Options'.

302 See *Uname Aumane and others v The State* [1980] PNGLR 510, per Kapi J (as he then was) at 537-538; *Investment Promotion Authority v Niugini Scrap Corporation Pty Ltd; Investment Promotion Authority v James Sinton Spence* (2001) N2104; *The State v Obert Poesan Pokanas* (2004) N2702 and *The State v Keputong Nagong* (1980) N225.

See also:

- *R v Storey* [1998] 1 VR 359 at 366 and *R v Radich* [1954] NZLR 86 at 87; and
- The Law Reform Commission of Ireland, 1996, 'Report of Sentencing', paragraph 2.1.

The need for deterrence involves:

> The imposition of a punishment that will ensure that the accused person and others do not commit like offences in the future (individual[303] and general[304] deterrence)[305], the so-called 'reductive' justification for prison sentences.[306]

The object of deterrent sentencing is to restrain or dissuade persons from future criminal action, either by:

- describing the potential punishment; or
- applying the punishment in order to engender fear.[307]

When determining an appropriate sentence whilst considering the need for deterrence a Court should not consider the:

- 'aggravating factors[308]';
- 'mitigating factors[309]'; or

[303] Individual deterrence is where the objective in choosing a specific sanction is to deter the particular accused person from engaging again in the offending conduct, see The Law Reform Commission of Ireland, 1996, 'Report of Sentencing', paragraph 2.43.

[304] General deterrence is used to describe threats directed at people who have not experienced the distasteful consequences of sentence, see The Law Reform Commission of Ireland, 1993, 'Consultation Paper on Sentencing', paragraph 4.33.

[305] See *The State v Iori Veraga* (2005) N2921, [2005] PGNC 43.

See also: *Veen v R (No. 2)* (1988) 164 CLR 465 at 476-477, (1988) 33 A Crim R 230, [1988] HCA 14; *Rex v Kenneth John Ball* (1951) 35 Cr App R 164 and *Tan Bok Yeng v Public Prosecutor* [1972] 1 MLJ 214, per Sharma J.

[306] See *Ryan v R* (2001) 206 CLR 267, (2001) 75 ALJR 815, (2001) 179 ALR 193, [2001] HCA 21, per McHugh J.

[307] See The Law Reform Commission of Ireland, 1993, 'Consultation Paper on Sentencing', paragraph 4.32.

[308] Refer also to the chapter titled 'Aggravating Factors'.

[309] Refer also to the chapter titled 'Mitigating Factors'.

- 'extenuating circumstances[310]'

because these types of sentences are based on the likelihood of the accused person or others re-offending, rather than on the gravity of the offence.[311]

Except in well-defined circumstances, such as:

- the youthfulness of the accused person[312]; or
- the mental incapacity of the accused person[313]

public deterrence is generally regarded as the main purpose of punishment.[314]

The subjective considerations relating to the particular accused person (however persuasive) are necessarily subsidiary to the duty of the Courts to see that the sentence which is imposed will operate as a powerful factor in preventing the commission of similar offences by those who may otherwise be tempted by the prospect that only light punishment will be imposed.[315]

---

[310] Refer also to the chapter titled 'Extenuating Circumstances'.

[311] See The Law Reform Commission of Ireland, 1996, 'Report of Sentencing', paragraph 3.9.

[312] Refer also to:

- the section titled 'Juvenile Courts Act' in the chapter titled 'Introduction To Sentencing'; and
- the section titled 'Youthfulness' in the chapter titled 'Mitigating Factors'.

[313] See *R v Engert* (1995) 84 A Crim R 67; *R v Henry and others* (1999) 46 NSWLR 346, [1999] NSWCCA 111; *R v Israil* [2002] NSWCCA 255; *R v Matthews* (2004) 145 A Crim R 445, [2004] NSWCCA 112, per Wood CJ at CL; *R v Scognamiglio* (1991) 56 A Crim R 81; *R v Anderson* [1981] VR 155 at 160-161, (1980) 2 A Crim R 379 at 383-384; *R v Champion* (1992) 64 A Crim R 244; *R v Kilmartin* (1989) 41 A Crim R 22 and *R v Verdins* [2007] VSCA 102.

Refer also to the subsection titled 'Mental Health' in the section titled 'Motive' in the chapter titled 'Extenuating Circumstances'.

[314] See *R v Gordon* (1994) 71 A Crim R 459 at 468 and *R v Cage* [2006] NSWCCA 304.

[315] See *R v Gordon* (1994) 71 A Crim R 459 at 468 and *R v Cage* [2006] NSWCCA 304.

OBJECTIVES OR PURPOSES OF SENTENCING

As regards the sentencing of children[316] general deterrence is, in most cases, of lesser significance then when sentencing an adult for the same offence.[317] But the significant public interest in deterring antisocial behaviour cannot be completely ignored.[318] Furthermore, deterrence is an important issue when a child commits a serious offence.[319]

---

316 Refer also to:

- the section titled 'Juvenile Courts Act' in the chapter titled 'Introduction To Sentencing'; and
- the section titled 'Youthfulness' in the chapter titled 'Mitigating Factors'.

317 See *KT v R* (2008) 182 A Crim R 571, [2008] NSWCCA 51; *R v GDP* (1991) 53 A Crim R 112 at 115-116; *R v E (a child)* (1993) 66 A Crim R 14 at 28 and *R v Adamson* (2002) 132 A Crim R 511, [2002] NSWCCA 349.

318 See *R v Pham and Ly* (1991) 55 A Crim R 128, per Lee CJ at CL at 135.

319 See *R v Williscroft* [1975] VR 292 at 299, [1975] Vic Rp 27.

EQUALITY IN SENTENCING

Each accused person should be treated equally before the law by being sentenced consistent with the principle of 'even-handedness' in sentencing which is fundamental to justice.[320]

'Equal justice' embodies the norm expressed in the term 'equality before the law'. It is an aspect of the 'Rule of Law'.[321]

The administration of criminal justice works as a system; not merely as a multiplicity of unconnected single instances.[322]

It should be systematically fair, and that involves, amongst other things, reasonable consistency.[323]

General concepts of 'systematic fairness' and 'reasonable consistency' apply to persons charged with similar offences arising out of unrelated events.[324]

The consistency they require is consistency in the application of the relevant legal principles, not some numerical or mathematical equivalence.[325]

There needs to be:

- equality between like offending; and
- a proportionality and relativity in respect of actual offences.[326]

---

[320] See *Republic v Lavalua* [1969-1982] NLR 99, [1980] NRSC 20.

Refer also to the section titled 'Disparity In Sentencing' in the chapter titled 'Appeals Against Sentence'.

[321] See *Green v R; Quinn v R* [2011] HCA 49.

[322] See *Hili v R* (2010) 272 ALR 465, [2010] HCA 45 and *Wong and Leung v R* (2001) 207 CLR 584, (2001) 76 ALJR 79, [2001] HCA 64, per Gleeson CJ.

[323] See *Hili v R* (2010) 272 ALR 465, [2010] HCA 45 and *Wong and Leung v R* (2001) 207 CLR 584, (2001) 76 ALJR 79, [2001] HCA 64, per Gleeson CJ.

[324] See *Green v R; Quinn v R* [2011] HCA 49.

[325] See *Green v R; Quinn v R* [2011] HCA 49.

[326] See *Saipir v Public Prosecutor* [1996] VUCA 7.

EQUALITY IN SENTENCING

The principle of 'proportionality' in sentencing will be offended by:

> the imposition of a sentence that exceeds that which can be justified as appropriate or proportionate to the gravity of the offence considered in the light of its objective circumstances[327],

even when imposing a disproportionate sentence is in order to achieve protection of society[328].[329]

The severity of the sentence imposed must be strictly proportionate to:

- the seriousness and gravity of the offence[330]; and

- the degree of culpability of the accused person[331].

---

[327] See *Hoare v R* (1989) 167 CLR 348 at 354, [1989] HCA 33.

[328] See *Lauritsen v R* (2000) 114 A Crim R 333, [2000] WASCA 203.

[329] See also: *Veen v R (No. 1)* (1979) 143 CLR 458, (1979) 53 ALJR 305, [1979] HCA 7; *Veen v R (No. 2)* (1988) 164 CLR 465 at 476-477, (1988) 33 A Crim R 230, [1988] HCA 14; *Chester v R* (1998) 165 CLR 611; *Ibbs v R; Baumer v R* (1988) 188 CLR 51 at 57, (1988) 83 ALR 8, [1988] HCA 67 and *Hoare v R; Bugmy v R* (1990) 169 CLR 525.

[330] See *Goli Golu v The State* [1979] PNGLR 653, [1979] PGSC 9 and *The State v Tom Keroi Gurua and others* (2002) N2312, [2002] PGNC 41.

See also: *Veen v R (No. 1)* (1979) 143 CLR 458, (1979) 53 ALJR 305, [1979] HCA 7.

The 'just deserts' principle of sentencing requires the severity of the sentence to be in proportion to the seriousness of the offending behaviour, although it is based on the harm caused or risked by the offending conduct and the culpability of the accused person in committing the crime, see The Law Reform Commission of Ireland, 1993, 'Consultation Paper on Sentencing', paragraph 4.75.

Refer also to the section titled 'Seriousness Of An Offence Generally' in the section titled 'Aggravating Factors'.

[331] See *R v Wilmott* (1966) 58 DLR (2d) 33; *R v Solowan* 2008 SCC 62, [2008] 3 SCR 309 and *R v Nasogaluak* 2010 SCC 6, [2010] 1 SCR 206.

Refer also to
- the section titled 'Role Played In The Commission Of An Offence' in the chapter titled 'Extenuating Circumstances'; and
- the section titled 'Member Of A Gang' in the chapter titled 'Aggravating Factors'.

EQUALITY IN SENTENCING

Equal justice according to law requires, where the law permits, differential treatment of persons according to differences between them relevant to the:

- scope;
- purpose; and
- subject matter

of the law.[332]

The 'parity rule' states:

> All parties to an offence must be equally punished on the basis of equal justice for all, subject to exceptions.

Where a Court is going to make exception and punish one or more outside the term imposed on the other co-accused, it must give its reasons for doing so.

---

[332] See *Green v R; Quinn v R* [2011] HCA 49.

EQUALITY IN SENTENCING

A Court must justify the disparity[333], otherwise all of the co-accused must receive an equal amount of punishment.[334]

The Court must impose a similar sentence on a co-accused, except where there are good reasons justifying disparate sentences.[335]

However, the sentences must not be of considerable disparity that it gives rise to a justifiable feeling of dissatisfaction and sense of injustice.[336]

A Court should take into account the sentences imposed on the other co-accused in the same case so that there is no objectionable disparity in the sentencing, provided that the other sentences were not inadequate.[337]

---

333 Disparity, simply put, is a difference in sentencing that cannot be justified, see The Law Reform Commission of Ireland, 1993, 'Consultation Paper on Sentencing', paragraph 2.25.

334 See *Max Sanawi v The State* (2010) SC1076, [2010] PGSC 31.

See also: *Denden Tom and others v The State* (2008) SC967; *Steven Loke Ume, Charles Patrick Kaona and Greg Wawa Kavoa v The State* (2006) SC836, [2006] PGSC 9; *Ignatius Natu Pomaloh v The State* (2006) SC834; *The State v Abel Airi* (2000) N2007; *The State v Morobet Awui Koma and Peter Kevin* [1987] PNGLR 262 at 263; *The State v Johnson Maurani* (2008) N3560, [2008] PGNC 191; *The State v Alphonse Polpolio and Jeffrey Baru* [2006] PGNC 16; *The State v Upano Manake (No. 1)* (2006) N3386, [2006] PGNC 166; *The State v Mathew Sabuin and others* [2006] PGNC 76; *The State v Alphonse Kaparo and John Loangesa* (2007) N3189, [2007] PGNC 79; *The State v Kevin Wakore* (2007) N3222, [2007] PGNC 61; *The State v Wesley Aldu* (2004) N2640; *The State v Jonathan Sengi* (2009) N3692, [2009] PGNC 91; *R v Herowa Poia and others* [1964] PNGLR 187; *The State v Tony Pandau Hahuahoru (No. 2)* (2002) N2186; *The State v Vincent Simbago* (2005) N2954, [2005] PGNC 3; *The State v Mark Kanupio and others* (2005) N2800, [2005] PGNC 159; *The State v Paul Yepei (No. 2)* (2004) N2571; *The State v Eki Kondi and others* (2004) N2543; *John Ini Lea v R* [1988-1989] SILR 134; *R v Belton and Petrow* [1997] 1 Cr App R (S) 215; *Kelly v DPP* [1991] SBHC 4; *Isaacs v R* (1997) 41 NSWLR 374 at 378 and *Cheung v R* (2001) 209 CLR 1 at 12-13, [2001] HCA 67.

See however: *Gimble v The State* [1988-89] PNGLR 271, (1988) SC369, [1988] PGSC 15; *Wesley Nobudi, John Evoa and Frank Yalikiti v The State* (2009) SC999, [2009] PGSC 20; *The State v Robert Bandi* (1990) N802; *The State v Jackson Nimai* (2008) N3355, [2008] PGNC 72; *The State v Danny Pakai* (2001) N2174 and *The State v Lawrie Patrick and others* [1995] PNGLR 195.

335 See *Uname Aumane and others v The State* [1980] PNGLR 510.

336 See *Uname Aumane and others v The State* [1980] PNGLR 510.

337 See *R v Coe* [1969] 1 All ER 65, per Parker LCJ at 68-69, (1969) 53 Cr App R 66, [1969] 1 All ER 65, [1968] 1 WLR 1950.

Refer also to the section titled 'Disparity In Sentencing' in the chapter titled 'Appeals Against Sentence'.

EQUALITY IN SENTENCING

The fact that a co-accused has not been brought to trial and may not be brought to trial is not a relevant matter going to mitigation.[338]

[338] See *Public Prosecutor v Ngudomp* [1982] PNGLR 357, [1982] PGSC 13.

DUTY OF THE PROSECUTION

The role of the prosecutor at sentencing is one of amicus (or partial adviser).[339]

It is the duty of the prosecutor[340] to:

- assist as much as possible in the sentencing process by providing such details and case authorities as is appropriate[341], including relevant sentencing principles[342] that might reasonably be thought to be relevant to the case[343] such as the need for general and/or personal deterrence[344];

- assist the Court to avoid an appealable error[345];

---

[339] As commented by Bingham LCJ in *R v Tolera* [1999] 1 Cr App R 29 at 32.

[340] As regards the 'Duty of the Prosecution', see also: *R v Heather MacNeil-Brown; R v Paul Wayne Piggott* [2008] VSCA 190; *R v Jones* [1984] WAR 175, per Burt CJ at 179-180; *R v Wilton* (1981) 28 SASR 362, per King CJ at 363-364; *R v Travers* (1983) 34 SASR 112, per Legoe J at 116-117; *R v Jermyn* (1985) 2 NSWLR 194, per Street CJ at 197-198 and McHugh JA at 203-204 and *R v Wilton* (1983) 34 SASR 112, per Legoe J at 116.

Refer also to the chapter titled 'Sentencing Submission'.

[341] See *Foli v R* [2004] SBHC 34.

[342] See also: section 15 of the Office of the Public Prosecutor, Prosecution Policy (2006).

Refer also to the chapter titled 'Objectives And Purposes Of Sentencing'.

[343] See *Acting Public Prosecutor v Uname Aumane and others* [1980] PNGLR 510 at 544.

See also: *R v Tait and Bartley* (1979) 24 ALR 473.

[344] See also: section 15 of the Office of the Public Prosecutor, Prosecution Policy (2006).

[345] Refer also to:
- the chapter titled 'Appeals Against Sentence'; and
- the chapter titled 'Appeals' in the text titled 'Injia on Criminal Practice and Procedure in Papua New Guinea and the Pacific'.

- make a submission as to sentence fairly[346] and in an even-handed manner[347];

- advise the Court of the matters or factors pertinent and relevant to appreciating the concerns and frustrations of members of the public as to their safety and security[348] and the public good generally[349], if relevant[350]; and

- advise the Court of any mitigating factors or extenuating circumstances, if an accused person is unrepresented[351].

---

[346] See *Whitehorn v R* (1983) 152 CLR 657, per Deane J at 663-664, per Dawson at 675, [1983] HCA 42; *R v Apostilides* (1984) 154 CLR 563 at 575-576, [1984] HCA 38; *Libke v R* (2007) 230 CLR 559, per Kirby and Callinan JJ at 576-577, per Hayne J at 586-587, [2007] HCA 30 and *Elias v R; Issa v R* [2013] HCA 31.

Refer also to the chapter titled 'Role Of The Prosecution' in the text titled 'Injia on Criminal Practice and Procedure in Papua New Guinea and the Pacific'.

[347] See *R v Tait and Bartley* (1979) 24 ALR 473.

[348] See *R v Tait and Bartley* (1979) 24 ALR 473.

[349] See *R v Melin* [1973] PNGLR 278, [1973] PGSC 33.

Refer also to the section titled 'Prevalence Of The Offence' in the chapter titled 'Aggravating Factors'.

[350] See section 15 of the Office of the Public Prosecutor, Prosecution Policy (2006).

[351] See section 17(5) of the *Professional Conduct Rules 1989*.

DUTY OF THE DEFENCE

It is the duty of a defence legal representative[352] to:

- assist as much as possible in the sentencing process by providing such details and case authorities as is appropriate[353], including relevant sentencing principles[354] that might reasonably be thought to be relevant to the case[355] such as the need for general and/or personal deterrence[356];

- assist the Court to avoid an appealable error[357];

- follow his or her client's instructions, and not to use devious means to obtain a favourable result for their client[358]; and

- not make any allegation that is merely scandalous or calculated to vilify or insult any person[359].

---

[352] As regards the 'Duty of the Defence', see also: *Giannarelli v Wraith* (1988) 165 CLR 543, per Brennan J at 579 and *R v Heather MacNeil-Brown; R v Paul Wayne Piggott* [2008] VSCA 190.

Refer also to the chapter titled 'Sentencing Submission'.

[353] See *Foli v R* [2004] SBHC 34.

[354] See also: section 15 of the Office of the Public Prosecutor, Prosecution Policy (2006).

Refer also to the chapter titled 'Objectives And Purposes Of Sentencing'.

[355] See *Acting Public Prosecutor v Uname Aumane and others* [1980] PNGLR 510 at 544.

See also: *R v Tait and Bartley* (1979) 24 ALR 473.

[356] See also: section 15 of the Office of the Public Prosecutor, Prosecution Policy (2006).

[357] Refer also to:

- the chapter titled 'Appeals Against Sentence'; and
- the chapter titled 'Appeals' in the text titled 'Injia on Criminal Practice and Procedure in Papua New Guinea and the Pacific'.

[358] See *The State v Nai'u Limgwe* [1976] PNGLR 314; *Nai'u Limgwe v The State* [1976] PNGLR 382 and *Awoda v The State* [1984] PNGLR 165.

[359] See section 16(11) of the *Professional Conduct Rules 1989*.

SENTENCING SUBMISSION

A suggested format for a sentencing submission is as follows:

Plea Bargain[360]

1. Advise the Court as to whether the charge been selected as a consequence of a plea bargain.

Outstanding Charges[361]

2. Advise the Court when there are other matters to be taken into account on sentence under section 603 of the *Criminal Code* (Ch. 262).

Maximum Sentence[362]

3. Advise the Court as to the maximum sentence that may be imposed for the offence/s whilst taking into consideration any circumstance of aggravation[363] as alleged in the charge/s.

---

360 Refer also to the chapter titled 'Plea Bargain'.

361 See section 15 of the Office of the Public Prosecutor, Prosecution Policy (2006).

Refer also to the chapter titled 'Outstanding Charges'.

362 See:

- *R v Clarke* (1974) 59 Cr App R 298; and
- section 15 of the Office of the Public Prosecutor, Prosecution Policy (2006).

Refer also to the chapter titled 'Maximum Sentence'.

363 Refer also to:

- the section titled 'General Principles' in the chapter titled 'Introduction To Sentencing';
- the section titled 'Circumstance Of Aggravation' in the chapter titled 'Aggravating Factors'; and
- the subsection titled 'Circumstances Of Aggravation' in the section titled 'Wording Of Charges' in the chapter titled 'Charges' in the text titled 'Injia on Criminal Practice and Procedure in Papua New Guinea and the Pacific'.

SENTENCING SUBMISSION

Minimum Sentence[364]

4. Advise the Court as to the minimum sentence that must be imposed as required by law, if applicable.

Sentencing Tariffs or Guidelines[365]

5. Advise the Court in relation to any sentencing tariff/s or guidelines as suggested by the National Court and Supreme Court.

Specific Issues[366]

6. Advise the Court as to any specific issues that should be considered in relation to the offence/s, other than the 'aggravating factors', 'mitigating factors' or 'extenuating circumstances'.

7. Advise the Court as to any consideration that may affect the interests of the accused person.[367]

Range of Sentences[368]

8. Outline to the Court the range of sentences that have been imposed for the offence/s based on previous cases.

---

[364] Refer also to the chapter titled 'Minimum Sentence'.

[365] Refer also to the chapter titled 'Comparative Sentences'.

[366] Refer also to the chapter titled 'Comparative Sentences'.

[367] See *R v Melin* [1973] PNGLR 278, [1973] PGSC 33.

[368] See *The State v Iori Veraga* (2005) N2921, [2005] PGNC 43.

See also:

- *R v Marshall* [1981] VR 725 at 735; *R v Casey and Wells* (1986) 20 A Crim R 191 and *R v Heather MacNeil-Brown; R v Paul Wayne Piggott* [2008] VSCA 190; and
- section 15 of the Office of the Public Prosecutor, Prosecution Policy (2006).

Refer also to the chapter titled 'Comparative Sentences'.

If the prosecution seeks a severe penalty then it must assist the Court towards this end by putting before it the true nature and extent of the heinousness involved in the commission of the offence[369].[370] Without an accurate appreciation of this, a Court falls into error that cannot be cured on appeal by the prosecution.[371]

However, neither the prosecution nor defence should suggest a precise period as being an appropriate term of imprisonment.[372]

Co-accused person[373]

9. Advise the Court as to the sentence/s imposed on any co-accused.

Pre-sentence Report[374]

10. Advise the Court as to whether a well-balanced pre-sentence report has been obtained.

---

[369] Refer also to the sections titled 'Seriousness Of An Offence Generally' and 'Prevalence Of The Offence' in the chapter titled 'Aggravating Factors'.

[370] See *R v Casey and Wells* (1986) 20 A Crim R 191.

[371] See *The State v Iori Veraga* (2005) N2921, [2005] PGNC 43.

See also: *R v Casey and Wells* (1986) 20 A Crim R 191.

[372] See *The State v Iori Veraga* (2005) N2921, [2005] PGNC 43.

See also: *R v Casey and Wells* (1986) 20 A Crim R 191.

Refer also to the section titled 'Imprisonment' in the chapter titled 'Sentencing Options'.

[373] Refer also to:
- the chapter titled 'Equality In Sentencing'; and
- the section titled 'Disparity In Sentencing' in the chapter titled 'Appeals Against Sentence'.

[374] Refer also to the chapter titled 'Pre-sentence Report'.

SENTENCING SUBMISSION

Victim Impact Statement[375]

11. Advise the Court as to the impact of the offence on the victim.

12. Advise the Court as to whether a victim impact statement has been prepared.

Age Of The Accused

13. Advise the Court as to the age of accused person.[376]

Aggravating Factors[377] (including)

14. What is the seriousness of the offence generally?

15. What is the prevalence of the offence?

16. Was the offence committed whilst the accused person was carrying, using or threatening to use a weapon?

17. Was there a breach of trust?

18. What is the accused person's character and antecedents, including prior criminal history and bad character?[378]

19. What was the duration of the offence?

20. Was the offence committed in the night-time?

---

[375] See section 15 of the Office of the Public Prosecutor, Prosecution Policy (2006).

Refer also to the chapter titled 'Victim Impact Statement'.

[376] See also: section 15 of the Office of the Public Prosecutor, Prosecution Policy (2006).

[377] See:

- section 15 of the Office of the Public Prosecutor, Prosecution Policy (2006); and
- *R v Van Pelz* (1942) 29 Cr App R 10, [1943] 1 All ER 36, [1943] KB 157.

Refer also to the chapter titled 'Aggravating Factors'.

[378] See section 15 of the Office of the Public Prosecutor, Prosecution Policy (2006).

21. Was the accused person under the effect of the consumption of alcohol when he or she committed the offence?

22. What was the age difference between the accused person and the victim?

23. Did the accused person show no remorse?

24. Is the accused person a law enforcement officer?

25. What was the degree of participation of the accused person?[379]

26. Was the accused person a member of a gang when he or she committed the offence?

27. Was the accused person a leader in a gang that committed the offence?

28. Was there any preplanning undertaken in order to commit the offence?

29. Is the offence involving an attack on a law enforcement officer?

30. Did the offence involve multiple or repeated sustained activity over a period of time?

31. Did the offence involve viciousness or a deliberate intention to harm or injure?

Mitigating Factors[380] (including)

32. Did the accused person enter a plea of guilty?

---

[379] See section 15 of the Office of the Public Prosecutor, Prosecution Policy (2006).

[380] See:
- section 15 of the Office of the Public Prosecutor, Prosecution Policy (2006); and
- *R v Van Pelz* (1942) 29 Cr App R 10, [1943] 1 All ER 36, [1943] KB 157.

Refer also to the chapter titled 'Mitigating Factors'.

33. Was the plea an indication of genuine remorse, repentance or contrition, including engaging in a peace and reconciliation ceremony or personally or publicly apologising for what he or she did?[381]

34. Did the accused person play a meaningful role in the payment of any customary compensation to the victim, including the amount paid, when, by whom and to whom?[382]

35. Was the plea in recognition of the strength of the prosecution case, including any admission made?

36. When did the accused person enter the plea of guilty?

37. What are the personal antecedents of the accused person, including good character, education, employment and Christian background?

38. Is the accused person a first time offender?[383]

39. Has the accused person co-operated by assisting the police in relation to the investigation of any offence?[384]

40. Did the accused person confess early to the investigating officer?

41. Does the age of the accused person warrant a mitigation of any sentence imposed?

42. Is the accused person currently suffering an illness that should mitigate any sentence imposed?

43. Has there been a delay between the date of arrest and sentence that warrants a mitigation of any sentence imposed?

44. Is there the risk of repetition in committing a similar offence by this accused person?

45. Are there any social or cultural pressures and isolation in relation to the accused person that warrants a mitigation of any sentence imposed?

---

[381] See *The State v Anton Towakra and others* (2009) N3845 and *The State v Bart Kiohin Mais and Henry Kevi* (2005) N2811, [2005] PGNC 142.

[382] Refer also to the section titled 'Compensation Order' in the chapter titled 'Sentencing Options.

[383] See section 15 of the Office of the Public Prosecutor, Prosecution Policy (2006).

[384] Refer also to the section titled 'Co-operation With Police' in the chapter titled 'Mitigating Factors'.

46. Did the accused person suffer any injuries as a consequence of the unlawful actions of a law enforcement officer because he or she committed this offence?

47. Did the accused person suffer any injuries as a consequence of the commission of this offence?

48. Did the accused person suffer any loss of property that was unlawfully destroyed as a consequence of the commission of this offence?

49. Was the accused person under the influence of drugs when he or she committed the offence under circumstances that warrant a mitigation of any sentence imposed?

Extenuating Circumstances[385] (including)

50. Did the accused person commit the offence as a consequence of de-facto provocation?

51. Did the accused person commit the offence as a consequence of duress or coercion?

52. What was the motive by which the accused person committed the offence?

53. Did the accused person commit the offence whilst suffering from a medical condition that warrants a reduction in any sentence imposed?

54. Did the accused person act impulsively in committing the offence in circumstances that warrant a mitigation of any sentence imposed?

55. Does the accused person have a lack of sophistication or traditional customs, practices and beliefs that resulted in the commission of the offence?

56. What was the role played by the accused person in the commission of the offence?[386]

57. Was the accused person under any pressure from his or her peers, family members or other social influences which compelled him or her to commit the offence?

---

[385] Refer also to the chapter titled 'Extenuating Circumstances'.

[386] See section 15 of the Office of the Public Prosecutor, Prosecution Policy (2006).

SENTENCING SUBMISSION

Disparity in Sentencing[387]

58. What was the sentence imposed on any co-accused?

59. Outline any differences in relation such a co-accused.

Imprisonment[388]

60. Advise the Court as to length of time that the accused person has already been in custody since being charged.

61. Advise the Court as to whether that period of custody can be deducted from the accused person's head sentence if a term of imprisonment is imposed.

No period of pre-trial custody can be deducted from a minimum penalty.

62. Advise the Court as to whether there are any grounds for not deducting that period from the accused person's head sentence if a term of imprisonment is imposed.

63. In relation to multiple offences advise the Court as to whether the terms of imprisonment that may be imposed should be concurrent or cumulative whilst taking into consideration the 'one transaction or continuing episode rule'.

64. Advise the Court as to the effect of the 'totality principle' on any terms of imprisonment if such a sentence was to be imposed.

Suspended Sentence[389]

65. Advise the Court as to whether as a matter of law any term of imprisonment that may be imposed can be suspended.

There is no power to suspend a sentence in relation to an offence not provided for by the *Criminal Code* (Ch. 262).

---

[387] Refer also to:
- the chapter titled 'Equality In Sentencing'; and
- the section titled 'Disparity In Sentencing' in the chapter titled 'Appeal Against Sentence'.

[388] Refer also to the section titled 'Imprisonment' in the chapter titled 'Sentencing Options'.

[389] Refer also to the subsection titled 'Suspended Sentence' in the section titled 'Imprisonment' in the chapter titled 'Sentencing Options'.

66. Advise the Court as to whether all or part of any term of imprisonment that may be imposed should be suspended.

67. Advise the Court as to whether there is any basis to suspend any term of imprisonment that may be imposed.

68. Outline to the Court any proposed conditions that the Court should consider if it intends to suspend any term of imprisonment.

Fine[390]

69. Does the accused person have the capacity to pay a fine?

70. What is the monthly income of the accused person?

71. What are the monthly expenses of the accused person?

72. Does the accused person have access to illegally obtained funds that could be used to pay a fine that the investigating officer may not be aware of?

Compensation Order[391]

73. Should the Court consider ordering the accused person pay compensation?

    When there has been no damage or injury then there should not be a compensation order.[392]

74. Advise the Court as to whether a payment of restitution/compensation has occurred.

75. Advise the Court as to whether the *Criminal Law (Compensation) Act 1995* would apply.[393]

---

[390] Refer also to the section titled 'Fine' in the chapter titled 'Sentencing Options'.

[391] Refer also to the section titled 'Compensation Order' in the chapter titled 'Sentencing Options'.

[392] See *The State v Peter Barnes and Douglas Ume* (1993) N1190.

[393] See section 15 of the Office of the Public Prosecutor, Prosecution Policy (2006).

Refer also to the section titled 'Compensation Order' in the chapter titled 'Sentencing Options'.

76. Is the victim willing to accept a payment of compensation?

77. What is the amount of compensation that the victim believes that he or she is realistically entitled to whilst not exceeding K5000 as a consequence of the commission of the offence?

78. What is the quantum of compensation that the Court should order whilst taking into consideration the factors as specified in the *Criminal Law (Compensation) Act 1995*, including:

> **78.1** what mental anguish has been caused to the victim as a consequence of the commission of this offence?;
>
> **78.2** is the victim suffering any on-going problems as a consequence of the commission of this offence?;
>
> and
>
> **78.3** did the victim suffer any loss of income as a consequence of the commission of this offence?

79. Is there any relevant custom that the Court should consider in relation to payment of compensation?

80. Does the accused person have the means himself or herself to pay compensation?

81. What is the monthly income of the accused person?

82. What are the monthly expenses of the accused person?

Probation Order[394]

83. Will the accused person consent to complying with the conditions of a Probation Order imposed under section 16 of the *Probation Act* (Ch. 381)?

84. What conditions should a Court consider when imposing a probation order?

[394] Refer also to the section titled 'Probation Order' in the chapter titled 'Sentencing Options'.

Restriction of Movement Order[395]

85. Advise the Court as to whether a restriction of movement order is appropriate.[396]

86. Will the accused person consent to complying with the conditions of a Restriction of Movement Order imposed under section 600 of the *Criminal Code* (Ch. 262) or section 205B of the *District Courts Act* (Ch. 40)?

Conditional Discharge[397]

87. On what basis should the accused person be conditionally discharged under section 602 of the *Criminal Code* (Ch. 262)?

The accused person must have been convicted of an offence relating to property and the victim must have received compensation to his or her satisfaction.

88. On what basis should the accused person be conditionally discharged under section 132 of the *District Courts Act* (Ch. 40)?

Property Order[398]

89. Is the accused person willing to return property that was unlawfully obtained and not currently in the possession of the investigating officer?

90. Should the property taken during the course of the commission of the offence be ordered to be returned to the accused person under section 21 of the *Goods Act* (Ch. 251)?

---

[395] Refer also to the section titled 'Restriction Of Movement Order' in the chapter titled 'Sentencing Options'.

[396] See section 15 of the Office of the Public Prosecutor, Prosecution Policy (2006).

Refer also to the section titled 'Restriction Of Movement Order' in the chapter titled 'Sentencing Options'.

[397] Refer also to the section titled 'Conditional Discharge' in the chapter titled 'Sentencing Options'.

[398] Refer also to the section titled 'Property Orders' in the chapter titled 'Sentencing Options'.

SENTENCING SUBMISSION

Disqualification Order[399]

91. Can the Court lawfully disqualify the driving licence of the accused person?

92. Should the driving licence of the accused person be disqualified?

Forfeiture Order

93. Should the Court order any property to be forfeited to the State that was unlawfully obtained or used?

[399] Refer also to the section titled 'Disqualification, Etc Of Driving Licence' in the chapter titled 'Sentencing Options'.

SENTENCING PROCEEDINGS

A sentencing hearing is:

- partly inquisitorial, ie., the Court actively elicits information from the parties and others[400]; and

- partly adversarial, ie., the Court is akin to an umpire which the conduct of the proceedings being left largely to the parties who present their cases as they think fit with the result that the information available to the Court is limited to that produced by the parties[401],

and the extent to which it is one or the other depends on whether and how far the facts about the offence, the accused person, and the victim are accepted or in dispute.[402]

The Court has the right to:

- inquire into any issue germane to sentence; and

- seek further information,

and is under a duty to do so if the accused person challenges any fact significant to the prosecutor's submissions as to sentence.[403]

---

[400] See New Zealand Law Commission, 2001, 'Proof of Disputed Facts on Sentence', Report 76, page 9.

[401] See New Zealand Law Commission, 2001, 'Proof of Disputed Facts on Sentence', Report 76, page 9.

[402] See:
- New Zealand Law Commission, 2001, 'Proof of Disputed Facts on Sentence', Report 76, page 8; and
- Allars, M, 'Neutrality, the Judicial Paradigm and Tribunal Procedure' (1991) 13 Sydney LR 377 at 379.

[403] See *R v Van Pelz* [1943] 1 KB 157, (1943) 29 Cr App R 10, per Viscount Caldecote LCJ and *R v Campbell* (1911) 6 Cr App R 131, per Lord Alverstone CJ at 132.

See also: New Zealand Law Commission, 2001, 'Proof of Disputed Facts on Sentence', Report 76, page 8.

SENTENCING PROCEEDINGS

The basic right of all persons under section 37(1) of the *Constitution of the Independent State of Papua New Guinea* is to the full protection of the law, especially when a person is charged with an offence. This suggests that the benefit of any reasonable doubt on issues of penalty should be given to those who have pleaded guilty.[404]

The effect of a plea of guilty is that an accused person admits to:

- the elements of the offence[405]; and
- the facts that have been put to him or her[406], including all of the essential facts necessary to constitute the offence[407].

A guilty plea however remains provisional and is open to be set aside if an accused person makes a statement at *allocatus* contradicting his or her earlier guilty plea.[408]

However, where the facts as presented by the prosecution are disputed then that should put the Court on alertness as to whether the plea of guilty is to be treated as an unequivocal admission of guilt.[409]

---

[404] See *The State v Aaron Lahu* (2005) N2798, [2005] PGNC 161 and *The State v Willie Dominic* (2005) N2938, [2005] PGNC 35.

See also: *R v Golathan* (1915) 11 Cr App R 79 at 80.

[405] See *R v Bryant* [1980] 1 NZLR 264 and *Curtis v Police* (1993) 10 CRNZ 28.

[406] See *Saperus Yalibakut v The State* (2006) SC890, [2006] PGSC 27 and *The State v Alphonse Polpolio and Jeffrey Baru* [2006] PGNC 16.

See also: *R v Hill* [1979] VR 311 at 312.

[407] See *R v Hill* [1979] VR 311 at 312; *Law v The State of Western Australia* [2009] WASCA 193 and *Harris v R* [2004] WASCA 292.

[408] See *The State v Joe Ivoro and Gemora Yavura* [1980] PNGLR 1 and *Gabriel Laku v The State* [1981] PNGLR 350.

[409] See *Apa v R* [1992] SBHC 47.

Refer also to:
- the section titled 'Plea Of Guilty' in the chapter titled 'Mitigating Factors'; and
- the subsection titled 'Plea Of Guilty' in the section titled 'Taking Of A Plea' in the chapter titled 'Court Procedure' in the text titled 'Injia on Criminal Practice and Procedure in Papua New Guinea and the Pacific'.

SENTENCING PROCEEDINGS

A plea of not guilty should not be entered in order to enable the Court to determine a question of fact that would not affect the outcome of such a trial.[410]

If on a plea of guilty an asserted fact is controverted then a Court may:

- hear evidence and come to a conclusion on the matter[411] (both sides calling witnesses and cross examining them in the usual way, if appropriate[412]).

  If either the version of the facts of the prosecution or defence is not accepted by the Court then it will be necessary to call evidence if that version of facts is to be accepted by the Court.[413]

  If an accused person's version of the facts is not accepted by the prosecution then the accused person should be given the opportunity of:

  - giving evidence; and/or
  - calling evidence to support his or her version of the facts.[414]

  The prosecution should oppose any assertion by the accused person that is inaccurate, misleading or unsubstantiated.[415]

---

[410] See *R v Milligan* (1982) 4 Cr App R (S) 2 and *R v Newton* (1983) 77 Cr App R 13, (1982) 4 Cr App R (S) 388, [1983] Crim LR 198.

See however: *R v Taggart* (1979) 1 Cr App R (S) 144.

[411] See *R v Gortat and Pirog* [1973] Crim LR 648.

See also: *R v Newton* (1983) 77 Cr App R 13, (1982) 4 Cr App R (S) 388, [1983] Crim LR 198; *R v Gravell* [1978] Crim LR 438; *R v Ball* [1983] Crim LR 198 and *R v Parker* [1984] Crim LR 763.

[412] See *R v McGrath and Casey* (1983) 5 Cr App R (S) 460.

[413] See *R v Olbrich* (1999) 199 CLR 270, [1999] HCA 54 and *Law v The State of Western Australia* [2009] WASCA 193.

[414] See *Koniel Alar and Hosea Biu v The State* [1979] PNGLR 300 at 307, [1981] PGSC 4; *Imiyo Wamela v The State* [1982] PNGLR 269 at 280, [1982] PGSC 24 and *The State v Ndrakum Pu-Uh* (2005) N2949, [2005] PGNC 172.

[415] See section 15.2 of the Office of the Public Prosecutor, Prosecution Policy (2006).

The normal standard of proof on the prosecution applies, ie., 'beyond reasonable doubt'.[416]

If the prosecution's version of the facts is not accepted by the defence then the prosecution should be given the opportunity of calling evidence on oath[417].[418]; or

- hear no evidence, but listen instead to the submissions of both the prosecution and defence and come to a conclusion.[419]

Where sworn evidence is not taken as to a contentious matter, a Court should apply the 'most favourable version' doctrine which involves:

---

[416] See:

- *R v McGrath and Casey* (1983) 5 Cr App R (S) 460; *R v Olbrich* (1999) 199 CLR 270, [1999] HCA 54; *R v Storey* [1998] 1 VR 359 at 369; *R v Gardiner* (1982) 140 DLR (3d) 612 at 641-648; *Law v The State of Western Australia* [2009] WASCA 193; *Anderson v R* (1993) 177 CLR 520 at 536; *Langridge v R* (1996) 17 WAR 346; *R v Isaacs* (1997) 41 NSWLR 374; *R v Morrison* [1998] QCA 162; *Cheung v R* (2001) 209 CLR 1, [2001] HCA 67; *O'Neil-Shaw v R* [2010] NSWCCA 42; *Select Rent Registry Ltd v Stevens* [1990] 2 NZLR 588; *R v Chamberlain* [1983] 2 VR 511; *R v Kerrigan* (1993) 14 Cr App R (S) 179 at 18 and *R v Tolera* [1999] 1 Cr App R (S) 29 at 33; and
- New Zealand Law Commission, 2001, 'Proof of Disputed Facts on Sentence', Report 76, page 12.

Refer also to the chapter titled 'Proof Of Issues' in the text titled 'Injia on Criminal Practice and Procedure in Papua New Guinea and the Pacific'.

[417] In this context this also refers to the taking of a solemn declaration or affirmation.

[418] See *R v Olbrich* (1999) 199 CLR 270, [1999] HCA 54 and *Law v The State of Western Australia* [2009] WASCA 193.

[419] See *R v Newton* (1983) 77 Cr App R 13, (1982) 4 Cr App R (S) 388, [1983] Crim LR 198.

See however:

- *R v Bryant* [1980] 1 NZLR 264; and
- New Zealand Law Commission, 2001, 'Proof of Disputed Facts on Sentence', Report 76, page 11.

Acting on the version of facts which, within the bounds of possibility, is most favourable to the accused person.[420]

If the latter course is followed, the benefit of any doubt must be given to the defence.[421]

For that purpose a Court may act on the version of facts as outlined in confessional evidence.[422]

However, the 'most favourable version' doctrine cannot be applied if an accused person on his or her plea and on his or her *allocutus* makes no challenge to the facts.[423] For the purpose of applying this principle the *allocutus* also includes statements made by a defence legal representative from the bar table.[424]

Whilst the sentencing stage is necessarily concerned with the finding of facts, the clearly defined procedural and evidentiary rules that apply to the earlier stage of determination of guilt are relaxed.[425]

---

420 See *Saperus Yalibakut v The State* (2006) SC890, [2006] PGSC 27; *John Baipu v The State* (2005) SC796, [2005] PGSC 19; *Imiyo Wamela v The State* [1982] PNGLR 269, [1982] PGSC 24; *Roger Jumbo and Aidan Awatan v The State* [1998] PNGLR 197, [1997] PGSC 25, (1997) SC516; *Koniel Alar and Hosea Biu v The State* [1979] PNGLR 300, [1979] PGSC 4; *Public Prosecutor v Tom Ake* [1978] PNGLR 469 and *R v Gabi Vagi* [1973] PNGLR 30, [1973] PGSC 51.

See also:

- *Weaver v Samuels* [1971] SASR 116 at 119 and *R v Tait and Bartley* (1979) 24 ALR 473; and
- section 27 of the *Juvenile Courts Act 1991* ['Procedure In Taking Plea Of Juvenile'].

421 See *R v Gortat and Pirog* [1973] Crim LR 648.

422 See *Koniel Alar and Hosea Biu v The State* [1979] PNGLR 300, [1979] PGSC 4; *Peremai Naroi v The State* [1987] PNGLR 293; *Public Prosecutor v Tom Ake* [1978] PNGLR 469; *The State v Lastin Inom* (1981) N329, [1981] PGNC 11 and *Leonard Sabadi v The Police* (2002) N2164, [2002] PGNC 44.

423 See *Public Prosecutor v Tom Ake* [1978] PNGLR 469 and *John Baipu v The State* (2005) SC796, [2005] PGSC 19.

424 See *John Baipu v The State* (2005) SC796, [2005] PGSC 19; *Koniel Alar and Hosea Biu v The State* [1979] PNGLR 300 at 307, [1979] PGSC 4 and *Imiyo Wamela v The State* [1982] PNGLR 269 at 280, [1982] PGSC 24.

425 See *Morris v The State* [1979] PNGLR 605.

See however: *R v Gabi Vagi* [1973] PNGLR 30, [1973] PGSC 51.

However, in sentencing proceedings 'hearsay evidence[426]', unless it is not objected to or conceded, should not be admitted.[427]

If the prosecution seeks to have a Court take a matter into account as an 'aggravating factor[428]', it must:

- bring that matter to the Court's attention; and, if necessary
- call evidence on it.[429]

But that will only be necessary if the Court is not prepared to act on the assertion, even though it is not disputed by the defence.[430]

If the defence seeks to have a Court take a matter into account as a 'mitigating factor[431]' or 'extenuating circumstance[432]', it must:

- bring that matter to the Court's attention; and, if necessary

---

426 As regards the law in relation to 'Hearsay Evidence', refer to the chapter titled 'Evidence' in the text titled 'Injia on Criminal Practice and Procedure in Papua New Guinea and the Pacific'.

427 See *R v Gabi Vagi* [1973] PNGLR 30, [1973] PGSC 51 and *Norris v The State* [1979] PNGLR 605, [1979] PGSC 18.

See also: *R v Traiconi* (1990) 49 A Crim R 417, per Gleeson CJ at 418-419; *Morse v R* [1977] WAR 151; *R v Newton* (1983) 77 Cr App R 13, (1982) 4 Cr App R (S) 388, [1983] Crim LR 198; *R v Lo Yim-kai* [1966] HKLR 414, per Blair-Kerr J at 423; *R v Nuku* [1969] NZLR 343 at 345 and *R v Bryant* [1980] 1 NZLR 264 [hearsay evidence is inadmissible].

See however:

- *R v Gardiner* (1982) 140 DLR (3d) 612 at 648 [the hearsay rule does not apply]; and
- New Zealand Law Commission, 2001, 'Proof of Disputed Facts on Sentence', Report 76, page 8.

428 Refer also to the chapter titled 'Aggravating Factors'.

429 See *R v Olbrich* (1999) 199 CLR 270, [1999] HCA 54 and *Law v The State of Western Australia* [2009] WASCA 193.

430 See *R v Olbrich* (1999) 199 CLR 270, [1999] HCA 54 and *Law v The State of Western Australia* [2009] WASCA 193.

431 Refer also to the chapter titled 'Mitigating Factors'.

432 Refer also to the chapter titled 'Extenuating Circumstances'.

- call evidence about it.[433]

But that will only be necessary if the Court is not prepared to act on the assertion, even though it is not disputed by the prosecution.[434]

The normal standard of proof on the defence applies, ie., on the 'balance of probabilities'.[435]

Court is however obliged to give notice to the defence if it is not prepared to act on an alleged:

- 'mitigating factor'; or
- 'extenuating circumstance'

that is not disputed by the prosecution.[436]

The giving of notice enables the defence to adduce evidence, for the purpose of establishing the 'mitigating factor' or 'extenuating circumstance', before sentence is imposed.[437]

a Court is not persuaded of the existence of a particular fact, whether mitigating, extenuating or aggravating:

- the absence of that fact does not prove the converse fact, adverse to or in favour of an accused person, as the case may be; and
- the fact does not exist for the purpose of sentencing.[438]

---

[433] See *R v Olbrich* (1999) 199 CLR 270, [1999] HCA 54 and *Law v The State of Western Australia* [2009] WASCA 193.

[434] See *R v Gabi Vagi* [1973] PNGLR 30, [1973] PGSC 51.

See also: *R v Olbrich* (1999) 199 CLR 270, [1999] HCA 54 and *Law v The State of Western Australia* [2009] WASCA 193.

[435] See *R v Olbrich* (1999) 199 CLR 270, [1999] HCA 54; *R v Storey* [1998] 1 VR 359 at 369 and *Law v The State of Western Australia* [2009] WASCA 193.

[436] See *Hutchins v The State of Western Australia* [2006] WASCA 258; *Nguyen v The State of Western Australia* [2009] WASCA 8; *CJ v The State of Western Australia* [2009] WASCA 42; *The State of Western Australia v Wickham* [2009] WASCA 137 and *Law v The State of Western Australia* [2009] WASCA 193.

[437] See *CJ v The State of Western Australia* [2009] WASCA 42 and *Law v The State of Western Australia* [2009] WASCA 193.

[438] See *R v Lobban* (2001) 80 SASR 550, [2001] SASC 392 and *Law v The State of Western Australia* [2009] WASCA 193.

SENTENCING PROCEEDINGS

As a consequence of a sentencing hearing being conducted and the version of an accused person being rejected, the impact of the plea of guilty by the accused person as a 'mitigating factor' should be reduced.[439]

[439] See *R v Hassell* [2000] 1 Cr App R (S) 67.

However, this sentencing principle is yet to find acceptance in Papua New Guinea.

PRE-SENTENCE REPORT

[1.0] ADULTS

If a Court is to consider imposing a lenient sentence, such as a 'suspended sentence[440]', as a consequence of 'mitigating factors[441]' and/or 'extenuating circumstances[442]', then it should be provided with a well-balanced pre-sentence report.[443]

A well-balanced pre-sentence report has inputs from:

- the accused person[444];
- the investigating officer[445];
- the accused person's relatives;
- the victim[446];
- the family of the victim, if the victim is deceased[447]; and

---

[440] Refer also to the subsection titled 'Suspended Sentence' in the section titled 'Imprisonment' in the chapter titled 'Sentencing Options'.

[441] Refer also to the chapter titled 'Mitigating Factors'.

[442] Refer also to the chapter titled 'Extenuating Circumstances'.

[443] See *Joe Giamur v The State* (2007) SC884, [2007] PGSC 7; *Richard Liri v The State* (2007) SC883, [2007] PGSC 3; *Daniel Ronald Walus v The State* (2007) SC882, [2007] PGSC 4; *Edmund Gima v The State; Suine Arnold v The State* (2003) SC730, [2003] PGSC 3; *Acting Public Prosecutor v Don Hale* (1998) SC564; *The State v Irox Winston* (2000) N2347; *The State v Jack Magal* (2008) CR No. 224 of 2006; *The State v Steven Molu Minji and others; The State v Didi Gelwak Sakol (No. 2)* (2009) N3794, [2009] PGNC 177; *The State v Wasa David Warifa* (2008) N3308, [2008] PGNC 32; *The State v Gerald Kirafe* (2005) N3660, [2005] PGNC 175; *The State v Andrew Yeskulu* (2003) N2410; *The State v Moki Lepi (No. 3)* (2004) N2734 and *The State v Ansong Ising* (2005) N2994, [2005] PGNC 14.

[444] Suspension based on circumstances personal to the accused person should be balanced against the community's concerns and interests, see *Tardrew v The State* [1986] PNGLR 91.

[445] See *The State v Joe Butema Arua* (2001) N2076.

[446] See *The State v Sylvester Heai Evore* (2006) N3236, [2006] PGNC 148; *The State v Jack Magal* (2008) CR No. 224 of 2006 and *The State v Steven Molu Minji and others; The State v Didi Gelwak Sakol (No. 2)* (2009) N3794, [2009] PGNC 177.

Refer also to the chapter titled 'Victim Impact Statement'.

[447] See *Kepa Wanege v The State* (2004) SC742, [2004] PGSC 22.

- independent members of the community in which the accused person lives[448];

and if the offence occurred within their community:

- what should be the appropriate punishment; and

- whether the community is prepared to assist with any community management of the accused person[449].

Sentencing is a community responsibility by virtue of section 158(1) of the *Constitution of the Independent State of Papua New Guinea*.[450]

Community involvement with the punishment of accused persons should be considered especially if a Court is considering returning an accused person to the community instead of imposing a term of imprisonment.[451] The Courts are bound to be in touch with the aspirations of the people, as mandated by the *Constitution of the Independent State of Papua New Guinea*, and if a criminal is to be sent back to the community, the community must have its say.[452]

[448] See *Kepa Wanege v The State* (2004) SC742, [2004] PGSC 22; *Sakarowa Koe v The State* (2004) SC739, [2004] PGSC 33; *The State v Fredinand Naka Penge* (2002) N2244; *The State v Rex Rongo* (2000) N2035; *The State v Jack Magal* (2008) CR No. 224 of 2006; *The State v Steven Molu Minji and others; The State v Didi Gelwak Sakol (No. 2)* (2009) N3794, [2009] PGNC 177 and *The State v Gibson Haulai* (2004) N2555.

[449] See *Acting Public Prosecutor v Don Hale* (1998) SC564; *Edmund Gima v The State; Suine Arnold v The State* (2003) SC730, [2003] PGSC 3; *Richard Liri v The State* (2007) SC883, [2007] PGSC 3; *The State v Irox Winston* (2000) N2347; *The State v Andrew Yeskulu* (2003) N2410; *The State v Moki Lepi (No. 3)* (2004) N2734 and *The State v Elizabeth Teka* (2008) N3509, [2008] PGNC 154.

[450] See *Acting Public Prosecutor v Don Hale* (1998) SC564; *The State v Jamie Campbell Fereka* (2003) N2359 and *The State v Gibson Haulai* (2004) N2555.

[451] See *Acting Public Prosecutor v Don Hale* (1998) SC564; *Edmund Gima v The State; Suine Arnold v The State* (2003) SC730, [2003] PGSC 3; *Richard Liri v The State* (2007) SC883, [2007] PGSC 3; *The State v William Chilen* (2008) N3549, [2008] PGNC 200 and *The State v Irox Winston* (2000) N2347.

[452] See *The State v William Chilen* (2008) N3549, [2008] PGNC 200; *The State v Zimma Munduai* (2000) N2036 and *The State v Scott Lalio* (2006) N2967, [2006] PGNC 27.

However, a return to the community should mean an appropriate report of the attitude of the community, including whether the community is prepared to:

- take some responsibility for their own offending members; and
- supervise any alternate punishment.[453]

A term of imprisonment should not be suspended, unless there is strong community support.[454]

A pre-sentence report:

- cannot substitute or dictate the kind of sentence to be imposed in any case[455];
- may assist a Court in the process of assessing what kind of sentence to impose[456]; and
- must be made available to the prosecution and the defence.[457]

Both the prosecution and defence should be given the opportunity to examine or cross-examine the author of the report in appropriate circumstances[458].

---

[453] See *Acting Public Prosecutor v Don Hale* (1998) SC564 and *The State v Jamie Campbell Fereka* (2003) N2359.

[454] See *Acting Public Prosecutor v Don Hale* (1998) SC564 and *The State v Louise Paraka* (2002) N2317.

[455] See *The State v Sul Kora* (2001) N2092, [2001] PGNC 93; *The State v Andrew Yeskulu* (2003) N2410 and *The State v Otom Masa* (2000) N2021.

[456] See *The State v Sul Kora* (2001) N2092, [2001] PGNC 93; *The State v Andrew Yeskulu* (2003) N2410 and *The State v Otom Masa* (2000) N2021.

[457] See *O'Keefe v Tankard* [1989] VR 371 at 381; *Stanton v Dawson* (1987) 31 A Crim R 104; *R v Jensen* (1996) 87 A Crim R 241; *R v Lucky* (1974) 12 SASR 136, per Bray CJ at 139; *R v Seres* [1980] Qd R 29 at 31 and *Stattery v Davis* (1993) 65 A Crim R 116, per Kearney J at 123.

[458] See *O'Keefe v Tankard* [1989] VR 371 at 381; *Stanton v Dawson* (1987) 31 A Crim R 104; *R v Jensen* (1996) 87 A Crim R 241; *R v Lucky* (1974) 12 SASR 136, per Bray CJ at 139; *R v Seres* [1980] Qd R 29 at 31 and *Stattery v Davis* (1993) 65 A Crim R 116, per Kearney J at 123.

PRE-SENTENCE REPORT

A defence legal representative should arrange for a pre-sentence report prior to sentencing.[459]

However, a Court may accept or reject a pre-sentence report for various reasons.[460]

[2.0] JUVENILES

Where:

- a Court is satisfied that an offence has been proven 'beyond reasonable doubt[461]'; or

- a juvenile admits the facts constituting the offence,

the Court shall, before imposing sentence, order the Juvenile Court Officer to prepare a pre-sentence report in respect of the juvenile.[462]

---

[459] See *The State v Louise Paraka* (2002) N2317; *The State v Jack Magal* (2008) CR No. 224 of 2006 and *The State v Steven Molu Minji and others; The State v Didi Gelwak Sakol (No. 2)* (2009) N3794, [2009] PGNC 177.

See however: *The State v Odei Boromake* (2006) N3159, [2006] PGNC 142.

[460] See *The State v Otom Masa* (2000) N2021.

[461] Refer also to the chapter titled 'Proof Of Issues' in the text titled 'Injia on Criminal Practice and Procedure in Papua New Guinea and the Pacific'.

[462] See section 29 of the *Juvenile Courts Act 1991* ['Pre-sentence Reports'].

PLEA BARGAIN

A plea bargain[463]:

- requires a Court to proceed to sentence for the lesser offence[464]; and
- entitles an accused person to a reduction from the maximum sentence[465].

It is not uncommon for plea discussions to be viewed as an evil-improper, unjust, secretive, unfair and irrational – though most would accept them as necessary, given the existing strain on the trial capacity of the courts.[466]

However, the need to maintain public confidence in the legal system may require that plea bargaining based on the appearance of having decisions on sentence made out of court between the prosecution and defence avoided.[467]

The Court is entitled to know as to whether there has been a plea bargain.[468]

---

[463] For the practice on plea bargaining, see *The State v Jack Gola and another* [1990] PNGLR 206.

Refer also to the chapter titled 'Role Of The Prosecution' in the text titled 'Injia on Criminal Practice and Procedure in Papua New Guinea and the Pacific'.

[464] See *The State v Paul Waiya* [2005] PGNC 176; *The State v Tikiria Amos* (2005) N2614 and *Mitige Neheye v The State; Martin Gawi v The State* [1994] PNGLR 71.

[465] See *Saperus Yalibakut v The State* (2006) SC890, [2006] PGSC 27 and *The State v Marcus Pitmete* (2007) N3229, [2007] PGNC 105.

See however: *Sakarowa Koe v The State* (2004) SC739, [2004] PGSC 33; *The State v Attiock Ishmel* (2001) N2294 and *The State v Michael Siwiri* (2006) N3382, [2006] PGNC 172.

[466] See The Law Reform Commission of Ireland, 1993, 'Consultation Paper on Sentencing', paragraph 12.5.

[467] See *The State v Jack Gola and another* [1990] PNGLR 206.

As to the practical benefits for the prosecution and defence, see The Law Reform Commission of Ireland, 1993, 'Consultation Paper on Sentencing', paragraphs 12.6 and 12.7.

[468] See *The State v James Gurave Guba* (2000) N2020.

See also: section 12 of the Office of the Public Prosecutor, Prosecution Policy (2006).

MAXIMUM SENTENCE

[1.0] STATUTORY PROVISION

Section 14 of the *Interpretation Act* (Ch. 2) states:

> 'Where a statutory provision specifies a penalty for an offence[469] against the provision, the penalty is the maximum penalty that may be imposed for that offence'.

[2.0] GENERAL PRINCIPLES

When an accused person commits an offence, he or she renders himself or herself liable to the maximum sentence that the Court can impose.[470]

The maximum penalty is one of many factors that bear on the ultimate discretionary determination of the sentence for the offence.[471]

A Court should pay careful attention to a maximum penalty for the following reasons:

- the legislature has legislated the maximum penalty[472].

  The legislature manifests its policy in the enactment of the maximum sentence that may be imposed.[473]

---

[469] The term 'offence' in relation to a law is defined in section 3(1) of the *Interpretation Act* (Ch. 2) as including:
'a breach or contravention of, or a failure to comply with, the law'.

The term 'law' is also defined in section 3(1) as meaning:
'a law of Papua New Guinea, and includes –
(a) the underlying law; and
(b) subordinate enactments'.

A 'subordinate enactment' is an instrument (whether of a legislative nature or not) made under an Act such as a regulation, see also section 3(1).

[470] See *Simon Kama v The State* (2004) SC740, [2004] PGSC 32.

See also: *DPP v Fritz* [1969-1982] NLR 107, [1981] NRSC 1.

[471] See *Elias v R; Issa v R* [2013] HCA 31.

[472] See *Markarian v R* (2005) 228 CLR 357, (2005) 215 ALR 213, [2005] HCA 25.

[473] See *Oliver* (1982) 7 A Crim R 174, per Street CJ at 177.

MAXIMUM SENTENCE

The Courts are, of course absolutely bound by:

- the statutory limit itself; and
- the legislative policy disclosed by the statutory limit[474];

- a maximum penalty invites comparison between:
  - the worst possible case; and
  - the case before the Court at the time[475]; and
- therefore, a maximum penalty does provide, when taken and balanced with all of the other relevant factors, a yardstick[476].

The principle that the maximum sentence should be reserved for the 'worst' type of case is:

> Not a rule of law, but a rule of practice adopted through the exercise of common sense in order to do justice.[477]

---

[474] See *Oliver* (1982) 7 A Crim R 174, per Street CJ at 177.

[475] See *Markarian v R* (2005) 228 CLR 357, (2005) 215 ALR 213, [2005] HCA 25.

[476] See *Markarian v R* (2005) 228 CLR 357, (2005) 215 ALR 213, [2005] HCA 25 and *Elias v R; Issa v R* [2013] HCA 31.

[477] See *SCR No. 1 of 1984; Re Maximum Penalty* [1984] PNGLR 418, [1984] PGSC 12.

MAXIMUM SENTENCE

The maximum sentence or a sentence close to the maximum sentence should be reserved for the most serious or 'worst' of cases.[478]

Such a sentence should be passed only in the most truly exceptional cases that are so serious that it is difficult to imagine a more serious example of the offence.[479]

A sentence that imposes the maximum sentence offends this principle only if the case is recognisably outside the worst category.[480]

However, when deciding whether to impose the maximum sentence the case does not necessarily have to be the worst imaginable.[481]

But the 'worst' type of cases may be where:

- an accused person had consistently been in breach of the law and is consistently coming back to Court on a particular type of offence; or
- an offence charged has severe 'aggravating factors[482], [483]'.

---

[478] See *Taiba Maima v Sma* [1971-1972] PNGLR 49; *Stanley Sabiu v The State* (2007) SC866; *Aloises Peter Irobo Kovei v The State* (2001) SC676; *Agiru Aieni and twelve others v Paul T. Tohain* [1978] PNGLR 37; *Goli Golu v The State* [1979] PNGLR 653, [1979] PGSC 9; *Avia Aihi v The State (No. 3)* [1983] PNGLR 92, [1982] PGSC 9; *Ure Hane v The State* [1984] PNGLR 105; *John Tolna and fourteen others v Paul Ari* (1980) N218; *Paia Lifi v Phillip Dege* (1980) N291(M); *Passingan v Beaton* [1971-72] PNGLR 206, [1971] PGSC 37; *Hen Kuru and nine others v Wass Kombra* (1981) N292(L); *The State v Robert Kawin* (2001) N2167; *The State v Obert Poesan Pokanas* (2004) N2702; *Election Amo v Monie Luke Raphael* (2002) N2300; *Bernard Vuga v Thoni Ribi* (1978) N141 and *The State v Steven Molu Minji and others; The State v Didi Gelwak Sakol (No. 2)* (2009) N3794, [2009] PGNC 177.

See also: *Veen v R (No. 2)* (1988) 164 CLR 465 at 478, (1988) 33 A Crim R 230, [1988] HCA 14; *Ibbs v R* (1987) 163 CLR 447, (1987) 61 ALJR 525 at 527, (1987) 74 ALR 1 at 5, [1987] HCA 46; *R v Amber* [1976] Crim LR 266; *Reynolds v Wilkinson* (1948) 51 WALR 17, per Dwyer CJ at 18; *Bensegger v R* [1979] WAR 65, per Burt CJ at 68; *R v Abdul Sherif* [2009] 2 Cr App R (S) 33; *The People (DPP) v Johnston* 3 Frewen 276; *Markarian v R* (2005) 228 CLR 357 and *Elias v R; Issa v R* [2013] HCA 31.

[479] See *R v Pinto* [2006] 2 Cr App R (S) 87.

[480] See *Veen v R* (No. 2) (1988) 164 CLR 465 at 478, (1988) 33 A Crim R 230, [1988] HCA 14.

[481] See *Bensegger v R* [1979] WAR 65, per Burt CJ at 68 and *R v Sherratt* (2000) 112 A Crim R 177.

[482] Refer also to the chapter titled 'Aggravating Factors'.

[483] See *Paia Lifi v Phillip Dege* (1981) N291(M); *Hen Kuru and nine others v Wass Kombra* (1981) N292(L) and *Election Amo v Monie Luke Raphael* (2002) N2300.

MAXIMUM SENTENCE

The fact that a case falls into the 'worst' type category does not necessarily mean that the maximum sentence will automatically apply.[484]

Irrespective, the Court must:

- consider the nature and circumstances of the offence[485]; and
- impose a sentence that is proportionate to the offence.[486]

Section 19 of the *Criminal Code* (Ch. 262) gives the Court a discretion to impose a lesser penalty upon an accused person if the factual circumstances do not establish a 'worst case' in relation to offences under that Code[487].[488]

---

[484] See *John Elipa Kalabus v The State* [1988-89] PNGLR 193 and *Election Amo v Monie Luke Raphael* (2002) N2300.

[485] See *Goli Golu v The State* [1979] PNGLR 653, [1979] PGSC 9, per Kearney J; *The State v Ure Hane of Gaire, Central Province* (1983) N442 and *Taiba Maima v Sma* [1971-1972] PNGLR 49.

See also: *Bensegger v R* [1979] WAR 65.

[486] See *Avia Aihi v The State (No. 3)* [1983] PNGLR 92 at 105, [1982] PGSC 9.

Refer also to the chapter titled 'Equality In Sentencing'.

[487] Section 2 of the *Criminal Code Act* (Ch. 262) states:

> 'The provisions contained in Schedule 1 are the law of Papua New Guinea with respect to the matters dealt with in that Schedule'.

As regards the law in relation to 'Acts in pari materia', refer to the section titled 'Extrinsic Aids' in the chapter titled 'Aids To Interpretation' in the text titled 'Injia on Statutory Interpretation in Papua New Guinea and the Pacific'.

[488] See *The State v Steven Molu Minji and others; The State v Didi Gelwak Sakol (No. 2)* (2009) N3794, [2009] PGNC 177.

However, that section only applies to the Code, see section 2 of the *Criminal Code Act* (Ch. 262) and the section itself.

MINIMUM SENTENCE

A minimum statutory penalty itself does not substantially impair and is not incompatible with the institutional integrity of the courts.[489]

A Court does not have any discretion, but to start with a minimum sentence.[490]

A Court may:

- still suspend the whole or part of a minimum sentence by virtue of section 19(1)(d) of the *Criminal Code* (Ch. 262)[491]; and
- must consider that option[492].

However, section 19 only applies to offences contained within the *Criminal Code* (Ch. 262).[493]

---

489 See *Palling v Corfield* (1970) 123 CLR 52 at 58, [1970] HCA 53 and *R v Ironside* (2009) 104 SASR 54, [2009] SASC 151.

490 See *Omaro Garo v The Police* [1985] PNGLR 320, [1985] PGSC 4; *SCR No 1 of 1984; Re Minimum Penalties Legislation* [1984] PNGLR 314, [1984] PGSC 13; *SCR No. 1 of 1985* [1984] PNGLR 314, (1984) SC280; *The State v Sunu, Walter, Gagoro and Haro; Reservation of Points of Law under section 21 Supreme Court Act (Ch 37)* [1983] PNGLR 396, [1983] PGSC 21; *The State v Aruve Waiba* (1994) CR No. 1 of 1994; *The State v Jack Moge* [1995] PNGLR 246, (1995) N1318; *The State v Inema Yawok* (1998) N1766 and *The State v Irox Winston* (2003) N2347.

491 See *The State v Sunu, Walter, Gagoro and Haro; Reservation of Points of Law under section 21 Supreme Court Act (Ch 37)* [1983] PNGLR 396, [1983] PGSC 21; *Edmund Gima v The State; Siune Arnold v The State* (2003) SC730, [2003] PGSC 3; *Alphonse Dambui v The State* (2003) SC724, [2003] PGSC 20; *The State v Ass Medron Nangil and others* (2005) N2823 and *The State v Thomas Waim, Tala Gena and Alois Wanpis* [1998] PNGLR 360, (1998) N750, (1998) PGNC 174.

Refer also to the subsection titled 'Suspended Sentence' in the section titled 'Imprisonment' in the chapter titled 'Sentencing Options'.

492 See *Alphonse Dambui v The State* (2003) SC724, [2003] PGSC 20.

493 Section 2 of the *Criminal Code Act* (Ch. 262) states:

> 'The provisions contained in Schedule 1 are the law of Papua New Guinea with respect to the matters dealt with in that Schedule'.

As regards the law in relation to 'Acts in pari materia', refer to the section titled 'Extrinsic Aids' in the chapter titled 'Aids To Interpretation' in the text titled 'Injia on Statutory Interpretation in Papua New Guinea and the Pacific'.

MINIMUM SENTENCE

A District Court should also consider a non-custodial discharge as provided for by section 138 of the *District Courts Act* (Ch. 40).[494].

[494] See *Henderson v Blackwell* [1977] PNGLR 223 at 225; *Laho Kerekere v Robin Miria* [1983] PNGLR 277 and *Boas Kuna v Police* (1994) N1296.

OUTSTANDING CHARGES

[1.0] STATUTORY PROVISION

Section 603 of the *Criminal Code* (Ch. 262)[495] states:

> '(1) Where the court before which a person is convicted on indictment[496] of an offence not punishable with death[497] or imprisonment for life[498] is satisfied that –
>
> (a) there has been filed in court a document in or to the effect of the prescribed form, signed by a member of the Police Force[499] and by the person so convicted, showing on the back of it a list of other indictable offences[500] not punishable with death or imprisonment for life with which he has been charged (whether or not he has been committed for trial in respect of those other offences); and
>
> (b) a copy of that document has been furnished to the person so convicted; and
>
> (c) in all the circumstances of the case it is proper to do so,

---

495 This statutory provision only applies in the National Court in relation to offences under the Code.

496 The term 'indictment' is defined in section 1(1) of the *Criminal Code* (Ch. 262) as meaning:

> 'a written charge preferred against an accused person in order to his trial before some court other than a court of summary jurisdiction'.

The term 'court of summary jurisdiction' is defined in section 3(1) of the *Interpretation Act* (Ch. 2) as meaning:

> 'a District Court'.

497 Refer also to the section titled 'Sentence Of Death' in the chapter titled 'Sentencing Options'.

498 Nor can any other offence be taken into account on sentence pursuant to the procedure in section 603 of the *Criminal Code* (Ch. 262) on a charge of 'Murder' which is clear from the opening words of that provision, see *John Baipu v The State* (2005) SC796, [2005] PGSC 19.

Refer also to the section titled 'Imprisonment' in the chapter titled 'Sentencing Options'.

499 The term 'the Police Force' is defined in section 3(1) of the *Interpretation Act* (Ch. 2) as meaning:

> 'the Police Force established by Section 188 (*establishment of the State Services*) of the *Constitution*'.

500 Crimes and misdemeanours are indictable offences, see section 3(2) of the *Criminal Code* (Ch. 262).

Refer also to the chapter titled 'Classification Of Offences' in the text titled 'Injia on Criminal Practice and Procedure in Papua New Guinea and the Pacific'.

the court may, with the consent of the State Prosecutor and before passing sentence on the person for the offence of which he has been convicted, ask the person whether he admits his guilt in respect of all or any of the offences specified in the list and wishes them to be taken into account in passing sentence on him.

(2) If the convicted person admits his guilt in respect of all or any of the offences specified in the list filed under Subsection (1) and wishes them to be taken into account by the court in passing sentence for the offence of which he has been convicted, the court may, if it thinks fit, take all or any of the offences in respect of which he has so admitted guilt into account.

(3) In a case to which Subsection (2) applies, the sentence passed on the convicted person shall not exceed the maximum sentence that may be passed in respect of the offence of which he has been convicted.

(4) The court shall certify on the document filed under Subsection (1) the offences specified in the list on the back of it that have, in respect of the conviction of the person concerned, been taken into account in passing sentence on that conviction, and afterwards proceedings or further proceedings on those offences shall not be taken against the person unless the conviction is quashed or set aside.

(5) An admission of guilt under and for the purposes of this section in respect of an offence is not admissible in evidence –

(a) in any proceedings or further proceedings taken under the exception to Subsection (4); or

(b) in any proceedings or further proceedings in respect of the offence if the offence was not taken into account under this section in passing sentence.

(6) An offence taken into account under this section in passing sentence on a person for another offence of which he has been convicted shall not, by reason of its being so taken into account, be regarded for any purpose as an offence of which he has been convicted.

(7) Where the court before which a person was convicted of an indictable offence took into account in accordance with this section, in passing sentence for the offence, any other offence or offences, then whenever in or in relation to any criminal proceedings –

(a) reference may lawfully be made to the fact that the person was convicted of the indictable offence, reference may also be made to the fact that that other offence or those other offences was or were so taken into account; and

(b) evidence may lawfully be given of the fact that that person was convicted of the indictable offence, evidence may also be given of the fact that that other offence or those other offences was or were so taken into account.[501]

(8) The fact that that other offence or the other offences was or were so taken into account may be proved in the same manner as the conviction for the indictable offence may be proved.

(9) Subsections (7) and (8) do not affect the operation of Subsection (6)'.

[2.0] GENERAL PRINCIPLES

Whether or not a Court takes into account other outstanding charges pursuant to section 603 of the *Criminal Code* (Ch. 262):

- is purely discretionary; and
- must be done with the consent of:
  - the State Prosecutor; and
  - the accused person himself or herself,

but not his or her legal representative being asked by the trial judge as to whether the accused person admits his or her guilt on outstanding charges and desires that they should be taken into account.[502]

The appropriate time for the prosecution to make such application is just prior to sentence.[503]

Where the prosecution is to resort to this procedural requirement it is well noted that an accused person:

- must have been first convicted upon indictment of an offence not punishable with death or life imprisonment; and

---

[501] Refer also to the chapter titled 'Double Jeopardy' in the text titled 'Injia on Criminal Practice and Procedure in Papua New Guinea and the Pacific'.

[502] See *Acting Public Prosecutor v Andrew Amona Yongga* [1981] PNGLR 314, [1981] PGSC 8 and *The State v Kopiwan Pupuni* (1998) N1709.

[503] See *The State v Kopiwan Pupuni* (1998) N1709.

- then asked about other outstanding charges that he or she:
    - admits his or her guilt; and
    - wishes to be taken into account.[504]

The Court can then determine a penalty appropriate and commensurate to the circumstances of the case for which he or she has been convicted, including those other outstanding charges. The sentence imposed must not, however, exceed the maximum prescribed penalty[505].[506]

When other offences are taken into account, there is an increase in the sentence.[507]

The preferred practice is for the Court to:

- nominate a term of imprisonment for the offence; and
- then allocate a term for the offence that is taken into account

before imposing a just over-all sentence that takes into account all of the factors and circumstances of the offences.[508]

[504] See *The State v Kopiwan Pupuni* (1998) N1709.

[505] Refer also to the chapter titled 'Maximum Sentence'.

[506] See *The State v Kopiwan Pupuni* (1998) N1709.

[507] See *Acting Public Prosecutor v Andrew Amona Yongga* [1981] PNGLR 314, [1981] PGSC 8, per Andrew and Pratt JJ.

[508] See *Acting Public Prosecutor v Andrew Amona Yongga* [1981] PNGLR 314, [1981] PGSC 8, per Andrew and Pratt JJ.

ATTEMPTS TO COMMIT AN OFFENCE

[1.0] GENERAL PRINCIPLE[509]

Generally speaking, an attempt should be punished with a lesser sentence than that for the completed offence.[510]

However, it is important to appreciate that where an attempt to commit a substantive offence is involved, it is relevant to consider, in evaluating the seriousness of the offence, inter alia:

- the offence was not completed;
- the chances of its success;
- the seriousness of the attempt;
- whether the attempt was sophisticated or naive;
- the competence of the attempt; and
- all the other surrounding circumstances.[511]

[2.0] CRIMINAL CODE

The following statutory provisions only apply to those offences as provided for by the *Criminal Code* (Ch. 262)[512], and do not refer to a simple offence.

---

[509] Refer also to the chapter titled 'Attempts To Commit Offences' in the text titled 'Injia on Criminal Offences in Papua New Guinea and the Pacific'.

[510] See *R v Pearce* [1952] 2 All ER 718; *Verrier v DPP* [1966] 3 WLR 924, [1967] AC 195, [1966] 3 All ER 586, (1966) 50 Cr App R 315 and *McKeagg v R* (2006) 162 A Crim R 51, [2006] WASCA 26.

See however: *Koraua and Kaitira v R* [1988-1989] SILR 4 at 5-6.

[511] See *R v Taouk* (1992) 65 A Crim R 387 at 390 and *R v Schofield* [2003] NSWCCA 3.

[512] Section 2 of the *Criminal Code Act* (Ch. 262) states:

> 'The provisions contained in Schedule 1 are the law of Papua New Guinea with respect to the matters dealt with in that Schedule'.

As regards the law in relation to 'Acts in pari materia', refer to the section titled 'Extrinsic Aids' in the chapter titled 'Aids To Interpretation' in the text titled 'Injia on Statutory Interpretation in Papua New Guinea and the Pacific'.

ATTEMPTS TO COMMIT AN OFFENCE

Section 509 of the *Criminal Code* (Ch. 262) states:

> '(1) A person who attempts to commit an indictable offence[513] is guilty of an indictable offence, that, unless otherwise stated, is a misdemeanour.
>
> (2) When a person who commits an indictable offence is punishable on summary conviction[514], a person who attempts to commit such an offence may also be summarily convicted'.

Section 510 states:

> '(1) A person who attempts to commit a crime[515] of such a kind that a person convicted of it is liable to the punishment of death or for imprisonment for life or for a term of 14 years or more, with or without any other punishment, is liable, if no other punishment is provided, to imprisonment for seven years.
>
> (2) A person who attempts to commit a crime of any other kind, is liable, if no other punishment is provided, to a punishment equal to one-half of the greatest punishment to which an accused person convicted of the crime that he attempted to commit is liable'.

Section 511 states:

> 'A person who attempts to commit a misdemeanour[516] is liable, if no other punishment is provided, to a punishment equal to one-half of the greatest punishment to which an accused person convicted of the offence that he attempted to commit is liable'.

---

513 Crimes and misdemeanours are indictable offences, see section 3(2) of the *Criminal Code* (Ch. 262).

Refer also to the chapter titled 'Classification Of Offences' in the text titled 'Injia on Criminal Practice and Procedure in Papua New Guinea and the Pacific'.

514 The term 'summary conviction' is defined in section 1(1) of the *Criminal Code* (Ch. 262) as meaning:
'conviction by a court of summary jurisdiction'.

The term 'court of summary jurisdiction' is defined in section 3(1) of the *Interpretation Act* (Ch. 2) as meaning:
'a District Court'.

515 Refer also to the chapter titled 'Classification Of Offences' in the text titled 'Injia on Criminal Practice and Procedure in Papua New Guinea and the Pacific'.

516 Refer also to the chapter titled 'Classification Of Offences' in the text titled 'Injia on Criminal Practice and Procedure in Papua New Guinea and the Pacific'.

ATTEMPTS TO COMMIT AN OFFENCE

Section 512 states:

'(1) Where a person is convicted of attempting to commit an offence, and it is proved that he desisted of his own motion from the further prosecution of his intention, without its fulfillment being prevented by circumstances independent of his will, he is liable to one-half of the punishment to which he would otherwise be liable.

(2) If the punishment referred to in Subsection (1) is imprisonment for life, the greatest punishment to which he is liable is imprisonment for seven years'.

VICTIM IMPACT STATEMENT

[1.0] INTRODUCTION

The position of the victim is in fact given special consideration by statute. Section 21A of the *Criminal Code* (Ch. 262) requires a Court to consider any victim impact statement that may have been prepared by the victim of crime. In a case where the victim is dead, ill or incapable of giving evidence, 'victim' includes the relatives of the deceased person.[517]

However, section 21A only applies to the offences as specified in the *Criminal Code* (Ch. 262).[518]

Section 21A requires a Court to consider any written statement of a victim of an offence which is to be in a prescribed form to be in accordance with procedures set down for that purpose.[519]

[2.0] STATUTORY PROVISION

Section 21A of the *Criminal Code* (Ch. 262) states:

> '(1) For the purposes of determining the sentence to be imposed on an offender, the court shall consider any statement that may have been prepared in accordance with Subsection (2) of a victim of the offence describing the harm done to, or loss suffered by, the victim arising from the commission of the offence.
>
> (2) A statement referred to in Subsection (1) must be --
>
> (a) prepared in writing in the form and in accordance with the procedures established for that purpose; and
>
> (b) filed with the court.

---

[517] See *Steven Loke Ume, Charles Patrick Kaona and Greg Wawa Kavoa v The State* (2006) SC836, [2006] PGSC 9.

[518] See *Steven Loke Ume, Charles Patrick Kaona and Greg Wawa Kavoa v The State* (2006) SC836, [2006] PGSC 9 and *The State v Blasius Bana* (2004) N2863, [2005] PGNC 108.

Section 2 of the *Criminal Code Act* (Ch. 262) states:

> 'The provisions contained in Schedule 1 are the law of Papua New Guinea with respect to the matters dealt with in that Schedule'.

As regards the law in relation to 'Acts in pari materia', refer to the section titled 'Extrinsic Aids' in the chapter titled 'Aids To Interpretation' in the text titled 'Injia on Statutory Interpretation in Papua New Guinea and the Pacific'.

[519] See *The State v Philip Peter* (2010) N4011, [2010] PGNC 48.

(3) A statement of the victim of an offence prepared and filed in accordance with Subsection (2) does not prevent the court from considering any other evidence concerning any victim of the offence for the purpose of determining the sentence to be imposed on the offender.

(4) For the purposes of this section, "Victim", in relation to any offence --

(a) means the person to whom harm was done or who suffered physical or emotional loss as a result of the commission of the offence; and

(b) where the person described in Paragraph (a) is dead, ill or otherwise incapable of making a statement referred to in Subsection (1), includes the spouse or any other relative of that person, anyone who has in law or fact the custody of that person or is responsible for the case[520] or support of that person or any dependent of that person'.

[3.0] FORM

Whilst a form of a Victim Impact Statement is yet to be prescribed by the Rules of Court, the form of a witness's statement prescribed under section 94(1)(d), (1A) and (1B) of the *District Courts Act* (Ch. 40) may be used as a guide. In practice, the form in use is as follows:

VICTIM IMPACT STATEMENT

Name: ....

The victim must be informed:

- that the information is being gathered for submission to the judicial officer sentencing an accused person if the accused person is found guilty or pleads guilty;
- that the information must be true;
- that the information must be recorded and may be verified in the manner set out at the bottom of this form; and

---

[520] However, in interpreting that section the word 'case' should be read as 'care' applying the purposive rule of statutory interpretation.

The law in relation to that rule is in the text titled 'Injia on Statutory Interpretation in Papua New Guinea and the Pacific'.

- about who may properly see or make copies of the information ascertained, and about the orders, directions, and conditions , relation to disclosure and distribution of it that may be made.

Statement to take story form and to cover the following:

Victims Details (if appropriate)

For example, age, occupation, sex, living arrangements, marital status, relation to the accused person (if any), ethnic origin

Physical Injuries

For example, type and extent of injuries, long and short term effects, what treatment was required, was hospitalisation required.

Financial Costs

For example, costs of treatment, replacement costs, repair costs, loss of wages or income, incidental costs and funeral costs.

Emotional Harm

For example, changes in behaviour, lifestyle and personal reaction and any treatment as a consequence.

Any other harm or effects

Attach any supporting documentation.

VICTIM IMPACT STATEMENT

Victim or other person making the Victim Impact Statement:	**OR (if it is not practicable for the victim to sign):**
I have given the information in this Victim Impact Statement knowing that it is for submission to the judicial officer sentencing the accused person and know that the information must be true. The information is true to the best of my knowledge and belief. I make it knowing that if it is tendered in evidence, I will be liable to prosecution if I have knowingly stated anything that is false or misleading in any particular.	I have advised the victim that the information in this Victim Impact Statement is for submission to the judicial officer sentencing the accused person and that the information must be true. I have read it to the victim and am satisfied that the victim approves of it. I make it knowing that if it is tendered in evidence, I will be liable to prosecution if I have knowingly stated anything that is false or misleading in any particular.
Signature/Mark: .... (victim)	Signature: ....
Name: .... (printed)	Name: .... (printed)
Date:	Designation: ....
	Date: ....

SENTENCING OPTIONS

[1.0] INTRODUCTION

Depending on the circumstances the options in sentencing that may be imposed include:

- Sentence of Death[521];
- Life Imprisonment[522];
- Imprisonment for a Term of Years[523];
- Suspended Sentence[524];
- Fine[525];
- Probation Order[526];
- Community Service Order[527];
- Good Behaviour Bond[528];
- Conditional Discharge[529];

---

[521] Refer also to the section titled 'Sentence Of Death' in this chapter.

[522] Refer also to the section titled 'Imprisonment' in this chapter.

[523] Refer also to the section titled 'Imprisonment' in this chapter.

[524] Refer also to the section titled 'Imprisonment' in this chapter.

[525] Refer also to the section titled 'Fine' in this chapter.

[526] Refer also to the section titled 'Probation Order' in this chapter.

[527] Refer also to the section titled 'Community Work Order' in this chapter.

[528] Refer also to the section titled 'Good Behaviour Bond' in this chapter.

[529] Refer also to the section titled 'Conditional Discharge' in this chapter.

SENTENCING OPTIONS

- Discharge Without Conviction[530];
- Enter Conviction but Impose No Further Order and Discharge The Juvenile[531];
- Compensation Order[532];
- Property Orders[533];
- Disqualification, etc of a Driving Licence[534];
- Restriction of Movement Order[535]; and
- Order a Juvenile to be a Ward of the Director of Child Welfare.[536]

A sentence may also commence or conclude with the 'Rising of the Court'[537].

---

[530] See section 30(2)(a) of the *Juvenile Courts Act 1991* ['Powers Of Court To Make Orders'].

Refer also to the section titled 'Juvenile Courts Act' in the chapter titled 'Introduction To Sentencing'.

[531] See section 30(2)(b) of the *Juvenile Courts Act 1991* ['Powers Of Court To Make Orders'].

Refer also to the section titled 'Juvenile Courts Act' in the chapter titled 'Introduction To Sentencing'.

[532] Refer also to the section titled 'Compensation Order' in this chapter.

[533] Refer also to the section titled 'Property Orders' in this chapter.

[534] Refer also to the section titled 'Disqualification, Etc Of A Driving Licence' in this chapter.

[535] Refer also to the section titled 'Restriction of Movement' in this chapter.

[536] See section 30(2)(iv) and (v) of the *Juvenile Courts Act 1991* ['Powers Of Court To Make Orders'].

Refer also to the section titled 'Juvenile Courts Act' in the chapter titled 'Introduction To Sentencing'.

[537] See *The State v James Hilux Palu* (2004) N2585, [2004] PGNC 182 and *The State v Anton Dima* (2007) N3119, [2007] PGNC 16.

See also: *Gerea and others v DPP* [1984] SILR 161, per Pratt JA at 174.

SENTENCING OPTIONS

[2.0] COMMUNITY WORK ORDER

[2.1] CRIMINAL CODE

A community work order is not a sentence that may be emposed under section 18 of the *Criminal Code* (Ch. 262).

[2.2] DISTRICT COURTS ACT

Section 199A of the *District Courts Act* (Ch. 40)[538] states:

> '(1) Where, under any law[539] a Court[540] may, after conviction, impose a fine[541] or imprisonment for an offence[542], it may, as well as imposing a fine, or instead of imposing a fine or imprisonment, order the offender to perform specified work for community purposes of a kind and in a manner approved by the Minister by notice in the National Gazette[543].

---

538 See also: section 205A of the *District Courts Act* (Ch. 40) ['Community Work Orders'].

539 The term 'law' is defined in section 3(1) of the *Interpretation Act* (Ch. 2) as meaning:
'a law of Papua New Guinea, and includes –
(a) the underlying law; and
(b) subordinate enactments'.

A 'subordinate enactment' is an instrument (whether of a legislative nature or not) made under an Act such as a regulation, see also section 3(1).

540 The term 'court' is defined in section 1 of the *District Courts Act* (Ch. 40) as meaning:
'the District Court'.

541 The term 'fine' is defined in section 1 of the *District Courts Act* (Ch. 40) as including:
'a pecuniary penalty, pecuniary forfeiture or pecuniary compensation payable under a conviction'.

542 The term 'offence', in relation to a law, is defined in section 3(1) of the *Interpretation Act* (Ch. 2) as including:
'a breach or contravention of, or a failure to comply with, the law.

543 The term 'the National Gazette' is defined in section 3(1) of the *Interpretation Act* (Ch. 2) as meaning:
'the official journal of that name of the National Government provided for by Section 252 (*the National Gazette*) of the *Constitution*, and includes any Special National Gazette, National Gazette Extraordinary or Supplement to the National Gazette'.

Section 52 of the *Evidence Act* (Ch. 48) states:
'The production of a paper purporting to be a Gazette is in all courts evidence that the paper is the Gazette and was published on the day on which it is dated'.

(2) Where a Court makes an order under Subsection (1), the work ordered to be performed shall not exceed –

(a) eight hours in any one day; and

(b) six days in any one week,

over a period not exceeding three months.

(3) Where a person fails to comply with an order under Subsection (1), the Court may order the person to be imprisoned for a term not exceeding two days for every day on which he fails to comply with the order.

(4) An order under Subsection (1) may include an anticipatory order under Subsection (3)'.

[3.0] COMPENSATION ORDER

[3.1] CRIMINAL LAW (COMPENSATION) ACT

[3.1.1] INTRODUCTION

A Court has the power to award a payment of customary compensation as a form of punishment under the *Criminal Law (Compensation) Act 1991*.

The terms of the *Criminal Law (Compensation) Act 1991* must be considered in every sentence by the National and the District Courts.[544]

However, a compensation order is not allowed in relation to offences involving victims of crime who are children.[545]

In *The State v Peter Kose Wena*[546] Kapi DepCJ (as he then was) stated:

> 'The primary decision the court needs to make is "whether in the circumstances of the case, compensation order should be ordered" (s. 2(2)). In considering this matter, s. 3(1) of the Act requires that the court shall take into account [a number of] factors.
>
> [...]

---

[544] See *Anna Max Marangi v The State* (2002) SC702 and *The State v Peter Kose Wena* [1993] PNGLR 168, (1993) N1184, [1993] PGNC 38.

[545] See *William Muma v The State* [1995] PNGLR 161 and *The State v Ebes Tiun* (2001) N2129.

[546] [1993] PNGLR 168 at 169-171, (1993) N1184, [1993] PGNC 38.

The secondary decision which the court has to make is the actual compensation order in terms of the period in which to pay, the form, manner of payment and the person or persons to be paid (s. 5, 6) and the amount of compensation and specify a default penalty in accordance with Schedule 1 of the Act (s. 6). The court shall request a means assessment report (s. 4(1) to enable it to make the appropriate compensation Order (s. 5(1)'.

In the circumstances in which an accused person does not wish to make a submission as to the amount of compensation it is appropriate for a Court to assess quantum on the basis of:

- the evidence[547]; and/or
- a submission from the prosecution[548].

It is proper to combine:

- a compensation order; and
- a sentence of significant imprisonment,

provided that an accused person has the capacity to pay the compensation ordered.[549]

However, it is inappropriate to make an order for compensation:

- if the victim is not willing to accept it[550];
- when there has been no damage or injury[551]; and

---

547 See *R v O'Rourke* [1990] 1 NZLR 155.

548 See *R v Gray* [1993] NZCA 356/93.

549 See *The State v Simam July Melly (No. 2)* (2009) N3779, [2009] PGNC 138.

See also: *Dorton* (1987) 9 Cr App R (S) 514.

550 See *The State v Prodie Akoi and Steven Akoi* (2004) N2584.

551 See *The State v Peter Barnes and Douglas Ume* (1993) N1190.

- against an accused person's spouse, relative, tribal or village group as there is no provision under the *Criminal Law (Compensation) Act 1991* for the making of such an order.[552]

[3.1.2] COMPENSATION AS PUNISHMENT

STATUTORY PROVISION

Section 2 of the *Criminal Law (Compensation) Act 1991* states:

> '(1) Notwithstanding that payment of compensation is not specified as a punishment for an offence, a court[553] may, in addition to any other punishments imposed, order an offender to pay compensation in accordance with this Act.
>
> (2) When a court is considering the punishment or punishments to be imposed for an offence, it shall also consider whether in the circumstances of the case, compensation should be ordered'.

GENERAL PRINCIPLE

A Court may make a compensation order under section 2 of the *Criminal Law (Compensation) Act 1991* notwithstanding that a 'No Means Assessment Report' has been prepared.[554]

---

552 See *The State v Margaret John (No. 1)* [1995] PNGLR 446 at 451, (1995) N1326; *The State v Margaret John (No. 2)* [1996] PNGLR 29; *The State v Henry Idab* (2001) N2172; *The State v Abel Airi* (2000) N2007 and *The State v Nickson Pari (No. 2)* (2001) N2033.

See however: *The State v Phillip Susuve Raipa* [1994] PNGLR 458.

553 The term 'court' is defined in section 1 of the *Criminal Law (Compensation) Act 1991* as meaning: 'the National Court or a District Court'.

554 See *The State v Simam July Melly (No. 2)* (2009) N3779, [2009] PGNC 138.

[3.1.3] FACTORS TO BE CONSIDERED

STATUTORY PROVISION

Section 3 of the *Criminal Law (Compensation) Act 1991* states:

> '(1) Where a court is deciding whether to make an order of compensation under Section 2, or is deciding upon the compensation to be ordered under Section 5, it shall take into account the following factors:–
>
> (a) the nature and seriousness of the offence;
>
> (b) the degree and nature of any personal injury or damage to property suffered by any person as a result of the commission of the offence;
>
> (c) any factors regarding the commission of the offence or the accused person's attitude which may be considered in mitigation or aggravation of the punishment;
>
> (d) any relevant custom regarding compensation, including but not limited to –
>
> (i) any custom regarding the nature, the amount, the method of payment and the appropriate person or persons to be paid the compensation; and
>
> (ii) any custom which relates the amount of compensation to the age or life expectancy of the person suffering injury or loss;
>
> (e) the information provided in the means assessment report, including any recommendations made by the Chief Probation Officer[555] in the means assessment report;

[555] The term 'Chief Probation Officer' is defined in section 1 of the *Criminal Law (Compensation) Act 1991* as meaning:

> 'the person appointed as such under the *Probation Act 1979*, or his delegate for the purposes of this Act'.

(f) any other relevant matter[556].

(2) In considering a matter under this section, a court is not bound to apply the technical rules of evidence but may act on such information as is available to it'.

GENERAL PRINCIPLE

A compensation order is not appropriate for serious crimes of violence such as aggravated robbery, rape, incest and homicide offences because the amount of compensation involved far exceed the monetary limit (K5,000) and default penalty (six months) prescribed by the *Criminal Law (Compensation) Act 1991*.[557]

[3.1.4] MEANS ASSESSMENT REPORT

STATUTORY PROVISION

Section 4 of the *Criminal Law (Compensation) Act 1991* states:

'(1) Where a court considers that an order for compensation should be made, it shall –

---

[556] The following factors may also be taken into account:

Mental Anguish Caused

- Outline whether the complainant has suffered mental anguish as a direct result of the commission of the offence.

On – Going Problems

- Outline as per medical and/or dental advice;
- Be specific as to the extent of such problems, duration of the problems and what treatment will be required in the future; and
- Outline medical and/or dental expenses currently incurred and to be incurred in the future.

Loss of Income

- Specify any loss of wages; and
- Explain why the complainant could not work.

[557] See *The State v Billy Kauwa* [1994] PNGLR 503.

(a) request the Chief Probation Officer to furnish to the court a means assessment report in respect of the offender[558]; and

(b) order the offender[559] to report to the Chief Probation Officer in order to determine the person's means and financial circumstances.

(2) Upon receiving a request under Subsection (1), the Chief Probation Officer shall –

(a) interview the offender and his immediate relatives[560] and report to the court on the means and financial circumstances of the offender; or

(b) advise the court that it is not practicable for him to furnish the report[561].

(3) A means assessment report may include a recommendation by the Chief Probation Officer as to the amount, nature and method of payment of the compensation to be ordered and any other matters in relation to the order which he considers relevant.

(4) Where the Chief Probation Officer advises the court that it is not practicable for him to furnish a means assessment report, the court may proceed under this Act without one'.

GENERAL PRINCIPLES

The issue for a Court to determine is whether realistically an accused person has the financial capacity to make a payment of compensation whilst taking into consideration:

- his or her income;
- his or her obligations; and

---

558 Section 1 of the *Criminal Law (Compensation) Regulation 1992* states:
'A request for a means assessment report under Section 4(1)(a) of the Act shall be in Form 1'.

559 The term 'offender' is defined in section 1 of the *Criminal Law (Compensation) Act 1991* as meaning:
'a person convicted of an offence'.

560 The term 'relative' is defined in section 1 of the *Criminal Law (Compensation) Act 1991* as meaning:
'father, mother, brother or sister'.

561 Section 2 of the *Criminal Law (Compensation) Regulation 1992* states:
'An advice to the court under Section 4(2)(b) of the Act that it is not practicable to furnish a report shall be in Form 2'.

- the maximum amount that he or she would realistically be able to pay.[562]

A compensation order should only be made under the *Criminal Law (Compensation) Act 1991* if an accused person has the means to pay compensation.[563]

In *The State v Peter Kose Wena*[564] Kapi DepCJ (as he then was) stated:

> 'The information contained in the means assessment report (s.3(1)(e)) is a factor to be taken into account when the court is considering the primary decision, namely, whether in the circumstances of a case, compensation order should be ordered. It would appear from this that a means assessment report should be provided before this primary decision is made.
>
> On the other hand, s. 4 which provides for the provision of a means assessment report, begins with the words:
>
> "(1) Where a court considers that an order for compensation should be made, it shall --
>
> (a) request the Chief Probation Officer to furnish to the court a means assessment report in respect of the accused person;"
>
> It would appear from this provision that a means assessment report is not relevant until the court has made the primary decision of whether, a compensation order should be made. This would appear to be inconsistent with s. 3(1)(e) in so far as the timing of the means assessment report is concerned.
>
> In resolving this apparent conflict, it may be helpful to examine the purpose or contents of the means assessment report. The report is requested to determine the accused person's:
>
> (a) Means and financial circumstances (s. 4(1)(b), 4(2(a)).
>
> (b) Ability to pay (amount), the nature and method of payment (s. 4(3)).

---

562 See *R v Jarvis* [1986] NZCA 306/86.

563 See *The State v Joe Butema Arua* (2001) N2076; *The State v Sam Piapin* (2009) N3585; *The State v Kennedy Arus* (2001) N2081; *The State v Eddie John Naopa* (2003) N2411; *The State v Raphael Kimba Aki (No. 2)* (2001) N2082 and *The State v Gore Yogal* (2001) N2080.

564 [1993] PNGLR 168 at 169-171, [1993] PGNC 38, (1993) N1184.

It is clear from this examination that a means assessment report contains relevant information applicable to what I have called the primary decision (whether or not a compensation order should be made) and the secondary decision (the actual order as to the amount, form, nature, method of payment, the period of payment, etc). The means assessment report is relevant to both stages (s. 3(1)). A single report would cover both stages of the decision.

The terms of s. 3 are couched in mandatory terms, that is, the court shall have regard to the information in the means assessment report. I have concluded from this that the court should request a means assessment report from the Chief Probation Officer for purposes of making the primary decision. That conclusion immediately raises practical difficulties. The court would adjourn further proceedings on sentence until the report is received. Can the Chief Probation Officer meet the demands of all National and District Courts throughout Papua New Guinea? There are many centres with no probation service. Even where there is a probation service, it may not be practicable to provide the report. The legislature was mindful of this. Under s. 4(4) of the Act, where it is not practicable, the court may proceed without the report. Where this is the case, the court can inquire into the means and financial and other relevant circumstances of the accused person by itself where the accused is not represented or through counsel for the accused'.

[3.1.5] COMPENSATION ORDERS

Section 5 of the *Criminal Law (Compensation) Act 1991* states:

'(1) Upon receipt of the means assessment report or the Chief Probation Officer's advice under Section 4(2), the court may, after taking into account the factors specified in Section 3–

(a) order the accused person to pay, within such period and in such manner as the court determines, compensation to a person or group of persons specified in the order[565]; and

(b) direct the Chief Probation Officer to supervise compliance with the compensation order.

(2) Subject to Subsection (3), compensation may be ordered in the form of cash, goods, services or any other kind or method of compensation which the court considers appropriate.

[565] Section 3 of the *Criminal Law (Compensation) Regulation 1992* states:
'A compensation order under Section 5(1)(a) at the Act shall be in Form 3'.

(3) No compensation ordered under this Act –

(a) shall include the use or payment of alcohol; and

(b) whether in the form of cash, goods, services or any other kind or method of compensation shall exceed in value K5,000.00,

and the value of any form of compensation other than cash shall be as determined by the court.'

[3.1.6] TERMS OF COMPENSATION ORDERS

STATUTORY PROVISION

Section 6(1) of the *Criminal Law (Compensation) Act 1991* states:

'A compensation order[566] shall –

(a) specify the nature and amount of the compensation to be paid; and

(b) specify a default penalty in accordance with Schedule 1; and

(c) specify the person or group of persons to whom the compensation is to be paid; and

(d) specify the date by which and the manner in which the compensation is to be paid.

Default Penalties [Schedule to the Act]

1. Where compensation is in the form of cash, the default penalty shall be as shown in the following table:–

Value Of Compensation	Default Term Of Imprisonment
Not exceeding K500.00	1 month
Exceeding K500.00 but not exceeding K1,000.00	2 months
Exceeding K1,000.00 but not exceeding K3,000.00	3 months
Exceeding K3,000.00	6 months

[566] The term 'compensation order' is defined in section 1 of the *Criminal Law (Compensation) Act 1991* as meaning:
'an order for compensation made under Section 5'.

See also: section 3 of the *Criminal Law (Compensation) Regulation 1992*.

2. Where compensation comprises or includes goods other than cash, the default penalty shall be in the discretion of the court, but in any case shall not exceed six months'.

OFFENCES

Section 6 of the *Criminal Law (Compensation) Act 1991* states (in part):

'(2) A person who, without reasonable excuse (proof of which is on him[567]) contravenes or fails to comply with a term of a compensation order, is guilty of an offence.

Penalty[568]: A fine not exceeding K400.00 or imprisonment for a term not exceeding six months.

(3) If, on information, it appears to a court that person has committed a breach of or has failed to comply with a term of a compensation order, the court may –

(a) issue a summons requiring the person to appear before it; or

(b) where the information is on oath[569] – issue a warrant for his arrest[570]'.

---

[567] This is a negative averment.

The onus is on the accused person to prove on the 'balance of probabilities' that he or she had a reasonable excuse for contravening or failing to comply with a term of a compensation order.

Refer also to the chapter titled 'Proof Of Issues' in the text titled 'Injia on Criminal Practice and Procedure in Papua New Guinea and the Pacific'.

[568] This is not an indictable offence [see section 21(b) of the *Interpretation Act* (Ch. 2)] and can be dealt with summarily [see section 22 of the Interpretation Act (Ch. 2)].

Refer also to the chapter titled 'Classification Of Offences' in the text titled 'Injia on Criminal Practice and Procedure in Papua New Guinea and the Pacific'.

[569] The term 'oath' is defined in section 3(1) of the *Interpretation Act* (Ch. 2), in the case of a person allowed by law to affirm, declare or promise, instead of swearing, as including:
'affirmation, declaration and promise'.

[570] As regards the law in relation to 'Arrest And Detain', refer to the chapter titled 'Police Powers' in the text titled 'Injia on Investigatory Practice in Papua New Guinea and the Pacific'.

WORDING OF CHARGES

'That on **[**Date**]** at **[**Place**]** in Papua New Guinea **[**Name of Accused Person**]** without reasonable excuse did **[**contravene **or** fail to comply with**]** a term of a compensation order.'

ELEMENTS

A. Date

B. Place

C. Accused Person

D. Without Reasonable Excuse

E. [1] Contravene

[2] Fail To Comply With

F. Term Of A Compensation Order

[3.1.7] REPORTING CONDITION

STATUTORY PROVISION

Section 7(1) of the *Criminal Law (Compensation) Act 1991* states:

> 'A compensation order shall contain a condition that the accused person shall report to the Chief Probation Officer at or within a specified time or times'.

SENTENCING OPTIONS

OFFENCES

Section 7 of the *Criminal Law (Compensation) Act 1991* states (in part):

> '(2) A person who, without reasonable excuse (proof of which is on him[571]), contravenes or fails to comply with the reporting condition of a compensation order, is guilty of an offence.
>
> Penalty[572]: A fine not exceeding K400.00 or imprisonment for a term not exceeding six months.
>
> (3) If, on information, it appears to a court that a person has committed a breach of or has failed to comply with, the reporting condition of a compensation order, the court may –
>
> (a) issue a summons requiring the person to appear before it; or
>
> (b) where the information is on oath – issue a warrant for his arrest[573]'.

WORDING OF CHARGES

'That on **[**Date**]** at **[**Place**]** in Papua New Guinea **[**Name of Accused Person**]** without reasonable excuse did **[**contravene **or** fail to comply with**]** the reporting condition of a compensation order.'

---

571 This is a negative averment.

The onus is on the accused person to prove on the 'balance of probabilities' that he or she had a reasonable excuse for contravening or failing to comply with a reporting condition.

Refer also to the chapter titled 'Proof Of Issues' in the text titled 'Injia on Criminal Practice and Procedure in Papua New Guinea and the Pacific'.

572 This is not an indictable offence [see section 21(b) of the *Interpretation Act* (Ch. 2)] and can be dealt with summarily [see section 22 of the Interpretation Act (Ch. 2)].

Refer also to the chapter titled 'Classification Of Offences' in the text titled 'Injia on Criminal Practice and Procedure in Papua New Guinea and the Pacific'.

573 As regards the law in relation to 'Arrest And Detain', refer to the chapter titled 'Police Powers' in the text titled 'Injia on Investigatory Practice in Papua New Guinea and the Pacific'.

ELEMENTS

A. Date

B. Place

C. Accused Person

D. Without Reasonable Excuse

E. [1] Contravene

[2] Fail To Comply With

F. Reporting Condition Of A Compensation Order

[3.2] CRIMINAL CODE[574]

The following statutory provisions only apply to those offences as provided for by the *Criminal Code* (Ch. 262).[575]

Section 421 of the *Criminal Code* (Ch. 262) states (in part):

> '(2) If the Court finds that the charge is proved, it may, whether it imposes a penalty or not, order the offender to make restitution of the property (if any) in respect of which the offence is committed, to its owner, and if the property is not at once restored, the Court may order the offender to pay the amount of its value assessed by the Court, to the owner either in one sum or by such instalments and at such times as the Court thinks fit'.

[574] Refer also to the chapters titled 'Good Behaviour Bond' and 'Conditional Discharge' in this chapter.

[575] Section 2 of the *Criminal Code Act* (Ch. 262) states:

> 'The provisions contained in Schedule 1 are the law of Papua New Guinea with respect to the matters dealt with in that Schedule'.

Section 6 of that Act states:

> 'This Act does not limit or affect in any way any provision of any other Act conferring on a court a power to pass a sentence or impose a punishment or make an order in addition to or instead of a sentence or punishment prescribed by the Code, or otherwise to deal with an offender'.

As regards the law in relation to 'Acts in pari materia', refer to the section titled 'Extrinsic Aids' in the chapter titled 'Aids To Interpretation' in the text titled 'Injia on Statutory Interpretation in Papua New Guinea and the Pacific'.

(3) Where, under Subsection (2), the Court has made an order in respect of property, with or without costs, and the offender has neglected or defaulted in carrying out the order, the offender is liable to imprisonment for such period as the Court, in its discretion, thinks fit, but not exceeding the maximum fixed by the following scale:–

Where the sum adjudged to be paid including costs	The period shall not exceed
Does not exceed K2.00	7 days
Exceeds K2.00 but does not exceed K4.00	14 days
Exceeds K4.00 but does not exceed K10.00	1 month
Exceeds K10.00 but does not exceed K40.00	2 months
Exceeds K40.00 but does not exceed K100.00	4 months
Exceeds K100.00 but does not exceed K200.00	8 months
Exceeds K200.00	12 months

Section 604 states:

'(1) Subject to Subsection (2), on a summary conviction[576] by which a penalty is imposed on the basis of–

(a) the value of any property taken, killed or destroyed; or

(b) the amount of any injury done to any property,

the value or amount shall be assessed by the convicting court and the amount, when recovered, shall be paid to the person aggrieved, unless he is unknown, or unless the property taken or injured is of a public nature, when it is to be applied in the same manner as other fines imposed by the court.

[576] The term 'summary conviction' is defined in section 1(1) of the *Criminal Code* (Ch. 262) as meaning:
'conviction by a court of summary jurisdiction'.

The term 'court of summary jurisdiction' is defined in section 3(1) of the *Interpretation Act* (Ch. 2) as meaning:
'a District Court'.

(2) When several persons join in the commission of the same offence, and on conviction a penalty is imposed on each of them on the basis of the value of the property or of the amount of the injury, no sum further than the value or amount shall be paid to the person aggrieved, and the remainder shall be applied in the same manner as other fines imposed by the court'.

Section 612 states:

'(1) When a person is convicted on indictment[577] of an indictable offence[578] relating to the person of any person, the court, on the application of the person aggrieved by the offence, may, in addition to any sentence that is passed on the accused person, order him to pay to the person aggrieved –

(a) his costs of prosecution; and

(b) a sum by way of compensation for any loss of time suffered by him by reason of the offence of which the accused person is convicted.

(2) An order under Subsection (1) for the payment of costs, or of any sum awarded by way of compensation may be enforced in the same manner as a judgement of the court given in civil proceedings.

(3) If any money was found on the person of the accused person on his arrest, the court may order it to be applied towards the payment of any money ordered under Subsection (1) to be paid by him'.

Section 623A states:

'(1) When a person is prosecuted, on the complaint of the owner of property or any person on whom the right to property has devolved by operation of law, on a charge or an indictable offence of which the unlawful acquisition of the property by him is an element, and is convicted of the offence on indictment, the court may order the property to be restored to the owner.

---

[577] The term 'indictment' is defined in section 1(1) of the *Criminal Code* (Ch. 262) as meaning:
'a written charge preferred against an accused person in order to his trial before some court other than a court of summary jurisdiction'.

The term 'court of summary jurisdiction' is defined in section 3(1) of the *Interpretation Act* (Ch. 2) as meaning:
'a District Court'.

[578] Crimes and misdemeanours are indictable offences, see section 3(2) of the *Criminal Code* (Ch. 262).

(2) An order made under Subsection (1) has the effect of a judgement, and is binding on the offender and any person claiming through him as determining the ownership of the property, but as regards any other person has the effect only of changing the possession of the property, and does not affect any right of property or right of action.

(3) In any case referred to in Subsection (1), the court before which the offender is convicted may order that any personal property which is found in his possession, and which appears to the court to have been derived, directly or indirectly, from such unlawful acquisition of property, shall be delivered to any person who appears to the court to be entitled to the property so unlawfully acquired.

(4) This section does not apply to a valuable security, if it appears that the security has been paid or discharged in good faith by some person liable to the payment of it, or, being a negotiable instrument, has been taken or received by transfer or delivery in good faith by some person for a valuable consideration without any notice and without any reasonable cause to suspect that the same had been so unlawfully acquired'.

[3.3] JUVENILE COURTS ACT

Subject to section 30 of the *Juvenile Courts Act 1991*, the Court may, in addition to any other powers under that Act or any other law enter a conviction and having regard to the ability of the juvenile to pay order the juvenile to pay damages of an amount not exceeding K200.00 to a person named in the order.[579]

[579] See section 30(2)(c)(ii) of the *Juvenile Courts Act 1991*.

SENTENCING OPTIONS

[4.0] CONDITIONAL DISCHARGE

[4.1] CRIMINAL CODE

The following statutory provision only applies to those offences as provided for by the *Criminal Code* (Ch. 262).[580]

Section 602 of the *Criminal Code* (Ch. 262) states:

> '(1) When a person is summarily convicted of an offence relating to property, the court that convicts him may discharge the offender, without inflicting any punishment, on his making such satisfaction to the person aggrieved for damages, with or without costs, as may be approved by the court.
>
> (2) When satisfaction in accordance with Subsection (1) has been made the offender is not liable to any civil proceedings for the same cause at the suit of the person aggrieved'.

---

[580] Section 2 of the *Criminal Code Act* (Ch. 262) states:

> 'The provisions contained in Schedule 1 are the law of Papua New Guinea with respect to the matters dealt with in that Schedule'.

As regards the law in relation to 'Acts in pari materia', refer to the section titled 'Extrinsic Aids' in the chapter titled 'Aids To Interpretation' in the text titled 'Injia on Statutory Interpretation in Papua New Guinea and the Pacific'.

[4.2] DISTRICT COURTS ACT

[4.2.1] STATUTORY PROVISION

Section 132 of the *District Courts Act* (Ch. 40) states:

> '(1) Where a person is charged before a Court[581] with a simple offence[582] or an indictable offence[583] triable summarily, and the Court thinks that the charge is proved but is of opinion that, having regard to –

---

[581] The term 'court' is defined in section 1 of the *District Courts Act* (Ch. 40) as meaning:
'the District Court'.

See also: *Public Prosecutor v Arthur Jawodimbari and Monty Derari* (2006) SC891, [2006] PGSC 28.

[582] The term 'simple offence' is defined in section 1 of the District Courts Act (Ch. 40) as meaning:
'an offence punishable on summary conviction before a court by fine, imprisonment or otherwise'.

[583] The term 'offence' in relation to a law is defined in section 3(1) of the *Interpretation Act* (Ch. 2) as including:
'a breach or contravention of, or a failure to comply with, the law'.

The term 'law' is also defined in section 3(1) as meaning:
'a law of Papua New Guinea, and includes –
(a) the underlying law; and
(b) subordinate enactments'.

A 'subordinate enactment' is an instrument (whether of a legislative nature or not) made under an Act such as a regulation, see also section 3(1).

(a) the character[584], antecedents[585], age[586], health[587] or mental condition[588] of the person charged; or

(b) the trivial nature of the offence[589]; or

(c) the extenuating circumstances under which the offence was committed[590],

it is inexpedient to inflict punishment, or other than a nominal punishment or that it is expedient to release the offender on probation, the Court may, without proceeding to conviction, make an order –

(d) dismissing the charge; or

---

[584] This refers to positively good character, as shown by, for example, voluntary work in the church or community. It means more than simply the absence of a prior conviction, see *Freda Nup v Chris Hambuga* [1984] PNGLR 206.

Refer also to:
- the section titled 'Good Character Generally' in the chapter titled 'Mitigating Factors'; and
- the section titled 'Character And Antecedents' in the chapter titled 'Aggravating Factors'.

[585] This refers to a prior conviction, if any, the existence of which would preclude application of this section and the absence of which does not automatically lead to the application of this section, see *Freda Nup v Chris Hambuga* [1984] PNGLR 206.

Refer also to:
- the section titled Criminal History' in the chapter titled 'Mitigating Factors'; and
- the section titled 'Character And Antecedents' in the chapter titled 'Aggravating Factors'.

[586] Refer also to the sections titled 'Youthfulness' and 'Advanced Age' in the chapter titled 'Mitigating Factors'.

[587] Refer also to the section titled 'Ill-Heath' in the chapter titled 'Mitigating Factors'.

[588] Refer also to the subsection titled 'Mental Health' in the section titled 'Motive' in the chapter titled 'Extenuating Circumstances'.

[589] This is to be ascertained separately from the place which the criminal conduct might occupy in the seriousness of the offences of that type, see *Freda Nup v Chris Hambuga* [1984] PNGLR 206.

[590] This refers to the circumstances that lessen the seeming magnitude of guilt by a partial excuse, and may include:
- non-legal or de-facto provocation ['Extenuating Circumstance']; and/or
- domestic or emotional stress, see *Freda Nup v Chris Hambuga* [1984] PNGLR 206.

Refer also to the chapter titled 'Extenuating Circumstances'.

(e) discharging the accused person conditionally on his entering into a recognizance, with or without sureties, to be of good behaviour and to appear for conviction and sentence when called on at any time during such period, not exceeding three years, as is specified in the order.

(2) An order made under Subsection (1) shall, for the purpose of –

(a) revesting or restoring stolen property; and

(b) enabling the Court to make orders as to the restitution or delivery of property to the owner; and

(c) the payment of money on or in connection with that restitution or delivery; and

(d) an appeal against conviction,

have the same effect as a conviction'.

[4.2.2] GENERAL PRINCIPLES

The requirements that must be satisfied in order to apply section 132 of the *District Courts Act* (Ch. 40) are as follows:

- that the charge is proven;
- that at least one of three matters as specified in that section is applicable; and
- that there are special features about the case that cause the magistrate to believe that it would not be proper or expedient:
    - to inflict punishment, other than nominal punishment; or
    - that the accused person should be released on probation[591].[592]

[591] Refer also to the section titled 'Probation Order' in this chapter.

[592] See *Ito Memairi and William Jiwaiba v Nelson Gua* [1984] PNGLR 66.

[5.0] DISQUALIFICATION, ETC OF DRIVING LICENCE

[5.1] MOTOR TRAFFIC ACT

[5.1.1] STATUTORY PROVISIONS

Section 35 of the *Motor Traffic Act* (Ch. 243) states:

> 'Where a person is convicted of an offence against Section 17(1)[593] or 18[594], the court that convicts him shall disqualify him from holding and obtaining a licence[595] for such period as it thinks proper, not being less than –
>
> (a) in the case of a first offence –
>
> (i) against Section 17(1) – three months; and
>
> (ii) against Section 18 – six months; and
>
> (b) in the case of a second or subsequent offence against either of those sections – 12 months'.

Section 36 states:

> '(1) Subject to Section 35, the court that convicts a person of an offence against this Act[596] may, in addition to any other punishment to which the person is liable under this Act in respect of the offence –
>
> (a) if he holds a licence or a permit under Section 11 –
>
> (i) suspend the licence or permit for such time as the court thinks proper and, if the court thinks fit, also direct that no licence and no such permit be granted to him during such further time after the expiration of the licence or permit as the court thinks proper; or
>
> (ii) cancel the licence or permit and, if the court thinks fit, declare him to be disqualified from obtaining a licence or such a permit for such time as the court thinks proper; and

---

[593] The heading to that section is 'Dangerous And Negligent Driving'.

[594] The heading to that section is 'Driving Under The Influence'.

[595] The term 'licence' is defined in section 1(1) of the *Motor Traffic Act* (Ch. 243) as meaning:
'a licence under the regulations [referring to the *Motor Traffic Regulation* (Ch. 243)'.

[596] The term 'this Act' is defined in section 1(1) of the *Motor Traffic Act* (Ch. 243) as including:
'the regulations [referring to the *Motor Traffic Regulation* (Ch. 243)'.

(b) if he does not hold a licence or a permit under Section 11 – direct that no licence or permit be granted to him during such time as the court thinks proper.

(2) A person whose licence or permit under Section 11 is suspended is, during the period of suspension, disqualified from obtaining a licence or permit'.

[5.1.2] GENERAL PRINCIPLE

Whilst section 36 of the *Motor Traffic Act* (Ch. 243) refers to a licence or a permit under section 11 of that Act, section 11 is only in relation to the issuance of a permit to drive an unregistered vehicle.[597]

[5.2] CRIMINAL CODE

The following statutory provision only applies to an accused person who is convicted on indictment of an offence in connection with or arising out of the driving of a motor vehicle by him or her as provided for by the *Criminal Code* (Ch. 262)[598]:

Section 330 of the *Criminal Code* (Ch. 262) states:

'(1) In this section, **"driver's licence"** includes any driving licence or driving permit deemed to be equivalent in Papua New Guinea to, and accepted in place of, a driver's licence for the purpose of authorising the holder to drive in Papua New Guinea any vehicle of the type or class to the driving of which the driving licence or driving permit is applicable.

---

[597] See *Fleming v Dau* [1983] PNGLR 339, [1983] PGNC 27, (1983) N436.

See however: *Kara Utala v Jacob Paula* (1986) N549(M).

[598] Section 2 of the *Criminal Code Act* (Ch. 262) states:

'The provisions contained in Schedule 1 are the law of Papua New Guinea with respect to the matters dealt with in that Schedule'.

As regards the law in relation to 'Acts in pari materia', refer to the section titled 'Extrinsic Aids' in the chapter titled 'Aids To Interpretation' in the text titled 'Injia on Statutory Interpretation in Papua New Guinea and the Pacific'.

(2) Where a person is convicted on indictment[599] of an offence in connection with or arising out of the driving of a motor vehicle by him, the court may, in addition to any sentence that it may pass, order that the accused person be, from the date of conviction, disqualified –

(a) absolutely; or

(b) for such period as the court shall specify in its order,

from holding or obtaining a driver's licence to operate a motor vehicle.

(3) A copy of an order under Subsection (2) shall be transmitted by the proper officer of the court to the Commissioner of Police'.

[5.3] LIQUOR (MISCELLANEOUS PROVISIONS) ACT

Section 6 of the *Liquor (Miscellaneous Provisions) Act* (Ch. 313) states (in part):

'(3) The driver of a vehicle who permits a person to drink liquor on his vehicle is guilty of an offence.

Penalty[600]: Disqualification of driving licence and imprisonment for a term not exceeding three months'.

---

[599] The term 'indictment' is defined in section 1(1) of the *Criminal Code* (Ch. 262) as meaning:

'a written charge preferred against an accused person in order to his trial before some court other than a court of summary jurisdiction'.

The term 'court of summary jurisdiction' is defined in section 3(1) of the *Interpretation Act* (Ch. 2) as meaning:

'a District Court'.

[600] This is not an indictable offence [see section 21(b) of the *Interpretation Act* (Ch. 2)] and can be dealt with summarily [see section 22 of the Interpretation Act (Ch. 2)].

Refer also to the chapter titled 'Classification Of Offences' in the text titled 'Injia on Criminal Practice and Procedure in Papua New Guinea and the Pacific'.

[5.4] GENERAL PRINCIPLES

An order for disqualification is not invalidated if an accused person is not asked, before a Court exercises its power to disqualify, if he or she has anything to say on the subject.[601]

However, it is desirable that:

- full particulars of an accused person's circumstances; and
- the accused person's comments upon the subject of disqualification

be obtained.[602]

A period of disqualification commences from the moment it is pronounced.

In cases where a sentence of imprisonment would be inappropriate, but a fine inadequate, it is proper to order disqualification from driving as a deterrent.[603]

However, a District Court has no power to disqualify or suspend an accused person from driving under section 330 of the *Criminal Code* (Ch. 262).[604]

[6.0] FINE

[6.1] CRIMINAL CODE

The following statutory provisions only apply to those offences as provided for by the *Criminal Code* (Ch. 262)[605].

---

[601] See *Arua v Bulanasoi* [1975] PNGLR 44, [1975] PGSC 2.

[602] See *Arua v Bulanasoi* [1975] PNGLR 44, [1975] PGSC 5.

[603] See *Agigo v The Republic of Nauru* [1969-1982] NLR 63, [1978] NRSC 4.

[604] See *Kara Utala v Jacob Paula* (1986) N549(M).

[605] Section 2 of the *Criminal Code Act* (Ch. 262) states:
'The provisions contained in Schedule 1 are the law of Papua New Guinea with respect to the matters dealt with in that Schedule'.

As regards the law in relation to 'Acts in pari materia', refer to the section titled 'Extrinsic Aids' in the chapter titled 'Aids To Interpretation' in the text titled 'Injia on Statutory Interpretation in Papua New Guinea and the Pacific'.

SENTENCING OPTIONS

Section 18 of the *Criminal Code* (Ch. 262) provides that a fine is a punishment that may be inflicted under that Code.

Section 19 states (in part):

'(1) In the construction of this Code, it is to be taken that, except when it is otherwise expressly provided –

(b) a person liable to imprisonment may be sentenced to pay a fine not exceeding K2,000.00 in addition to, or instead of, imprisonment; and

(c) a person sentenced on conviction on indictment to pay a fine may be sentenced –

(i) to be imprisoned until the fine is paid, in addition to any other punishment to which he is sentenced; and

(ii) instead of being sentenced to be imprisoned until the fine is paid – to be imprisoned for a term (not exceeding the term provided for in Subparagraph (i)) if the fine is not paid within a specified period (which period may be extended as the court thinks fit); and

(2) Imprisonment in accordance with Subsection (1)(c)(i), for non-payment of the fine –

(a) shall not extend for a term longer than two years; and

(b) shall not together with the fixed term of imprisonment (if any) extend for a term longer than the longest term for which he might be sentenced to be imprisoned without fine.

(3) In a case to which Subsection (1)(c) applies, the court may give such directions as it thinks proper as to the enforcement of the sentence of imprisonment, including a direction that the person sentenced appear at some future sittings of the court or when called on, by notice in the prescribed form, to show cause why the sentence of imprisonment should not be executed because of the non-payment of the fine within the specified period or any extension of that period.

(4) If under Subsection (3) a person directed to appear, or called on by notice in the prescribed form, to show cause why the sentence of imprisonment should not be executed because of the non-payment of the fine within the specified period, or any extension of that period, does not appear at the required time and place, a Judge[606] may issue a warrant to arrest him and to bring him before a Judge'.

---

[606] The term 'Judge' is defined in section 3(1) of the *Interpretation Act* (Ch. 2) as meaning: 'a Judge of the Supreme Court or of the National Court'.

[6.2] DISTRICT COURTS ACT[607]

Section 165 of the *District Courts Act* (Ch. 40) states (in part):

> '(1) Where, by a conviction [...], a fine[608] [...] is [...] ordered to be paid, the Court[609] may do all or any of the following things:–
>
> (a) allow time for the payment;
>
> (b) direct the payment to be made by installments;
>
> (c) direct that the person liable to pay is at liberty to give security for the payment.
>
> (2) Where a fine [...] is [...] directed to be paid by installments, the instalments shall be paid to the Clerk[610] or to such other person as the Court orders and, if default is made in the payment of an installment, the same proceedings may be taken to recover the amount then remaining due as if an order for payment by installments had not been made'.

---

607 As regards:

- the 'transfer of jurisdiction as to enforcement of a fine', see section 166 of the *District Courts Act* (Ch. 40);
- the sentence of 'imprisonment for non-payment of a fine', see section 167 of the *District Courts Act* (Ch. 40);
- a 'Court imposing imprisonment in default of a fine', see section 168 of the *District Courts Act* (Ch. 40);
- a Warrant of Commitment, see sections 169, 170, 171, 172, 173, 202, 203, 204 and 207 of the *District Courts Act* (Ch. 40); and
- the 'reduction of imprisonment on part payment of a fine', see section 202 of the *District Courts Act* (Ch. 40).

608 The term 'fine' is defined in section 1 of the *District Courts Act* (Ch. 40) as including:
'a pecuniary penalty, pecuniary forfeiture or pecuniary compensation payable under a conviction'.

609 The term 'court' is defined in section 1 of the *District Courts Act* (Ch. 40) as meaning:
'the District Court'.

610 The term 'Clerk' is defined in section 1 of the *District Courts Act* (Ch. 40) as meaning:
'the Clerk of a District Court'.

SENTENCING OPTIONS

Section 200 states (in part):

'(2) Subject to Subsection (3), where a Court, under any law[611], may impose a penalty for an offence punishable on summary conviction[612] but has no power to impose a fine for that offence, it may impose a fine not exceeding K200.00, but not being such an amount as would subject the offender, in default of payment of the fine, to a term of imprisonment longer than that to which he is liable under the first-mentioned law, if it considers that the justice of the case would be met better by a fine than by imprisonment.

(3) Subsection (2) does not apply in the case of an offence for which a minimum sentence of imprisonment is prescribed'.[613]

Section 201 states (in part):

'(1) Where –

(a) under this Act or any other law, the payment of –

(i) a fine; or

adjudged to be paid by a conviction, is authorized to be enforced by imprisonment; and

---

[611] The term 'law' is defined in section 3(1) of the *Interpretation Act* (Ch. 2) as meaning:
'a law of Papua New Guinea, and includes –
(a) the underlying law; and
(b) subordinate enactments'.

A 'subordinate enactment' is an instrument (whether of a legislative nature or not) made under an Act such as a regulation, see also section 3(1).

[612] The term 'summary conviction' is defined in section 1 of the *District Courts Act* (Ch. 40) as meaning:
'conviction by a court of summary jurisdiction'.

The term 'court of summary jurisdiction' is defined in section 3(1) of the *Interpretation Act* (Ch. 2) as meaning:
'a District Court'.

[613] Therefore:

- if the penalty to be imposed for an offence does not specify a fine then a Court may impose a fine not exceeding K200, provided that the default period does not exceed the specified term of imprisonment as prescribed for the offence [see section 200(2)]; and
- if the penalty to be imposed for an offence does not specify a fine then a Court may impose a fine not exceeding K200, provided that the default period is not less than the minimum sentence of imprisonment if such a sentence is prescribed [see section 200(3)].

(b) a term of imprisonment is not prescribed by the law authorising the making of the conviction,

the imprisonment shall be for such period, not exceeding the maximum specified in Subsection (2), as the Court thinks fit.

(2) Imprisonment imposed under Subsection (1) shall not exceed the maximum period fixed by the following scale:–

where the sum adjudged to be paid, including costs–	The period shall not exceed–
Does not exceed K50.00	14 days
Exceeds K50.00 but does not exceed K200.00	28 days
Exceeds K200.00	60 days'.

[6.3] JUVENILE COURTS ACT

Subject to section 30 of the *Juvenile Courts Act 1991*, the Court may, in addition to any other powers under that Act or any other law enter a conviction and having regard to the ability of the juvenile to pay order the juvenile to pay a fine of an amount not exceeding K200.00.[614]

[6.4] GENERAL PRINCIPLES

A Court cannot impose a fine in excess of the maximum sentence prescribed by law.[615]

A fine is a sentence, but it is to be regarded as a less severe form of punishment than a custodial sentence.[616]

A fine as an alternative to a term of imprisonment must be a true alternative.[617]

614 See section 30(2)(c)(i) of the *Juvenile Courts Act 1991*.

615 See *R v Tuto* [1980-1981] SILR 19.

616 See *SCR No. 1 of 1984; Re Maximum Penalty* [1984] PNGLR 418, [1984] PGSC 12.

617 See *R v Hall* (1968) 52 Cr App R 736 at 738.

SENTENCING OPTIONS

The maximum fine may be imposed in the worst type of case.[618]

A Court may impose a fine as well as a term of imprisonment, provided that the combination of the two sentences reflects the overall criminality of the offending.[619]

The default penalty is merely a threat that if the fine is not paid the defaulter will go to jail; it need not be equated with the maximum fine specified in any particular case.[620]

The maximum 'in default' provision should only be reserved for the case where there is a real doubt that the fine imposed, after due consideration of capacity to pay, will not be paid.[621]

In considering a default penalty a Court should consider:

- the circumstances of the case and the accused person before it[622]; and
- the maximum default period as provided by law.

When considering that the *Criminal Code* (Ch. 262) does not specify default periods for the payment of a fine, a Court should apply the default periods as specified in section 201(2) of the *District Courts Act* (Ch. 40) so as to ensure that there is consistency in sentencing.

It is wrong to impose a substantial fine, unless a Court is satisfied that:

- it is; or
- is at least likely to be,

within an accused person's capacity to pay.[623]

---

618 See *SCR No. 1 of 1984; Re Maximum Penalty* [1984] PNGLR 418, [1984] PGSC 12.

Refer also to the chapter titled 'Maximum Sentence'.

619 See *R v Jury* [2002] NZCA 225.

620 See *SCR No. 1 of 1984; Re Maximum Penalty* [1984] PNGLR 418, [1984] PGSC 12.

621 See *SCR No. 1 of 1984; Re Maximum Penalty* [1984] PNGLR 418, [1984] PGSC 12.

622 See *Garry Kulau v Kevin Alile* (1990) N869.

623 See *Idau Gabe v Mevum Griffin* [1977] PNGLR 492.

See also: *R v Hewitt* [1971] Crim LR 492; *Kabook v The Republic of Nauru* [1969-1982] NLR 24, [1974] NRSC 5; *R v Rollo* [1981] 2 NZLR 667 and *R v Churchill* [1966] 2 All ER 215 at 221.

In the absence of a reasonable explanation to the contrary, past receipt of illegally obtained funds will often — but not always — support an inference that the accused person still possesses sufficient funds to pay a fine at the time of sentencing.[624]

But the strength of that inference will:

- depend on the circumstances; and
- vary from case to case.[625]

[7.0] GOOD BEHAVIOUR BOND

[7.1] CRIMINAL CODE[626]

The following statutory provisions only apply to those offences as provided for by the *Criminal Code* (Ch. 262).[627]

Section 18 of the *Criminal Code* (Ch. 262) provides that the punishments that may be inflicted under that Code include 'finding security to keep the peace and be of good behaviour'.

Section 19 states (in part):

> '(1) In the construction of this Code, it is to be taken that, except when it is otherwise expressly provided –

---

[624] See *R v Grimberg* (2002) 155 OAC 296; *R v Desjardins* (1996) 182 NBR (2d) 321; *R v Dow* (1976) 1 CR (3d) S-9; *R v Noseworthy* 2000 NFCA 45, 192 Nfld & PEIR 120 and *R v Guppy* (1995) 16 Cr App R (S) 25.

[625] See *R v Topp* [2011] 3 SCR 119.

[626] See also: section 344(2) of the *Criminal Code* (Ch. 262).

[627] Section 2 of the *Criminal Code Act* (Ch. 262) states:

> 'The provisions contained in Schedule 1 are the law of Papua New Guinea with respect to the matters dealt with in that Schedule'.

As regards the law in relation to 'Acts in pari materia', refer to the section titled 'Extrinsic Aids' in the chapter titled 'Aids To Interpretation' in the text titled 'Injia on Statutory Interpretation in Papua New Guinea and the Pacific'.

(d) a person convicted on indictment[628] of an offence not punishable with death may –

(i) instead of, or in addition to, any punishment to which he is liable – be ordered to enter into his own recognizance, with or without sureties, in such amount as the court thinks proper, to keep the peace and be of good behaviour for a time fixed by the court; and

(ii) comply with such other conditions as the court may, in its discretion, impose; and

(e) a person convicted of any offence on summary conviction[629] may, instead of being sentenced to any punishment to which he is liable, be discharged on his entering into his own recognizances, with or without sureties, in such amount as the court thinks proper, to keep the peace and be of good behaviour for a term not exceeding one year; and

(f) when a person is convicted of an offence not punishable with death, the court may instead of passing sentence, discharge the accused person on his entering into his own recognizance, with or without sureties, in such sum as the court thinks proper, conditioned that –

(i) he shall appear and receive judgement at some future sittings of the court or when called on within a period specified by the court; and

(ii) if the court thinks fit, he shall in the meantime keep the peace and be of good behaviour and comply with such other conditions as the court, in its discretion, imposes.

(5) Imprisonment under Subsection (1)(d) for not entering into a recognizance –

(a) shall not extend for a term longer than one year; and

---

[628] The term 'indictment' is defined in section 1(1) of the *Criminal Code* (Ch. 262) as meaning:
'a written charge preferred against an accused person in order to his trial before some court other than a court of summary jurisdiction'.

The term 'court of summary jurisdiction' is defined in section 3(1) of the *Interpretation Act* (Ch. 2) as meaning:
'a District Court'.

[629] 'The term 'summary conviction' is defined in section 1(1) of the *Criminal Code* (Ch. 262) as meaning:
'conviction by a court of summary jurisdiction'.

The term 'court of summary jurisdiction' is defined in section 3(1) of the *Interpretation Act* (Ch. 2) as meaning:
'a District Court'.

(b) shall not together with the fixed term of imprisonment (if any) extend for a term longer than the longest term for which he might be sentenced to be imprisoned without fine.

(6) When a court sentences any person convicted under Subsection (1)(d) to a term of imprisonment, it may further order that –

(a) the offender be imprisoned for such portion of that term as it thinks proper; and

(b) the execution of the sentence for the remaining portion of the sentence be suspended on his entering into a recognizance, with sureties if so directed, in accordance with Subsection (1)(d) but further conditioned that, if called on, he shall appear and receive judgement in respect of his service of the portion of the sentence.

(7) A Judge[630] may, on being satisfied that the offender has committed a breach of any of the conditions of a recognizance under Subsection (6), forfeit the recognizance and commit him to prison to undergo the suspended portion of his sentence or any part of it'.

Section 601 states:

'(1) When a person who has not been previously convicted in Papua New Guinea or elsewhere of an offence[631] of such a nature that, on conviction, a sentence may be imposed restricting the liberty of the offender for a period of six months or upwards, is convicted of any offence of such a nature that he may be sentenced on the conviction, to imprisonment for a period not exceeding three years, then, if in the opinion of the court that convicts him a sentence of imprisonment for a period not exceeding three years is an adequate punishment, the court –

(a) shall proceed to pass sentence on the offender in the usual form; and

(b) may, if it thinks fit, suspend the execution of the sentence on the offender entering into a recognizance in accordance with Subsection (2), in such amount as the court directs.

---

[630] The term 'Judge' is defined in section 3(1) of the *Interpretation Act* (Ch. 2) as meaning:
'a Judge of the Supreme Court or of the National Court'.

[631] Section 2 of the *Criminal Code* (Ch. 262) states:
'An act or omission that makes the person doing or making it liable to punishment is called an offence'.

However, this statutory provision only applies to offences contained in the *Criminal Code* (Ch. 262), see section 2 of the *Criminal Code Act* (Ch. 262).

The law in relation to 'Acts in pari materia' is examined in the section titled 'Extrinsic Aids' in the chapter titled 'Aids To Interpretation' in the text titled 'Injia on Statutory Interpretation in Papua New Guinea and the Pacific'.

(2) A recognizance under Subsection (1)(b) shall be conditioned that the offender shall –

(a) be of good behaviour; and

(b) comply with such other conditions as the court, in its discretion, imposes,

for –

(c) a period from the date of the sentence equal to the term of the sentence; or

(d) if the term of the sentence is less than 12 months – for the period of 12 months,

and will not during that period do or omit to do any act by which the recognizance would become liable to be forfeited under this section.

(3) The court may, if it thinks fit, instead of proceeding in accordance with Subsection (1)(b) direct that –

(a) the offender be imprisoned for such portion of the term of sentence as it thinks proper; and

(b) execution of the remaining portion of the sentence be suspended on the offender entering into a recognizance in accordance with Subsection (4) in such amount as the court directs.

(4) A recognizance under Subsection (3)(b) shall be conditioned that the offender shall–

(a) be of good behaviour; and

(b) comply with such other conditions as the court in its discretion imposes,

for –

(c) a period from the termination of his imprisonment equal to the term of the remaining portion of his sentence; or

(d) if the remaining portion is less than 12 months – for the period of 12 months, and shall not during that period do or omit to do any act by which the recognizance would become liable to be forfeited under this section.

(5) When a recognizance is entered into under Subsection (1) or (3), the accused person shall be discharged from custody, but is liable to be committed to prison to undergo his sentence, if, during the period specified in the recognizance, any of the conditions specified in the subsequent provisions of this section happens with respect to him.

(6) A written notice shall be given to the offender on his discharge specifying the conditions under which he will become liable to be committed to prison in accordance with Subsection (5).

(7) When an offender is committed to prison in accordance with Subsection (5), the term of the sentence begins to run from the commencement of his custody on the commitment, but the term of the imprisonment does not extend beyond the period specified in the recognizance, and at the expiration of that period the offender shall be released.

(8) If the offence –

(a) has relation to property; or

(b) is an offence against the person,

the court may, on suspending the execution of the sentence under Subsection (1)(b) or (3)(b) order the offender –

(c) to make restitution of the property in respect of which the offence was committed; or

(d) to pay compensation for –

(i) the injury done to the property; or

(ii) the injury done to the person injured,

as the case may be,

and may –

(e) assess the amount to be paid by the offender in any such case; and

(f) direct when, to whom and in what instalments the amount is to be paid.

(9) An order under Subsection (8) may be enforced in the same manner as orders made by magistrates on summary convictions.

(10) The court may –

(a) require the offender to give security for the performance of an order under Subsection (8); and

(b) make the discharge of the offender from custody conditional on such security being given.

(11) An offender discharged under this section must, once at least in every three months during the period specified in the recognizance, report his address and occupation to the member of the Police Force[632] in charge at the place where he was convicted, or at such other place as the Commissioner of Police appoints.

(12) A report referred to in Subsection (11) may be made either by the offender –

(a) personally attending; or

(b) by letter signed by him and addressed to the member of the Police Force referred to in that subsection,

unless in any case the Head of State, acting on advice[633], directs that the report be made by the accused person personally, in which case it must be made in that manner only.

(13) If, during the period specified in the recognizance –

(a) it is proved to a magistrate in a court of summary jurisdiction that an offender discharged under this section has failed to report his address and occupation to the person, at the times and in the manner prescribed by Subsections (11) and (12); and

(b) an offender discharged under this section is charged by a member of the Police Force with getting his livelihood by dishonest means, and, on his being brought before a magistrate in a court of summary jurisdiction[634], it appears to the magistrate that there are reasonable grounds for believing that he is getting his livelihood by dishonest means; or

---

632 The term 'the Police Force' is defined in section 3(1) of the *Interpretation Act* (Ch. 2) as meaning:
'the Police Force established by Section 188 (*establishment of the State Services*) of the Constitution'.

633 The term 'the Head of State, acting on advice' is defined in section 3(1) of the *Interpretation Act* (Ch. 2) as meaning:
'the Head of State, acting with, and in accordance with, the advice of the National Executive Council'.

The term 'the National Executive Council' is also defined in section 3(1) as meaning:
'the National Executive Council established by Section 149 (*the National Executive Council*) of the *Constitution*'.

634 The term 'court of summary jurisdiction' is defined in section 3(1) of the *Interpretation Act* (Ch. 2) as meaning:
'a District Court'.

(c) an offender discharged under this section is charged with an offence punishable on indictment or summary conviction, and, on his being required by the magistrate before whom he is charged to give his name and address, he refuses to do so, or gives a false name or a false address; or

(d) an offender discharged under this section is convicted of –

(i) an indictable offence[635], whether on indictment or summarily; or

(ii) an offence punishable on summary conviction for which imprisonment for a period exceeding one month may be imposed,

the court or magistrate before whom the offender is charged or convicted may –

(e) forfeit the recognizance; and

(f) commit him to prison to undergo his original sentence, or so much of it (if any) as remains to be undergone under the provisions of this section; and

(g) grant any necessary warrant for his committal.

(14) If during the period specified in the recognizance none of the events referred to in Subsection (13) happens –

(a) the offender is discharged from the original sentence; and

(b) the conviction on which the sentence was imposed is not, on any subsequent conviction against him, to be treated as a previous conviction for the purposes of any law under which a greater punishment may be inflicted on a person who has been previously convicted'.

[7.2] CRIMINAL PRACTICE RULES

Order 3, Division 5 of the *Criminal Practice Rules 1987* states:

'17. Upon proof by affidavit or otherwise that a convicted person who entered into a recognizance as ordered by the Court is in breach of the conditions of the recognizance, the Court may issue a warrant for his arrest.

18. A person arrested upon warrant issued under Rule 17 shall –

---

[635] Crimes and misdemeanours are indictable offences, see section 3(2) of the *Criminal Code* (Ch. 262).

(a) be brought before the Court or a Judge[636] as soon as possible; or

(b) if compliance with sub-rule (a) is not possible, then the person arrested shall be brought before a Magistrate to be dealt with according to law.

19. A warrant under Rule 17 shall be in accordance with Form 8'.

[7.3] DISTRICT COURTS ACT

Section 200(1) of the *District Courts Act* (Ch. 40) states:

> 'Where imprisonment or a fine[637] may be imposed by a Court[638] under any law[639] and there is prescribed by that law a requirement for the offender to enter into his recognizance and to find securities for keeping the peace, or being of good behaviour, and observing some other condition, or to do any of those things, the Court may dispense with any such requirement wholly or in part'.[640]

---

[636] The term 'Judge' is defined in Order 1, Division 2, rule 5 of the *Criminal Practice Rules 1987* as meaning:

> 'a judge or acting judge of the National Court of Justice'.

[637] The term 'fine' is defined in section 1 the *District Courts Act* (Ch. 40) as meaning:

> 'a pecuniary penalty, pecuniary forfeiture or pecuniary compensation payable under a conviction'.

[638] The term 'court' is defined in section 1 the *District Courts Act* (Ch. 40) as meaning:

> 'the District Court'.

[639] The term 'law' is defined in section 3(1) of the *Interpretation Act* (Ch. 2) as meaning:

> 'a law of Papua New Guinea, and includes –
> (a) the underlying law; and
> (b) subordinate enactments'.

A 'subordinate enactment' is an instrument (whether of a legislative nature or not) made under an Act such as a regulation, see also section 3(1).

[640] Refer also to the chapter titled 'Conditional Discharge'.

SENTENCING OPTIONS

[8.0] IMPRISONMENT

[8.1] CONSTITUTIONAL PROVISION

Section 42 of the *Constitution of the Independent State of Papua New Guinea* states (in part):

'(1) No person shall be deprived of his personal liberty except–

(b) in the execution of the sentence or order of a court in respect of an offence of which he has been found guilty, or in the execution of the order of a court of record[641] punishing him for contempt of itself or another court or tribunal[642]'.

[8.2] STATUTORY PROVISIONS

[8.2.1] INTERPRETATION ACT

Section 17 of the *Interpretation Act* (Ch. 2) states:

'Where under a statutory provision imprisonment may be awarded for an offence, it may be awarded with or without hard labour'.

---

[641] Refer also to the chapter titled 'Criminal Jurisdiction Of The Courts' in the text titled 'Injia on Criminal Practice and Procedure in Papua New Guinea and the Pacific'.

[642] Refer also to the chapter titled 'Contempt Of Court' in the text titled 'Injia on Criminal Practice and Procedure in Papua New Guinea and the Pacific'.

[8.2.2] CRIMINAL JUSTICE (SENTENCES) ACT

Section 3 of the *Criminal Justice (Sentences) Act 1986* states:

> '(1) A sentence imposed by a court in the National Judicial System[643] shall take effect from the beginning of the day on which it is imposed, unless a law[644] otherwise provides.
>
> (2) There may be deducted from the length or any term of imprisonment imposed by the sentence of any court any period before the sentence was imposed during which the accused person was in custody in connection with the offence for which the sentence was imposed'.

Section 4 states:

> 'At the time of imposing a sentence in any court in the National Judicial System, the judicial officer imposing the sentence shall specify –
>
> (a) the length of the sentence imposed; and
>
> (b) the length of any period to be deducted from the sentence under Section 3(2); and
>
> (c) the resultant length of the sentence to be served'.

---

[643] Refer also to the chapter titled 'Criminal Jurisdiction Of The Courts' in the text titled 'Injia on Criminal Practice and Procedure in Papua New Guinea and the Pacific'.

[644] The term 'law' is defined in section 3(1) of the *Interpretation Act* (Ch. 2) as meaning:
'a law of Papua New Guinea, and includes –
(a) the underlying law; and
(b) subordinate enactments'.

A 'subordinate enactment' is an instrument (whether of a legislative nature or not) made under an Act such as a regulation, see also section 3(1).

[8.2.3] CRIMINAL CODE

The following statutory provisions only apply to those offences as provided for by the *Criminal Code* (Ch. 262).[645]

Section 18 of the *Criminal Code* (Ch. 262) provides that a sentence of imprisonment is a punishment that may be inflicted under that Code.

Section 19 states (in part):

> '(1) In the construction of this Code, it is to be taken that, except when it is otherwise expressly provided –
>
> (aa) a person liable to death[646] may be sentenced to imprisonment for life or for any shorter term; and
>
> (a) a person liable to imprisonment for life or for any other period, may be sentenced to imprisonment for any shorter term; and
>
> (b) a person liable to imprisonment may be sentenced to pay a fine not exceeding K2,000.00 in addition to, or instead of, imprisonment'.

---

[645] Section 2 of the *Criminal Code Act* (Ch. 262) states:

> 'The provisions contained in Schedule 1 are the law of Papua New Guinea with respect to the matters dealt with in that Schedule'.

Section 6 of that Act states:

> 'This Act does not limit or affect in any way any provision of any other Act conferring on a court a power to pass a sentence or impose a punishment or make an order in addition to or instead of a sentence or punishment prescribed by the Code, or otherwise to deal with an offender'.

As regards the law in relation to 'Acts in pari materia', refer to the section titled 'Extrinsic Aids' in the chapter titled 'Aids To Interpretation' in the text titled 'Injia on Statutory Interpretation in Papua New Guinea and the Pacific'.

[646] Refer also to the section titled 'Sentence Of Death' in this chapter.

SENTENCING OPTIONS

Section 20 states:

'(1) Where a person who is convicted of an offence[647] is undergoing, or has been sentenced to undergo, for another offence, a sentence involving deprivation of liberty[648], the punishment to be inflicted on him for the first-mentioned offence may be directed to take effect from the expiration of the deprivation of liberty for the last-mentioned offence.

(2) Subject to Subsection (1), a sentence of imprisonment –

(a) on a conviction on indictment[649] – takes effect from the first day of the sittings of the court at which the offender is convicted; and

(b) on a summary conviction[650] – takes effect from the commencement of the offender's custody under the sentence.

---

647 Section 2 of the *Criminal Code* (Ch. 262) states:

'An act or omission that makes the person doing or making it liable to punishment is called an offence'.

However, this statutory provision only applies to offences contained in the *Criminal Code* (Ch. 262), see section 2 of the *Criminal Code Act* (Ch. 262).

The law in relation to 'Acts in pari materia' is examined in the section titled 'Extrinsic Aids' in the chapter titled 'Aids To Interpretation' in the text titled 'Injia on Statutory Interpretation in Papua New Guinea and the Pacific'.

648 The law in relation to the offence of 'Deprivation Of Liberty' is examined in the chapter titled 'Offences Against The Person' in the text titled 'Injia on Criminal Offences in Papua New Guinea and the Pacific'.

649 The term 'indictment' is defined in section 1(1) of the *Criminal Code* (Ch. 262) as meaning:

'a written charge preferred against an accused person in order to his trial before some court other than a court of summary jurisdiction'.

The term 'court of summary jurisdiction' is defined in section 3(1) of the *Interpretation Act* (Ch. 2) as meaning:

'a District Court'.

650 The term 'summary conviction' is defined in section 1(1) of the *Criminal Code* (Ch. 262) as meaning:

'conviction by a court of summary jurisdiction'.

The term 'court of summary jurisdiction' is defined in section 3(1) of the *Interpretation Act* (Ch. 2) as meaning:

'a District Court'.

(3) A person who escapes from lawful custody[651] while undergoing a sentence involving deprivation of liberty is liable on recapture to undergo the punishment that he was undergoing at the time of his escape, for a term equal to the period during which he was absent from prison after the escape and before the expiration of the term of his original sentence whether or not at the time of his recapture the term of that sentence had or has not expired'.

Section 420(2) states:

'Subject to Section 421(4), where –

(a) a charge for an offence is dealt with under Subsection (1); and

(b) the maximum penalty provided in this Code for that offence is imprisonment for a term exceeding 10 years,

the maximum penalty which may be imposed by a Principal Magistrate[652] is imprisonment for a term not exceeding 10 years, notwithstanding anything to the contrary in this Code'.

[8.2.4] DISTRICT COURTS ACT

Section 171 of the *District Courts Act* (Ch. 40) states:

'(1) Where –

(a) a conviction does not adjudge the payment of a fine, but that the offender be imprisoned for his offence; or

(b) a Court[653] orders the doing of an act other than the payment of a fine or sum of money or costs and directs that, in case of the offender's neglect or refusal to do the act, he shall be imprisoned, and the offender neglects or refuses to do the act,

---

[651] The law in relation to the offence of 'Escaping From Lawful Custody' is examined in the chapter titled 'Miscellaneous Offences' in the text titled 'Injia on Criminal Offences in Papua New Guinea and the Pacific'.

[652] As appointed under section 1A of the *District Courts Act* (Ch. 40).

Refer also to the section titled 'District Court' in the chapter titled 'Criminal Jurisdiction Of The Courts' in the text titled 'Injia on Criminal Practice and Procedure in Papua New Guinea and the Pacific'.

[653] The term 'court' is defined in section 1 of the *District Courts Act* (Ch. 40) as meaning:
'the District Court'.

the Court or a Magistrate[654] may issue a warrant of commitment for the imprisonment of the offender for such time as the conviction directs.

(2) If, by a conviction or order referred to in Subsection (1), costs are also adjudged to be paid by the offender to the complainant[655], and the offender does not pay the costs in accordance with the terms of the conviction or order, a Magistrate, by warrant, may commit the offender to a correctional institution or police lock-up, there to be kept according to the terms of the conviction or order, unless he sooner pays the costs'.

[8.2.5] CRIMINAL LAW (BAIL) ACT

The *Criminal Law (Bail) Act 1969* states:

'(1) Where in a criminal proceeding an accused person is released on bail or on recognizance, whether pending the hearing and determination of an appeal or otherwise, including the case where an appellant is released under Section 223 of the District Courts Act, any period during which he was so released shall not, unless a court having jurisdiction in the matter otherwise orders, be taken into account in calculating the length of any sentence of imprisonment to be served by him.

(2) Imprisonment, whether under the sentence passed by the court of trial or the sentence passed by a court on appeal, shall, subject to any order made under Subsection (1), be deemed to be resumed or to begin to run, as the case requires, as from the day when the person concerned is received into prison under the sentence'.

---

654 The term 'Magistrate' is defined in section 1 of the *District Courts Act* (Ch. 40) as meaning:
'a Magistrate appointed under the *Magisterial Service Act 1975* and includes a Deputy Chief Magistrate, a Principal Magistrate, a District Court Magistrate and a Reserve Magistrate [as appointed under section 3]'.

Refer also to the section titled 'District Court' in the chapter titled 'Criminal Jurisdiction Of The Courts' in the text titled 'Injia on Criminal Practice and Procedure in Papua New Guinea and the Pacific'.

655 The term 'Complainant' is defined in section 1 of the *District Courts Act* (Ch. 40) as including:
'informant'.

[8.2.6] JUVENILE COURTS ACT

Subject to sections 30, 31 and 30(5) of the *Juvenile Courts Act 1991*, the Court may, in addition to any other powers under that Act or any other law enter a conviction and sentence a juvenile to a term of imprisonment in the juvenile section of a corrective institution.[656]

[8.3] GENERAL PRINCIPLES

The intention of section 36(1) of the *Constitution of the Independent State of Papua New Guinea* is to prohibit cruel, degrading and inhumane treatment that features pain and suffering caused to the human person either physically or mentally: it is not intended to prohibit custodial sentences.[657]

Certainly in the case of serious offences the starting point in the consideration of the punishment must be that of imprisonment.[658]

However, there must be the power to impose a term of imprisonment, otherwise the sentence is a nullity.[659]

At common law there is no limit to the term of imprisonment that may be imposed.[660]

The purpose of imprisonment is to:

- deter accused persons from re-offending[661]; and

---

[656] See section 30(2)(c)(iii) of the *Juvenile Courts Act 1991*.

Refer also to the section titled 'Juvenile Courts Act' in the chapter titled 'Introduction To Sentencing'.

[657] See SCR No. 1 of 1984; *Re Minimum Penalties Legislation* [1984] PNGLR 314, [1984] PGSC 13.

As regards the imposition of a sentence of imprisonment, see *SCR No. 2 of 1989; Special Reference pursuant to Section 19 of the Constitution Reference by the Principal Legal Adviser; Re Village Courts Act (Ch. No. 44)* [1988-89] PNGLR 491.

[658] See *Harris v The DPP (Nauru)* [1998] NRSC 2.

[659] See *Boas Kuna v Police* (1994) N1296.

[660] See *R v Castro* 5 QBD 490.

See also: *The People (Attorney-General) v Giles* [1974] IR 422.

[661] Refer also to the chapter titled 'Objectives And Purposes Of Sentencing'.

- rehabilitate accused persons[662].[663]

Before a custodial sentence is imposed a Court must satisfy itself that no other method of dealing with the accused person is appropriate.[664]

There should be limited use of 'arithmetical deduction' in determining an appropriate sentence.[665]

A Court should have regard to the circumstances that would make imprisonment more arduous for a particular accused person than is normal.[666]

When imposing a fine together with a term of imprisonment the combination of the two sentences should reflect the overall criminality of the offending.[667]

A Court should not impose a 'crushing sentence' that is manifestly excessive.[668]

When the prisons are overcrowded the Courts must be particularly careful to examine each case to ensure, if an immediate custodial sentence is necessary, that the sentence is as short as possible, consistent only with the duty to:

---

[662] As regards the 'rehabilitive or reformative' objective or purpose of sentencing, refer to the chapter titled 'Objectives And Purposes Of Sentencing'.

[663] See *R v Tau and 16 others* [1996] SBHC 1.

[664] See *Kenilaua v R* [2004] SBHC 64.

[665] See *Markarian v R* (2005) 228 CLR 357, (2005) 215 ALR 213, [2005] HCA 25.

[666] See *Houghton v The State of Western Australia* (2006) 32 WAR 260, [2006] WASCA 143; *R v Eliasen* (1991) 53 A Crim R 391 at 395 and *R v Vachalec* [1981] 1 NSWLR 351 at 353.

Refer also to:
- the section titled 'Mentally-ill' in the chapter titled 'Extenuating Circumstances'; and
- the sections titled 'Advanced Age' and 'Social And Cultural Isolation' in the chapter titled 'Mitigating Factors'.

[667] See *R v Jury* [2002] NZCA 225.

[668] See *The State v Anton Towakra and others* (2009) N3845.

Refer also to:
- the subsection titled 'Totality Principle' in this section; and
- the chapter titled 'Appeals Against Sentence'.

- protect the interests of the public; and
- punish and deter the criminals.[669]

The term of a sentence of imprisonment imposed by the National Court, other than a sentence directed to be served cumulatively, must be calculated from the first day of the sittings of the court.[670]

[8.4] GENERAL PROCEDURE

The following procedure should be followed when determining a sentence of imprisonment[671]:

Step 1

What is the maximum sentence for the offence as provided for by the statutory provision?[672]

Step 2

What is a proper starting point for each offence, ie., the most serious punishment imposed based on previous cases in similar circumstances?[673]

---

[669] See *R v Bibi* (1980) 71 Cr App R 160, per Lane LCJ and *R v Kefford* [2002] EWCA Crim 519, [2002] 2 Cr App R (S) 106, per Woolf LCJ.

[670] See *Saki v The State* [1980] PNGLR 33, [1980] PGSC 16.

[671] See *The State v Anton Towakra and others* (2009) N3845; *The State v Judah Lusan Piries* (2007) CR No. 886 of 2007 and *The State v Michael Keari and others* (2007) CR No. 868 of 2007.

See also: *Emil Kongian and others v The State* (2007) SC928, [2007] PGSC 45.

[672] Refer also to the chapter titled 'Maximum Sentence'.

[673] Refer also to:
- the chapter titled 'Comparative Sentences'; and
- the chapter titled 'Maximum Sentence'.

Step 3

What sentences have been imposed for equivalent offences based on all previous cases[674] and sentencing tariffs[675]?

Step 4

What weight should be given to 'aggravating factors[676]', 'mitigating factors[677]' and 'extenuating circumstances[678]' in order to determine the head sentence?[679]

A Court should specify all 'mitigating' and 'extenuating' factors in favour of an accused person and then make a general deduction without any particularisation as to the sentence of imprisonment imposed.[680]

A Court should also specify all 'aggravating factors' without any particularisation as to the sentence of imprisonment imposed.

---

674 Refer also to the chapter titled 'Comparative Sentences'.

Reference should also be made to any relevant tariffs and guidelines issued by the Supreme Court.

As regards the disadvantages of the tariff system, see *Griffiths v R* (1977) 137 CLR 293, (1977) 51 ALJR 749 at 765, [1977] HCA 44.

675 Refer also to section titled 'General Principles' in this chapter.

676 Refer also to the chapter titled 'Aggravating Factors'.

677 Refer also to the chapter titled 'Mitigating Factors'.

678 Refer also to the chapter titled 'Extenuating Circumstances'.

679 See *Puka Babai v The State* (1995) SC493.

680 See *Kesino Apo v The State* [1988-89] PNGLR 182 and *Puka Babai v The State* (1995) SC493.

SENTENCING OPTIONS

Step 5

What sentences should be imposed for each offence?[681]

Step 6

Should the sentences be served concurrently or cumulatively? [multiple sentences][682]

Step 7

What is the effect of the 'totality principle'? [multiple sentences][683]

Step 8

Should the pre-sentence period in custody be deducted?

In accordance with the provisions of section 3(2) of the *Criminal Justice (Sentences) Act 1986* it is a well accepted practice for a Court to have a pre-trial custody period deducted from any sentence imposed on an accused person.[684]

---

[681] See *Pearce v R* (1998) 194 CLR 610 at 624; *Mill v R* (1988) 166 CLR 59, (1998) 83 ALR 1, [1988] HCA 70 and *Johnson v R* (2004) 78 ALJR 616, (2004) 205 ALR 346, [2004] HCA 15.

Whilst the fixing of an appropriate sentence for each offence before turning to questions of accumulation or concurrency is orthodox, such an approach is not immutable, see *McNamara v The State of Western Australia* [2010] WASCA 193, per McLure P; *KC v The State of Western Australia* [2008] WASCA 216 and *R v Abboud* [2005] NSWCCA 251.

To extract individual sentences out of context and suggest that those sentences are excessive can involve a high level of artificiality and obscure the real objective where multiple offences are part of a course of conduct, see *McMahon v R* [2011] NSWCCA 147.

[682] Refer also to the subsection titled 'Concurrent Or Cumulative Sentences' in this section.

[683] Refer also to the subsection titled 'Concurrent Or Cumulative Sentences' in this section.

[684] See *Joe Giamur v The State* (2007) SC884, [2007] PGSC 7.

The only period to be deducted from the head sentence is the pre-trial custody period.[685]

If however a Court decides not to deduct the period of pre-trial custody then reasons should be given.[686]

No period of pre-trial custody can be deducted from a minimum penalty.[687]

Step 9

Should all or part of the sentence/s be suspended?

[8.5] SUSPENDED SENTENCE

[8.5.1] STATUTORY PROVISIONS

CRIMINAL CODE

The power to suspend a term of imprisonment is derived from:

- section 19(1)(d)[688];
- section 19(1)(f)[689]; and
- section 19(6)(b)[690]

[685] See *Babai v The State* [1995] PNGLR 179, [1995] PGSC 10.

[686] See *Pogu v The State* [1986] PNGLR 203, [1986] PGSC 7.

[687] See *The State v Mathew Peters* [1984] PNGLR 387, [1984] PGSC 10.

[688] See *Tom Longman Yaul v The State* (2005) SC803, [2005] PGSC 29.

[689] See *Acting Public Prosecutor v John Airi* (1981) SC214; *Public Prosecutor v Thomas Vola* [1981] PNGLR 412, [1981] PGSC 26 and *Daniel Ronald Walus v The State* (2007) SC882, [2007] PGSC 4.

[690] See *Joe Giamur v The State* (2007) SC884, [2007] PGSC 7.

of the *Criminal Code* (Ch. 262).[691]

Section 19 states (in part):

'(1) In the construction of this Code, it is to be taken that, except when it is otherwise expressly provided –

(d) a person convicted on indictment[692] of an offence not punishable with death may –

(i) instead of, or in addition to, any punishment to which he is liable – be ordered to enter into his own recognizance, with or without sureties, in such amount as the court thinks proper, to keep the peace and be of good behaviour for a time fixed by the court; and

(ii) comply with such other conditions as the court may, in its discretion, impose; and

(f) when a person is convicted of an offence not punishable with death, the court may instead of passing sentence, discharge the offender on his entering into his own recognizance, with or without sureties, in such sum as the court thinks proper, conditioned that –

(i) he shall appear and receive judgement at some future sittings of the court or when called on within a period specified by the court; and

(ii) if the court thinks fit, he shall in the meantime keep the peace and be of good behaviour and comply with such other conditions as the court, in its discretion, imposes.

---

691 However, section 19 of the *Criminal Code* (Ch. 262) only applies in relation to the Code.

Section 2 of the *Criminal Code Act* (Ch. 262) states:
'The provisions contained in Schedule 1 are the law of Papua New Guinea with respect to the matters dealt with in that Schedule'.

As regards the law in relation to 'Acts in pari materia', refer to the section titled 'Extrinsic Aids' in the chapter titled 'Aids To Interpretation' in the text titled 'Injia on Statutory Interpretation in Papua New Guinea and the Pacific'.

692 The term 'indictment' is defined in section 1(1) of the *Criminal Code* (Ch. 262) as meaning:
'a written charge preferred against an accused person in order to his trial before some court other than a court of summary jurisdiction'.

The term 'court of summary jurisdiction' is defined in section 3(1) of the *Interpretation Act* (Ch. 2) as meaning:
'a District Court'.

(6) When a court sentences any person convicted under Subsection (1)(d) to a term of imprisonment, it may further order that –

(a) the offender be imprisoned for such portion of that term as it thinks proper; and

(b) the execution of the sentence for the remaining portion of the sentence be suspended on his entering into a recognizance, with sureties if so directed, in accordance with Subsection (1)(d) but further conditioned that, if called on, he shall appear and receive judgement in respect of his service of the portion of the sentence'.

CRIMINAL PRACTICE RULES

Order 3, Division 4 of the *Criminal Practice Rules 1987* states:

'12. Upon conclusion of a trial in which a convicted person is sentenced to a term of imprisonment with or without part suspension, the Associate[693] shall prepare --

(a) four copies of a warrant for imprisonment; and

(b) four copies of any recognizance as directed,

for signature by the trial judge and the convicted person where necessary.

13. After the signing of the warrant and recognizance, the Associate shall hand the original warrant and recognizance to the Corrective Institution Officer by whom the convicted person is to be taken into custody.

14. In the absence of such officer, the documents referred to in Rule 13 shall be given to the senior policeman present in Court, or the Sheriff.

15. Copies of the documents referred to in Rule 13 shall be distributed --

(a) to the Prosecutor; and

---

693 The term 'Associate' is defined in Order 1, Division 2, rule 5 as meaning:
'a person appointed to act as an Associate to a Judge'.

An 'Associate' is appointed by the Judicial and Legal Services Commission, see section 7(1) of the *National Court Act* (Ch. 38).

The term 'Judge' is also defined in rule 5 as meaning:
'a judge or acting judge of the National Court of Justice'.

(b) to the Registrar[694], after placing them in the Court Papers; and

(c) a copy of the recognizance, to the convicted person.

16. The documents in this Division shall be in Forms 5, 6, 7, as applicable'.

Division 5 states:

'17. Upon proof by affidavit or otherwise that a convicted person who entered into a recognizance as ordered by the Court is in breach of the conditions of the recognizance, the Court may issue a warrant for his arrest.

18. A person arrested upon warrant issued under Rule 17 shall --

(a) be brought before the Court or a Judge as soon as possible; or

(b) if compliance with sub-rule (a) is not possible, then the person arrested shall be brought before a Magistrate to be dealt with according to law.

19. A warrant under Rule 17 shall be in accordance with Form 8'.

[8.5.2] GENERAL PRINCIPLES

The suspension of a sentence is usually arrived at in consideration of future commitments required of an accused person aimed at assisting him or her to rehabilitate[695], and not to re-offend, based on a pre-sentence report[696].[697]

---

[694] The term 'Registrar' is defined in Order 1, Division 2, rule 5 as meaning:
'the Registrar of the National Court'.

The 'Registrar' is appointed by the Judicial and Legal Services Commission, see section 7(1) of the *National Court Act* (Ch. 38).

[695] See *The State v Allan Nareti and Amstrong Kupe* (2004) N2582.

Refer also to the section titled 'The Need For Reformation Or Rehabilitation' in the chapter titled 'Objectives And Purposes Of Sentencing'.

[696] Refer also to the chapter titled 'Pre-sentence Report'.

[697] See *Joe Giamur v The State* (2006) SC884, [2007] PGSC 7.

SENTENCING OPTIONS

A Court should determine the length of a sentence of imprisonment before deciding whether to suspend it.[698]

The fact that a sentence is to be suspended does not justify passing a sentence longer than would be imposed if the sentence were to be served immediately.[699]

A term of imprisonment should not be suspended, unless there is a basis to do so.[700]

The following factors should be considered by a Court when deciding whether to impose a suspended sentence:

- whether such a sentence will promote the personal deterrence[701] and reformation[702] of the accused person[703];
- assist in the rehabilitation of the accused person[704];

---

698 See *R v Mah Wing* 5 Cr App R (S) 347, per Griffiths LJ.

See also: The Law Reform Commission of Ireland, 1996, 'Report of Sentencing', paragraph 11.6.

699 See *R v Mah Wing* 5 Cr App R (S) 347, per Griffiths LJ.

See also: The Law Reform Commission of Ireland, 1996, 'Report of Sentencing', paragraph 11.6.

700 See *The State v Robert Lorou Sevese* (2006) N3453, [2006] PGNC 101.

701 Refer also to the section titled 'The Need For Deterrence' in the chapter titled 'Objectives And Purposes Of Sentencing'.

702 Refer also to the section titled 'The Need For Reformation Or Rehabilitation' in the chapter titled 'Objectives And Purposes Of Sentencing'.

703 See *Public Prosecutor v Tardrew* [1986] PNGLR 91, [1986] PGSC 10.

704 See *Joe Giamur v The State* (2007) SC884, [2007] PGSC 7; *Richard Liri v The State* (2007) SC883, [2007] PGSC 3; *The State v Sylvester Heai Evore* (2006) N3236, [2006] PGNC 148; *The State v Andrew Yeskulu* (2003) N2410; *The State v Salle Sorowi* (2007) N3467; *The State v Gibson Haulai* (2004) N2555 and *The State v Dobi Ao (No. 2)* (2002) N2247.

Refer also to the section titled 'The Need For Reformation Or Rehabilitation' in the chapter titled 'Objectives And Purposes Of Sentencing'.

- whether such a sentence will promote the repayment or restitution of stolen money or goods[705];

- whether such a sentence will prevent an accused person from re-offending[706] which a term of imprisonment, standing alone, seldom does[707];

- whether an accused person is of:

    - good character[708]; and

    - good family background[709];

- whether an accused person is a first time accused person[710] aged 18 years and below[711]; and

---

[705] See *Public Prosecutor v Tardrew* [1986] PNGLR 91, [1986] PGSC 10.

See for example, *The State v Gibson Haulai* (2004) N2555.

[706] See *Joe Giamur v The State* (2007) SC884, [2007] PGSC 7; *Richard Liri v The State* (2007) SC883, [2007] PGSC 3 and *The State v Frank Kagai* [1987] PNGLR 320.

[707] See *The State v Frank Kagai* [1987] PNGLR 320; *The State v Moki Lepi (No. 3)* (2004) N2734; *The State v Micky John Lausi* (2001) N2073; *The State v Jimmy Solomon* (2001) N2100 and *The State v Mahuva Jimmy and Uta Helisha* (2004) N2632.

[708] See *The State v Micky John Lausi* (2001) N2073; *The State v Jimmy Solomon* (2001) N2100; *The State v Mahuva Jimmy and Uta Helisha* (2004) N2632; *The State v Frank Kagai* [1987] PNGLR 320 and *The State v Justin Vincent Nyama* [1991] PNGLR 127.

Refer also to the section titled 'Good Character Generally' in the chapter titled 'Mitigating Factors'.

[709] See *The State v Frank Kagai* [1987] PNGLR 320; *The State v Justin Vincent Nyama* [1991] PNGLR 127; *The State v Thomas Waim, Tala Gena and Alois Wanpis* [1998] PNGLR 360, (1998) N750, (1998) PGNC 174 and *The State v Salle Sorowi* (2007) N3467.

Refer also to the chapter titled 'Mitigating Factors'.

[710] Refer also to the section titled 'Good Character Generally' in the chapter titled 'Mitigating Factors'.

[711] See *Gimble v The State* [1988-89] PNGLR 271 at 275, (1988) SC369, [1988] PGSC 15 and *The State v Thomas Waim, Tala Gena and Alois Wanpis* [1998] PNGLR 360, (1998) N750, (1998) PGNC 174.

Refer also to the section titled 'Youthfulness' in the chapter titled 'Mitigating Factors'.

- whether a term of imprisonment has the potential to positively damage an accused person[712], such as:
    - the potential of causing an excessive degree of suffering to the particular accused person, for example because of his or her poor physical or mental health not being able to be properly treated whilst in incarceration[713];

      However, a Court should be careful not to give a double reduction in relation to an accused person's ill-health[714]; and
    - turning an accused person into an hard-core criminal[715].

---

[712] See *The State v Frank Kagai* [1987] PNGLR 320; *The State v Moki Lepi (No. 3)* (2004) N2734; *The State v Micky John Lausi* (2001) N2073; *The State v Jimmy Solomon* (2001) N2100 and *The State v Mahuva Jimmy and Uta Helisha* (2004) N2632.

[713] See *Public Prosecutor v Tardrew* [1986] PNGLR 91, [1986] PGSC 10; *The State v Thomas Waim, Tala Gena and Alois Wanpis* [1998] PNGLR 360, (1998) N750, (1998) PGNC 174; *The State v Salle Sorowi* (2007) N3467; *The State v Moki Lepi (No. 3)* (2004) N2734; *The State v Micky John Lausi* (2001) N2073; *The State v Jimmy Solomon* (2001) N2100 and *The State v Mahuva Jimmy and Uta Helisha* (2004) N2632.

Refer also to:
- the section titled 'Ill-health' in the chapter titled 'Mitigating Factors'; and
- the subsection titled 'Mental Health' in the section titled 'Motive' in the chapter titled 'Extenuating Circumstances'.

[714] See *Public Prosecutor v Tardrew* [1986] PNGLR 91, [1986] PGSC 10 and *Public Prosecutor v Thomas Vola* [1981] PNGLR 412 at 414, [1981] PGSC 26.

[715] See *The State v Sul Kora* (2001) N2092, [2001] PGNC 93.

SENTENCING OPTIONS

A Court should not consider imposing a suspended sentence when there is no proper basis to make such an order[716] because there is no well-balanced pre-sentence report[717].

Imposing a suspended sentence is not a 'soft option' or an exercise in leniency[718], but a form of punishment.[719]

In imposing a suspended sentence a Court must outline the factors which it considered in making such an order.[720]

A term of imprisonment may be suspended:

- in whole; or
- in part

depending on the circumstances of the commission of the offence.[721]

---

[716] See *Public Prosecutor v Thomas Vola* [1981] PNGLR 412, [1981] PGSC 26; *Edmund Gima v The State; Siune Arnold v The State* (2003) SC730, [2003] PGSC 3; *Richard Liri v The State* (2007) SC883, [2007] PGSC 3; *The State v Thomas Waim, Tala Gena and Alois Wanpis* [1998] PNGLR 360, (1998) N750, (1998) PGNC 174 and *The State v Salle Sorowi* (2007) N3467.

[717] See *Joe Giamur v The State* (2007) SC884, [2007] PGSC 7; *Richard Liri v The State* (2007) SC883, [2007] PGSC 3; *Edmund Gima v The State; Siune Arnold v The State* (2003) SC730, [2003] PGSC 3; *Acting Public Prosecutor v Don Hale* (1998) SC564; *The State v Irox Winston* (2000) N2347; *The State v Jack Magal* (2008) CR No. 224 of 2006; *The State v Steven Molu Minji and others; The State v Didi Gelwak Sakol (No. 2)* (2009) N3794, [2009] PGNC 177; *The State v Wasa David Warifa* (2008) N3308, [2008] PGNC 32; *The State v Gerald Kirafe* (2005) N3660, [2005] PGNC 175; *The State v Andrew Yeskulu* (2003) N2410 and *The State v Moki Lepi (No. 3)* (2004) N2734.

Refer also to the chapter titled 'Pre-sentence Report'.

[718] See *The State v Frank Kagai* [1987] PNGLR 320 and *The State v Sylvester Heai Evore* (2006) N3236, [2006] PGNC 148.

[719] See *Richard Liri v The State* (2007) SC883, [2007] PGSC 3; *The State v Sul Kora* (2001) N2092, [2001] PGNC 93; *The State v Andrew Yeskulu* (2003) N2410; *The State v Moki Lepi (No. 3)* (2004) N2734; *The State v Micky John Lausi* (2001) N2073; *The State v Jimmy Solomon* (2001) N2100 and *The State v Mahuva Jimmy and Uta Helisha* (2004) N2632.

[720] See *Richard Liri v The State* (2007) SC883, [2007] PGSC 3.

[721] See *Tom Longman Yaul v The State* (2005) SC803, [2005] PGSC 29.

The power to suspend part of an accused person's sentence is not dependent on the accused person serving a portion of the sentence. If suspension of a part of a sentence is warranted, a Court must exercise the power to do so at the time of the pronouncement of sentence, and not at a later time.[722]

An accused person must, as part of an actual suspension package, as opposed to an expected suspension, be ordered to:

- enter into his or her own recognizance to keep the peace and be of good behaviour for a time fixed by the Court; and
- comply with such other conditions as the Court may, in its discretion, impose.[723]

An accused person is required to:

- enter into his or her own recognizance; and
- accept any other terms of suspension

before the decision to suspend is pronounced.[724]

Conditions must be imposed during the period of suspension in order to demonstrate that a suspended sentence of imprisonment is an alternative to a term of imprisonment[725].[726]

The conditions on which a sentence is suspended must be designed and have the ability to show:

- that the sentence is a form of punishment; and

---

[722] See *Daniel Ronald Walus v The State* (2007) SC882, [2007] PGSC 4.

[723] See *Daniel Ronald Walus v The State* (2007) SC882, [2007] PGSC 4.

[724] See *Daniel Ronald Walus v The State* (2007) SC882, [2007] PGSC 4.

[725] See *Richard Liri v The State* (2007) SC883, [2007] PGSC 3 and *The State v Guise Jopping* (2004) N2678.

[726] See for example: *The State v Gibson Haulai* (2004) N2555; *The State v Mahuva Jimmy and Uta Helisha* (2004) N2632; *The State v Anton Towakra and others* (2009) N3845 and *The State v Obert Poesan Pokanas* (2004) N2702, [2004] PGNC 75.

- that the sentence is not an immediate grant of liberty and excuse from committing an offence.[727]

Hence, the conditions must:

- reflect the fact that an accused person is allowed to serve his or her sentence outside the prison system which gives the community the opportunity to see the accused person serve his or her sentence; and

- help in the accused person's rehabilitation[728].[729]

Such a sentence also has the potential to even deter[730] an accused person and other possible accused persons from committing any offence after seeing an accused person serving his or her time before their eyes.[731]

Such additional conditions may include:

- a requirement to pay compensation according to specified conditions;

- a requirement to perform a specified period of free community service under the supervision and direction of the Probation Service;

- a requirement to remain at a specified residence during specified hours, subject to exemptions as approved by the Probation Service;

- a requirement to reside at a place as approved by the Probation Service or the Court;

- a requirement not to leave a particular village or province, otherwise than as approved by the Probation Service or the Court;

---

[727] See *The State v Gibson Haulai* (2004) N2555 and *The State v Salle Sorowi* (2007) N3467.

[728] Refer also to the section titled 'The Need For Reformation Or Rehabilitation' in the chapter titled 'Objectives And Purposes Of Sentencing'.

[729] See *The State v Salle Sorowi* (2007) N3467.

[730] Refer also to the section titled 'The Need For Deterrence' in the chapter titled 'Objectives And Purposes Of Sentencing'.

[731] See *The State v Salle Sorowi* (2007) N3467.

- a requirement to report within a specified period of time after release from custody to the Probation Service and submit to directions from the Senior Probation Officer;
- a requirement to participate in a reconciliation ceremony supervised by local community leaders and witnessed by a Probation Officer within a specified period of time;
- a requirement to attend a specified Church every weekend for service and worship and submit to counselling;
- a requirement to report to a specified Probation Office on specified days and between specified times;
- a requirement not to consume alcohol or unlawful drugs;
- a requirement not to associate with known criminals;
- a requirement to have satisfactory probation reports which are submitted to the Court Registry as directed;
- a requirement to allow for and permit the Probation Service to visit his or her home in order to monitor compliance with the conditions;
- a requirement to serve the balance of the term of the suspended sentence if there is a breach of the conditions[732];
- a requirement not to leave a specified location without the prior written approval of a Court;
- an acknowledgement that any member of the accused person's family may report any non-compliance with the conditions; and
- an entitlement to apply for a review and/or variation of any of the conditions to the Court[733].

---

[732] However, section 19 of the *Criminal Code* (Ch. 262) does not specify what action may be taken by a Court if there is a breach of section 19(1)(f), unlike section 19(1)(d).

[733] A Court is vested with power under section 19 of the *Probation Act* (Ch. 381) to vary any conditions of a suspended sentence, see *The State v Elizabeth Teka (No. 2)* (2009) N3604, [2009] PGNC 46.

An accused person so released has an obvious incentive not to re-offend. Therefore, the Court should ensure that there should be no misconceptions as to what will occur if he or she does.[734]

If any of the conditions are breached, any person may report the matter to:

- the police;
- any person nominated to supervise the accused person; or
- the Probation Office,

any of whom may bring the matter to the attention of the National Court.[735]

An application to dissolve a suspended sentence and for an order that an accused person be re-committed to custody should be made either by:

- originating summons; or
- dispensing with that requirement in accordance with Order 1, Rules 11 and 12 of the *Criminal Practice Rules 1987*.[736]

In either case there should be an affidavit or oral evidence of the alleged breach of the conditions of the suspended sentence.[737]

---

[734] See *The State v Moki Lepi (No. 3)* (2004) N2734; *The State v Micky John Lausi* (2001) N2073; *The State v Jimmy Solomon* (2001) N2100 and *The State v Mahuva Jimmy and Uta Helisha* (2004) N2632.

However, section 19 of the *Criminal Code* (Ch. 262) does not specify what action may be taken by a Court if there is a breach of section 19(1)(f), unlike section 19(1)(d).

See however: *The State v Elizabeth Teka (No. 2)* (2009) N3604, [2009] PGNC 46.

See also: *R v Ithell* [1969] 2 All ER 249.

[735] See *The State v Anton Towakra and others* (2009) N3845 and *The State v Jelio Yawi* (2009) N3631, [2009] PGNC 44.

[736] See *Tom Longman Yaul v The State* (2005) SC803, [2005] PGSC 29.

However, section 19 of the *Criminal Code* (Ch. 262) does not specify what action may be taken by a Court if there is a breach of section 19(1)(f), unlike section 19(1)(d).

[737] See *Tom Longman Yaul v The State* (2005) SC803, [2005] PGSC 29.

However, section 19 of the *Criminal Code* (Ch. 262) does not specify what action may be taken by a Court if there is a breach of section 19(1)(f), unlike section 19(1)(d).

The Court may then issue a warrant for arrest of the accused person and the accused person can be brought before the Court to show cause why he or she should not be sent to jail to serve the rest of his or her sentence.[738]

However, the prosecution has to prove on the 'balance of probabilities' that a condition has not been complied with before a suspended sentence can be revoked.[739]

If an accused person who commits a further offence during the period of a suspended sentence then the entire period of imprisonment that was suspended should be served.[740]

An accused person whose suspended sentence is proposed to be dissolved on the ground that he or she has breached the conditions of his or her suspended sentence has a right to be heard:

- on whether he or she has, in fact, breached the conditions; and
- why he or she ought not to be re-committed to custody.[741]

[8.6] CONCURRENT OR CONSECUTIVE SENTENCES

[8.6.1] INTRODUCTION

A Court sentencing an accused person for more than one offence should:

- fix an appropriate sentence for each offence: and then
- consider questions of cumulation and concurrence; and then

---

[738] See *The State v Anton Towakra and others* (2009) N3845 and *The State v Jelio Yawi* (2009) N3631, [2009] PGNC 44.

[739] See *The State v Linden Alphonse* (2008) N3533, [2008] PGNC 177.

[740] See *R v Fitton* 11 Cr App R (S) 350.

[741] See *Tom Longman Yaul v The State* (2005) SC803, [2005] PGSC 29.

However, section 19 of the *Criminal Code* (Ch. 262) does not specify what action may be taken by a Court if there is a breach of section 19(1)(f), unlike section 19(1)(d).

- apply the 'totality principle'[742]; and then
- consider whether the application of the 'totality principle' would result in an appropriate measure of the total criminality involved[743].[744]

What is important is:

> That the punishment imposed upon an accused person reflects the total criminality of what he or she did.[745]

A Court has a discretion as whether to impose:

- concurrent sentences; or

---

[742] See *Pearce v R* (1998) 194 CLR 610 at 624, [1998] HCA 57.

There is, however, some flexibility in the application of that principle, see *Johnson v R* (2004) 78 ALJR 616, (2004) 205 ALR 346, [2004] HCA 15; *Markarian v R* (2005) 228 CLR 357, (2005) 215 ALR 213, [2005] HCA 25 and *R v Abboud* [2005] NSWCCA 251.

[743] See *R v White* [2002] WASCA 112; *R v Faithful* (2004) 142 A Crim R 554, [2004] WASCA 39 and *R v Wilson* [2005] NSWCCA 219.

[744] See *R v Knight* (2005) 155 A Crim R 252, [2005] NSWCCA 253 and *R v Hamid* (2006) 164 A Crim R 179, [2006] NSWCCA 302.

[745] See *Ian Napolean Setep v The State* (2001) SC666, [2001] PGSC 14; *Acting Public Prosecutor v Konis Haha* [1981] PNGLR 205 at 214, [1981] PGSC 6; *Paul Mase and Kope Lore John v The State* [1991] PNGLR 88; *The Public Prosecutor v Sidney Kerua and Billy Kerua* [1985] PNGLR 85, [1985] PGSC 8; *Emil Kongian and others v The State* (2007) SC928, [2007] PGSC 45; *The State v John Pesa* [1994] PNGLR 317; *The State v Peter Tulemanil* (2008) N3685, [2008] PGNC 233 and *The Public Prosecutor v Terrance Kaveku* [1977] PNGLR 110, [1977] PGSC 8.

See also: *Pearce v R* (1998) 194 CLR 610 at 623, [1998] HCA 57; *Walgar v The State of Western Australia* [2007] WASCA 241; *R v Kalache* (2000) 111 A Crim R 152 at 184, [2000] NSWCCA 2; *R v Knight* (2005) 155 A Crim R 252, [2005] NSWCCA 253; *R v Hamid* (2006) 164 A Crim R 179, [2006] NSWCCA 302; *R v Weldon; R v Carberry* (2002) 136 A Crim R 55 at 62, [2002] NSWCCA 475; *R v Wilson* [2005] NSWCCA 219; *Mill v R* (1988) 166 CLR 59, (1998) 83 ALR 1, [1988] HCA 70; *R v Stevens* [1997] 2 Cr App R (S) 180; *Postiglione v R* (1997) 189 CLR 295, per McHugh J at 307-308, (1997) 145 ALR 408, (1997) 71 ALJR 875, [1997] HCA 26; *Roffey v The State of Western Australia* [2007] WASCA 246 and *Jarvis v R* (1993) 20 WAR 201, per Ipp J at 206-207.

- cumulative sentences.[746]

However, that discretion has to be exercised in accordance with well-established principles.[747]

There is however no general rule that determines whether sentences ought to be imposed:

- concurrently; or

- consecutively.[748]

The mechanism of making some sentences cumulative and others concurrent (or partly so) may be used where the aggregate of sentences imposed in respect of each count exceeds the appropriate total sentence.[749]

At the same time, it is necessary to ensure public confidence in the administration of justice by imposing sentences which do not suggest that multiple offences will be punished in the same way as one or two offences.[750]

A sentence of imprisonment should be made cumulative if the offences were committed whilst on bail.[751]

---

[746] See *The State v Irox Winston* (2003) N2347.

See also: *Cahyadi v R* (2007) 168 A Crim R 41, per Howie J at 47, [2007] NSWCCA 1 and *R v Hammoud* (2000) 118 A Crim R 66, [2000] NSWCCA 540.

[747] See *Emil Kongian and others v The State* (2007) SC928, [2007] PGSC 45 and *The State v Irox Winston* (2003) N2347.

[748] See *Cahyadi v R* (2007) 168 A Crim R 41, [2007] NSWCCA 1.

[749] See *R v Myers* [2002] NSWCCA 162; *R v Knight* (2005) 155 A Crim R 252, [2005] NSWCCA 253 and *R v Hamid* [2006] NSWCCA 302.

[750] See *R v Wheeler* [2000] NSWCCA 34; *R v Knight* (2005) 155 A Crim R 252, [2005] NSWCCA 253 and *R v Hamid* [2006] NSWCCA 302.

[751] See *R v Young* [1973] Crim LR 585 and *Hennessy* (1970) 51 Cr App R 148.

See also: *Mill v R* (1988) 166 CLR 59, (1998) 83 ALR 1, [1988] HCA 70; *R v Wallace* [1983] NZLR 758; *R v Richards* [1981] 2 NSWLR 464; *R v Kain* (1985) 38 SASR 309; *Clark* (1994) 15 Cr App R (S) 852; *Hammond* (1995) 16 Cr App R (S) 142; *R v Lucky* (1974) 12 SASR 136; *R v Knight* (1981) 26 SASR 573; *R v Bradley* [1979] 1 NZLR 262; *Postiglione v R* (1997) 189 CLR 295, per McHugh J at 307-308, (1997) 145 ALR 408, (1997) 71 ALJR 875, [1997] HCA 26 and *Krishna v R* (1962) 8 Fiji LR 236.

SENTENCING OPTIONS

It should be expressed with clarity by a Court:

- the sentences imposed in respect of each charge/count; and
- whether those sentences were to run:
  - concurrently; or
  - consecutively.[752]

[8.6.2] ONE TRANSACTION OR CONTINUING EPISODE RULE

The 'one transaction or continuing episode' rule states:

> When a number of offences arise out of 'one transaction or continuing episode', any terms of imprisonment are usually made concurrent[753], but not necessarily so[754,755].

---

[752] See *R v Anthony* [1962] Crim LR 259.

[753] See *R v Peter John Kastercum* (1972) 56 Cr App R 298 at 299-300; *R v Faulkner* (1972) 56 Cr App R 594 and *R v Skinner* (1968) 8 Cr App R (S) 166.

See also: *Hassan v The State of Western Australia* [2006] WASCA 139; *R v Wheatley* (1983) 5 Cr App R (S) 417; *Public Prosecutor v Law Aik Meng* [2007] 2 SLR(R) 814; *Maideen Pillai v Public Prosecutor* [1995] 3 SLR(R) 706; *Kanagasuntharam v Public Prosecutor* [1991] 2 SLR(R) 874; *Jeffery bin Abdullah v Public Prosecutor* [2009] 3 SLR(R) 414 and *V Murugesan v Public Prosecutor* [2006] 1 SLR(R) 388.

[754] See *R v White* [2002] WASCA 112; *Ruane v R* (1979) 1 A Crim R 284; *R v Faithfull* (2004) 142 A Crim R 554, [2004] WASCA 39; *Nguyen v R* [2007] NSWCCA 14 and *R v Weldon; R v Carberry* (2002) 136 A Crim R 55, [2002] NSWCCA 475.

[755] See *Ian Napolean Setep v The State* (2001) SC666, [2001] PGSC 14; *Acting Public Prosecutor v Konis Haha* [1981] PNGLR 205, [1981] PGSC 6; *Public Prosecutor v Kerua and Kerua* [1985] PNGLR 85, [1985] PGSC 8; *Paul Mase and Kope Lore John v The State* [1991] PNGLR 88; *Tremellan v R* [1973] PNGLR 116 at 119-120, [1973] PGSC 49; *The State v Timothy Bipi* (2009) N3608, [2009] PGNC 55; *The State v Philip Eki Vaki* (2007) N3464, [2007] PGNC 163; *The State v Irox Winston* (2003) N2347; *The State v Henry Eliakim* (2007) N3190, [2007] PGNC 76; *The State v Sottie Apusa* [1988-89] PNGLR 170; *The State v Ilam Peter* (2006) N3090, [2006] PGNC 80; *The State v Seth Ujan Talil* (2010) N4159 and *The State v Steven Tari Nangimon Garasai* (2010) N4155.

See also: *Dickens v R* (2004) 147 A Crim R 343, [2004] WASCA 179; *Borbil v Western Australia* (2007) 169 A Crim R 152, [2007] WASCA 24; *R v Faithfull* (2004) 142 A Crim R 554, [2004] WASCA 39; *LJM (A child) v The State of Western Australia* (2005) 30 WAR 38, [2005] WASCA 172; *Walgar v The State of Western Australia* [2007] WASCA 241; *The State of Western Australia v Amoore* (2008) 182 A Crim R 165, [2008] WASCA 65 and *Dicker v Asherton* (1974) 65 LSJS 150 at 151.

That rule, however, is not carved in stone, and nor is it an absolute rule. There may be situations where consecutive sentences are necessary to discourage the type of criminal conduct being punished.[756]

It is a general rule, and what has been described as a good working rule.[757]

The 'one transaction or continuing episode rule' has been described as applying:

- when a number of offences arise out of substantially the same:
    - act;
    - circumstances; or
    - series of occurrences[758];
- when there is one multi-faceted course of criminal conduct[759]; or
- if the offences are considered to be manifestations of the one criminal:
    - enterprise;
    - transaction; or
    - episode[760].

  It is not infrequent that, where the offences arise out of one criminal enterprise concurrent sentences will be imposed, but:

    - this is not an inflexible rule; and

[756] See *R v Peter John Kastercum* (1972) 56 Cr App R 298.

See also: *V Murugesan v Public Prosecutor* [2006] 1 SLR(R) 388.

[757] See *Ruane v R* (1979) 1 A Crim R 284.

[758] See *Brown v Lynch* (1982) 5 A Crim R 404 at 407.

[759] See *Attorney-General v Tichy* (1982) 30 SASR 84 at 92-93.

[760] See *Pearce v R* (1994) 194 CLR 610, per Kirby J at 650, [1998] HCA 57.

- the practice should not be followed where wholly concurrent sentences would fail to take account of differences in conduct.[761]

Each case however depends upon its own circumstances and it is for the Court to determine whether the application of the rule would result in an appropriate measure of the total criminality involved in the conduct.[762]

Where there are truly two or more incursions into criminal conduct, consecutive sentences will generally be appropriate. Where, whatever the number of technically identifiable offences committed, an accused person was truly engaged upon one multi-faceted course of criminal conduct a Court is likely to find concurrent sentences just and convenient.[763]

Successive crimes, each involving the commission of the same or closely related offences, committed within a short space of time, are regarded as appropriate for concurrent sentences.[764]

Even distinct and unrelated offences have sometimes been treated as if they were related for the purpose of concurrency because they were committed within a short period of time.[765]

However, the fact that offences are committed:

- soon after one another; or
- simultaneously,

does not necessarily make them part of a single transaction for the purpose of the 'one transaction or continuing episode' rule.[766]

---

[761] As commented by Ipp JA in *R v Weldon; R v Carberry* (2002) 136 A Crim R 55, [2002] NSWCCA 475.

[762] See *R v Faithfull* (2004) 142 A Crim R 554, [2004] WASCA 39; *R v White* [2002] WASCA 112; *R v O'Rourke* [1997] 1 VR 246 at 253 and *R v O'Brien and Gloster* [1997] 2 VR 714 at 720-721.

[763] See *Attorney-General v Tichy* (1982) 30 SASR 84, per Wells J at 92-93; *Worthington v Western Australia* (2005) 152 A Crim R 585 at 590-591 and *Johnson v R* (2004) 78 ALJR 616, per Gleeson CJ at 618, (2004) 205 ALR 346, [2004] HCA 15.

[764] See *John Sil Kawage v Gagorine Yube and Stephen Tifai* [1976] PNGLR 604.

See also: *Pepper v Western Australia* (2005) 30 WAR 447, per Roberts-Smith JA at 471.

[765] See *Western Australia v Miller* (2005) 30 WAR 38 at 42, [2005] WASCA 53 and *Worthington v Western Australia* (2005) 152 A Crim R 585 at 591.

[766] See *Shaw* (1989) 39 A Crim R 343, per Brinsden J at 347 and *Pepper v Western Australia* (2005) 30 WAR 447, per Roberts-Smith JA at 471.

SENTENCING OPTIONS

Sentences imposed whilst taking into consideration the 'one transaction or continuing episode rule' do not have to be concurrent, although may be so.[767]

Ultimately, justice requires due consideration of:

- whether, and to what extent, an accused person was truly engaged upon one multi-faceted course of criminal conduct; and

- whether the sentences imposed properly reflected the outcome of that consideration.[768]

[8.6.3] CUMULATIVE SENTENCES

Cumulative sentences are normally applicable where the offences are:

- so different in character; or

- in relation to different victims.[769]

---

[767] See *R v White* [2002] WASCA 112; *Ruane v R* (1979) 1 A Crim R 284; *Attorney-General v Tichy* (1982) 30 SASR 84 at 92-93; *Pearce v R* (1998) 194 CLR 610 at 623, [1998] HCA 57; *Johnson v R* (2004) 78 ALJR 616, (2004) 205 ALR 346, [2004] HCA 15; *Koushappis* (1988) 34 A Crim R 419 at 422; *Western Australia v Miller* (2005) 30 WAR 38 at 42, [2005] WASCA 53; *Worthington v Western Australia* (2005) 152 A Crim R 585 at 591 and *Pepper v Western Australia* (2005) 30 WAR 447, per Roberts-Smith JA at 471.

[768] See *Johnson v R* (2004) 78 ALJR 616, per Gleeson CJ at 618, (2004) 205 ALR 346, [2004] HCA 15.

[769] See *Ian Napolean Setep v The State* (2001) SC666, [2001] PGSC 14; *Public Prosecutor v Kerua and Kerua* [1985] PNGLR 85, [1985] PGSC 8; *Paul Mase and Kope Lore John v The State* [1991] PNGLR 88; *Mugining v R* [1975] PNGLR 352; *Acting Public Prosecutor v Konis Naha* [1981] PNGLR 205, [1981] PGSC 6; *The State v Irox Winston* (2003) N2347; *The State v Henry Eliakim* (2007) N3190, [2007] PGNC 76; *The State v John Pesa* [1994] PNGLR 317; *The State v James Gurave Guba* (2000) N2020 and *The State v Peter Tulemanil* (2008) N3685, [2008] PGNC 233.

For example, burglary and violence to a householder, an assault plus escaping from custody[770] or sexual assaults on different victims.[771]

Where there are multiple victims a Court should order consecutive sentences, otherwise there would be a failure to acknowledge the harm done to the individual victims.[772]

The power to make two or more sentences cumulative should however only be exercised in exceptional cases.[773]

Where two offences committed during the course of a single episode are:

- of a completely different nature; and
- each individually involving significant or extreme gravity,

it is likely that some accumulation will be necessary to address the criminality of the two.[774]

[8.6.4] TOTALITY PRINCIPLE

The effect of the 'totality principle' is to require a Court that has passed a series of sentences, each properly:

- calculated in relation to the offence for which it is imposed; and

---

770 Section 20(3) of the *Criminal Code* (Ch. 262) states:

> 'A person who escapes from lawful custody while undergoing a sentence involving deprivation of liberty is liable on recapture to undergo the punishment that he was undergoing at the time of his escape, for a term equal to the period during which he was absent from prison after the escape and before the expiration of the term of his original sentence whether or not at the time of his recapture the term of that sentence had or has not expired'.

771 See *Ian Napolean Setep v The State* (2001) SC666, [2001] PGSC 14; *Public Prosecutor v Kerua and Kerua* [1985] PNGLR 85, [1985] PGSC 8; *Paul Mase and Kope Lore John v The State* [1991] PNGLR 88; *Mugining v R* [1975] PNGLR 352; *Acting Public Prosecutor v Konis Naha* [1981] PNGLR 205, [1981] PGSC 6; *The State v Irox Winston* (2003) N2347; *The State v Henry Eliakim* (2007) N3190, [2007] PGNC 76; *The State v John Pesa* [1994] PNGLR 317; *The State v James Gurave Guba* (2000) N2020 and *The State v Peter Tulemanil* (2008) N3685, [2008] PGNC 233.

772 See *R v Wilson* [2005] NSWCCA 219 and *Vaovosa v R* [2007] NSWCCA 253.

773 See *Passingan v Beaton* [1971-72] PNGLR 206, [1971] PGSC 37.

774 See *Nguyen v R* [2007] NSWCCA 14, per Howie J.

- made consecutive or concurrent in accordance with the 'single transaction or continuing episode rule',

to:

- review the aggregate sentence; and
- consider whether the sentence is just and appropriate.[775]

The total sentence imposed must properly reflect the 'totality' of the criminality.[776]

There is no principle that no matter:

- how many offences are committed;
- how long the period over which the offences are committed; or
- how much is involved

cumulative sentences exceeding the maximum permissible for a single offence should never be imposed.[777]

---

[775] See The Law Reform Commission of Ireland, 1993, 'Consultation Paper on Sentencing', paragraph 1.154.

See also: *R v French* (1982) 4 Cr App R (S) 57, per Lane LCJ.

[776] See *Ian Napolean Setep v The State* (2001) SC666, [2001] PGSC 14; *Acting Public Prosecutor v Konis Haha* [1981] PNGLR 205 at 214, [1981] PGSC 6; *Paul Mase and Kope Lore John v The State* [1991] PNGLR 88; *The Public Prosecutor v Sidney Kerua and Billy Kerua* [1985] PNGLR 85, [1985] PGSC 8; *Emil Kongian and others v The State* (2007) SC928, [2007] PGSC 45; *The State v John Pesa* [1994] PNGLR 317; *The State v Peter Tulemanil* (2008) N3685, [2008] PGNC 233 and *The Public Prosecutor v Terrance Kaveku* [1977] PNGLR 110, [1977] PGSC 8.

See also: *Pearce v R* (1998) 194 CLR 610 at 623, [1998] HCA 57; *Walgar v The State of Western Australia* [2007] WASCA 241; *R v Kalache* (2000) 111 A Crim R 152 at 184, [2000] NSWCCA 2; *R v Knight* (2005) 155 A Crim R 252, [2005] NSWCCA 253; *R v Hamid* (2006) 164 A Crim R 179, [2006] NSWCCA 302; *R v Weldon; R v Carberry* (2002) 136 A Crim R 55 at 62, [2002] NSWCCA 475; *R v Wilson* [2005] NSWCCA 219; *Mill v R* (1988) 166 CLR 59, (1998) 83 ALR 1, [1988] HCA 70; *R v Stevens* [1997] 2 Cr App R (S) 180; *Postiglione v R* (1997) 189 CLR 295, per McHugh J at 307-308, (1997) 145 ALR 408, (1997) 71 ALJR 875, [1997] HCA 26; *Roffey v The State of Western Australia* [2007] WASCA 246 and *Jarvis v R* (1993) 20 WAR 201, per Ipp J at 206-207.

[777] See *Johnson v R* (2004) 78 ALJR 616, per Gleeson CJ at 618, [2004] HCA 15; *Attorney-General v Tichy* (1982) 30 SASR 84, per Wells J at 92-93 and *R v Daswani* [2005] QCA 167, per McMurdo P.

SENTENCING OPTIONS

It is necessary to ensure that:

- the punishment imposed is proportionate to the total criminality; and
- it is permissible to achieve this by requiring some sentences to be cumulative upon others.[778]

The 'totality principle' usually applies where:

- an accused person is serving a term of imprisonment, at the time of sentencing, for another offence.[779]

  It is the application of the 'totality principle' that will generally determine the extent to which a particular sentence is to be served concurrently or cumulatively with an existing sentence.[780]

  When a Court imposes a sentence of imprisonment on an accused person who is already subject to an existing sentence for other offences, and orders the new sentence to run consecutively to the existing sentence, the Court should also consider the propriety of the aggregate sentence taken as a whole[781]; and

- an accused person is to be sentenced for more than one offence.

  When a Court has:

  - arrived at appropriate head sentences; and
  - decided whether those sentences should be concurrent or cumulative,

  it must then look at the total sentence to see if it is:

---

[778] See *Johnson v R* (2004) 78 ALJR 616, per Gleeson CJ at 618, [2004] HCA 15; *Attorney-General v Tichy* (1982) 30 SASR 84, per Wells J at 92-93 and *R v Daswani* [2005] QCA 167, per McMurdo P.

[779] See *Mill v R* (1988) 166 CLR 59 at 66, (1998) 83 ALR 1, [1988] HCA 70; *Barnes v The State of Western Australia* [2004] WASCA 258 and *Carr v The State of Western Australia* (2006) 166 A Crim R 1, [2006] WASCA 125.

[780] See *Mill v R* (1988) 166 CLR 59, (1998) 83 ALR 1, [1988] HCA 70; *Pearce v R* (1998) 194 CLR 610; *Johnson v R* (2004) 205 ALR 346, [2004] HCA 15 and *R v MMK* [2006] NSWCCA 272.

[781] See *R v Jones* (1996) 1 Cr App R (S) 153; *R v Millen* (1980) 2 Cr App R (S) 357; *Nollen v Police* (2001) 120 A Crim R 64; *R v Postiglione* (1997) 189 CLR 295, per McHugh J at 307-308, (1997) 145 ALR 408, (1997) 71 ALJR 875, [1997] HCA 26 and *R v Gordon* (1994) 71 A Crim R 459, per Hunt CJ at CL at 466.

- just; and
- appropriate.[782]

If it is not, it must vary one or more sentences to get a just total.[783]

Unless it can be said that each offence is committed as part of a single criminal activity, the sentences should be determined:

- without reference to each other; and then
- by imposing the sentences wholly or partially concurrently,

thereby enabling the Court to achieve the necessary degree of punishment for the total criminal conduct.[784]

If the sentence for one offence can comprehend and reflect the criminality of the other, then the sentences ought to be concurrent, otherwise there is a risk that the combined sentences will exceed that which is warranted to reflect the totality of the two offences.[785]

---

[782] See *Ian Napolean Setep v The State* (2001) SC666, [2001] PGSC 14; *The State v Irox Winston* (2003) N2347; *The State v A Juvenile, 'TAA'* (2006) N3017; *The State v Henry Eliakim* (2007) N3190, [2007] PGNC 76; *The State v Steven Siname* (2009) N3908; *The Public Prosecutor v Terrence Kaveku* [1977] PNGLR 110, [1977] PGSC 8; *Paul Mase and Kope Lore John v The State* [1991] PNGLR 88 and *Ando Kenene v Gabriel Simon, Alois Gabuor and George Taper* [1983] PNGLR 179, [1983] PGSC 14.

See also: *Pearce v R* (1998) 194 CLR 610, [1998] HCA 57; *Johnson v R* (2004) 78 ALJR 616, (2004) 205 ALR 346, [2004] HCA 15; *Markarian v R* (2005) 228 CLR 357, (2005) 215 ALR 213, [2005] HCA 25 and *R v Abboud* [2005] NSWCCA 251.

[783] See *Ian Napolean Setep v The State* (2001) SC666, [2001] PGSC 14; *The State v Irox Winston* (2003) N2347; *The State v A Juvenile, 'TAA'* (2006) N3017; *The State v Henry Eliakim* (2007) N3190, [2007] PGNC 76; *The State v Steven Siname* (2009) N3908; *The Public Prosecutor v Terrence Kaveku* [1977] PNGLR 110, [1977] PGSC 8; *Paul Mase and Kope Lore John v The State* [1991] PNGLR 88 and *Ando Kenene v Gabriel Simon, Alois Gabuor and George Taper* [1983] PNGLR 179, [1983] PGSC 14.

See also: *Pearce v R* (1998) 194 CLR 610, [1998] HCA 57; *Johnson v R* (2004) 78 ALJR 616, (2004) 205 ALR 346, [2004] HCA 15; *Markarian v R* (2005) 228 CLR 357, (2005) 215 ALR 213, [2005] HCA 25 and *R v Abboud* [2005] NSWCCA 251.

[784] See *Pearce v R* (1998) 194 CLR 610, [1998] HCA 57; *Mill v R* (1988) 166 CLR 59, (1998) 83 ALR 1, [1988] HCA 70 and *Johnson v R* (2004) 205 ALR 346, (2004) 78 ALJR 616, [2004] HCA 15.

[785] See *Cahyadi v R* (2007) 168 A Crim R 41, per Howie J at 47, [2007] NSWCCA 1.

If not, the sentence should be at least partially cumulative otherwise there is a risk that the total sentence will fail to reflect the total criminality of the two offences. This is so regardless of whether the two offences:

- represent two discrete acts of criminality; or
- can be regarded as part of a single episode of criminality.[786]

Whether the sentence for one offence can comprehend and reflect the criminality of the other sentence/s calls for the identification and an evaluation of relevant factors pertaining to the offences. These will include:

- the nature; and
- the seriousness

of each offence.[787]

It is proper practice to pass a sentence that each of the offences merit and making those sentences concurrent, rather than passing short sentences and making those consecutive.[788]

It should be expressed with clarity by a Court:

- the sentences imposed in respect of each charge/count; and
- whether those sentences were to run:
  - concurrently; or
  - consecutively.[789]

---

[786] See *Cahyadi v R* (2007) 168 A Crim R 41, per Howie J at 47, [2007] NSWCCA 1.

[787] As commented by Hall J in *R v XX* [2009] NSWCCA 115.

[788] See *R v Dolby* (1989) 11 Cr App R (S) 335.

[789] See *R v Anthony* [1962] Crim LR 259.

When applying the principle of totality, the question to be posed is:

> Can the sentence for one offence can comprehend and reflect the criminality of the other offence/s?[790]

The 'totality principle' is comprised of the following limbs:

- The total effective sentence must bear a proper relationship to the overall criminality involved in all of the offences:
    - viewed in their entirety; and
    - having regard to the circumstances of the case, including those that are personal to an accused person.[791]

  The sentence must therefore be:
    - just; and
    - appropriate.[792]

---

[790] See *R v MMK* [2006] NSWCCA 272 and *Cahyadi v R* (2007) 168 A Crim R 41, [2007] NSWCCA 1.

[791] See *Smith v R* [1972] Crim LR 124.

See also: *Woods v R* (1994) 14 WAR 341, per Anderson J at 352; *R v Faithfull* (2004) 142 A Crim R 554, [2004] WASCA 39; *R v White* [2002] WASCA 112; *R v O'Rourke* [1997] 1 VR 246 at 253; *R v O'Brien and Gloster* [1997] 2 VR 714 at 720-721; *Pearce v R* (1998) 194 CLR 610, [1998] HCA 57; *Western Australia v Miller* (2005) 30 WAR 38, [2005] WASCA 53; *Johnson v R* (2004) 78 ALJR 616, (2004) 205 ALR 346, [2004] HCA 15; *Mill v R* (1998) 166 CLR 59 at 63, (1998) 83 ALR 1, [1988] HCA 70; *Angitalo and others v R* [2005] SBHC 5; *R v Holder and Johnston* [1983] 3 NSWLR 245 at 260, (1983) 13 A Crim R 375; *R v Glenister* [1980] 2 NSWLR 597 at 612; *R v Smith and Shoesmith* (1983) 32 SASR 219; *Wise v R* [1965] Tas SR 196 at 209; *Kelly v R* (1992) 33 FCR 536 at 541, [1992] FCA 7; *Pollock v The State of Western Australia* [2009] WACA 121; *Roffey v The State of Western Australia* [2007] WASCA 246; *Giglia v The State of Western Australia* [2010] WACA 9; *Postiglione v R* (1997) 189 CLR 295, per McHugh J at 307-309, (1997) 145 ALR 408, (1998) 71 ALJR 875, [1997] HCA 26; *Jarvis v R* (1993) 20 WAR 201, per Anderson J at 216 and *Carr v The State of Western Australia* (2006) 166 A Crim R 1, [2006] WASCA 125.

[792] See *Ian Napolean Setep v The State* (2001) SC666, [2001] PGSC 14.

In other words, the final sentence must not be

- inadequate; or
- excessive[793].[794]

Whether or not the aggregate effect of a sentence is inadequate or excessive depends on the facts of each case[795]; and

- The Court should not impose a 'crushing' sentence, ie., a sentence that will have a crushing effect upon an accused person.[796]

'Crushing' has long been used as a pejorative adjective in relation to sentences.[797]

The word 'crushing' in this context connotes the destruction of any reasonable expectation of a useful life after release.[798]

An extremely long total sentence may be 'crushing' upon an accused person in the sense that it will:

- induce a feeling of hopelessness; and

---

[793] See *R v Bocskei* (1970) 54 Cr App R 519.

[794] See *The Public Prosecutor v Terrence Kaveku* [1977] PNGLR 110, [1977] PGSC 8.

Refer also to the chapter titled 'Appeals Against Sentence'.

[795] See *Acting Public Prosecutor v Konis Haha* [1981] PNGLR 205, per Kapi J (as he then was).

[796] See *The State v Anton Towakra and others* (2009) N3845; *The State v Seth Ujan Talil* (2010) N4159 and *The State v Steven Tari Nangimon Garasai* (2010) N4155.

See also: *R v Smith* [1972] Crim LR 124; *Martino v The State of Western Australia* [2006] WASCA 78; *Jarvis v R* (1993) 20 WAR 201, per Anderson J at 216; *Postiglione v R* (1997) 189 CLR 295 at 304, (1997) 145 ALR 408, (1997) 71 ALJR 875, [1997] HCA 26; *R v Schmidt* [2011] QCA 133; *Heromanley v Public Prosecutor* [2010] VUCA 25; *Kalfau v Public Prosecutor* [1990] VUCA 9; *Pollock v The State of Western Australia* [2009] WACA 121; *Roffey v The State of Western Australia* [2007] WASCA 246; *Giglia v The State of Western Australia* [2010] WACA 9; *Johnson v R* (2004) 78 ALJR 616, (2004) 205 ALR 346, [2004] HCA 15 and *Carr v The State of Western Australia* (2006) 166 A Crim R 1, [2006] WASCA 125.

[797] See *Cranssen v R* (1936) 55 CLR 509 at 521, [1936] HCA 42 and *R v Schmidt* [2011] QCA 133.

[798] See *Martino v The State of Western Australia* [2006] WASCA 78.

- destroy any expectation of useful life after release.[799]

The effect of such a sentence:

- increases the severity of the sentence to be served; and

- destroys such prospects as there may be of reformation and rehabilitation[800].[801]

Of course, in many cases of multiple offending, an accused person may not be entitled to the element of mercy entailed in adopting such a constraint.[802]

However, an aggregate sentence may be inappropriately long under the first limb even if it cannot be described as 'crushing'.[803]

The practical effect of the 'totality principle' is:

> Ordinarily to arrive at an aggregate sentence that is less than that which would be arrived at by simply adding up all the terms appropriate for the individual offences.[804]

However, a Court must in each case consider whether the application of that general rule would result in an appropriate measure of the total criminality involved in the conduct.[805] If not, then the appropriate result should be achieved, if practicable, by making the sentences wholly or partially concurrent, rather than by adjusting the otherwise appropriate sentence.[806]

---

799 See *R v MAK* (2006) 167 A Crim R 159, [2006] NSWCCA 381.

800 Refer also to the section titled 'The Need For Reformation Or Rehabilitation' in the chapter titled 'Objectives And Purposes Of Sentencing'.

801 See *R v MAK* (2006) 167 A Crim R 159, [2006] NSWCCA 381.

802 See *R v MAK* (2006) 167 A Crim R 159, [2006] NSWCCA 381.

803 See *Jarvis v R* (1998) 20 WAR 201 at 216; *Roffey v The State of Western Australia* [2007] WASCA 246 and *Giglia v The State of Western Australia* [2010] WACA 9.

804 See *R v Holder and Johnston* [1983] 3 NSWLR 245, per Street CJ at 260, (1983) 13 A Crim R 375 and *Giglia v The State of Western Australia* [2010] WACA 9.

805 See *R v White* [2002] WASCA 112.

806 See *Mill v R* (1988) 166 CLR 59 at 63, (1998) 83 ALR 1, [1988] HCA 70.

Where the principle of totality comes into effect, it is of little importance how the ultimate aggregate is made up.[807]

It is wrong in principle to:

> Impose a series of fines and cumulative default sentences when in reality there is no prospect of an accused person being able to pay the fines.[808]

If a fine is the appropriate sentence it should be made alternative to imprisonment.[809]

A sentence of imprisonment should be made cumulative if the offences were committed whilst on bail.[810]

[9.0] PROBATION ORDER

[9.1] PROBATION ACT

[9.1.1] PROBATION ORDER

Section 16 of the *Probation Act* (Ch. 381) states:

> '(1) In this section, **"offence"** does not include an offence for which a mandatory minimum sentence is provided for by any law.

---

[807] See *R v Holder and Johnston* [1983] 3 NSWLR 245 at 260, (1983) 13 A Crim R 375 and *Giglia v The State of Western Australia* [2010] WACA 9.

[808] See *Kenene v Samon; Gabour and Tapu* [1983] PNGLR 179, [1983] PGSC 14.

[809] See *Kenene v Samon; Gabour and Tapu* [1983] PNGLR 179, [1983] PGSC 14.

[810] See *R v Young* [1973] Crim LR 585.

See also: *Mill v R* (1988) 166 CLR 59, (1998) 83 ALR 1, [1988] HCA 70; *R v Wallace* [1983] NZLR 758; *R v Richards* [1981] 2 NSWLR 464; *R v Kain* (1985) 38 SASR 309; *Clark* (1994) 15 Cr App R (S) 852; *Hammond* (1995) 16 Cr App R (S) 142; *R v Lucky* (1974) 12 SASR 136; *R v Knight* (1981) 26 SASR 573; *R v Bradley* [1979] 1 NZLR 262; *Postiglione v R* (1997) 189 CLR 295, per McHugh J at 307-308, (1997) 145 ALR 408, (1997) 71 ALJR 875, [1997] HCA 26; *Hennessy* (1970) 51 Cr App R 148 and *Krishna v R* (1962) 8 Fiji LR 236.

(2) Subject to Subsection (3), where a person, is convicted of an offence punishable by imprisonment or a fine or both imprisonment and a fine, the court convicting him may by probation order[811] –

(a) impose a sentence but suspend committing him to imprisonment or a fine or both imprisonment and a fine; or

(b) defer sentencing him to imprisonment or a fine or both imprisonment and a fine,

and release him on probation for a period specified in the order, being a period of not less than six months and not more than five years.

(3) [Repealed]

(4) Subsection (2) does not prevent the court –

(a) imposing and requiring the payment by the probationer[812] of a fine authorized by law; or

(b) in accordance with any law – disqualifying the probationer from holding or obtaining a licence to drive a motor vehicle under the *Motor Traffic Act 1950*.

(5) A probation order takes effect from such date as may be determined by the Court or, where the Court makes no determination as to the date, from the date of the making of the order.

(6) Subsection (2) shall not be construed as derogating from the powers of any court conferred by any other law to release a person on probation for such period and on such conditions as are specified in that law.

(7) Notwithstanding Subsection (6), where a law provides for –

(a) probation; or

(b) a person to be placed on probation,

this Act[813] shall apply in the absence of any express provisions to the contrary in that law'.

---

[811] The term 'probation order' is defined in section 2 of the *Probation Act* (Ch. 381) as meaning: 'an order made under Section 16(2)'.

[812] The term 'probationer' is defined in section 2 of the *Probation Act* (Ch. 381) as meaning: 'a person in relation to whom a probation order is in force'.

[813] The term 'this Act' is defined in section 2 of the *Probation Act* (Ch. 381) as including: 'the regulations'.

[9.1.2] CONDITIONS OF PROBATION

Section 17 of the *Probation Act* (Ch. 381) states:

'(1) A probation order shall –

(a) specify the address to which the probationer is to go and remain on release until he is contacted by a probation officer[814]; and

(b) require the probationer to report to a probation officer as and when he is required by the probation officer to do so; and

(c) require the probationer to keep the peace and to be of good behaviour; and

(d) direct that –

(i) the probationer shall not change his address, other than the address referred to in Paragraph (a), unless he has given to a probation officer reasonable notice of his intention to do so and the reasons for the proposed change; and

(ii) where by virtue of the change of address, the probationer has moved to another declared area[815] – he shall, within 48 hours of arrival, report to a probation officer in that area and advise that officer of the nature and place of his employment and of his new address in that area; and

(e) direct that the probationer shall give to a probation officer reasonable notice of his intention to change his employment and advise him of the nature and place of his proposed employment; and

(f) require that the probationer shall, for the purposes of this Act, allow a probation officer to enter his home during reasonable hours.

(2) In Subsection (1)(a), (b), (e) and (f), **"probation office"** includes a voluntary probation officer[816]'.

---

814 The term 'probation officer' is defined in section 2 of the *Probation Act* (Ch. 381) as meaning:
'a person referred to in Section 5(b)'.

815 The term 'declared area' is defined in section 2 of the *Probation Act* (Ch. 381) as meaning:
'an area declared under Section 3'.

816 The term 'voluntary probation officer' is defined in section 2 of the *Probation Act* (Ch. 381) as meaning:
'a person appointed under Section 6(1)'.

[9.1.3] ADDITIONAL CONDITIONS

Section 18 of the *Probation Act* (Ch. 381) states:

'(1) In addition to the conditions set out in Section 17(1), the court may impose all or any of the following conditions:–

(a) that a probationer shall not, except with the permission of a probation officer and in accordance with such directions as the probation officer may give, leave any specified area;

(b) that a probationer shall pay, within such period and by such instalments as the court determines, damages for injury, or compensation for loss, suffered by any person by virtue of the offence for which the probationer is convicted or shall carry out work in restitution for such injury, compensation or loss;

(c) that a probationer shall travel to and reside in a specific area;

(d) that a probationer shall perform community work under the provisions of any law;

(e) that a probationer shall pay, within such period and by such instalments as the court determines, compensation according to custom to any person or persons.

(2) Subsection (1) does not prevent the court imposing such other conditions as are necessary in the circumstances of the case for ensuring compliance by the probationer with the conditions of the order and for his good conduct and welfare.

(3) Where a probationer is performing community work or work by way of restitution, the probationer shall be deemed to be employed by the State for the purposes of the *Workers Compensation Act* 1978'.

[9.1.4] VARIATION AND DISCHARGE

Section 19 of the *Probation Act* (Ch. 381) states:

'(1) Subject to Subsection (6), a relevant court[817] may, on application by a probationer, suspend or vary the conditions of the probation order which relates to that probationer.

---

[817] The term 'relevant court' in relation to an application, or other matter, connected with a probation order, is defined in section 2 of the Probation Act (Ch. 381) as meaning:
'a court exercising the same jurisdiction as the court that made the order'.

(2) A probationer who has served not less than half the period of probation[818] may, subject to Subsection (6), apply to a relevant court for the discharge of the probation order relating to him and the court may discharge the order.

(3) Subject to Subsection (6), a probation officer may, in relation to a probation order, apply to a relevant court for –

(a) suspension or variation of the conditions of the order; or

(b) imposition of additional conditions; or

(c) extension of the period of probation where that period is less than five years; or

(d) the discharge of the order.

(4) On the hearing of an application under Subsection (3), the court, having regard to the information before it in relation to the probationer, may –

(a) do all, or any of the following things:–

(i) suspend or vary any conditions of the probation order;

(ii) impose any additional conditions;

(iii) subject to Subsection (5) – extend the period of probation; or

(b) discharge the order.

(5) A period of probation shall not be extended beyond the period of five years from the date when the probation order in which that period is specified first took effect.

(6) Except with the written consent of the Chief Probation Officer[819], an application under Subsection (1), (2) or (3) shall not be made to a court unless that court exercises jurisdiction in a declared area[820]'.

---

[818] The term 'period of probation' is defined in section 2 of the *Probation Act* (Ch. 381) as meaning:
'a period specified in a probation order in accordance with Section 16(2) and, includes, where the period has been extended under this Act, the extension'.

[819] The term 'Senior Probation Officer' is defined in section 2 of the *Probation Act* (Ch. 381) as meaning:
'a person referred to in Section 5(b)'.

[820] The term "declared area" is defined in section 2 of the *Probation Act* (Ch. 381) as meaning:
'an area declared under Section 3'.

[9.1.5] BREACH OF CONDITIONS OF PROBATION[821]

STATUTORY PROVISION

Section 20 of the *Probation Act* (Ch. 381) states:

'(1) A probationer who contravenes, or fails to comply with, a condition of a probation order that relates to him commits an offence.

(2) An offence under Subsection (1) may be heard by a relevant court or a court exercising jurisdiction superior to the relevant court and the court may, on conviction of the probationer–

(a) extend the period of probation where that period is less than five years; or

(b) vary any condition of the probation order; or

(c) impose additional conditions; or

(d) where in accordance with Section 16(2)(a) sentence to imprisonment was suspended – commit the probationer to imprisonment for the whole or part of that sentence; or

(e) where in accordance with Section 16(2)(b) sentence was deferred – sentence the probationer to imprisonment for the offence for which he was originally convicted; or

(f) impose the penalty of a fine of not exceeding K200.00 or imprisonment for a term not exceeding four months.

(3) Section 19(5) applies to an extension under Subsection (2)(a).

(4) Where the court has proceeded in accordance with Subsection (2)(d) or (e), the court shall discharge the probation order'.

WORDING OF CHARGES

'That on **[**Date**]** at **[**Place**]** in Papua New Guinea **[**Name of Accused Person**]** being a probationer did **[**contravene **or** fail to comply with**]** a condition of a probation order to wit **[**specify the condition that was contravened **or** not complied with**]**.'

---

[821] See *Thomas J Bolkings v Mathas Ambane Bare* (1992) N1099.

ELEMENTS

A. Date

B. Place

C. Accused Person

D. Probationer

E. [1] Contravene

[2] Fail To Comply With

F. A Condition Of A Probation Order

[9.1.6] ARREST OF PROBATIONER

Section 21 of the *Probation Act* (Ch. 381) states:

> '(1) A member of the Police Force[822] who, on reasonable grounds, believes that a probationer has committed a breach of a condition of a probation order relating to that probationer may, subject to the *Arrest Act 1977*[823] and the *Bail Act 1977*[824], arrest him without a warrant.
>
> (2) If, on information, it appears to a relevant court that a probationer has committed a breach of, or has failed to comply with, a condition of the probation order relating to him, the court may –
>
> (a) issue a summons requiring the probationer to appear before it; or

---

[822] The term 'the Police Force' is defined in section 3(1) of the *Interpretation Act* (Ch. 2) as meaning:
'the Police Force established by Section 188 (*establishment of the State Services*) of the *Constitution*'.

[823] As regards the law in relation to 'Arrest And Detain', refer to the chapter titled 'Police Powers' in the text titled 'Injia on Investigatory Practice in Papua New Guinea and the Pacific'.

[824] As regards the law in relation to 'Right To Bail', refer to the chapter titled 'Rights Of An accused person' in the text titled 'Injia on Criminal Practice and Procedure in Papua New Guinea and the Pacific'.

(b) where the information is on oath[825] – issue a warrant for his arrest'.

[9.1.7] SUBSEQUENT SENTENCE

Section 22 of the *Probation Act* (Ch. 381) states:

> '(1) Where a probationer is sentenced to imprisonment for a subsequent offence, other than an offence under Section 20, the period of probation shall continue to run while the probationer is under that imprisonment, and on release he shall serve the unexpired period of probation (if any).
>
> (2) Subsection (1) does not prevent a court dealing with the probationer in accordance with Section 20 for an offence under that section'.

[9.2] JUVENILE COURTS ACT

Subject to sections 30 and 32 of the *Juvenile Courts Act 1991*, the Court may, in addition to any other powers under this Act or any other law enter a conviction and order that a juvenile be placed on probation in accordance with the *Probation Act 1979* for a period of not less than six months, but not more than three years.[826]

---

[825] The term 'oath' is defined in section 3(1) of the *Interpretation Act* (Ch. 2) in the case of a person allowed by law to affirm, declare or promise, instead of swearing as including:
'affirmation, declaration and promise'.

[826] See section 30(2)(c)(iii) of the *Juvenile Courts Act 1991*.

[10.0] PROPERTY ORDERS

[10.1] STOLEN GOODS[827]

[10.1.1] STATUTORY PROVISIONS

Section 21 of the *Goods Act* (Ch. 251) states:

'(1) Subject to this Part, where goods[828] are sold by a person who –

(a) is not the owner; and

(b) does not sell them under the authority or with the consent of the owner,

the buyer[829] acquires no better title to the goods than the seller[830] had unless the owner of the goods is precluded by his conduct from denying the seller's authority to sell.

(2) This Part does not affect –

(a) the provisions of Part III. or any enactment enabling the apparent owner of goods to dispose of them as if he were the true owner of the goods; or

(b) the validity of a contract of sale[831] under–

(i) a special, common law or statutory power of sale; or

(ii) an order of a court'.

---

[827] See also: section 132(2) of the *District Courts Act* (Ch. 40).

[828] The term 'goods' is defined in section 1(1) of the *Goods Act* (Ch. 251) as including:
'(a) all chattels personal other than things in action and money; and
(b) emblements and things attached to or forming part of any land that are agreed to be severed before sale or under the contract of sale'.

[829] The term 'buyer' is defined in section 1(1) of the *Goods Act* (Ch. 251) as meaning:
'a person who buys or agrees to buy goods'.

[830] The term 'seller' is defined in section 1(1) of the *Goods Act* (Ch. 251) as meaning:
'a person who sells or agrees to sell goods'.

[831] The term 'contract of sale' is defined in section 1(1) of the *Goods Act* (Ch. 251) as including:
'an agreement to sell and a sale'.

Section 24(1) states:

> 'Where goods[832] have been stolen[833] and the offender is convicted, the property in the goods stolen revests in the person who was the owner of the goods or his personal representative, notwithstanding any intermediate dealing with them'.

[10.1.2] GENERAL PRINCIPLES

Section 21 of the *Goods Act* (Ch. 251) provides that a seller, who is:

- not the owner; or
- not selling with the owner's consent or authority,

confers no better title on the buyer than he or she had himself or herself, unless the owner is stopped by his or her conduct from denying the seller's authority to sell.[834]

This general rule is subject to several exceptions, the most important of which are set out in sections 22, 23, 24 and 25 of that Act.[835]

When property has been stolen then the ownership of that property remains with the rightful owner, irrespective of whether the thief sells the property to another person.

In such circumstances the prosecutor should apply to the Court for an order as to a return of the property to the complainant.

---

832 The term 'goods' is defined in section 1(1) of the *Goods Act* (Ch. 251) as including:
'(a) all chattels personal other than things in action and money; and
(b) emblements and things attached to or forming part of any land that are agreed to be severed before sale or under the contract of sale'.

833 Refer also to the section titled 'Stealing' in the chapter titled 'Offences Against Property' in the text titled 'Injia on Offences in Papua New Guinea and the Pacific'.

834 See *Shem Pake v Daniel Tulapi and Jimmy Arete* (2003) N2375.

835 See *Shem Pake v Daniel Tulapi and Jimmy Arete* (2003) N2375.

[10.2] FRAUDULENTLY OBTAINED GOODS

[10.2.1] STATUTORY PROVISION

Section 24(2) of the *Goods Act* (Ch. 251) states:

> 'Notwithstanding any other enactment, where goods[836] have been obtained by fraud or other wrongful means not amounting to larceny[837] the property in the goods does not revest in the person who was the owner of the goods or his personal representative by reason only of the conviction of the offender'.

[10.2.2] GENERAL PRINCIPLE

When an accused person obtains property by means of a fraud or other wrongful means not amounting to 'Stealing' the ownership in the property transfers from the rightful owner to the accused person.

In such circumstances the prosecutor should apply for compensation to an equal value of the property.

---

836 The term 'goods' is defined in section 1(1) of the *Goods Act* (Ch. 251) as including:
'(a) all chattels personal other than things in action and money; and
(b) emblements and things attached to or forming part of any land that are agreed to be severed before sale or under the contract of sale'.

837 Refer also to the chapter titled 'Offences Against Property' in the text titled 'Injia on Offences in Papua New Guinea and the Pacific'.

[11.0] RESTRICTION OF MOVEMENT ORDER

[11.1] CRIMINAL CODE

[11.1.1] STATUTORY PROVISIONS

The following statutory provisions only apply to those offences as provided for by the *Criminal Code* (Ch. 262).[838]

Section 18 of the *Criminal Code* (Ch. 262) provides that restriction of movement is a punishment that may be inflicted under that Code.

Section 19 states (in part):

> '(9) Notwithstanding that restriction of movement is not specified as a punishment for an offence, a court may, in addition to any other punishment or punishments imposed, also impose restriction of movement in accordance with Section 600.
>
> (10) When a court is considering the punishment or punishments to be imposed in any case it shall also consider whether, in the circumstances of the case, restriction of movement is an appropriate punishment'.

Section 600 states:

> '(1) For the purposes of this section –
>
> **"home"**, in relation to a person, means –
>
> (a) the place (if any) where he has resided continuously during the period of five years immediately preceding the date of the offence giving rise to the conviction in respect of which a punishment under this section is being imposed; or
>
> (b) an area of customary land on which he may by custom build or occupy a house or garden, whether in his own right or in right of his spouse or some other relation; or
>
> (c) an area of customary land owned by a linguistic or cultural group with which he or his spouse has customary affiliations involving usage rights in land; or

---

[838] Section 2 of the *Criminal Code Act* (Ch. 262) states:

'The provisions contained in Schedule 1 are the law of Papua New Guinea with respect to the matters dealt with in that Schedule'.

As regards the law in relation to 'Acts in pari materia', refer to the section titled 'Extrinsic Aids' in the chapter titled 'Aids To Interpretation' in the text titled 'Injia on Statutory Interpretation in Papua New Guinea and the Pacific'.

(d) an area of land leased for a term of not less than 12 months or held in freehold by him or his spouse under a Law in force in the country; or

(e) in a particular case where the provisions of Paragraph (a), (b), (c) or (d) are inapplicable–any other place with which he or his spouse has connections such that it should, in the opinion of the court, be reasonably regarded as his home;

"Probation Officer" means a probation officer appointed under the *Probation Act 1979*.

(2) Where a person is convicted of an offence, the court that convicts him may, in addition to or instead of any other punishment that may be imposed, order him–

(a) not to come or be within such part of the country as the court specifies; or

(b) to be returned to his home, as specified by the court,

during such period, not exceeding five years, as is specified by the court.

(3) An order under Subsection (2) –

(a) may be made subject to such exceptions and conditions as to the court seem proper, including a condition requiring the person to report his presence at regular intervals to a District Officer or Probation Officer or member of the Police Force; and

(b) remains in force for such period as is specified.

(4) An order made under Subsection (2)(b) does not operate so as to hinder or prevent a person from leaving the country.

(5) A person who, without reasonable excuse (proof of which is on him), contravenes or fails to comply with an order made under Subsection (2) is guilty of an offence.

Penalty[839]: Imprisonment for a term not exceeding six months.

(6) A person who is convicted of an offence against Subsection (5) is liable to be again removed from the part of the country specified in the order, or to be removed to the part of the country specified by the court, as the case may be, or a new order under this section may be made against him'.

---

[839] This is not an indictable offence [see section 3(3) of the *Criminal Code* (Ch. 262)] and can be dealt with summarily [see section 3(4) of the Criminal Code (Ch. 262)].

Refer also to the chapter titled 'Classification Of Offences' in the text titled 'Injia on Criminal Practice and Procedure in Papua New Guinea and the Pacific'.

[11.1.2] DISOBEY COURT ORDER

OFFENCES

Section 600(5) of the *Criminal Code* (Ch. 262) states:

> 'A person who, without reasonable excuse (proof of which is on him), contravenes or fails to comply with an order made under Subsection (2) is guilty of an offence.
>
> Penalty[840]: Imprisonment for a term not exceeding six months'.

WORDING OF CHARGES

'That on **[**Date**]** at **[**Place**]** in Papua New Guinea **[**Name of Accused Person**]** without reasonable excuse did **[**contravene **or** fail to comply**]** with an order made under section 600(2) of the *Criminal Code* (Ch. 262) by the **[**location of court**]** on **[**date that order was made**]**.'

ELEMENTS

A. Date

B. Place

C. Accused Person

D. Without Reasonable Excuse

E. [1] Contravene

[2] Fail

F. Order Made Under Section 600(2)

---

840 This is not an indictable offence [see section 3(3) of the *Criminal Code* (Ch. 262)] and can be dealt with summarily [see section 3(4) of the Criminal Code (Ch. 262)].

Refer also to the chapter titled 'Classification Of Offences' in the text titled 'Injia on Criminal Practice and Procedure in Papua New Guinea and the Pacific'.

SENTENCING OPTIONS

WITHOUT REASONABLE EXCUSE

This is a negative averment.

The onus is on the accused person to prove on the 'balance of probabilities' that he or she had a reasonable excuse for:

- contravening; or
- failing to comply with

the order made under section 600(2) of the *Criminal Code* (Ch. 262).[841]

COURT ORDER

When a Court makes an order against an accused person a minute or memorandum of the order shall be made and signed by the presiding Judge or Magistrate constituting the Court.

[11.2] DISTRICT COURTS ACT

[11.2.1] STATUTORY PROVISION

Section 205B of the *District Courts Act* (Ch. 40) states:

> '(1) Notwithstanding that restriction of movement is not specified as a punishment for an offence, a District Court may, in addition to any other punishment or punishments imposed, also impose restriction of movement in accordance with this section.
>
> (2) When a District Court is considering the punishment or punishments to be imposed in any case it shall also consider whether, in the circumstances of the case, restriction of movement is an appropriate punishment.
>
> (3) Where a person is convicted of an offence, the District Court that convicts him may, in addition to or instead of any other punishment that may be imposed, order him –

[841] Refer also to the chapter titled 'Proof Of Issues' in the text titled 'Injia on Criminal Practice and Procedure in Papua New Guinea and the Pacific'.

(a) not to come or be within such part of the country as the District Court specifies; or

(b) to be returned to his home, as specified by the District Court,

during such period, not exceeding five years, as is specified by the court.

(4) An order under Subsection (3) –

(a) may be made subject to such exceptions and conditions as to the District Court seem proper, including a condition requiring the person to report his presence at regular intervals to a District Officer or Probation Officer or member of the Police Force; and

(b) remains in force for such period as is specified.

(5) An order made under Subsection (3)(b) does not operate so as to hinder or prevent a person from leaving the country.

(6) A person who, without reasonable excuse (proof of which is on him), contravenes or fails to comply with an order made under Subsection (3) is guilty of an offence.

Penalty[842]: Imprisonment for a term not exceeding six months.

(7) A person who is convicted of an offence against Subsection (6) is liable to be again removed from the part of the country specified in the order, or to be removed to the part of the country specified by the District Court, as the case may be, or a new order under this section may be made against him.

(8) For the purposes of this section –

"home", in relation to a person, means –

(a) the place (if any) where he has resided continuously during the period of five years immediately preceding the date of the offence giving rise to the conviction in respect of which a punishment under this section is being imposed; or

(b) an area of customary land on which he may by custom build or occupy a house or garden, whether in his own right or in right of his spouse or some other relation; or

(c) an area of customary land owned by a linguistic or cultural group with which he or his spouse has customary affiliations involving usage rights in land; or

---

[842] This is not an indictable offence [see section 21(b) of the *Interpretation Act* (Ch. 2)] and can be dealt with summarily [see section 22 of the *Interpretation Act* (Ch. 2)].

Refer also to the chapter titled 'Classification Of Offences' in the text titled 'Injia on Criminal Practice and Procedure in Papua New Guinea and the Pacific'.

(d) an area of land leased for a term of not less than 12 months or held in freehold by him or his spouse under a law in force in the country; or

(e) in a particular case where the provisions of Paragraph (a), (b), (c) or (d) are inapplicable –any other place with which he or his spouse has connections such that it should, in the opinion of the court, be reasonably regarded as his home;

"Probation Officer" means a probation officer appointed under the *Probation Act 1979'*.

[11.2.2] DISOBEY COURT ORDER

OFFENCES

Section 205B(6) of the *District Courts Act* (Ch. 40) states:

> 'A person who, without reasonable excuse (proof of which is on him), contravenes or fails to comply with an order made under Subsection (3) is guilty of an offence.
>
> Penalty[843]: Imprisonment for a term not exceeding six months'.

WORDING OF CHARGES

'That on **[**Date**]** at **[**Place**]** in Papua New Guinea **[**Name of Accused Person**]** without reasonable excuse did **[**contravene **or** fail to comply**]** with an order made under section 205B(3) of the *District Courts Act* (Ch. 40) by the **[**location of court**]** on **[**date that order was made**]**.'

---

[843] This is not an indictable offence [see section 21(b) of the *Interpretation Act* (Ch. 2)] and can be dealt with summarily [see section 22 of the *Interpretation Act* (Ch. 2)].

Refer also to the chapter titled 'Classification Of Offences' in the text titled 'Injia on Criminal Practice and Procedure in Papua New Guinea and the Pacific'.

SENTENCING OPTIONS

ELEMENTS

A. Date

B. Place

C. Accused Person

D. Without Reasonable Excuse

E. [1] Contravene

[2] Fail

F. Order Made Under Section 205B(3)

WITHOUT REASONABLE EXCUSE

This is a negative averment.

The onus is on the accused person to prove on the balance of probabilities that he or she had a reasonable excuse for:

- contravening; or
- failing to comply with

the order made under section 205B(3) of the *District Courts Act* (Ch. 40).[844]

COURT ORDER

When a Court makes an order against an accused person a minute or memorandum of the order shall be made and signed by the presiding Magistrate constituting the Court.[845]

---

[844] Refer also to the chapter titled 'Proof Of Issues' in the text titled 'Injia on Criminal Practice and Procedure in Papua New Guinea and the Pacific'.

[845] See section 160 of the *District Courts Act* (Ch. 40) ['Minute Of Decision To Be Made'].

See also: sections 7 ['Authentication Of Acts Of Magistrate Or Clerk'] and 161 ['Formal Convictions And Orders'].

SENTENCING OPTIONS

[12.0] SENTENCE OF DEATH

[12.1] CONSTITUTIONAL PROVISION

Section 35(1) of the *Constitution of the Independent State of Papua New Guinea* states (in part):

> 'No person shall be deprived of his life intentionally except –
>
> (a) in execution of a sentence of a court following his conviction of an offence for which the penalty of death is prescribed by law'.

[12.2] STATUTORY PROVISIONS

Section 18 of the *Criminal Code* (Ch. 262) provides that a sentence of death is a punishment that may be inflicted under that Code.

A Court has a discretion whether to impose:

- a sentence of death;
- imprisonment for life; or
- imprisonment for any shorter term for an offence for which an accused person is liable to death.[846]

[846] Section 19(1)(aa) of the *Criminal Code* (Ch. 262) states:

> 'In the construction of this Code, it is to be taken that, except when it is otherwise expressly provided –
>
> (aa) a person liable to death may be sentenced to imprisonment for life or for any shorter term'.

SENTENCING OPTIONS

Section 597 of the *Criminal Code* (Ch. 262)[847] states:

> 'Subject to Section 598, the sentence to be pronounced on a person who is convicted of a crime[848] punishable with death is that he be returned to his former custody, and that at a time and place to be appointed by the Head of State, acting on advice[849], on the mode of execution of the death sentence from any one of those stated under Section 614 Subsection (1)'.

Section 598 states:

> '(1) When a person is convicted of any crime punishable with death, except treason and wilful murder, if the court is of opinion that, under the circumstances of the case, it is proper that the offender should be recommended for mercy[850], the court may, if it thinks fit, direct the proper officer, instead of asking the offender whether he has anything to say why sentence of death should not be passed on him, to ask the offender, and that officer shall ask the offender, whether he has anything to say why judgement of death should not be recorded against him.
>
> (2) In a case referred to in Subsection (1) the court may abstain from pronouncing sentence of death, and may, instead, order judgement of death to be entered on record.
>
> (3) On an order under Subsection (2) the proper officer is to enter judgement of death on record against the offender in the usual form, as if sentence of death had actually been pronounced by the court against the offender in open court.
>
> (4) A record of a judgement of death entered under this section has the same effect as if sentence of death had been pronounced in open court'.

---

[847] As amended by the *Criminal Code (Amendment) Act 2013.*

However, this textbook was published prior to the enactment of the *Criminal Code (Amendment) Act 2013.*

[848] Refer also to the chapter titled 'Classification Of Offences' in the text titled 'Injia on Criminal Practice and Procedure in Papua New Guinea and the Pacific'.

[849] The term 'the Head of State, acting on advice' is defined in section 3(1) of the *Interpretation Act* (Ch. 2) as meaning:

> 'the Head of State, acting with, and in accordance with, the advice of the National Executive Council'.

The term 'the National Executive Council' is also defined in that section as meaning:

> 'the National Executive Council established by Section 149 (*the National Executive Council*) of the *Constitution*'.

[850] See sections 151 and 152 of the *Constitution of the Independent State of Papua New Guinea* and the *Organic Law on the Advisory Committee on the Power of Mercy.*

SENTENCING OPTIONS

Section 599 states:

'(1) When sentence of death is passed on a woman, she may apply for an order to stay execution on the ground that she is pregnant.

(2) If an application is made under Subsection (1), the court shall direct one or more medical practitioners to be sworn to examine the woman in some private place either together or successively, and to ascertain whether or not she is pregnant.

(3) If on the report of an examination conducted in pursuance of a direction under Subsection (2), verified on oath, it appears that the woman is pregnant, the court shall order that execution of the sentence be postponed until –

(a) she is delivered of a child; or

(b) it is no longer possible in the course of nature that she should be so delivered'.

Section 614[851] states:

'(1) The punishment of death shall be carried out by any one of the following methods as determined by the Head of State acting on advice from the National Executive Council

(a) hanging the offender by the neck until the person is dead; or

(b) administration of anesthetics followed by lethal injection; or

(c) medial death through anesthetic administration and deprivation of oxygen; or

(d) death via a firing squad.

(2) The time and place of execution shall be appointed by the Head of State, acting on advice.

(3) The Sheriff, or a Sheriff's officer appointed by the Sheriff, shall be present at the execution.

(4) The officer-in-charge and the proper officers of the correctional institution (including the visiting medical officer), all justices who wish to be present, and such members of the Police Force as the Sheriff or Sheriff's officer allow may also be present.

---

[851] As amended by the *Criminal Code (Amendment) Act 2013*.

However, this textbook was published prior to the enactment of the *Criminal Code (Amendment) Act 2013*.

(5) All the persons attending the execution shall remain in the enclosure until the execution has been carried out according to law, and until the visiting medical officer has signed a certificate in the following form –

"I, ... , the visiting medical officer of the ... Correctional Institution, certify that I have today witnessed the execution of ... , lately, as I am informed, convicted and duly sentenced to death by the National Court and I further certify that he was, in pursuance of the sentence, hanged by the neck until he was dead.

Dated ... 20 ...

Visiting Medical Officer."

(6) The Sheriff or Sheriff's officer, the officer-in-charge and officers of the correctional institution, and the members of the Police Force who are present shall sign, before leaving the correctional institution, a declaration in the following form adding their description –

"We declare and testify that we were this day present when the extreme penalty of the law was executed on ..., lately, as we are informed, convicted by the National Court, and duly sentenced to death on ... 20 , and that he was, in pursuance of the sentence, hanged by the neck until he was dead.

(*Signatures of Witnesses.*)"

(7) Every certificate and declaration under this section shall be transmitted by the Sheriff, Sheriff's officer, or deputy of the Sheriff, whichever of them is present at the execution, to the Registrar of the National Court and shall be entered and kept in his office as a record of the Court, and a copy of it is to be twice published in the National Gazette.

(8) The body of the offender shall be buried at such place as the Head of State, acting on advice, directs'.

[12.3] GENERAL PRINCIPLES[852]

In Papua New Guinea a sentence of death is constitutionally valid.[853]

[852] See also: section 16 of the Office of the Public Prosecutor Prosecution Policy (2006).

[853] See *Steven Loke Ume, Charles Patrick Kaona and Greg Wawa Kavoa v The State* (2006) SC836, [2006] PGSC 9 and *Alois Erebebe and Taros Togot v The State* (2013) SC1228.

See also: *Ernest Lockhart v R* [2011] UKPC 33.

However, the death penalty should not be imposed on a mentally impaired person.[854]

The death penalty is prescribed for the following offences:

- 'Piracy', section 81 of the *Criminal Code* (Ch. 262);
- 'Attempted Piracy', section 82 of the *Criminal Code* (Ch. 262);
- 'Treason', section 37 of the *Criminal Code* (Ch. 262);
- 'Wilful Murder', section 299(2) of the *Criminal Code* (Ch. 262).

  The death penalty may be considered appropriate in a wilful murder case which is the premeditated, vicious and brutal killing in cold blood of:

  - an innocent and defenceless or harmless person; or
  - a person in authority or position of responsibility in the community,

  with complete and blatant disregard for the sanctity of human life and for which there is no motive or lawful motive for taking away the life of another person.[855]

  The killing is 'unthinkable', 'consciousless', 'senseless', 'pitiless' and 'unnecessarily torturous'[856];
- 'Wilful Murder Of A Person On Account Of Accusation Of Sorcery', section 229A of the *Criminal Code* (Ch. 262)[857];

---

[854] See *R v Pritchard* (1836) 7 C & P 303.

See also: Blackstone's Commentaries on the Laws of England, Lord Hale's Pleas of the Crown and *Atkins v Virginia* (2002) 536 US 304.

[855] See *Steven Loke Ume, Charles Patrick Kaona and Greg Wawa Kavoa v The State* (2006) SC836, [2006] PGSC 9 and *Alois Erebebe and Taros Togot v The State* (2013) SC1228, [2013] PGSC 9.

[856] See *Steven Loke Ume, Charles Patrick Kaona and Greg Wawa Kavoa v The State* (2006) SC836, [2006] PGSC 9 and *Alois Erebebe and Taros Togot v The State* (2013) SC1228, [2013] PGSC 9.

[857] As amended by the *Criminal Code (Amendment) Act 2013*.

However, this textbook was published prior to the enactment of the *Criminal Code (Amendment) Act 2013*.

- 'Aggravated Rape', section 347A of the *Criminal Code* (Ch. 262)[858]; and
- 'Robbery', section 386 of the *Criminal Code* (Ch.262)[859].

The death penalty has been imposed in the following cases:

- *Alois Erebebe and Taros Togot v The State* (2013) SC1228, [2013] PGSC 9
- *Manu Kovi v The State* (2005) SC789, [2005] PGSC 34
- *The State v Gregory Kiapkot and others* (2011) N4381, [2011] PGNC 108
- *The State v Clarence Tema Mongi* (2007) N3259, [2007] PGNC 135
- *The State v Sedoki Lota and Fred Abenko* (2007) N3183, [2007] PGNC 167
- *The State v Mark Poroli* (2004) N2655
- *The State v Ben Simakot Simbu (No. 2)* (2004) N2546
- *The State v Kepak Langa* (2003) N2462
- *The State v Arua Maraga Hariki* (2002) N2332
- *The State v Ambrose Lati (No. 2)* (2009) N3740, [2009] PGNC 121

---

858 As amended by the *Criminal Code (Amendment) Act 2013*.

However, this textbook was published prior to the enactment of the *Criminal Code (Amendment) Act 2013*.

859 As amended by the *Criminal Code (Amendment) Act 2013*.

However, this textbook was published prior to the enactment of the *Criminal Code (Amendment) Act 2013*.

AGGRAVATING FACTORS

[1.0] INTRODUCTION

Whilst a Court[860] should advise an accused person that the 'mitigating factors[861]' and 'extenuating circumstances[862]' will result in a reduced sentence, it should also advise the accused person that the 'aggravating factors' will result in:

> a more severe sentence than would otherwise be imposed.

The more mitigating factors that are present, the more likely it is that the head sentence will be reduced. The more aggravating factors present, the more likely it is the head sentence will be lifted above the starting point. However, sentencing is not an exact science. It is a discretionary process. When a factor is marked as mitigating or aggravating it does not mean necessarily that it is given the same weight as another mitigating or aggravating factor. Some mitigating factors may be 'strongly mitigating'. Others maybe 'mildly mitigating'. The same goes for aggravating factors.[863]

It is the duty of a defence legal representative to advise the accused person as to the effect of mitigating factors, extenuating circumstances and aggravating factors.

Where an accused person is unrepresented, the Court should take on that responsibility before the administration of the *allocatus*.

A Court can only take into account aggravating factors if it is satisfied of the existence of such factors 'beyond reasonable doubt'.[864]

Aggravating factors include:

- the seriousness of the offence generally;
- the prevalence of the offence;
- whether the offence involved the carrying of, using or threatening to use a weapon;

---

[860] See *R v Aroride* [1999] 2 Cr App R (S) 406 and *R v Fearon* [1996] 2 Cr App R (S) 25.

[861] Refer also to the chapter titled 'Mitigating Factors'.

[862] Refer also to the chapter titled 'Extenuating Circumstances'.

[863] See *The State v Paul Nelson* (2005) N2844 and *The State v Jacky Moses* (2012) N4886, [2012] PGNC 213.

[864] See *R v Olbrich* (1999) 199 CLR 270, [1999] HCA 54; *R v Storey* [1998] 1 VR 359 at 369 and *Law v The State of Western Australia* [2009] WASCA 193.

AGGRAVATING FACTORS

- whether there was a breach of trust;
- the accused person's character and antecedents, including prior criminal history and bad character;
- the duration of the offence;
- whether the offence occurred in the night-time;
- whether the consumption of alcohol influenced the actions of the accused person;
- the age difference between the accused person and the victim;
- whether the accused person showed no remorse;
- whether the accused person was a law enforcement officer;
- whether the accused person was a member of a gang that committed the offence;
- whether the accused person provided leadership in a gang that committed the offence;
- whether there was any preplanning;
- whether the offence involved an attack on a law enforcement officer;
- whether there were multiple or a repeated sustained activity over a period of time; and
- whether the offence involved viciousness or a deliberate intention to harm or injure.

AGGRAVATING FACTORS

The following should not be considered as an aggravating factor:

- the entering of a plea of not guilty.[865]

  An accused person should be entitled to plead not guilty and to defend himself or herself without attracting the risk of a higher penalty.[866]

  A sentence should not be increased in order to mark the Court's disapproval of an accused person for having put the issues to proof[867]; and

- how a particular defence was conducted[868].

  A sentence should not be increased in order to mark the Court's disapproval of an accused person for having presented a time-wasting or even a scurrilous defence.[869]

---

865 See *R v Cervetto and Ibara; ex parte Madaha* [1965-66] PNGLR 110, [1965] PGSC 8; *Siganto v R* (1998) 194 CLR 656 at 663, (1998) 105 A Crim R 184, [1998] HCA 74; *Cameron v R* (2002) 209 CLR 339, (2002) 76 ALJR 382, [2002] HCA 6; *Castlemaine Tooheys Ltd v South Australia* (1990) 169 CLR 436 at 478-479; *R v Gray* [1977] VR 225 at 231; *R v David Dickson Jabaltjari* (1989) 64 NTR 1, [1989] NTSC 38, per Asche CJ; *R v Richmond* [1920] VLR 9, per Cussen J at 12; *H v The State of Western Australia* (2006) 163 A Crim R 151, [2006] WASCA 53; *R v Harper* [1968] 2 QB 108 at 110 and *Hryczszyn v R* [1976] Tas SR 10 at 13-14.

See however: *The State v Eddy Kava Laura (No. 2)* [1988-89] PNGLR 98; *Emil Kongian and others v The State* (2007) SC928, [2007] PGSC 45; *The State v Steven Molu Minji and others; The State v Didi Gelwak Sakol (No. 2)* (2009) N3794, [2009] PGNC 177; *The State v Simam July Melly (No. 2)* (2009) N3779, [2009] PGNC 138; *The State v Steven Tabogani and others* (2008) N3559, [2008] PGNC 194; *The State v Amos Young* (2008) N3548, [2008] PGNC 212; *The State v Upano Manake (No. 2)* (2006) N3504, [2006] PGNC 174; *The State v Jimmy Ketu (No. 2)* (2007) N3394, [2007] PGNC 153; *The State v Wesley Ignas* [2007] PGNC 115; *The State v Alexander Junior Nara (No. 2)* (2007) N3214, [2007] PGNC 86; *The State v Richard Saku and others* (2006) N3284, [2006] PGNC 162; *The State v John Wanimba and others* (2005) N2863, [2005] PGNC 108; *The State v Steven Mul Mangi (No. 2)* (2005) N2993, [2005] PGNC 12; *The State v Iori Veraga* (2005) N2921, [2005] PGNC 43; *The State v Henry Nandiro (No. 2)* (2004) N2668; *The State v Donald Poni* (2004) N2663; *The State v Eki Kondi and others* (2004) N2543; *The State v Cherobim Kani Peso* (2003) N2412; *The State v Micky John Lausi* (2001) N2073;.

866 See *Siganto v R* (1998) 194 CLR 656 at 663, (1998) 105 A Crim R 184, [1998] HCA 74.

867 See *R v Gray* [1977] VR 225 at 231.

868 See *R v Harper* [1968] 2 QB 108 at 110 and *Hryczszyn v R* [1976] Tas SR 10 at 13-14.

869 See *R v Gray* [1977] VR 225 at 231.

AGGRAVATING FACTORS

[2.0] CIRCUMSTANCE OF AGGRAVATION[870]

If a 'circumstance of aggravation'[871] is to be taken into account for the purpose of increasing the maximum sentence above what it would otherwise be then it must be:

- specified or particularised in the charge and proven 'beyond reasonable doubt[872]' as an element of the charge[873]; or

- admitted on a plea of guilty upon a Court accepting the plea[874] and entering a conviction[875] or otherwise found guilty beyond reasonable doubt[876].

---

[870] As regards the law in relation to 'Wording Of Charges', refer to the chapter titled 'Charges' in the text titled 'Injia on Criminal Practice and Procedure in Papua New Guinea and the Pacific'.

[871] As defined in section 1(1) of the *Criminal Code* (Ch. 262).

As regards the law in relation to 'Wording Of Charges', refer to the chapter titled 'Charges' in the text titled 'Injia on Criminal Practice and Procedure in Papua New Guinea and the Pacific'.

[872] Refer also to the chapter titled 'Proof Of Issues' in the text titled 'Injia on Criminal Practice and Procedure in Papua New Guinea and the Pacific'.

[873] See *Paul Palma v The State* (2008) SC1214, [2008] PGSC 56; *The State v Marcus Yame* (2010) N4131; *The State v Dibol Petrus Kopal* (2004) N2778 and *The State v James Yali* (2006) N2989, [2006] PGNC 26.

See also: *R v Bright* [1916] 2 KB 441 and *R v De Simoni* (1981) 147 CLR 383, per Gibbs CJ at 389, [1981] HCA 31.

[874] Refer also the subsection titled 'Plea Of Guilty' in the section titled 'Taking Of A Plea' in the chapter titled 'Court Procedure' in the text titled 'Injia on Criminal Practice and Procedure in Papua New Guinea and the Pacific'.

[875] See *SCR No. 2 of 1981; Re s19(1)(f) Criminal Code (Ch. 262)* [1982] PNGLR 150, per Kearney J at 156, [1982] PGSC 18; *R v Ebulya* [1964] PNGLR 200, per Smithers J at 231 and *The State v Binga Thomas* (2005) N2828, [2005] PGNC 189.

[876] See *Jack Mari v The State* (2007) SC 1147, [2007] PGSC 49; *The State v Michael Butemo Jiregari* [1984] PNGLR 62; *The State v Dibol Petrus Kopal* (2004) N2778; *The State v Binga Thomas* (2005) N2828; *The State v James Yali* (2006) N2989 and *The State v Jeffery Wangi* (2006) N3016.

See also: sections 528 ['Form Of Indictment'] and 538 ['Offences Involving Circumstances Of Aggravation'] of the *Criminal Code* (Ch. 262).

Refer also to the chapter titled 'Proof Of Issues' in the text titled 'Injia on Criminal Practice and Procedure in Papua New Guinea and the Pacific'.

AGGRAVATING FACTORS

If a circumstance of aggravation is not specified or particularised in a charge, it may nonetheless be taken into account as an aggravating factor when deciding on a sentence within the allowable range.[877]

However, a circumstance of aggravation must not be taken into account:

- if it constitutes a separate offence with which the accused person has not been convicted[878];
- if it does not form part of the offence with which the accused person has been convicted[879]; or
- if the accused person has not asked it to be taken into consideration in accordance with the procedure as set out in section 603 of the *Criminal Code* (Ch. 262)[880].[881]

[3.0] SERIOUSNESS OF AN OFFENCE GENERALLY

Assessment of and the attribution of due weight to the objective gravity of an offence is fundamental to the sentencing process.[882]

---

[877] See *The State v Marcus Yame* (2010) N4131 and *The State v Mark Samuel Haupas* (2007) N3186, [2007] PGNC 81.

[878] See *R v De Simoni* (1981) 147 CLR 383 at 389, [1981] HCA 31.

[879] See *John Baipu v The State* (2005) SC796, [2005] PGSC 19 and *Ben Wafia and others v The State* (2006) SC851, [2006] PGSC 19.

See also: *Lane v Auckland City Council* [1975] 1 NZLR 353 and *R v Pattison* (2002) 19 CRNZ 407.

[880] Refer also to the chapter titled 'Outstanding Charges'.

[881] See *John Baipu v The State* (2005) SC796, [2005] PGSC 19 and *Ben Wafia and others v The State* (2006) SC851, [2006] PGSC 19.

See also: *Lane v Auckland City Council* [1975] 1 NZLR 353 and *R v Pattison* (2002) 19 CRNZ 407.

[882] See *Markarian v R* (2005) 228 CLR 357, (2005) 215 ALR 213, [2005] HCA 25; *R v Geddes* (1936) 36 SR (NSW) 554; *R v Khoury* [2011] NSWCCA 118; *R v Dodd* (1991) 57 A Crim R 349 at 354; *R v Gordon* (1994) 71 A Crim R 459 at 468 and *R v Cage* [2006] NSWCCA 304.

See also: *Mulato v R* [2006] NSWCCA 282.

AGGRAVATING FACTORS

The seriousness of an offence can be reflected by:

- the maximum sentence that may be imposed.[883]

  It represents the legislature's assessment of the seriousness of the offence and for this reason provides a sentencing yardstick.[884]

  Whilst prima facie the seriousness of an offence is reflected by what the law imposes as the maximum punishment[885], the other applicable aggravating factors and any 'mitigating factors[886]' and 'extenuating circumstances[887]' will assist a Court in determining the degree of seriousness for the offence in question[888].

  However, a Court dealing on indictment with a matter which was capable of summary disposal may have regard to that fact on sentence[889], but it is not a factor that operates universally to reduce a sentence[890].

  The significance of the loss of a chance to be dealt with summarily will vary from case to case[891];

---

[883] Refer also to the chapter titled 'Maximum Sentence'.

[884] See *Muldrock v R* (2011) 244 CLR 120 at 133, [2001] HCA 39 and *Elias v R; Issa v R* [2013] HCA 31.

[885] See *Koniel Alar and Hosea Biu v The State* [1979] PNGLR 300, [1979] PGSC 4; *The Public Prosecutor v Vangu'u Ame* [1983] PNGLR 424, [1983] PGSC 23; *Jack Tanga v The State* [1999] PNGLR 216; *Ruddy Yekat v The State* [2000] PNGLR 225, (2000) SC665 and *Ian Napoleon Setep v The State* (2001) SC666, [2001] PGSC 14.

See also: *Tamana v R* [1995] SBHC 42; *Hola v R* [1993] SBHC 9; *R v Tait and Bartley* (1979) 24 ALR 473 at 483-484; *Ibbs v R* (1987) 163 CLR 447, (1987) 61 ALJR 525 at 527, (1987) 74 ALR 1 at 5, [1987] HCA 46 and *Gilson v R* (1991) 172 CLR 353 at 364, [1991] HCA 24.

[886] Refer also to the chapter titled 'Mitigating Factors'.

[887] Refer also to the chapter titled 'Extenuating Circumstances'.

[888] See The Law Reform Commission of Ireland, 1996, 'Report of Sentencing', paragraph 3.6.

[889] See *R v El Masri* [2005] NSWCCA 167; *R v Sandford* (1994) 72 A Crim R 160 at 195; *R v Griggs* (1999) 109 A Crim R 484 at 485-486, [1999] NSWCCA 381; *R v LPY* (2002) 135 A Crim R 237 at 240, [2002] NSWCCA 464 and *Dagdanasar v R* [2010] NSWCCA 310.

[890] See *R v Sandford* (1994) 72 A Crim R 160 at 195; *R v El Masri* [2005] NSWCCA 167 and *Dagdanasar v R* [2010] NSWCCA 310.

[891] See *R v Depoma* [2003] NSWCCA 382.

- the range of sentences that have been imposed[892];

- the value of property involved in the commission of the offence[893] and whether it has been recovered[894];

- the extent and nature of injuries suffered by a victim as a consequence of the commission of the offence[895];

- the location where the offence occurred[896];

- whether the victim was weak, defenceless or vulnerable.

  Offences against weak, defenceless or vulnerable persons are, in principle, worse than offences against persons who might have a real, in principle, opportunity of defending themselves or escaping the consequences of the offending behaviour because there is disparity between the positions of the accused person and the victim[897];

- the effect of the offence on the victim.

---

[892] Refer also to the chapter titled 'Comparative Sentences'.

[893] See *The State v Oa Seseka* (1990) N921.

See also: *R v Topilu* [1995] SBHC 7.

[894] See *The State v Philip Saku and others* (2011) N4355, [2011] PGNC 78.

[895] See *The State v Grace John (No. 3)* (2011) N4371, [2011] PGNC 104; *The State v Fidelis Kiatni* (2011) N4331, [2011] PGNC 67; *The State v Dilu Kimam* (2011) N4323, [2011] PGNC 58; *The State v Jacob Aku Matai* (2011) N4256, [2011] PGNC 26; *The State v Billy Turmur and Sou Mesak* (2011) N4349, [2011] PGNC 92 and *The State v Peter Jai* (2011) 4391.

See also: *DPP (Victoria) v Cook* (2004) 141 A Crim R 579, per Eames JA at 586-587; *R v Webb* [1971] VR 147; *R v Malinder* (1986) 23 A Crim R 179; *R v Funifaka and others* [1997] SBHC 31 and *Kwaifanabo and Kwatebeo v DPP* (Solomon Islands Criminal Appeal Case No. 16 of 1984).

[896] See *The State v Fanundi Badi Moibamo (No. 3)* (2011) N4372, [2011] PGNC 105.

[897] See The Law Reform Commission of Ireland, 1993, 'Consultation Paper on Sentencing', paragraph 5.35.

In determining sentence, any detrimental, prejudicial or deleterious effect that may have been produced on the victim by the commission of the offence should be taken into consideration.[898]

The suffering of psychological problems by a victim, especially in relation to sexual offences, is an aggravating factor.[899] This is of particular significance due to general unavailability of appropriate medical services in Papua New Guinea.[900]

However, the distress caused to a victim by having to give evidence should not be taken into account as an 'aggravating factor'[901], although it is a factor to be taking into account when considering what reduction in sentence should be given to an accused person who has pleaded guilty because the victim does not have to relive the trauma of the offence in the witness box[902];

- whether the offence was committed for pleasure or excitement.

---

[898] See *R v Webb* [1971] VR 147 at 151 and *Porter v R* [2008] NSWCCA 145.

Refer also to the chapter titled 'Victim Impact Statement'.

[899] See *Lawrence Hindemba v The State* (1998) SC593, [1999] PGSC 48; *The State v Ereman Kepas* (2007) N3192, [2007] PGNC 77; *The State v Alexander Junior Nara (No. 2)* (2007) N3214, [2007] PGNC 86; *The State v Damien Mangawi* (2003) N2419; *The State v Otto Paulus* (2002) N2241; *The State v Joe Sime* [2006] PGNC 73; *The State v Pais Steven Sow* (2004) N2588; *The State v Maxon Nanguan* (2009) N3689, [2009] PGNC 82; *The State v Kiddi Sorari* (2004) N2553; *The State v Philip Soni and Tony Ilong* (2008) N3694, [2008] PGNC 237 and *The State v Tonny Kupin* (2009) N3641.

See also: *Stanley Bade v R* [1988-1989] SILR 121 at 125.

[900] See *The State v Peter Yawoma* (2001) N2032 and *The State v Donald Angavia and others* (2004) N2590.

[901] See *Siganto v R* (1998) 194 CLR 656 at 663, (1998) 105 A Crim R 184, [1998] HCA 74 and *Harris v R* [1967] SASR 316 at 328.

[902] See *The State v Chan Alois And Augustine Tutut* (2008) N3668, [2008] PGNC 180 and *The State v Tonny Kupin* (2009) N3641.

See also:
- *Burenikarawa v R* [2006] SBCA 4 and *R v Churches* [2002] NZCA 78; and
- The Law Reform Commission of Ireland, 1993, 'Consultation Paper on Sentencing', paragraph 5.79.

Inherent in this factor is the notion that accused persons who commit offences merely for 'thrills' or for 'kicks' show complete disregard of accepted community standards and the law.[903]

Their behaviour is the most wanton and flagrant breach of the law imaginable, and their conduct is deliberate, calculated, wholly unjustifiable and inexcusable[904]; and

- whether the offence was committed whilst on bail which reveals a blatant disregard for the law.[905]

[4.0] PREVALENCE OF THE OFFENCE

The prevalence of a particular offence must play some part in the sentencing process, particularly in emphasising the importance of:

- general deterrence[906]; and
- denunciation[907].[908]

[903] See The Law Reform Commission of Ireland, 1993, 'Consultation Paper on Sentencing', paragraph 5.42.

[904] See The Law Reform Commission of Ireland, 1993, 'Consultation Paper on Sentencing', paragraph 5.42.

[905] See *Pop v R* (2000) 116 A Crim R 398, [2000] WASCA 283; *Colangelo v The State of Western Australia* [2004] WASCA 294; *The State of Western Australia v Wynne* (2008) 188 A Crim R 502, [2008] WASCA 195 and *The State of Western Australia v Atherton* (2009) 197 A Crim R 119, [2009] WASCA 148.

[906] Refer also to the section titled 'The Need For Deterrence' in the chapter titled 'Objectives And Purposes Of Sentencing'.

[907] Refer also to the chapter titled 'Objectives And Purposes Of Sentencing'.

[908] See *R v Peterson* [1984] WAR 329, per Burt CJ at 332; *Giles v Barnes* [1967] SASR 174; *Braslin and Cowen v Tasmania* [2010] TASCCA 1 and *R v Downie and Dandy* [1998] 2 VR 517, per Calloway JA at 520-522.

AGGRAVATING FACTORS

Where an offence is prevalent the Courts must be severe in their punishment[909], but should not make one accused person a scapegoat for others.[910]

The circumstances of:

- the offence; and
- the accused person

must also be given due weight.[911]

Youthful accused persons[912] should not receive special treatment where the offence charged is prevalent.[913]

The assertion of increased prevalence may be borne out by:

- an analysis of the Court records[914]; and
- other information[915].

---

[909] See *Paulus Mandatititip and another v The State* [1978] PNGLR 128, [1978] PGSC 5 and *Kali Mari v The State* (1980) SC175.

[910] See *Wilkeson v Grant; Stephens v Grant; Michalov v The State* [1967-68] PNGLR 112, [1967] PGSC 47.

[911] See *Wilkeson v Grant; Stephens v Grant; Michalov v The State* [1967-68] PNGLR 112, [1967] PGSC 47.

[912] Refer also to the section titled 'Youthfulness' in the chapter titled 'Mitigating Factors'.

[913] See *Rakatani v The State* [1979] PNGLR 556, [1979] PGSC 21; *Paulus Mandatititip and another v The State* [1978] PNGLR 128, [1978] PGSC 5; *Peter Naibiri and Kutoi Soti Apia v The State* (1978) SC178 and *The State v Donald Angavia and others* (2004) N2590.

[914] See *Braslin and Cowen v Tasmania* [2010] TASCCA 1.

[915] See *HKSAR v Ma Suet-chun* [2001] 4 HKC 337.

AGGRAVATING FACTORS

The following offences have been held to be prevalent:

- Arson[916];
- Break and Enter[917];
- Conspiracy To Defraud[918];
- Dangerous Driving Causing Death[919];
- False Pretences[920];
- Forgery[921];
- Grievous Bodily Harm[922];
- Grievous Bodily Harm with Intent[923];

---

916 See *The State v Prodie Akoi and Steven Akoi* (2004) N2584 [Sepik and Highlands Provinces] and *The State v Robin Warren and others (No. 2)* (2003) N2418.

917 See *Mandatititip v The State* [1978] PNGLR 128, [1978] PGSC 5; *Bakiri Pena v The State* (1980) SC183, [1980] PGSC 2; *Acting Public Prosecutor v Mailai* [1981] PNGLR 258, [1981] PGSC 7; *Acting Public Prosecutor v Kasen* (1981) SC205, [1981] PGSC 4; *The State v Michael Kamban Mani* (2002) N2246; *The State v Jonah Yohang Monalen* (2004) N2677 and *The State v Ian Bob Wali* (2004) N2580.

918 See *The State v Martha Agua* (2011) N4499, [2011] PGNC 207.

919 See *The State v Philip Iparu* (2005) N2995, [2005] PGNC 11.

920 See *The State v John Bolkun* (2012) N4689, [2012] PGNC 75.

921 See *The State v Andrew Aopo Lengade* (2012) N4690, [2012] PGNC 76.

922 See *The State v Maggie Rumints* (2012) N4900, [2012] PGNC 275; *The State v Willie Boi and Ikupu Iru* (2012) N4781, PGNC 204; *The State v Iso Bamaru* (2006) N3390, [2006] PGNC 168; *The State v Peter Mol* (2008) N3707, [2008] PGNC 239; *The State v Tamumei Lawrence and others* (2006) N3117, [2007] PGNC 17 and *The State v Ambe Tu* (2008) N3306, [2008] PGNC 37.

923 See *The State v Oliver Toluana and Penias Kivung (*2011) N4417, [2011] PGNC 138 and *The State v Peter Pepa* (2010) N4146.

AGGRAVATING FACTORS

- Harbouring Escaped Prisoner[924];
- Incest[925];
- Killings on the High Seas[926];
- Manslaughter[927];
- Misappropriation[928];
- Murder[929];
- Persistent Sexual Abuse of a Child[930];

---

924 See *The State v Collin Paino; The State v David Paino; The State v Michael Paino and The State v Rose Todi Paino* (2007) N3199, [2007] PGNC 88.

925 See *The State v Sevi Kwetok* (2006) N3389, [2006] PGNC 167; *The State v Michael Siwiri* (2006) N3382, [2006] PGNC 172; *The State v Tom Feri* (2008) N3305, [2008] PGNC 30; *The State v Francis Angosiwen (No. 2)* (2004) N2670 and *The State v Samuel Kawar* (2011) N4234, [2011] PGNC 22.

926 See *The State v Selmon Amos and Misialsi Amos (No. 3)* (2012) N5073, [2012] PGNC 289.

927 See *Sakarowa Koe v The State* (2004) SC739, [2004] PGSC 33; *The State v Wamaong Robert* (2010) N4065, [2010] PGNC 100; *The State v Peter Wanam* (2010) N3981, [2010] PGNC 31; *The State v Juvenile 'D'* (2008) N3508, [2008] PGNC 153; *The State v Tony Dom* (2012) N4767, [2012] PGNC 97 and *The State v Jackson Peng* (2012) N4737, [2012] PGNC 110.

928 See *The State v Tony Baik* (1999) N1930; *The State v Alice Wilmot* (2005) N2857, [2005] PGNC 105; *The State v Imoi Maino* (2004) N2773; *The State v Simam July Melly (No. 2)* (2009) N3779, [2009] PGNC 138; *The State v David Kang* (2009) N3603, [2009] PGNC 47 and *The State v Peman Etami* (2012) N4769, [2012] PGNC 96.

929 See *Joseph Enn v The State* (2004) SC738; *Simon Kama v The State* (2004) SC740, [2004] PGSC 32; *The State v Ladimat Kilala and others* (2012) N5080, [2012] PGNC 282; *The State v Philip Eki Vaki* (2007) N3464, [2007] PGNC 163; *The State v Charlie Langu (No. 2)* (2004) N2652; *The State v Paul Potape Huliya* (2005) N2872, [2005] PGNC 77 and *The State v Baika Martin and others* (2008) N3312, [2008] PGNC 29.

930 See *The State v Ben Sakias* (2011) N4238, [2011] PGNC 37.

AGGRAVATING FACTORS

- Rape[931];
- Receiving[932];
- Robbery[933];
- sexual abuse of children generally[934];
- sexual offences generally[935];
- Sexual Penetration[936];
- Sexual Touching[937];

---

[931] See *Lawrence Hindemba v The State* (1998) SC593, [1999] PGSC 48; *John Aubuku v The State* [1987] PNGLR 267; *The State v Kenneth Penias* [1004] PNGLR 48; *James Mora Maeoa v The State* [1986] PNGLR 280; *The State v Ludwig Camilus* (2009) N3760, [2009] PGNC 144; *The State v Lucas Dabo and Alista Gele* [2006] PGNC 97; *The State v Henry Nandiro (No. 2)* (2004) N2668; *The State v Bernard Nanau Porai* (2005) N2944, [2005] PGNC 30; *The State v Donald Poni* (2004) N2663; *The State v Siro Waida* (2008) N3311, [2008] PGNC 38; *The State v Dilu Kimam* (2011) N4323, [2011] PGNC 58; *The State v Jacob Aku Matai* (2011) N4256, [2011] PGNC 26; *The State v Billy Turmur and Sou Mesak* (2011) N4349, [2011] PGNC 92; *The State v Nick Teptep and Kindis Mis* (2004) N2612 and *The State v Clarence Tema Mongi* (2011) N4364, [2011] PGNC 88.

[932] See *The State v Tony Mwayawa* (2008) N3557, [2008] PGNC 199.

[933] See *Bobolan Mebu Peter v The State* (2007) SC894, [2007] PGSC 28; *Richard Liri v The State* (2007) SC883, [2007] PGSC 3; *The State v Clinton Tikambari* (2011) N4553, [2011] PGNC 224; *The State v Petrus Abai* (2010) N4132, [2010] PGNC 137; *The State v Patrick Puppy Kaikara Loavi* (2006) N3384, [2006] PGNC 104; *The State v Jackson Nimai* (2008) N3355, [2008] PGNC 72; *The State v Andrew Nane John (No. 2)* (2007) N3197, [2007] PGNC 84; *The State v Philip Eki Vaki* (2007) N3464, [2007] PGNC 163; *The State v Nipi Beo Bayu* [2006] PGNC 96; *The State v Vincent Malara* (2002) N2188 and *The State v Paul Maima Yogol and Dama Teiye* (2004) N2583.

[934] See *The State v Arthur Tangi (No. 3)* (2012) N5075, [2012] PGNC 280.

[935] See *The State v David Kang* (2009) N3603, [2009] PGNC 47; *The State v Simam July Melly (No. 2)* (2009) N3779, [2009] PGNC 138 and *The State v Chris Nawa (No. 2)* (2009) N3732, [2009] PGNC 11.

[936] See *The State v Siro Waida* (2008) N3311, [2008] PGNC 38 and *The State v Bernard Soeka Hela* (2012) N4788, [2012] PGNC 228.

[937] See *The State v Tala John* (2012) N4630, [2012] PGNC 197; *The State v George Philip* (2012) N4829, [2012] PGNC 165; *The State v Jack Andy* (2012) N4779, [2012] PGNC 227; *The State v Brady Meki* (2006) N3391, [2006] PGNC 169; *The State v Wasa David Warifa* (2008) N3308, [2008] PGNC 32 and *The State v Garry Pokas* (2011) N4375, [2011] PGNC 106.

AGGRAVATING FACTORS

- Stealing[938];
- Stealing as a Servant[939];
- unlawful killings generally[940];
- Unlawful Use of a Motor Vehicle[941];
- violent offences generally[942]; and
- Wilful Murder[943].

[5.0] DURATION OF AN OFFENCE

The duration of an offence may be considered as an aggravating factor depending on the circumstances of the offence.[944]

---

938 See *Public Prosecutor v Aia and Pino* [1978] PGSC 2; [1978] PNGLR 224; *Seo Ross v The State* (1999) SC605, [1999] PGSC 10; *The State v Simam July Melly (No. 2)* (2009) N3779, [2009] PGNC 138; *The State v Johnson Maurani* (2008) N3560, [2008] PGNC 191; *The State v Allan Nareti and Amstrong Kupe* (2004) N2582 and *The State v David Kang* (2009) N3603, [2009] PGNC 47.

939 See *Secretary for Law v Linhardt* [1975] PNGLR 132, [1975] PGSC 33 and *The State v Neville Miria* (2013) N5102, [2013] PGNC 37.

940 See *Simon Kama v The State* (2004) SC740, [2004] PGSC 32; *The State v Wesley Ignas* [2007] PGNC 115; *The State v Timothy Diwa* (2005) N3381, [2005] PGNC 184; *The State v Jimmy Ketu (No. 2)* (2007) N3394, [2007] PGNC 153 and *The State v Carol Alfred* (2009) N3602, [2009] PGNC 143.

941 See *The State v Thomas Wakai and others* (2006) N3360, [2006] PGNC 165.

942 See *Public Prosecutor v Goina, Vele, Leva and Wari* (1982) SC230, [1982] PGSC 4; *Max Java v The State* (2002) SC701; *Mary Bomai Michael v The State* (2004) SC737, [2004] PGSC 37; *Joseph Nimagi, Tom Gurua Kerui and David Bawai Laiam v The State* (2004) SC741, [2004] PGSC 31; *Kepa Wanege v The State* (2004) SC742, [2004] PGSC 22; *The State v Charles Langu (No. 2)* (2004) N2652 and *The State v Ladimat Kilala and others* (2012) N5080, [2012] PGNC 282.

943 See *The State v Clarence Tema Mongi* (2007) N3259, [2007] PGNC 135.

944 See *Wellington Belawa v The State* [1988-89] PNGLR 496, [1988] PGSC 6; *The State v Henry Matatenge* (2007) N3218, [2007] PGNC 59; *The State v Oa Seseka* (1990) N921; *The State v Penias Mokei* (2002) N2635 and *The State v Isaac Kuila (No. 2)* (2009) N3736, [2009] PGNC 110.

See also: *R v Topilu* [1995] SBHC 7 and *R v Farobo* (Solomon Islands Criminal Case No. 19 of 1986).

AGGRAVATING FACTORS

[6.0] CARRYING, USING OR THREATENING TO USE A WEAPON

The use of a weapon in the commission of an offence will generally be considered as an aggravating factor.[945]

It is clear that an accused person who uses violence to further an offence should be considered more culpable than other accused persons who commit the same offence without violence. Not only are those accused persons flagrantly defying the law, but they are also prepared to defy it still further to ensure success or non-detection.[946]

However, the carrying and threatened use of a weapon should also be viewed as a factor which aggravates culpability.[947]

The carrying of a weapon aggravates culpability because:

- it indicates that the accused person:
  - contemplated the use of violence; and
  - had prepared himself or herself for it,

  unless there is a credible excuse of self-protection against an anticipated attack;
- it makes it more likely that violence will result – thus the harm risked by the accused person is greater and the seriousness of the offence is aggravated; and
- a person faced by an accused person with a weapon is at a great disadvantage and this disparity should be viewed as more serious than offences where the parties meet on equal terms.[948]

---

[945] See *Manu Kovi v The State* (2005) SC789, [2005] PGSC 34; *Acting Public Prosecutor v Don Hale* (1998) SC564; *Ivoro Kaumin Lupu v The State* (1997) SCRA No. 2 of 1997 and *Hawai John v The State* (1998) SCR No. 9 of 1995.

See also: *R v Durbarree* (1968) 52 Cr App R 238.

[946] See The Law Reform Commission of Ireland, 1993, 'Consultation Paper on Sentencing', paragraph 5.38.

[947] See The Law Reform Commission of Ireland, 1993, 'Consultation Paper on Sentencing', paragraph 5.40.

[948] See The Law Reform Commission of Ireland, 1993, 'Consultation Paper on Sentencing', paragraph 5.40.

AGGRAVATING FACTORS

[7.0] BREACH OF TRUST

People who occupy a position of confidence or trust are in such positions on condition that they maintain that confidence or trust.[949]

If an accused person takes advantage of that position to further personal ends then:

- he or she not only commits the offence charged; but also
- breaches the trust placed in him or her by:
    - society; and
    - the victims of the offence.[950]

Such breaches are also usually deliberate, thus they indicate a high degree of intent.[951]

Therefore, the commission of an offence that involved a breach of trust will generally be considered as an aggravating factor.[952]

The higher the position of trust, the greater the responsibility.[953]

Breach of trust is of the most severe kind where sexual abuse takes place in a homely environment.[954]

---

[949] See The Law Reform Commission of Ireland, 1993, 'Consultation Paper on Sentencing', paragraph 5.36.

[950] See The Law Reform Commission of Ireland, 1993, 'Consultation Paper on Sentencing', paragraph 5.36.

[951] See The Law Reform Commission of Ireland, 1993, 'Consultation Paper on Sentencing', paragraph 5.36.

[952] See *Wellington Belawa v The State* [1988-89] PNGLR 496, [1988] PGSC 6 and *James Mova Meaoa v The State* [1996] PNGLR 280.

See also: *Edward Fiuadi v R* [1988-1989] SILR 150 at 152.

As regards incest cases, see *Mitige Neheye v The State; Martin Gawi v The State* [1994] PNGLR 71.

[953] See *The State v Oa Seseka* (1990) N921.

[954] See *The State v Arthur Tangi (No. 3)* (2012) N5075, [2012] PGNC 280.

A sentence of imprisonment will generally be appropriate in relation to any offence where there has been a breach of trust.[955]

[8.0] CHARACTER AND ANTECEDENTS

The character and antecedents of an accused person are, to the extent that they are relevant, to be taken into account in fixing the sentence to be imposed.[956]

The term 'character and antecedents' includes:

- previous criminal history; and
- matters revealed in the commission of the offence that reflects on the character of an accused person.[957]

An accused person's criminal history[958] is relevant to show whether:

- the current offence is an uncharacteristic aberration; or
- the accused person has manifested in his or her commission of the current offence a continuing attitude of disobedience of the law.[959]

An accused person who has been convicted of, or admits to, the commission of other offences will, all other things being equal, ordinarily receive a heavier sentence than an accused person who has previously led a blameless life.[960]

---

[955] See *Edward Fiuadi v R* [1988-1989] SILR 150 at 152.

[956] See *Weininger v R* (2003) 212 CLR 629 at 640, [2003] HCA 14.

[957] See *R v King's Lynn Justices; ex parte Carter and others* [1968] 3 All ER 858, per Parker LCJ at 862.

See also: *R v Lymm Justices; ex parte Brown* [1973] 1 All ER 716.

[958] As regards the law in relation to a previous conviction, refer to the subsection titled 'Previous Convictions' in the section titled 'Wording Of Charges' in the chapter titled 'Charges' in the text titled 'Injia on Criminal Practice and Procedure in Papua New Guinea and the Pacific'.

[959] See *Veen v R (No. 2)* (1988) 164 CLR 465, (1988) 33 A Crim R 230, [1988] HCA 14.

[960] See *Weininger v R* (2003) 212 CLR 629 at 640, [2003] HCA 14.

AGGRAVATING FACTORS

More weight should be given to previous convictions for offences of the same character as that for which the accused person is to be punished than to convictions for offences of a different character.[961]

A previous conviction is a special aggravating factor that is given greater weight than other aspects of an accused person's character.[962]

A repeat accused person is likely to receive a higher sentence.[963]

An adverse criminal record may impact on the sentencing process in a number of ways, including:

- as an indicator of an accused person's moral culpability[964] and if this is the case, then the seriousness of the offence is increased, and so too must be the sentence in proportion to it.[965]

  Previous criminal history is relevant to culpability, in that exposure on a previous occasion to the system of sanctions should have brought home to the accused person dramatically and personally that his or her criminal conduct was offensive to society.[966]

  The seriousness of a prior offence may have some bearing on the culpability of an accused person because such an accused person should have known better than to engage in further serious offences.[967]

---

[961] See *Crayson v R* (1920) 22 WALR 37, per McMillan CJ at 38.

[962] See *Gimble v The State* [1988-89] PNGLR 271 at 278, (1988) SC369, [1988] PGSC 15 and *Lawrence Hindemba v The State* (1998) SC593.

[963] See *Gimble v The State* [1988-89] PNGLR 271 at 278, (1988) SC369, [1988] PGSC 15 and *Lawrence Hindemba v The State* (1998) SC593.

[964] See *Veen v R (No. 2)* (1988) 164 CLR 465, (1988) 33 A Crim R 230, [1988] HCA 14.

[965] See The Law Reform Commission of Ireland, 1993, 'Consultation Paper on Sentencing', paragraph 6.2.

[966] See *The People (DPP) v Tiernan* [1988] IR 250, [1989] ILRM 149.

See also: The Law Reform Commission of Ireland, 1996, 'Report of Sentencing', paragraph 3.19.

[967] See The Law Reform Commission of Ireland, 1993, 'Consultation Paper on Sentencing', paragraph 6.6.

AGGRAVATING FACTORS

An accused person with a number of relevant prior convictions may be viewed as more culpable because such an accused person should have known not to engage in criminal conduct.[968]

Retribution[969], deterrence[970] and protection of society may all indicate that a more severe penalty is warranted[971];

- as an indicator of an accused person's prospects of rehabilitation[972];
- as an indicator of the dangerous propensity of an accused person and the community's need for protection to deter the accused person and other accused persons from committing further offences[973]; and
- the increased importance of specific deterrence as a factor in sentencing whilst having regard to the failure of more moderate penalties as a means of deterrence[974].

Whilst a Court is entitled to take into account a previous conviction for a similar offence a Court must be careful not to place too much weight on it.[975]

---

968 See The Law Reform Commission of Ireland, 1993, 'Consultation Paper on Sentencing', paragraph 6.6.

969 Refer also to the section titled 'The Need For Retribution' in the chapter titled 'Objectives And Purposes Of Sentencing'.

970 Refer also to the section titled 'The Need For Deterrence' in the chapter titled 'Objectives And Purposes Of Sentencing'.

971 See *Veen v R (No. 2)* (1988) 164 CLR 465, (1988) 33 A Crim R 230, [1988] HCA 14.

972 Refer also to the section titled 'The Need For Reformation Or Rehabilitation' in the chapter titled 'Objectives And Purposes Of Sentencing'.

973 See *Veen v R (No. 2)* (1988) 164 CLR 465, (1988) 33 A Crim R 230, [1988] HCA 14.

Refer also to the section titled 'The Need For Deterrence' in the chapter titled 'Objectives And Purposes Of Sentencing'.

974 See *R v O'Brien and Gloster* [1997] 2 VR 714 at 718.

See also: *R v Fuller-Cust* (2006) 6 VR 496, per Batt JA at 514.

Refer also to the section titled 'The Need For Deterrence' in the chapter titled 'Objectives And Purposes Of Sentencing'.

975 See *Gregory Kasen v The State* (2001) N2133.

AGGRAVATING FACTORS

No principle of sentencing requires that more severe sanctions be administered to those who persist in their criminal behaviour.[976]

A criminal history is relevant, not to punish an accused person for his or her past offences, but to demonstrate whether the current offence is:

- uncharacteristic; or
- a continuing attitude of disobedience of the law warranting a more serious penalty[977],

particularly when an accused person has committed the same type of offence previously.[978]

However, a previous conviction cannot justify a sentence longer than is appropriate whilst taking into consideration the gravity of the current offence[979], in order either to:

- extend the period of protection to society from the risk of recidivism by an accused person; or
- act as a general deterrent.[980]

---

[976] See *R v O'Brien and Gloster* [1997] 2 VR 714 at 718.

[977] See *R v Queen* [1928] Crim LR 56.

See also: *Veen v R (No. 2)* (1988) 164 CLR 465 at 477-478, (1988) 33 A Crim R 230, [1988] HCA 14 and *O'Donnel v Perkins* [1908] VR 537.

[978] See *R v Howe* [1982] 1 NZLR 618; *R v Casey* [1931] NZLR 594, per Myers CJ at 597 and *R v Ward* [1976] 1 NZLR 588, per McCarthy P at 591.

[979] See *DPP v Ottewell* [1970] AC 642 at 650.

See also: *R v McNaughton* [2006] NSWCCA 242 and *Veen v R (No. 2)* (1988) 164 CLR 465, (1988) 33 A Crim R 230, [1988] HCA 14.

[980] See *Ibbs v R; Baumer v R* (1988) 188 CLR 51 at 57, (1988) 83 ALR 8, [1988] HCA 67; *Veen v R (No. 2)* (1988) 164 CLR 465 at 477-478, (1988) 33 A Crim R 230, [1988] HCA 14 and *R v Aston (No. 2)* [1991] 1 Qd R 375.

But a repeat accused person may be given a far sterner sentence[981], especially if he or she has recently been released from jail[982].

The staleness of a previous conviction should also be taken into consideration. As the time between the past and current offence increases, the culpability of the accused person decreases.[983] The more distant the conviction the less plausible it is to claim that it dramatically and personally calls to the accused person's attention the fact that the current offence is condemned by the criminal law. Similarly, the age of the accused person at the time of commission of the previous offences should also be of relevance since an offence committed when a minor casts less light on the present character of the accused person.[984]

A previous conviction in another country may be considered.[985]

A previous conviction must be proven in accordance with the law.[986]

[9.0] NIGHT-TIME

The commission of an offence in the night-time may be considered as an aggravating factor.[987]

---

981 See *The State v Urika Iari* (2006) N3238, [2006] PGNC 152.

See also: *Ibbs v R; Baumer v R* (1988) 188 CLR 51 at 57, (1988) 83 ALR 8, [1988] HCA 67.

982 See *The State v Bani Basil* (2008) N3671, [2008] PGNC 228.

983 See *R v Sukina* [1998] SBHC 60.

984 See The Law Reform Commission of Ireland, 1993, 'Consultation Paper on Sentencing', paragraph 6.5.

985 See *R v Ford* (1921) 15 Cr App R 176.

986 See *R v Finney* (1924) 18 Cr App R 41.

See also: *Ex parte Kelly; Re Teece* (1966) 85 WN (Pt. 1) NSW 151 at 153-156.

987 See *The State v Donald Poni* (2004) N2663.

See also: *Ironimo v R* [1996] SBHC 63 and *R v Su'Umania* (Solomon Islands Criminal Case No. 2 of 1987).

AGGRAVATING FACTORS

[10.0] EFFECT OF ALCOHOL CONSUMPTION

The consumption of alcohol may sometimes assist in assessing the degree of deliberation involved in the commission of an offence.[988]

The relevance of intoxication also goes to the question of culpability. The rationale is that if an accused person offends while under the influence of alcohol his or her self control is affected.[989]

Therefore, the voluntary consumption of alcohol may be considered as an aggravating factor.[990]

[11.0] NO REMORSE

A failure to show genuine remorse is a matter that may be considered as an aggravating factor.[991]

---

988 See *R v Coleman* (1990) 47 A Crim R 306 at 327.

989 See *Kesino Apo v The State* [1988-89] PNGLR 182 at 182-183, [1988] PGSC 4.

990 See *The State v Abel Airi* (2000) N2007; *The State v Gerald Kirafe* (2005) N3660, [2005] PGNC 175; *John Elipa Kalabus v The State* [1988-89] PNGLR 193; *The State v Jimmy Morgan* (2001) N2171; *The State v Jimmy Ketu (No. 2)* (2007) N3394, [2007] PGNC 153; *Mase and another v The State* [1991] PNGLR 88; *The State v Ian Bob Wali* (2004) N2580; *The State v Newman Saimon Bonga* (2007) N3388, [2007] PGNC 154; *The State v Abel Airi* (2000) N2007; *The State v Gilbert Peter Diga* (2000) N1991; *The State v Jerry Mana* (2003) N2367; *The State v Grace John (No. 3)* (2011) N4371, [2011] PGNC 104 and *The State v Clarence Tema Mongi* (2011) N4364, [2011] PGNC 88.

See also: *Campbell v R* [1994] SBCA 3; *R v Patua, Kukiti, Ngelea and Manegaua* (Solomon Islands Criminal Case No. 6 of 1989) and *Hu'ahulu v Police* [1994] Tonga LR 93, per Ward CJ at 95.

991 See *The State v Kopol Hiol* (2008) CR No. 538 of 2007; *The State v Steven Molu Minji and others; The State v Didi Gelwak Sakol (No. 2)* (2009) N3794, [2009] PGNC 177; *The State v Jonathan Sengi* (2009) N3692, [2009] PGNC 91; *The State v Alexander Junior Nara (No. 2)* (2007) N3214, [2007] PGNC 86; *The State v Wesley Ignas* [2007] PGNC 115; *The State v Henry Matatenge* (2007) N3218, [2007] PGNC 59; *The State v Ereman Kepas* (2007) N3192, [2007] PGNC 77 and *The State v Kenneth Baupo and Fabian Girida* (1989) N795.

AGGRAVATING FACTORS

[12.0] OFFENCES COMMITTED BY LAW ENFORCEMENT OFFICER

It is essential for the upholding of law and order that the special position of trust that law enforcement officers hold be maintained.[992]

Therefore, when an offence is committed by a law enforcement officer that may be considered as an aggravating factor.[993]

[13.0] REPEATED ACTS CAUSING MULTIPLE INJURIES OR LOSS OF PROPERTY

Repeated acts constituting the offence committed over time is an aggravating factor.[994]

---

[992] See The Law Reform Commission of Ireland, 1993, 'Consultation Paper on Sentencing', paragraph 5.36.

[993] See *The State v John Wanimba and others* (2005) N2863, [2005] PGNC 108; *The State v Peni Bilak* (2005) N2866, [2005] PGNC 92; *The State v Jimmy Naime* (2005) N2873, [2005] PGNC 76 and *The State v Robin Warren and others (No. 2)* (2003) N2418.

As regards the improper use of confidential police information, see *R v Kasim* [2006] 1 Cr App R (S) 12 and *Attorney-General's Reference No. 1 of 2007* [2007] 2 Cr App R (S) 86.

[994] See *The State v Binga* (2005) N2828, [2005] PGNC 189; *The State v Peter Lare* (2004) N2557 and *The State v Ilam Peter* (2006) N3090, [2006] PGNC 80.

[14.0] MEMBER OF A GANG

The commission of an offence whilst a member of a gang may be considered as an aggravating factor because accused persons who are commit offences together give strength and encouragement to each other.[995]

[15.0] PRE-PLANNING OR PRE-MEDITATON

Since the determination of seriousness relies on an assessment of the culpability of an accused person it is axiomatic that the greater the planning or pre-meditation, the greater the culpability of the accused person because it is more likely that the offence was deliberate and intentional.[996]

An accused person who plans his or her offence is not only coolly defying the law but is going to some lengths to ensure that he or she succeeds and, sometimes, such an accused person is not detected. Such an accused person clearly and unequivocally places his or her interests above the constraints imposed by society on him or her and all others.[997]

---

[995] See *The State v Peter Yandi* (2010) N4064, [2010] PGNC 50; *The State v Jonathan Sengi* (2009) N3692, [2009] PGNC 91; *The State v Tomkuk Herman Itagau* [2006] PGNC 105; *The State v Terence Ago* (2004) N2673, [2004] PGNC 92; *The State v Upano Manake (No. 2)* (2006) N3504, [2006] PGNC 174; *The State v Philip Eki Vaki* (2007) N3464, [2007] PGNC 163; *The State v Terence Ago* (2004) N2673, [2004] PGNC 92; *The State v James Gatana and others* (2001) N2127; *The State v Patrick Puppy Kaikara Loavi* (2006) N3384, [2006] PGNC 104 and *The State v Baika Martin and others* (2008) N3312, [2008] PGNC 29.

Refer also to:

- the chapter titled 'Equality In Sentencing'; and
- the section titled 'Disparity In Sentencing' in the chapter titled 'Appeals Against Sentence'.

[996] See The Law Reform Commission of Ireland, 1993, 'Consultation Paper on Sentencing', paragraph 5.33.

[997] See The Law Reform Commission of Ireland, 1993, 'Consultation Paper on Sentencing', paragraph 5.33.

Therefore, evidence of pre-planning or pre-meditation may be considered as an aggravating factor.[998]

[16.0] AGE DIFFERENCE

The age difference between an accused person and a victim the cases involving violence may be considered as an aggravating factor.[999]

[17.0] ATTACKS ON LAW ENFORCEMENT OFFICERS

An unlawful attack on a law enforcement officer, including a judge, magistrate, police officer and prison officer may be considered as an aggravating factor.[1000]

---

[998] See *The State v Neiman Dua* (2013) N4957, [2013] PGNC 8; *The State v Francis Waka Sapu* (2012) N4533, [2012] PGNC 290; *The State v Andrew Aopo Lengade* (2012) N4690, [2012] PGNC 76; *The State v Langalen Yandan (No. 2)* (2012) N4833, [2012] PGNC 158; *The State v Andrew Jessie* (2012) N4904, [2012] PGNC 239; *The State v David Wilfred Yahresase* (2012) N4803, [2012] PGNC 233; *The State v Clinton Tikambari* (2011) N4553, [2011] PGNC 224; *The State v Alphonse Asarombo and Timothy Asarombo* (2010) N4121, [2010] PGNC 132 and *The State v Moli Mumugap and Jessica Wunol* (2008) N3546.

[999] See *The State v Sottie Apusa* [1988-89] PNGLR 170; *The State v Jerome Deila* (2009) N3804; *The State v Mitige Neheya* [1988-89] PNGLR 174; *The State v Brown Kawage* (2009) N3696, [2009] PGNC 87; *The State v Tonny Kupin* (2009) N3641; *The State v Waninara Judas Liligau* (2007) N3195, [2007] PGNC 87; *The State v Alois Dick* (2007) N3220, [2007] PGNC 58; *The State v John Seregat* (2007) N3266, [2007] PGNC 133; *The State v Joe Sime* [2006] PGNC 73; *The State v David Duna Burua* (2006) CR No. 829 of 2005; *The State v Henry Matatenge* (2007) N3218, [2007] PGNC 59; *The State v Binga Thomas* (2005) N2828, [2005] PGNC 189; *The State v Penias Mokei* (2002) N2635; *The State v Ereman Kepas* (2007) N3192, [2007] PGNC 77; *The State v Chris Nawa (No. 2)* (2009) N3732, [2009] PGNC 115; *The State v Jerry Kui* (2011) N4367, [2011] PGNC 85 and *The State v Tonai Kuse* (2011) N4304, [2011] PGNC 54.

See also: *R v Pillar and others* [1984] 1 NZLR 248; *R v Te Pou and others* [1985] 2 NZLR 508 and *R v Potatau* (1989) 4 CRNZ 2.

[1000] See *Secretary for Law v Peter* [1974] PNGLR 99, [1974] PGSC 33; *Peter Naibiri and Kutoi Soti Apia v The State* (1978) SC137; *Ure Hane v The State* [1984] PNGLR 105 at 107; *Joe Foe Leslie Leslie v The State* (1998) SC560; *The State v Elizah Ute* (2004) N2550; *The State v Henry Idab* (2001) N2172 and *The State v John Pais Kawage* (2009) N3626, [2009] PGNC 37.

AGGRAVATING FACTORS

[18.0] VICIOUSNESS OR DELIBERATE INTENTION TO HARM

Viciousness or deliberate intention to harm is an aggravating factor.[1001]

[19.0] LEADERSHIP IN A GANG

Leadership in a gang during the course of the commission of an offence may be considered as an aggravating factor.[1002]

Leadership infers a degree of planning and premeditation, and therefore a greater intention to break the law and to succeed in its commission.[1003]

By acting as ringleader and instigating others to join in the commission of the offence it is the ringleader who is the major cause of the offending behaviour. The ringleader is thus responsible for greater harm since he or she has encouraged others to offend.[1004]

[1001] See *Rex Lialu v The State* [1990] PNGLR 487; *Anna Max Marangi v The State* (2002) SC702; *Manu Kovi v The State* (2005) SC789, [2005] PGSC 34 and *Timothy Diwai v The State* (2007) SC892, [2007] PGSC 30.

[1002] See *Ian Napoleon Setep v The State* (2001) SC666, [2001] PGSC 14; *The State v Tony Pandau Hahuahoru (No. 2)* (2002) N2186; *The State v Tom Keroi Gurua and others* (2002) N2312, [2002] PGNC 41, *Andrew Uramani and others v The State* [1996] PNGLR 287, [1996] PGSC 33 and *Winugini Urugitaru v R* [1974] PNGLR 283 at 286, [1974] PGSC 38.

See also: *Lowe v R* (1984) 154 CLR 606, [1984] HCA 46; *Postiglione v R* (1997) 189 CLR 295, (1998) 71 ALJR 875, [1997] HCA 26; *R v Kollas and Mitchell* [2002] NSWCCA 491, per Wood CJ at CL; *R v MacGowan* (1986) 42 SASR 580, per King CJ at 582-583; *R v Olbrich* (1999) 199 CLR 270, [1999] HCA 54; *R v Coe* [1969] 1 All ER 65, (1969) 53 Cr App R 66, [1969] 1 All ER 65, [1968] 1 WLR 1950; *Van der Worp v R* [2000] WASCA 154; *McPherson v R* [2002] WACA 287 and *R v Wright* (1991) 7 CRNZ 624.

Refer also to:
- the chapter titled 'Equality In Sentencing'; and
- the section titled 'Disparity In Sentencing' in the chapter titled 'Appeals Against Sentence'.

[1003] See The Law Reform Commission of Ireland, 1993, 'Consultation Paper on Sentencing', paragraph 5.43.

[1004] See The Law Reform Commission of Ireland, 1993, 'Consultation Paper on Sentencing', paragraph 5.43.

EXTENUATING CIRCUMSTANCES

[1.0] INTRODUCTION

There is a distinction between extenuating circumstances and mitigating factors, although both have the same desired effect of reducing the punishment.[1005]

'Extenuating circumstances' are:

> The particular circumstances in which the offence was committed that have the effect of reducing or diminishing the gravity of an offence.[1006]

However, mitigating factors are usually unrelated to the circumstances of the offence.[1007]

In order for a Court to act fairly and, in principle, to be seen to act fairly, a full opportunity must be given to allow 'extenuating circumstances' to be put to the Court.[1008]

A Court should not particularise specific periods of deductions from the head sentence based on specific extenuating circumstances, for example, that two years be deducted for de-facto provocation.

No specific amount of sentence should be deducted for any specific extenuating circumstance.

The only specific period to be deducted from the head sentence is the time an accused person has served in custody prior to sentence.[1009]

1005 See *John Elipa Kalabus v The State* [1988-89] PNGLR 19.

1006 See *Steven Loke Ume, Charles Patrick Kaona and Greg Wawa Kavoa v The State* (2006) SC836, [2006] PGSC 9.

1007 See *John Elipa Kalabus v The State* [1988-89] PNGLR 19.

1008 Section 59(2) of the *Constitution of the Independent State of Papua New Guinea* states:

> 'The minimum requirement of natural justice is the duty to act fairly and, in principle, to be seen to act fairly'.

See also: *The State v Aaron Lahu* (2005) N2798, [2005] PGNC 161.

1009 See *Babai v The State* [1995] PNGLR 179, [1995] PGSC 10.

Section 3(2) of the *Criminal Justice (Sentences) Act 1986* states:

> 'There may be deducted from the length or any term of imprisonment imposed by the sentence of any court any period before the sentence was imposed during which the offender was in custody in connection with the offence for which the sentence was imposed'.

EXTENUATING CIRCUMSTANCES

Extenuating circumstances may include:

- de-facto provocation[1010];
- duress or coercion[1011];
- an accused person's motive for committing an offence, including:
    - an accused person's medical condition, such as a psychopathic personality[1012];
    - an accused person's emotional problems; and
    - impulsive conduct[1013];
- an accused person's lack of sophistication.[1014]

  However, this extenuating circumstance should not be over-emphasised because the law must still be complied with[1015];

[1010] See *Steven Loke Ume, Charles Patrick Kaona and Greg Wawa Kavoa v The State* (2006) SC836, [2006] PGSC 9 and *Denden Tom and others v The State* (2008) SC967.

[1011] See *Steven Loke Ume, Charles Patrick Kaona and Greg Wawa Kavoa v The State* (2006) SC836, [2006] PGSC 9 and *Denden Tom and others v The State* (2008) SC967.

[1012] See *Steven Loke Ume, Charles Patrick Kaona and Greg Wawa Kavoa v The State* (2006) SC836, [2006] PGSC 9 and *Denden Tom and others v The State* (2008) SC967.

[1013] See *R v Henry and others* (1999) 46 NSWLR 346, [1999] NSWCCA 111, per Spigelman CJ.

[1014] See *Steven Loke Ume, Charles Patrick Kaona and Greg Wawa Kavoa v The State* (2006) SC836, [2006] PGSC 9; *Denden Tom and others v The State* (2008) SC967 and *The State v Jackson Peng* (2012) N4737, [2012] PGNC 110.

See however: *The Public Prosecutor v Apava Keru; Public Prosecutor v Aia Moroi* [1985] PNGLR 78, [1985] PGSC 7.

[1015] See *The Pubic Prosecutor v Tumu Waria of Yogos* [1977] PNGLR 170, [1977] PGSC 18.

- an accused person's traditional customs, practices and beliefs[1016].

  Custom should not be taken into account, unless there is proper evidence thereof.[1017]

  However, this extenuating circumstance should not be over-emphasised because the law must still be complied with[1018]; and

- the role that the accused person played in the commission of the offence.

[2.0] DE-FACTO PROVOCATION

'De-factor provocation' is:

> A wrongful act that provokes an accused person's conduct in a non-legal sense[1019].[1020]

Such provocation reduces the degree of culpability of the accused person.[1021]

The weight to be given to this extenuating circumstance will depend on a number of factors, including:

- whether the victim was violent towards the accused person[1022];

1016 See *Steven Loke Ume, Charles Patrick Kaona and Greg Wawa Kavoa v The State* (2006) SC836, [2006] PGSC 9 and *Denden Tom and others v The State* (2008) SC967.

See however: *The Public Prosecutor v Apava Keru; Public Prosecutor v Aia Moroi* [1985] PNGLR 78, [1985] PGSC 7.

1017 See *The Public Prosecutor v Vangu'u Ame* [1983] PNGLR 424 at 427, [1983] PGSC 23.

1018 See *The Pubic Prosecutor v Tumu Waria of Yogos* [1977] PNGLR 170, [1977] PGSC 18.

1019 The law in relation to the defence of 'Provocation' is examined in the chapter titled 'Offences Against The Person' in the text titled 'Injia on Criminal Offences in Papua New Guinea and the Pacific'.

1020 See *Emil Kongian and others v The State* (2007) SC928, [2007] PGSC 45 and *Public Prosecutor v Apava Keru; Public Prosecutor v Aia Moroi* [1985] PNGLR 78.

1021 See *Emil Kongian and others v The State* (2007) SC928, [2007] PGSC 45 and *Public Prosecutor v Apava Keru; Public Prosecutor v Aia Moroi* [1985] PNGLR 78.

1022 See *The State v Francis Giru* (1997) N1661 and *The State v Issau Parao* (2009) N3625, [2009] PGNC 38.

- the degree of provocation offered[1023] which when great has the tendency of reducing the objective gravity of the offence[1024];

- the extent of the loss of the power of self-control suffered which when great has the tendency of reducing the objective gravity of the offence[1025]; and

- the time between:

    - the provocation (whether isolated or cumulative in its effect); and

    - the loss of the power of self-control

  which when short has the tendency of reducing the objective gravity of the offence[1026].

1023 As regards:

- a dispute over land with the victim, see *The State v James Agamp Make, William Dot and Norman Pokop* (1998) N1748;
- substantial loss of property caused by the victim, see *The State v Mathias Inabari* (2004) N2587;
- an extramarital affair, see *The State v Philipa Kawage* (2008) CR No. 1386 of 2006; and
- an unproven allegation of adultery, see *The State v Noelyn Anton* (2012) N4828, [2012] PGNC 120.

1024 See *R v Morabito* (1992) 62 A Crim R 83 at 86 and *R v Alexander* (1994) 78 A Crim R 141, per Hunt CJ at CL at 144.

See also: The Law Reform Commission of Ireland, 1993, 'Consultation Paper on Sentencing', paragraph 5.55.

1025 See *R v Morabito* (1992) 62 A Crim R 83 at 86 and *R v Alexander* (1994) 78 A Crim R 141, per Hunt CJ at CL at 144.

See also: The Law Reform Commission of Ireland, 1993, 'Consultation Paper on Sentencing', paragraph 5.55.

1026 See *The State v Eliesa Kopeia Madiroto* (1997) N1554 and *The State v Tumu Luna* (2002) N2205.

See also:

- *R v Morabito* (1992) 62 A Crim R 83 at 86; and
- The Law Reform Commission of Ireland, 1993, 'Consultation Paper on Sentencing', paragraph 5.55.

See however: *Public Prosecutor v Apava Keru; Public Prosecutor v Aia Moroi* [1985] PNGLR 78.

It is at least clear that:

- swift and impulsive retaliation is far less blameworthy than planned and premeditated revenge; and
- offences motivated by strong provocation are less blameworthy than unprovoked offences because it is the provocation, rather than an intention to flagrantly disobey the authority of the law, that is the primary motivation for the offending conduct[1027].

An accused person who commits a payback murder in accordance with his or her custom may be entitled to some reduction in sentence for de-facto provocation.[1028]

[3.0] DURESS OR COERCION

The commonsense starting point of the common law is that adults of sound mind are ordinarily to be held responsible for the offences that they commit.[1029]

To this general principle there has, since the fourteenth century, been a recognised, but limited, exception in favour of those persons who commit offences because they are forced or compelled to do so against their will by the threats of another.[1030]

Such persons are said, in the language of the criminal law, to act as they do because they are subject to duress.[1031]

1027 See The Law Reform Commission of Ireland, 1993, 'Consultation Paper on Sentencing', paragraph 5.55.

1028 See *Public Prosecutor v Apava Keru; Public Prosecutor v Aia Moroi* [1985] PNGLR 78, [1985] PGSC 7.

1029 See *R v Z* (2005) 2 AC 467, per Lord Bingham of Cornwall at 489, [2005] UKHL 22.

1030 See *R v Z* (2005) 2 AC 467, per Lord Bingham of Cornwall at 489, [2005] UKHL 22.

1031 See *R v Z* (2005) 2 AC 467, per Lord Bingham of Cornwall at 489, [2005] UKHL 22.

EXTENUATING CIRCUMSTANCES

Where an accused person commits an offence whilst acting under duress that falls short of a complete defence to the charge[1032] then that duress is capable of being a factor that reduces a sentence that would otherwise be applied.[1033]

The onus lies upon the accused person to establish the relevant facts.[1034]

[4.0] MOTIVE

[4.1] INTRODUCTION

The motive of an accused person for committing an offence may be considered as an 'extenuating circumstance' in appropriate circumstances.

The absence of motive however does not aggravate the offence and nor does it provide a significant mitigating factor.[1035]

Motive may be an extenuating circumstance if it impinges upon the moral culpability of the accused person[1036] in so far as the accused person's capacity to:

- reason;
- appreciate fully the rightness or wrongness of a particular act; or

---

[1032] Refer also to the defence of 'Compulsion' as provided for by section 32 of the *Criminal Code* (Ch. 262).

The law in relation to that defence is examined in the chapter titled 'Criminal Responsibility' in the text titled 'Injia on Criminal Offences in Papua New Guinea and the Pacific'.

[1033] See *Steven Loke Ume, Charles Patrick Kaona and Greg Wawa Kavoa v The State* (2006) SC836, [2006] PGSC 9 and *Denden Tom and others v The State* (2008) SC967.

See also: *R v Olbrich* (1999) 199 CLR 270 at 281, [1999] HCA 54; *Trocko* (1988) 142 LSJS 412, per King CJ and *R v Day* [2009] SASC 84.

[1034] See *R v Olbrich* (1999) 199 CLR 270 at 281, [1999] HCA 54.

[1035] See *Willy Kelly Goya v The State* [1987] PNGLR 51.

[1036] See *R v Henry and others* (1999) 46 NSWLR 346, [1999] NSWCCA 111, per Spigelman CJ.

- exercise appropriate powers of control has been affected.[1037]

This can include:

- emotional problems[1038] where it is causally related to the commission of the offence[1039];

- medical problems[1040], such as mental health, where it is causally related to the commission of the offence[1041]; and

- impulsive conduct[1042].

The degree to which motive may be pertinent must however depend on the whole of the circumstances.[1043]

Such matters can be classified as circumstances of the offence, and not merely circumstances of the accused person that might go to the appropriate level of punishment.[1044]

Questions of motive must however be treated with great care. It is possible that an accused person may come up with a heart-breaking motive for the simple purpose of making a ploy for leniency.[1045]

1037 See *Channon v R* (1978) 20 ALR 1, (1978) 33 FLR 433, [1978] FCA 16 and *R v Engert* (1995) 84 A Crim R 67.

1038 See *R v Henry and others* (1999) 46 NSWLR 346, [1999] NSWCCA 111, per Spigelman CJ.

1039 See *Channon v R* (1978) 20 ALR 1, (1978) 33 FLR 433, [1978] FCA 16 and *R v Engert* (1995) 84 A Crim R 67.

1040 See *R v Henry and others* (1999) 46 NSWLR 346, [1999] NSWCCA 111, per Spigelman CJ.

1041 See *Channon v R* (1978) 20 ALR 1, (1978) 33 FLR 433, [1978] FCA 16 and *R v Engert* (1995) 84 A Crim R 67.

1042 See *R v Henry and others* (1999) 46 NSWLR 346, [1999] NSWCCA 111, per Spigelman CJ.

1043 See *R v Henry and others* (1999) 46 NSWLR 346, [1999] NSWCCA 111, per Spigelman CJ.

1044 See *Al v R; R v SB and Al* [2011] NSWCCA 95.

1045 See *Qila v R* [1995] SBHC 44.

A Court must, therefore, continue to:

- guard against such abuses and excuses; and
- be vigilant, in detecting and separating the genuine from the false.[1046]

[4.2] MENTAL HEALTH

The existence of a mental illness is always a relevant factor in the sentencing process, but its impact upon:

- the sentencing process; and
- the various issues that arise in sentencing

will vary considerably according to the circumstances of each individual case.[1047]

In respect to a mental health issue there must always be clear medical evidence.[1048]

There is, of course, a distinction between:

- mental illness that has been self-induced (for example, by the ingestion of alcohol or illicit drugs); and
- mental illness that has not been self-induced.[1049]

It is well-established that where an accused person's mental illness or psychological difficulties have been self-induced (for example, by the ingestion of alcohol or illicit drugs), his or her condition is not generally to be regarded as mitigating the offence. In these circumstances the accused person is generally to be regarded as morally responsible for his or her condition.[1050]

1046 See *Qila v R* [1995] SBHC 44.

1047 See *R v Wiskich* (2000) 207 LSJS 431, per Martin J at 457-458, [2000] SASC 64.

1048 See *Rojumana v R* [1990] SILR 132; *R v Irlam; ex parte Attorney-General* [2002] QCA 235; *R v Verschaffelt* [2002] 3 NZLR 772 and *R v Bernard* [1997] 1 Cr App R (S) 135.

1049 See *Smith v The State of Western Australia* [2010] WASCA 176.

1050 See *R v Wright* (1997) 93 A Crim R 48; *R v Martin* (2007) 20 VR 14, [2007] VSCA 291; *Damiani v The State of Western Australia* [2006] WASCA 47 and *Butler v The State of Western Australia* [2010] WASCA 104.

However, where an accused person's mental illness or psychological difficulties have not been self-induced his or her condition is a mitigating factor in the sentencing process.[1051]

Psychiatric abnormality falling short of insanity[1052] is frequently found to be a cause of, or factor contributing to, criminal conduct. The sentencing of an accused person in cases of that kind is inevitably difficult.[1053]

Persons of reduced mental capacity cannot be said to be fully responsible for their offences and some allowance should be made in mitigation in recognition of their reduced intent.[1054]

The assessment that an accused person suffers from a 'mild intellectual disability' should not obscure the fact that he or she is mentally retarded. The condition of mental retardation is classified according to its severity as mild, moderate, severe or profound. Mental retardation is defined by reference to both significantly subaverage general intellectual functioning and significant limitations in adaptive functioning. 'Significantly subaverage intellectual functioning' is defined as an intelligence quotient (IQ or IQ-equivalent) of about 70 or below.[1055]

A temporary mental disorder or diminished responsibility of the mind may be taken into consideration.[1056]

However, it does not inevitably follow that the existence of some mental illness must result in a lesser sentence.[1057]

[1051] See *Phillips v The State of Western Australia* [2011] WASCA 69.

[1052] The law in relation to the defence of 'Insanity' is examined in the chapter titled 'Criminal Responsibility' in the text titled 'Injia on Criminal Offences in Papua New Guinea and the Pacific'.

[1053] As noted by Brennan J in *Channon v R* (1978) 20 ALR 1, (1978) 33 FLR 433 at 436-437, [1978] FCA 16.

[1054] See The Law Reform Commission of Ireland, 1993, 'Consultation Paper on Sentencing', paragraph 5.57.

[1055] See *Muldrock v R* (2011) 85 ALJR 1154, [2011] HCA 39.

[1056] See *The State v Opoyua Helai* (1997) N1533; *The State v Eric Gordon Berry* [1977] PNGLR 128 and *The State v Justus Taimbari Kauri* (1987) N684.

Diminished responsibility is not a defence under the *Criminal Code* (Ch. 262), see *Nicholas Wesley v The State* [1999] PNGLR 452, [1999] PGSC 57, (1999) SC662; *Kutapa Keapu v The State* [1994] PNGLR 135 at 136-137, [1994] PGSC 10; *The State v Joseph Makapi* (1980) N214; *R v Peter Ivoro* [1971-72] PNGLR 374; *The State v Eric Gordon Berry* [1977] PNGLR 128 and *The State v Ure Hane Of Gaire, Central Province* (1983) N442.

[1057] See *Courtney v R* [2007] 172 A Crim R 371, [2007] NSWCCA 195.

EXTENUATING CIRCUMSTANCES

The effect of mental illness or psychological difficulties (falling short of insanity) on the moral blameworthiness or culpability of an accused person is variable.[1058]

It depends upon the nature, effect and severity of the condition and its symptoms.[1059]

An accused person who seeks to rely on mental illness or psychological difficulties as a factor which reduces his or her moral blameworthiness or culpability must prove on the 'balance of probabilities' that:

> the condition impaired his or her mental functioning to such an extent as to reduce the blameworthiness or culpability of the offending behaviour.[1060]

In order for a mental illness to mitigate punishment there must be a causal connection between:

- the condition; and
- the commission of the offence

that reduces an accused person's moral culpability in respect to the offence.[1061]

However, a mental illness does not have to be:

- the sole cause of the commission of an offence; or
- a cause of the commission of an offence,

[1058] See *R v Verdins* (2007) 16 VR 269, (2007) 169 A Crim R 581, [2007] VSCA 102 and *Wheeler v R [No. 2]* [2010] WASCA 105.

[1059] See *R v Verdins* (2007) 16 VR 269, (2007) 169 A Crim R 581, [2007] VSCA 102 and *Wheeler v R [No. 2]* [2010] WASCA 105.

[1060] See *Wheeler [No. 2]* [2010] WASCA 105.

[1061] See *Veen v R (No. 2)* (1988) 164 CLR 465 at 476, (1988) 33 A Crim R 230, [1988] HCA 14; *Channon v R* (1978) 20 ALR 1, [1978] FCA 16, (1978) 33 FLR 433 at 436-437, per Brennan J at 436-437; *R v Paparone* (2000) 112 A Crim R 190, per Murray J at 199-200, [2000] WASCA 127; *T v The State of Western Australia* [2005] WASCA 237, per Roberts-Smith JA; *Kiesey v The State of Western Australia* [2005] WASCA 229, per Roberts-Smith JA; *Orchard v R* [2004] WASCA 23; *R v Tsiaras* [1996] 1 VR 398 at 400; *Lauritsen v R* (2000) 22 WAR 442 at 456-459, (2000) 114 A Crim R 333, [2000] WASCA 203; *R v Payne* (2002) 131 A Crim R 432; *R v Richards* [1999] WASCA 105; *R v Juli* (1990) 50 A Crim R 31 at 37; *R v Hurd* (1988) 38 A Crim R 454 at 461 and 465; *R v Balchin* (1974) 9 SASR 64 at 68; *R v Reynolds* (1983) 10 A Crim R 30; *R v Scognamiglio* (1991) 56 A Crim R 81 at 86; *Anderson v R* [1981] VR 155 at 159; *R v Engert* (1995) 84 A Crim R 67, per Gleeson CJ at 70-71; *R v Bridger* [2003] 1 NZLR 636 at 648; *R v Abraham* (1993) 10 CRNZ 336 and *Muldrock v R* (2011) 85 ALJR 1154, [2011] HCA 39.

in order to be relevant to sentencing.[1062]

Mental illness may be relevant as follows:

- where the illness contributes to the commission of an offence in a material way and an accused person's moral culpability in the offence, as distinct from the accused person's legal responsibility, is reduced[1063];

  To the extent that there is a moral lessening of culpability, that should be reflected in the penalty imposed[1064], but not necessarily so[1065];

[1062] See *Benitez v R* (2006) 160 A Crim R 166, [2006] NSWCCA 21 and *R v Engert* (1995) 84 A Crim R 67, per Gleeson CJ at 71.

[1063] See *R v Henry and others* (1999) 46 NSWLR 346, [1999] NSWCCA 111; *Jiminez* [1999] NSWCCA 7; *R v Tsiaras* [1996] 1 VR 398 at 400; *Lauritsen v R* (2000) 22 WAR 442 at 456-459, (2000) 114 A Crim R 333, [2000] WASCA 203; *R v Israil* [2002] NSWCCA 255; *R v Pearson* [2004] NSWCCA 129; *R v Swan* [2006] NSWCCA 47, per Spigelman CJ; *R v Hemsley* [2004] NSWCCA 228, per Sperling J; *R v Wright* (1997) 93 A Crim R 48; *R v Verdins* (2007) 16 VR 269, (2007) 169 A Crim R 581, per Maxwell P at 588-589, [2007] VSCA 102; *R v Hamid* (2006) 164 A Crim R 179 at 197, [2006] NSWCCA 302; *Orchard v R* [2004] WASCA 23; *Thompson v R* (2005) 157 A Crim R 385, [2005] WASCA 223; *R v Richards* [1999] WASCA 105; *R v Paparone* (2000) 112 A Crim R 190, per Murray J, [2000] WASCA 127; *R v Payne* (2002) 131 A Crim R 432; *F v The State of Western Australia* (2008) 184 A Crim R 125, [2008] WASCA 100; *Krijestorac v The State of Western Australia* [2010] WASCA 35; *Wheeler v R [No. 2]* [2010] WASCA 105 and *Gok v R* [2010] WASCA 185.

[1064] See *R v Juli* (1990) 50 A Crim R 31 at 37; *R v Hurd* (1988) 38 A Crim R 454 at 461 and 465; *R v Tsiaras* [1996] 1 VR 398 at 400; *R v Balchin* (1974) 9 SASR 64 at 68; *R v Reynolds* (1983) 10 A Crim R 30; *Lauritsen v R* (2000) 22 WAR 442 at 456-459, (2000) 114 A Crim R 333, [2000] WASCA 203; *Orchard v R* [2004] WASCA 23 and *R v Payne* (2002) 131 A Crim R 432.

[1065] See *R v Scognamiglio* (1991) 56 A Crim R 81; *R v Engert* (1995) 84 A Crim R 67; *R v Champion* (1992) 64 A Crim R 244; *R v Wright* (1997) 93 A Crim R 48 and *Courtney v R* (2007) 172 A Crim R 371, [2007] NSWCCA 195.

- the nature and severity of the illness may render an accused person inappropriate for general deterrence[1066].[1067]

  General deterrence should often be given very little weight in the case of an accused person suffering from a mental illness because such an accused person is not an appropriate medium for making an example to others.[1068]

  However, where an accused person understands:

  - what he or she is doing; and

  - the gravity of his or her actions,

  general deterrence may be of continuing significance[1069];

[1066] Refer also to the section titled 'The Need For Deterrence' in the chapter 'Objectives And Purposes Of Sentencing'.

[1067] See *R v Engert* (1995) 84 A Crim R 67, per Gleeson CJ at 71; *R v Israil* [2002] NSWCCA 255; *R v Pearson* [2004] NSWCCA 129; *R v Swan* [2006] NSWCCA 47, per Spigelman CJ; *R v Hemsley* [2004] NSWCCA 228, per Sperling J; *R v Verdins* (2007) 16 VR 269, (2007) 169 A Crim R 581, [2007] VSCA 102; *R v Scognamiglio* [1991] 56 A Crim R 81; *R v Tsiaras* [1996] 1 VR 398 at 400*; R v Neumann; ex parte Attorney-General (Queensland)* [2007] 1 Qd R 53, [2005] QCA 362; *F v The State of Western Australia* (2008) 184 A Crim R 125, [2008] WASCA 100; *Krijestorac v The State of Western Australia* [2010] WASCA 35; *Wheeler v R [No. 2]* [2010] WASCA 105; *Gok v R* [2010] WASCA 185 and *Thompson v R* (2005) 157 A Crim R 385, [2005] WASCA 223.

[1068] See *R v Scognamiglio* (1991) 56 A Crim R 81 at 86; *R v Engert* (1995) 84 A Crim R 67, per Gleeson CJ at 70-71; *R v Anderson* [1981] VR 155 at 160-161, (1980) 2 A Crim R 379 at 383-384; *R v Pitt* [2005] NSWCCA 304; *R v Kilmartin* (1989) 41 A Crim R 22; *Man* (1990) 50 A Crim R 79; *R v Matthews* (2004) 145 A Crim R 445, [2004] NSWCCA 112, per Wood CJ; *R v Champion* (1992) 64 A Crim R 244; *R v Henry and others* (1999) 46 NSWLR 346, [1999] NSWCCA 111, per Wood CJ at CL; *Muldrock v R* (2011) 85 ALJR 1154, [2011] HCA 39; *Veen v R (No. 2)* (1988) 164 CLR 465 at 476-477, (1988) 33 A Crim R 230, [1988] HCA 14; *R v Wright* (1997) 93 A Crim R 48 and *Minehan v R* (2010) 201 A Crim R 243, [2010] NSWCCA 140.

[1069] See *R v Wright* (1997) 93 A Crim R 48 at 51; *R v Henry and others* (1999) 46 NSWLR 346, [1999] NSWCCA 111; *R v Matthews* (2004) 145 A Crim R 445, [2004] NSWCCA 112 and *R v Hemsley* [2004] NSWCCA 228.

- specific deterrence[1070] may be more difficult to achieve and is often not worth pursuing as such.[1071]

  Whether specific deterrence should be:

  - moderated; or
  - eliminated

  as a sentencing consideration depends upon:

  - the nature; and
  - the effect

  of the illness.[1072]

  Personal deterrence does assume some rational analysis or reasoning by the accused person in comparing:

  - the likely gains from the offence;

    against

  - the prospect, and likely severity, of punishment.[1073]

  Where the illness affects an accused person's ability to make an analysis, that consideration may be afforded less significance than it would in the case of a well person[1074];

[1070] Refer also to the section titled 'The Need For Deterrence' in the chapter 'Objectives Or Purposes Of Sentencing'.

[1071] See *R v Tsiaras* [1996] 1 VR 398 at 400; *F v The State of Western Australia* (2008) 184 A Crim R 125, [2008] WASCA 100; *Krijestorac v The State of Western Australia* [2010] WASCA 35; *Wheeler v R [No. 2]* [2010] WASCA 105; *Gok v R* [2010] WASCA 185 and *Thompson v R* (2005) 157 A Crim R 385, [2005] WASCA 223.

[1072] See *R v Verdins* (2007) 16 VR 269, (2007) 169 A Crim R 581, [2007] VSCA 102.

[1073] See *Thompson v R* (2005) 157 A Crim R 385, [2005] WASCA 223.

[1074] See *Thompson v R* (2005) 157 A Crim R 385, [2005] WASCA 223.

- psychiatric illness may mean that a given sentence will weigh more heavily on an accused person than it would on a person in normal health[1075];

- whether a custodial sentence may have a significant adverse effect on the mental health of an accused person[1076];

- the level of danger that an accused person presents to the community[1077]; and

- as to what is the most appropriate sentence[1078].

Ultimately, however, in the application of these principles, it is a matter of balancing the relevant factors in a manner no different from that which is involved in every sentencing exercise.[1079]

[4.3] IMPULSIVENESS

Impulsive reactions are generally the least blameworthy kind of intentional act since there has not been a careful decision to defy the law.[1080]

[1075] See *R v Tsiaras* [1996] 1 VR 398 at 400; *F v The State of Western Australia* (2008) 184 A Crim R 125, [2008] WASCA 100; *Krijestorac v The State of Western Australia* [2010] WASCA 35; *Wheeler v R [No. 2]* [2010] WASCA 105; *Gok v R* [2010] WASCA 185 and *Thompson v R* (2005) 157 A Crim R 385, [2005] WASCA 223.

[1076] See *R v Tsiaras* [1996] 1 VR 398 at 40, (2007) 169 A Crim R 581, [2007] VSCA 102; *Jiminez* [1999] NSWCCA 7; *R v Israil* [2002] NSWCCA 255; *R v Swan* [2006] NSWCCA 47, per Spigelman CJ; *R v Hemsley* [2004] NSWCCA 228, per Sperling J and *R v Verdins* (2007) 169 A Crim R 581, [2007] VSCA 102.

[1077] See *Veen v R (No. 2)* (1988) 164 CLR 465 at 476, (1988) 33 A Crim R 230, [1988] HCA 14; *R v Israil* [2002] NSWCCA 255; *Channon v R* (1978) 20 ALR 1, per Brennan J at 4-5, (1978) 33 FLR 433, [1978] FCA 16 and *Lauritsen v R* (2000) 22 WAR 442, (2000) 114 A Crim R 333, [2000] WASCA 203.

[1078] See *R v Verdins* (2007) 16 VR 269, (2007) 169 A Crim R 581, [2007] VSCA 102; *R v Tsiaras* [1996] 1 VR 398 at 400; *F v The State of Western Australia* (2008) 184 A Crim R 125, [2008] WASCA 100; *Krijestorac v The State of Western Australia* [2010] WASCA 35; *Wheeler v R [No. 2]* [2010] WASCA 105; *Gok v R* [2010] WASCA 185 and *Thompson v R* (2005) 157 A Crim R 385, [2005] WASCA 223.

[1079] See *R v Engert* (1995) 84 A Crim R 67 at 71.

[1080] See The Law Reform Commission of Ireland, 1993, 'Consultation Paper on Sentencing', paragraph 5.56.

Impulse is, thus, the corollary of planning and premeditation which acts as an 'aggravating factor'[1081] [1082].

However, impulse can only be a significant mitigating factor if the accused person was unaware of the impulsive reaction about to take place – if, say, the accused person had a history of violent reactions and knew of the types of situation likely to trigger off these reactions, then he or she may be regarded as being more culpable.[1083]

As a general rule drug addiction should not be a factor in reducing a sentence[1084], unless:

- the addiction commenced at a very young age[1085]; or
- the addiction was a consequence of medical treatment over which an accused person had no control[1086] [1087].

1081 Refer also to the section titled 'Pre-planning And Pre-meditation' in the chapter titled 'Aggravating Factors'.

1082 See The Law Reform Commission of Ireland, 1993, 'Consultation Paper on Sentencing', paragraph 5.56.

1083 See The Law Reform Commission of Ireland, 1993, 'Consultation Paper on Sentencing', paragraph 5.56.

1084 See *R v Henry and others* (1999) 46 NSWLR 346, [1999] NSWCCA 111.

As regards the consumption of an illegal drug prior to the commission of an offence, see *The State v Clarence Tema Mongi* (2007) N3259, [2007] PGNC 135. Refer also to the section titled 'Effect Of Consumption Of Alcohol' in the chapter titled 'Aggravating Factors' because the consumption of an illegal drug may also be considered as an aggravating factor based on those principles that apply to the consumption of alcohol.

1085 See *SS v R; JC v R* [2009] NSWCCA 114; *R v Henry and others* (1999) 46 NSWLR 346, [1999] NSWCCA 111, per Wood CJ at CL and *R v Todorovic* [2008] NSWCCA 49, per Hulme J.

1086 See *R v Todorovic* [2008] NSWCCA 49, per Hulme J and *SS v R; JC v R* [2009] NSWCCA 114, per Price J.

1087 See however: *Brewster and others* [1998] 1 Cr App R 220 (self-induced addiction is not a mitigating factor under any circumstances).

However, a drug addiction may be considered in terms of the objective criminality of an offence, including:

- by determining whether the offence was impulsive or planned[1088];
- by determining the state of mind of an accused person at the time of the commission of an offence[1089]; and
- by determining whether an accused person was unable to control his or her own behaviour at the time of the commission of an offence[1090].

[5.0] BELIEF IN SORCERY

The Courts recognise the existence and influence of sorcery without acknowledging and accepting that sorcery and its powers exist as a fact.[1091]

The belief in sorcery is a factor in sentencing because it controls the thinking and actions of those who believe and act on it[1092], provided that the belief was the cause for the commission of the offence.[1093]

[1088] See *R v Bouchard* (1996) 84 A Crim R 499 at 501-502 and *R v Henry and others* (1999) 46 NSWLR 346, [1999] NSWCCA 111.

[1089] See *R v Henry and others* (1999) 46 NSWLR 346, [1999] NSWCCA 111.

[1090] See *R v Hammond* (1996) 92 A Crim R 450 at 455.

See however: *Anna Le v R* [2006] NSWCCA 136.

[1091] See *The State v Aiaka Karavea and another* (1983) N452(M), per Kidu CJ; *The State v Jude Gena and four others* (2004) N2649, per Kapi CJ; *Albert Toti Yohannes v The State* (1998) SC577, [1998] PGSC 30; *The State v Alphonse Aia Mohavila* (2006) N3385, [2006] PGNC 106 and *The State v Maraka Jackson* (2006) N3237, [2006] PGNC 154.

[1092] See *The State v Aiaka Karavea and another* (1983) N452(M), per Kidu CJ; *The State v Jude Gena and four others* (2004) N2649, per Kapi CJ; *Albert Toti Yohannes v The State* (1998) SC577, [1998] PGSC 30; *The State v Alphonse Aia Mohavila* (2006) N3385, [2006] PGNC 106 and *The State v Maraka Jackson* (2006) N3237, [2006] PGNC 154.

[1093] See *Acting Public Prosecutor v Uname Aumane and others* [1980] PNGLR 510; *Kwayawaka and five others v The State* [1990] PNGLR 6, [1990] PGSC 15; *Roger Jumbo and Aidan Awatan v The State* [1998] PNGLR 197, (1997) SC516, [1997] PGSC 25; *The State v Alphonse Aia Mohavila* (2006) N3385, [2006] PGNC 106 and *The State v Maraka Jackson* (2006) N3237, [2006] PGNC 154.

However, a Court must be satisfied that there is some reasonable basis for holding such a belief[1094], ie., that it was a genuine belief[1095].

Otherwise, an accused person may use a claim of a belief in sorcery as an excuse to explain away the commission of an offence. This is a 'question of fact' that a Court can determine on the evidence presented before it.[1096]

Where an accused person only puts sorcery forward as a possible explanation for his or her conduct and there is another equally plausible explanation, it is open to the Court to reject the sorcery explanation.[1097]

But if a belief in sorcery is put forward and it is not beyond the bounds of reasonable possibility a Court ought not to reject it without giving the accused person the opportunity to establish his or belief on oath together with such witnesses as he or she may wish to call.[1098]

The weight to be attached to such a belief depends on the facts of the case.[1099]

However, it should no longer be assumed that a belief in sorcery will be treated as a significant factor in sentencing in every case.[1100]

1094 See *Public Prosecutor v Apava Keru; Public Prosecutor v Aia Moroi* [1985] PNGLR 78 at 80; *The State v Alphonse Aia Mohavila* (2006) N3385, [2006] PGNC 106 and *The State v Maraka Jackson* (2006) N3237, [2006] PGNC 154.

1095 See *The State v Isak Wapsi* (2009) N3695, [2009] PGNC 84.

1096 See *Roger Jumbo and Aidan Awatan v The State* [1998] PNGLR 197, (1997) SC516, [1997] PGSC 25; *The State v Alphonse Aia Mohavila* (2006) N3385, [2006] PGNC 106 and *The State v Maraka Jackson* (2006) N3237, [2006] PGNC 154.

1097 See *John Baipu v The State* (2005) SC796, [2005] PGSC 19 and *Albert Toti Johannes v The State* (1998) SC577, [1998] PGSC 30.

1098 See *Roger Jumbo and Aidan Awatan v The State* [1998] PNGLR 197 and *John Baipu v The State* (2005) SC796, [2005] PGSC 19.

1099 See *John Baipu v The State* (2005) SC796, [2005] PGSC 19 and *Irai Thomas v The State* (2007) SC867.

1100 See *John Baipu v The State* (2005) SC796, [2005] PGSC 19.

EXTENUATING CIRCUMSTANCES

Actions taken on the spur of the moment[1101] motivated by fear and self-preservation and which have parallels to but perhaps do not amount to provocation as contemplated by section 16 of the *Sorcery Act* (Ch. 274)[1102] are likely to increase the degree of mitigation.[1103]

But such factors as educational level of the accused person, the place of residence with the availability of village councillors, village courts, police, churches, other educational influences such as radio and television, and other aspects of good order and government that give an accused person alternate remedies to self-help and the knowledge that it is unacceptable, may be factors which reduce the mitigating effect of the belief in sorcery. Not because the belief in the effectiveness of sorcery may be diminished, but because the belief that taking the law into the accused person's own hands as the only effective means of dealing with the problem should and ought to be diminished.[1104]

However, a genuine belief in sorcery does not substantially reduce the sentence in relation to a homicide offence.[1105]

Killing someone is against the law and the Courts have a responsibility in demonstrating through the penalties they impose that the law does not approve of killing of sorcerers, no matter how much people believe in sorcery.[1106] A strong punitive and deterrent sentence is required to punish such accused persons and to send a clear message to their own community who apparently seem to think that it is alright to kill a sorcerer or a reputed sorcerer for that matter; that it is wrong to kill another person including a sorcerer, reputed or not, and that they will be punished by the Courts, if they do.[1107]

[1101] See *The State v Isak Wapsi* (2009) N3695, [2009] PGNC 84.

[1102] The *Sorcery Act* (Ch. 274) had not been repealed by the *Sorcery (Repeal) Act 2013* prior to the publication of this textbook.

[1103] See *John Baipu v The State* (2005) SC796, [2005] PGSC 19.

[1104] See *John Baipu v The State* (2005) SC796, [2005] PGSC 19.

[1105] See *Irai Thomas v The State* (2007) SC867, [2007] PGSC 26; *John Baipu v The State* (2005) SC796, [2005] PGSC 19; *Agoara Kelo and another v The State* (1981) SC198; *The State v Baika Martin and others* (2008) N3312, [2008] PGNC 29 and *The State v Sedoki Lota and Fred Abenko* (2007) N3183, [2007] PGNC 167.

[1106] See *The State v Sedoki Lota and Fred Abenko* (2007) N3183, [2007] PGNC 167.

[1107] See *The State v Boat Yokum and six others* (2002) N2337; *The State v Urari Siviri* (2004) N2747 and *The State v Saweno Visari and Ragu Maioi* [2006] PGNC 61.

EXTENUATING CIRCUMSTANCES

[6.0] ROLE PLAYED IN THE COMMISSION OF AN OFFENCE

In certain circumstances, the fact that an accused person played a minor role in the commission of an offence may mean that he or she is less culpable than some of the other co-accused who participated in the offence.[1108]

Fringe members of a group should be treated as less culpable than co-accused who participate more fully or lead the others.[1109]

1108 See The Law Reform Commission of Ireland, 1993, 'Consultation Paper on Sentencing', paragraph 5.63.

Refer also to the sections titled 'Leadership In A Gang' and 'Member Of A Gang' in the chapter titled 'Aggravating Factors'.

1109 See The Law Reform Commission of Ireland, 1993, 'Consultation Paper on Sentencing', paragraph 5.63.

Refer also to the sections titled 'Leadership In A Gang' and 'Member Of A Gang' in the chapter titled 'Aggravating Factors'.

MITIGATING FACTORS

[1.0] INTRODUCTION

There is a distinction between extenuating circumstances and mitigating factors, although both have the same desired effect of reducing the punishment.[1110]

'Extenuating circumstances' are:

> The particular circumstances in which the offence was committed that have the effect of reducing or diminishing the gravity of an offence.[1111]

However, mitigating factors are usually unrelated to the circumstances of the offence.[1112]

The term 'mitigate' from which 'mitigation' is derived means:

> To lessen the seriousness of evil, harm, pain, etc.[1113]

Thus, circumstances or factors of mitigation are intended to make an offence less serious, and thereby lessen the severity or rigors of the prescribed sanction.[1114]

The more mitigating factors that are present, the more likely it is that the head sentence will be reduced. The more aggravating factors present, the more likely it is the head sentence will be lifted above the starting point. However, sentencing is not an exact science. It is a discretionary process. When a factor is marked as mitigating or aggravating it does not mean necessarily that it is given the same weight as another mitigating or aggravating factor. Some mitigating factors may be 'strongly mitigating'. Others maybe 'mildly mitigating'. The same goes for aggravating factors.[1115]

1110 See *John Elipa Kalabus v The State* [1988-89] PNGLR 19.

1111 See *Steven Loke Ume, Charles Patrick Kaona and Greg Wawa Kavoa v The State* (2006) SC836, [2006] PGSC 9.

1112 See *John Elipa Kalabus v The State* [1988-89] PNGLR 19.

1113 See *The State v Iori Veraga* (2005) N2921, [2005] PGNC 43.

1114 See *The State v Iori Veraga* (2005) N2921, [2005] PGNC 43.

1115 See *The State v Paul Nelson* (2005) N2844 and *The State v Jacky Moses* (2012) N4886, [2012] PGNC 213.

MITIGATING FACTORS

In order for a Court to act fairly and, in principle, to be seen to act fairly, a full opportunity must be given to allow mitigating factors to be put to the Court.[1116]

The 'mitigating factors' pertinent to an accused person are always a major factor to be weighed in sentencing by reducing punishment[1117], but the mitigating factors need to be assessed properly.[1118]

A Court should take into consideration mitigating factors:

- even though the maximum sentence for a particular offence may be considered too low[1119]; and
- prior to making the decision whether to impose a custodial sentence.[1120]

A Court should not particularise specific periods of deductions from the head sentence based on specific mitigating factors, for example, that two years be deducted for advanced age.[1121]

[1116] See *Moses Aikaba and others v Tami* [1971-72] PNGLR 155, [1971] PGSC 2; *Agiru Aieni and twelve others v Paul T Tahain* [1978] PNGLR 37; *Michael Gende v The State* (1999) SC626, [1999] PGSC 25; *Tom Longman Yaul v The State* (2005) SC803, [2005] PGSC 29 and *The State v Justin Komboli* (2005) N2891, [2005] PGNC 61.

Section 59(2) of the *Constitution of the Independent State of Papua New Guinea* states:

> 'The minimum requirement of natural justice is the duty to act fairly and, in principle, to be seen to act fairly'.

[1117] See *Harris v The DPP (Nauru)* [1998] NRSC 2.

[1118] See *Bock v R* [1993] SBHC 56.

[1119] See *R v Carroll* (1995) 16 Cr App R (S) 488.

[1120] See *R v Hori; R v Melody* [1993] SBHC 52 and *R v Mani* [1998] SBHC 77.

[1121] See *Babai v The State* [1995] PNGLR 179, [1995] PGSC 10 and *Acting Public Prosecutor v Nitak Mangilonde Taganis of Tambitanis* [1982] PNGLR 299, [1982] PGSC 6.

See however: *R v Taueki* [2005] 3 NZLR 372.

MITIGATING FACTORS

The only specific period to be deducted from the head sentence is the time period that an accused person has served in custody prior to sentence.[1122]

Mitigating factors include:

- the entering of a plea of guilty[1123];
- the accused person's personal antecedents, including good character, education, employment[1124] and Christian background[1125];
- whether the accused person has no or limited previous convictions (first time offender[1126]);
- whether the accused person co-operated with police and the extent thereof[1127];
- whether the accused person made an early confession to police[1128];

[1122] Section 3(2) of the *Criminal Justice (Sentences) Act 1986* states:

> 'There may be deducted from the length or any term of imprisonment imposed by the sentence of any court any period before the sentence was imposed during which the offender was in custody in connection with the offence for which the sentence was imposed'.

See also: *Babai v The State* [1995] PNGLR 179, [1995] PGSC 10.

[1123] See *Steven Loke Ume, Charles Patrick Kaona and Greg Wawa Kavoa v The State* (2006) SC836, [2006] PGSC 9 and *Denden Tom and others v The State* (2008) SC967.

Refer also to the subsection titled 'Plea Of Guilty' in the section titled 'Taking Of A Plea' in the chapter titled 'Court Procedure' in the text titled 'Injia on Criminal Practice and Procedure in Papua New Guinea and the Pacific'.

[1124] However, a reduction in sentence when an accused person's job is in jeopardy leads to the introduction of social inequality into sentencing, see The Law Reform Commission of Ireland, 1993, 'Consultation Paper on Sentencing', paragraph 5.103.

[1125] See *Steven Loke Ume, Charles Patrick Kaona and Greg Wawa Kavoa v The State* (2006) SC836, [2006] PGSC 96 and *Denden Tom and others v The State* (2008) SC967.

[1126] See *Steven Loke Ume, Charles Patrick Kaona and Greg Wawa Kavoa v The State* (2006) SC836, [2006] PGSC 9 and *Denden Tom and others v The State* (2008) SC967.

[1127] See *Steven Loke Ume, Charles Patrick Kaona and Greg Wawa Kavoa v The State* (2006) SC836, [2006] PGSC 9 and *Denden Tom and others v The State* (2008) SC967.

[1128] See *Steven Loke Ume, Charles Patrick Kaona and Greg Wawa Kavoa v The State* (2006) SC836, [2006] PGSC 9 and *Denden Tom and others v The State* (2008) SC967.

MITIGATING FACTORS

- whether the accused person has expressed genuine remorse for committing the offence[1129];
- the youthfulness of the accused person[1130];
- whether the accused person has a good personal and family background[1131];
- whether the accused person is suffering from ill-health and the extent thereto[1132];
- whether the accused person has paid restitution or compensation[1133];
- whether there has been a delay between the commission of the offence and sentencing and the reasons thereof;
- whether there is any risk of repetition;
- the impact of social or cultural pressures and isolation on the accused person; and
- whether the accused person has suffered extra-curial punishment as a consequence of committing the offence.

[1129] See *Steven Loke Ume, Charles Patrick Kaona and Greg Wawa Kavoa v The State* (2006) SC836, [2006] PGSC 9 and *Denden Tom and others v The State* (2008) SC967.

[1130] See *Steven Loke Ume, Charles Patrick Kaona and Greg Wawa Kavoa v The State* (2006) SC836, [2006] PGSC 9 and *Denden Tom and others v The State* (2008) SC967.

[1131] See *Steven Loke Ume, Charles Patrick Kaona and Greg Wawa Kavoa v The State* (2006) SC836, [2006] PGSC 9 and *Denden Tom and others v The State* (2008) SC967.

[1132] See *Steven Loke Ume, Charles Patrick Kaona and Greg Wawa Kavoa v The State* (2006) SC836, [2006] PGSC 9 and *Denden Tom and others v The State* (2008) SC967.

[1133] See *Manu Kovi v The State* (2005) SC789, [2005] PGSC 34; *Steven Loke Ume, Charles Patrick Kaona and Greg Wawa Kavoa v The State* (2006) SC836, [2006] PGSC 9 and *Denden Tom and others v The State* (2008) SC967.

Refer also to the section titled 'Compensation Order' in the chapter titled 'Sentencing Options'.

MITIGATING FACTORS

Mitigating factors that are not accepted by either:

- the Court; or
- the prosecution

need to be proven on the 'balance of probabilities'.[1134]

A Court may remark on the absence of mitigating factors that attract leniency.[1135]

[2.0] PLEA OF GUILTY

A plea of guilty is an admission of guilt of the elements of the charge as presented and it must be clearly unequivocal before it is accepted by the Court.[1136]

A guilty plea is indicative of the accused person's acceptance of responsibility for his or her wrong, his or her repentence and remorse, his or her willingness to change his or her criminal behaviour and saves of enormous benefit to the Court and the prosecution in terms of saving valuable time and costs of running a prosecution and trial.

A plea of guilty is therefore a 'mitigating factor'.

That a plea of guilty should result in a reduced sentence is a well-established principle.

[1134] See *R v Olbrich* (1999) 199 CLR 270, [1999] HCA 54; *R v Storey* [1998] 1 VR 359 at 369 and *KS v The State of Western Australia* [2011] WASCA 85, per Hall J.

[1135] See *Siganto v R* (1998) 194 CLR 656 at 664, (1998) 105 A Crim R 184, [1998] HCA 74.

[1136] Refer also to the subsection titled 'Plea Of Guilty' in the section titled 'Taking Of A Plea' in the chapter titled 'Court Procedure' in the text titled 'Injia on Criminal Practice and Procedure in Papua New Guinea and the Pacific'.

MITIGATING FACTORS

The effect of a plea of guilty is that an accused person admits to:

- the elements of the offence; and
- the facts that have been put to him or her[1137], including all of the essential facts necessary to constitute the offence[1138].

The plea also negatives all defences.[1139]

A plea of guilty does not, however, constitute an admission of all of the facts stated in the:

- prosecution's depositions; or
- witness statements.[1140]

An accused person who has pleaded guilty is to be given the benefit of the doubt on 'mitigating factors' raised in the depositions, the *allocutus* or in submissions that are not contested by the prosecution.[1141]

In determining the amount of reduction to be given for entering a plea of guilty a Court should examine the circumstances surrounding the plea.[1142]

[1137] See *Saperus Yalibakut v The State* (2006) SC890, [2006] PGSC 27 and *The State v Alphonse Polpolio and Jeffrey Baru* [2006] PGNC 16.

See also: *R v Hill* [1979] VR 311 at 312.

[1138] See *R v Hill* [1979] VR 311 at 312; *Law v The State of Western Australia* [2009] WASCA 193 and *Harris v R* [2004] WASCA 292.

[1139] See *Schugman v Menz* [1970] SASR 381, per Bray CJ at 381-382 and *Harris v R* [2004] WASCA 292.

[1140] See *R v Hill* [1979] VR 311 at 312.

[1141] See *Saperus Yalibakut v The State* (2006) SC890, [2006] PGSC 27; *The State v Jelio Yawi* (2009) N3631, [2009] PGNC 44 and *The State v Lawrence Giobun* (2009) N3728, [2009] PGNC 119.

Refer also to the chapter titled 'Sentencing Proceedings'.

[1142] See *Wilson v R* [2000] NZCA 60.

MITIGATING FACTORS

The fact that an accused person pleads guilty has no bearing on:

- the circumstances of the offence; or
- the accused person's personal characteristics.[1143]

Making allowance for a reduction in sentence for a plea of guilty is a purely practical concern based on the following factors:

- it may be indicative of:

  An acceptance of and a willingness to facilitate the course of justice[1144];

- there is recognition for the fact that the accused person has foregone the right to trial on the presumption of innocence[1145];
- it avoids inconvenience to witnesses[1146];
- it reduces court delays[1147];

[1143] See The Law Reform Commission of Ireland, 1993, 'Consultation Paper on Sentencing', paragraph 5.79.

[1144] See *Cameron v R* (2002) 209 CLR 339, (2002) 76 ALJR 382, [2002] HCA 6 and *H v The State of Western Australia* (2006) 163 A Crim R 151, [2006] WASCA 53.

[1145] See The Law Reform Commission of Ireland, 1993, 'Consultation Paper on Sentencing', paragraph 5.80.

[1146] See *R v Shannon* (1979) 21 SASR 442 at 448 and 451; *R v Morton* [1986] VR 863 at 867; *Dodge* (1988) 34 A Crim R 325 at 331; *Winchester* (1992) 58 A Crim R 345 at 350; *R v Atholwood* (1999) 109 A Crim R 465 at 467 and *R v Shannon* (1979) 21 SASR 442, per King CJ at 454-453.

[1147] See *R v Shannon* (1979) 21 SASR 442 at 448 and 451; *R v Morton* [1986] VR 863 at 867; *Dodge* (1988) 34 A Crim R 325 at 331; *Winchester* (1992) 58 A Crim R 345 at 350 and *R v Atholwood* (1999) 109 A Crim R 465 at 467.

See also: The Law Reform Commission of Ireland, 1996, 'Report of Sentencing', paragraph 6.1 and The Law Reform Commission of Ireland, 1993, 'Consultation Paper on Sentencing', paragraph 5.79.

- there is the resultant savings in court time and expense[1148]; and
- it avoids the victim having to relive the trauma of the offence in the witness box[1149].

A plea of guilty may be taken into account in mitigation, even though it is solely motivated by self-interest.[1150]

[1148] See *The State v Bernard Soeka Hela* (2012) N4788, [2012] PGNC 228; *The State v Esther Koite Nokup* (2012) N4787, [2012] PGNC 225; *The State v Tony Dom* (2012) N4767, [2012] PGNC 97; *The State v Kapaka Roga and others* (2012) N4804, [2012] PGNC 223; *The State v John Bolkun* (2012) N4689, [2012] PGNC 75; *The State v Peter Pendin* (2012) N4541, [2012] PGNC 292; *The State v Andrew Aopo Lengade* (2012) N4690, [2012] PGNC 76; *The State v Seke Kapieng* (2012) N4695, [2012] PGNC 102 and *The State v Tala John* (2012) N4630, [2012] PGNC 197.

See also:
- *R v Fraser* [1982] 4 Cr App R (S) 254; *Dodge* (1988) 34 A Crim R 325, per Kirby P at 331; *R v Atholwood* (1999) 109 A Crim R 465 at 467; *Cameron v R* (2002) 209 CLR 339, (2002) 76 ALJR 382, [2002] HCA 6; *Siganto v R* (1998) 194 CLR 656, (1998) 105 A Crim R 184, [1998] HCA 74; *R v Churches* [2002] NZCA 78; *R v Shannon* (1979) 21 SASR 442 at 448 and 451; *R v Morton* [1986] VR 863 at 867; *Winchester* (1992) 58 A Crim R 345 at 350 and *AB v R* (1999) 198 CLR 111, per Hayne J at 155, [1999] HCA 46; and
- The Law Reform Commission of Ireland, 1993, 'Consultation Paper on Sentencing', paragraph 5.79.

[1149] See *The State v Tala John* (2012) N4630, [2012] PGNC 197; *The State v Seke Kapieng* (2012) N4695, [2012] PGNC 102; *The State v Levi Ateika* (2010) N3962, [2010] PGNC 25; *The State v Chan Alois And Augustine Tutut* (2008) N3668, [2008] PGNC 180 and *The State v Tonny Kupin* (2009) N3641.

See also:
- *Burenikarawa v R* [2006] SBCA 4 and *R v Churches* [2002] NZCA 78; and
- The Law Reform Commission of Ireland, 1993, 'Consultation Paper on Sentencing', paragraph 5.79.

The extra stress that giving evidence can cause to a victim of a rape means that a plea of guilty perhaps more so than other cases, should normally result in reduction from what would otherwise be the appropriate sentence, see *John Aubuku v The State* [1987] PNGLR 267 at 269.

[1150] See *Rigby v The State of Western Australia* [2005] WASCA 134.

MITIGATING FACTORS

The degree of weight to be given to a plea of guilty is subject to a number of factors, including:

- whether the plea is an indication of genuine remorse[1151], repentance or contrition.[1152]

  The traditional justification for allowing a reduction in sentence for an expression of remorse, ie., that it indicates a likelihood of successful re-integration into society.[1153]

  Whilst remorse will be a major factor in determining whether an accused person is unlikely to re-offend and has good prospects of rehabilitation[1154], without true remorse it is difficult to see how either finding could be made.[1155]

  A Court is not bound to accept assertions by an accused person that he or she is remorseful, even when that assertion is made in the witness box.[1156]

[1151] See *The State v Michael Tangip* (2012) N4782, [2012] PGNC 205.

See also: *Pavlic v R* (1995) 5 Tas R 186, [1995] TASSC 96 and *Ferguson v R* [2001] TASSC 20.

[1152] See *Emil Kongian and others v The State* (2007) SC928, [2007] PGSC 45; *Acting Public Prosecutor v John Airi* (1981) SC241 and *Wellington Belewa v The State* [1988-89] PNGLR 496, [1988] PGSC 6.

See also: *R v Neal* (1982) 42 ALR 609, per Murphy J at 617; *R v Beri* [1987] 1 NZLR 46 at 48; *R v Rapira* [2003] NZCA 217; *R v Winchester* (1992) 58 A Crim R 345, per Hunt CJ at CL at 350; *R v Holder and Johnston* [1983] 3 NSWLR 245, (1983) 13 A Crim R 375; *R v Morton* [1986] VR 863; *Pavlic v R* (1995) 5 Tas R 186; *Ferguson v R* [2001] TASSC 20; *R v Shannon* (1979) 21 SASR 442 at 454-453; *Siganto v R* (1998) 194 CLR 656 at 663-664, (1998) 105 A Crim R 184 at 189-190, [1998] HCA 74; *Cameron v R* (2002) 209 CLR 339, (2002) 76 ALJR 382, [2002] HCA 6; *H v The State of Western Australia* (2006) 163 A Crim R 151, [2006] WASCA 53 and *AB v R* (1999) 198 CLR 111, per Hayne J at 155, [1999] HCA 46.

However, genuine remorse is not a pre-condition for the mitigatory effect of a plea of guilty, see *Hooper v R* (2003) 27 WAR 264; *Rigby v The State of Western Australia* [2005] WASCA 134; *Winchester* (1992) 58 A Crim R 345 at 350; *Verschuren v R* (1996) 17 WAR 467 at 473; *R v Atholwood* (1999) 109 A Crim R 465 at 467; *Kalache* (2000) 111 A Crim R 152, [2000] NSWCCA 2; *Pop v R* (2000) 116 A Crim R 398, [2000] WASCA 283 and *Aconi v R* [2001] WASCA 211.

[1153] See The Law Reform Commission of Ireland, 1993, 'Consultation Paper on Sentencing', paragraph 5.88.

[1154] Refer also to the section titled 'The Need For Reformation And Rehabilitation' in the chapter titled 'Objectives And Purposes Of Sentencing'.

[1155] See *R v MAK* (2006) 167 A Crim R 159 at 169-170, [2006] NSWCCA 381.

[1156] See *Alvares v R* [2011] NSWCCA 33 and *R v Stafrace* (1997) 96 A Crim R 452.

MITIGATING FACTORS

A Court necessarily assumes the role or attitude of a 'doubting Thomas'.[1157]

Caution is appropriate whether the statement is made to:

- a psychiatrist or psychologist[1158];
- to an officer preparing a presentence report[1159]; or
- in a letter from the accused person to the Court[1160].

Such out-of-court statements are made in circumstances where they are unlikely to be challenged, and when an accused person does not give viva voce evidence the Court does not have the assistance of demeanour in evaluating the correctness of asserted remorse.[1161]

It is difficult to justify a deduction in sentence simply because the accused person shows remorse or denounces his or her offending conduct, especially if the accused person has done nothing else to show remorse, other than to simply express remorse. An inherent difficulty with this factor is that an expression of remorse *per se* is very difficult to prove or disprove whilst at the same time being very easy to make.[1162]

[1157] See *The State v Iori Veraga* (2005) N2921, [2005] PGNC 43.

See also: *Pham v R* [2010] NSWCCA 208, per Simpson J.

[1158] See *R v Qutami* (2001) 127 A Crim R 369, [2001] NSWCCA 353, per Spigelman CJ and Smart AJ and *R v McGourty* [2002] NSWCCA 335, per Wood CJ at CL.

[1159] See *R v Palu* (2002) 134 A Crim R 174, [2002] NSWCCA 381, per Howie J and *TS v R* [2007] NSWCCA 194, per Giles JA.

[1160] See *R v Elfar* [2003] NSWCCA 358, per Whealy J.

[1161] As McClelland CJ at CL pointed out in *Pfitzner v R* [2010] NSWCCA 314.

[1162] See The Law Reform Commission of Ireland, 1993, 'Consultation Paper on Sentencing', paragraph 5.87.

Concrete evidence of contrition is required, such as:

- the payment of restitution or compensation[1163]; or
- co-operation with the police and the prosecution[1164], including the admission of other offences.[1165]

Depending on the circumstances of the offence, an expression of remorse should be accompanied or supported by:

- a payment of compensation; or
- such other ways of restoring damages done by the commission of an offence,

otherwise a mere expression of remorse is meaningless.[1166]

To merely say sorry means nothing.[1167]

The sooner the compensation is paid the greater the weight it should be given.[1168]

If it is made on the day of trial or immediately after conviction it does not show remorse.[1169]

[1163] Refer also to the subsection titled 'Customary Compensation' in the section titled 'Compensation Order' in the chapter titled 'Sentencing Options'.

[1164] Refer also to the section titled 'Co-operation With Police' in this chapter.

[1165] See *The State v Iori Veraga* (2005) N2921, [2005] PGNC 43.

[1166] See *Ala Peter Utieng v The State* (2000) SCRA No. 15 of 2000; *Rudy Yekat v The State* (2000) SC665, (2000) SC665; *The State v Lucas Yovura* (2003) N2366; *The State v Enni Mathew and others (No. 2)* (2003) N2563; *The State v Sailor Peter Tatanu* (2006) N3392, [2006] PGNC 170; *The State v Patrick Puppy Kaikara Loavi* (2006) N3384, [2006] PGNC 104; *The State v Fredinand Naka Penge* (2002) N2244; *The State v Kevin Anis and Martin Ningigan* (2003) N2360; *The State v Tau Karo* (2004) N2600; *The State v Donald Poni* (2004) N2663 and *The State v Donald Angavia and others (No. 2)* (2004) N2590.

Refer also to the section titled 'Compensation Order' in the chapter titled 'Sentencing Options'.

[1167] See *The State v Donald Poni* (2004) N2663 and *The State v Donald Angavia and others (No. 2)* (2004) N2590.

[1168] See *Wellington Belawa v The State* [1988-89] PNGLR 496, [1988] PGSC 6, per Bredmeyer J.

[1169] See *The State v Oa Seseka* (1990) N921.

However, remorse is not necessarily shown by a plea of guilty and may be contested by the prosecution as to whether it is genuine.[1170] In such circumstances an accused person must be given the opportunity to prove otherwise.[1171]

Irrespective, it may be difficult for a Court to determine whether remorse is genuine[1172];

- whether the plea was in recognition of the inevitable.[1173]

  However, even when the prosecution case is strong a plea of guilty should still be considered as a mitigating factor[1174]; and

- the timing of the plea.[1175]

  Whether remorse or contrition is shown by a plea of guilty depends upon:

  - the time; and
  - the circumstances

[1170] See *R v Olbrich* (1999) 199 CLR 270 at 286, [1999] HCA 54.

[1171] See *R v Olbrich* (1999) 199 CLR 270 at 286, [1999] HCA 54 and *Nash v Haas* [1972] Tas SR 1.

[1172] See *R v Riki Rapira and others* [2003] NZCA 217.

[1173] See *The State v Oa Seseka* (1990) N921.

See also: *Shannon* (1979) 21 SASR 442 at 452; *Ellis* (1986) 6 NSWLR 603, per Hunt CJ at CL at 604; *R v Winchester* (1992) 58 A Crim R 345 at 350; *R v Henry* [1996] 1 Cr App R (S) 167; *Burenikarawa v R* [2006] SBCA 4 and *Tyler v R; R v Chalmers* [2007] NSWCCA 247.

[1174] See *R v Atholwood* (1999) 109 A Crim R 465, per Ipp J at 467.

[1175] See *R v McGrath* [1971-72] PNGLR 247; *The State v Neville Miria* (2013) N5102, [2013] PGNC 37; *The State v Neiman Dua* (2013) N4957, [2013] PGNC 8; *The State v Sali Kevin Mavuug* (2012) N4898, [2012] PGNC 255; *The State v Mason Kinjon Karato (No. 2)* (2012) N4832, [2012] PGNC 157 and *The State v Tony Pinuana* [2007] PGNC 119.

See also: *Wilson v R* [2000] NZCA 60; *R v Orchard* [1991] 1 NZLR 320 at 321; *R v Moevasa* [2002] NZCA 72; *Cardile v R* [2003] WASCA 72; *R v Holder* [1983] 3 NSWLR 245, (1983) 13 A Crim R 375; *Bulger* [1990] 2 Qd R 559, (1990) 48 A Crim R 239; *R v Atholwood* (1999) 109 A Crim R 465; *R v Winchester* (1992) 58 A Crim R 345, per Hunt CJ at CL at 350; *DPP v G* [1994] IR 587 and *The People (DPP) v Tiernan* [1988] IR 250, [1989] ILRM 149 at 159.

in which the plea is advanced.[1176]

The entry of an early plea is the most compelling evidence of acceptance of responsibility, remorse and contrition.[1177]

The earlier the plea after the commission of an offence the more favourable it will be for an accused person.[1178]

When a plea comes very late and is not indicative of genuine remorse, the weight to be given should generally be greatly reduced.[1179]

An expression of remorse after conviction following a trial loses its significance.[1180]

The weight given to a plea is reduced where:

- there has been a plea bargain[1181]; or
- the accused person has delayed the plea to obtain some forensic advantage[1182].

1176 See *John Elipa Kalabus v The State* [1988-89] PNGLR 193, per Kidu CJ at 197.

See also: *Ruddy Yekat v The State* [2000] PNGLR 225, (2000) SC665; *Allan Peter Utieng v The State* (2001) SCR No. 15 of 2000; *The State v Tumu Luna* (2002) N2205; *The State v Maria Paul* (2003) N2434; *The State v Donald Angavia and others (No. 2)* (2004) N2590; *The State v Misack Kilik* (2004) N2749 and *The State v Moki Lepi (No. 3)* (2004) N2734.

1177 See *R v Accused* (1997) 14 CRNZ 645 at 647.

1178 See *John Elipa Kalabus v The State* [1988-89] PNGLR 193, per Kidu CJ at 197.

See also: *Ruddy Yekat v The State* [2000] PNGLR 225, (2000) SC665; *Allan Peter Utieng v The State* (2001) SCR No. 15 of 2000; *The State v Tumu Luna* (2002) N2205; *The State v Maria Paul* (2003) N2434; *The State v Donald Angavia and others (No. 2)* (2004) N2590; *The State v Misack Kilik* (2004) N2749 and *The State v Moki Lepi (No. 3)* (2004) N2734.

1179 See *H v The State of Western Australia* (2006) 163 A Crim R 151, [2006] WASCA 53.

1180 See *The State v Tumu Luna* (2002) N2205.

1181 See *Dib* [2003] NSWCCA 117 and *Ahmad* [2006] NSWCCA 177.

Refer also to the chapter titled 'Plea Bargain'.

1182 See *Stambolis* [2006] NSWCCA 56; *Saad* [2007] NSWCCA 98; *Chiekh and Hoete* [2004] NSWCCA 448 and *R v Borkowski* [2009] NSWCCA 102.

However, even a late plea should still be considered as a mitigating factor.[1183]

The reason for the delay in entering a plea is generally irrelevant.[1184]

The amount of the deduction is discretionary and a Court must be accorded a wide measure of latitude which will be respected by an appellate Court.[1185]

However, no specific amount of sentence is to be deducted for any specific mitigating factor.[1186]

The entering of a plea does not alleviate an accused person from being sentenced to a lengthy term of imprisonment.[1187]

Depending on the circumstances of a case no weight may be given to a plea of guilty.[1188]

The reduction is not as a favour to an accused person, but in the public interest.[1189]

[1183] See *R v Atholwood* (1999) 109 A Crim R 465, per Ipp J at 467; *Dodge* (1988) 34 A Crim R 325 at 331; *Heferen v R* (1999) 106 A Crim R 89 at 92; *Thomson and Houlton* (2000) 115 A Crim R 104 at 134, (2000) 49 NSWLR 383, [2000] NSWCCA 309; *The People (DPP) v Tiernan* [1988] IR 250, per Finlay CJ at 255, [1989] ILRM 149; *DPP v G* [1994] 1 IR 587, per Finlay CJ at 591; *The People (DPP) v M* [1994] 3 IR 306, per Denham J at 319; *R v Raymond Everest Hessell* [2009] NZCA 450; *Forbes* [2005] NSWCCA 377 and *R v Borkowski* [2009] NSWCCA 102.

[1184] See *Stambolis* [2006] NSWCCA 56; *Giac* [2008] NSWCCA 280 and *R v Borkowski* [2009] NSWCCA 102.

[1185] See *Postiglione v R* (1997) 189 CLR 295, per Kirby J at 336, (1997) 145 ALR 408, (1998) 71 ALJR 875, [1997] HCA 26 and *Lowndes v R* (1999) 195 CLR 665 at 671-672, [1999] HCA 29.

[1186] See *Babai v The State* [1995] PNGLR 179, [1995] PGSC 10.

[1187] See *John Elipa Kalabus v The State* [1988-89] PNGLR 193.

[1188] See *Thomson and Houlton* (2000) 115 A Crim R 104 at 134, (2000) 49 NSWLR 383, [2000] NSWCCA 309; *Kalache* (2000) 111 A Crim R 152, [2000] NSWCCA 2; *El-Andouri* [2004] NSWCCA 178; *Moody v French* (2008) 36 WAR 393, [2008] WASCA 67; *Sau Soo Kim v Public Prosecutor* [1975] 2 MLJ 134; *Melvani v Public Prosecutor* [1971] 1 MLJ 137; *Public Prosecutor v Sulaiman bin Ahmad* [1993] 1 MLJ 74 and *Public Prosecutor v Ravindran and others* [1993] 1 MLJ 45.

See however: *Pitamama v R* [2005] SBHC 45 and *R v Ball* [1998] EWCA Crim 3182.

[1189] See *R v de Haan* [1967] 3 All ER 618, [1968] 2 QB 108, per Edmund-Davies LJ at 111.

MITIGATING FACTORS

[3.0] GOOD CHARACTER GENERALLY

In determining whether an accused person has good character, the Court should not consider the accused person's character for the offence for which he or she is being sentenced.[1190]

If an accused person is of otherwise good character, then a Court is bound to take that into account in the sentence that it imposes. The weight that must be given to an accused person's otherwise good character will vary according to all of the circumstances.[1191]

In its strict sense, character refers to:

> The inherent moral qualities of a person.[1192]

What makes a person of otherwise good character will necessarily vary according to the individual who stands for sentence.[1193]

It is impossible to state a universal rule.[1194]

There is no hard and fast rule as to what constitutes evidence of character at the sentencing stage[1195], but generally included are:

- whether an accused person can demonstrate good personal qualities and conduct[1196];
- the accused person's personal details such as age, family background, education and work record[1197]; and

---

[1190] See *Ryan v R* (2001) 206 CLR 267, (2001) 75 ALJR 815, (2001) 179 ALR 193, [2001] HCA 21, per *McHugh J and Ziems v The Prothonotary of the Supreme Court of New South Wales* (1957) 97 CLR 279, per Kitto J at 299.

[1191] See *Ryan v R* (2001) 206 CLR 267, (2001) 75 ALJR 815, (2001) 179 ALR 193, [2001] HCA 21, per McHugh J.

[1192] See *Melbourne v R* (1999) 198 CLR 1 at 15.

[1193] See *Melbourne v R* (1999) 198 CLR 1 at 15.

[1194] See *Melbourne v R* (1999) 198 CLR 1 at 15.

[1195] See The Law Reform Commission of Ireland, 1993, 'Consultation Paper on Sentencing', paragraph 1.21.

[1196] See *Ryan v R* (2001) 206 CLR 267, (2001) 75 ALJR 815, (2001) 179 ALR 193, [2001] HCA 21.

- other details such as income and personal situation since arrest, including whether or not the accused person was on bail or in custody[1198].

Good character is therefore not simply an absence of a criminal history.[1199]

A Court should give credit for previous good character.[1200]

The age of an accused person is an important consideration in determining for what period of time an accused person has been of good character.[1201]

The period of time between:

- the date of the commission of an offence; and

- the date of sentencing

is of particular importance if that is a lengthy period and an accused person did not commit any offences during that period.[1202]

The rules of evidence are relaxed in relation to character evidence, so that 'hearsay evidence[1203]' may be relied upon.[1204]

1197 See The Law Reform Commission of Ireland, 1993, 'Consultation Paper on Sentencing', paragraph 1.21.

1198 See The Law Reform Commission of Ireland, 1993, 'Consultation Paper on Sentencing', paragraph 1.21.

1199 See *Ryan v R* (2001) 206 CLR 267, (2001) 75 ALJR 815, (2001) 179 ALR 193, [2001] HCA 21.

1200 See *The State v Maniwogin* (2004) N2750, [2004] PGNC 32 and *The State v Jackson Peng* (2012) N4737, [2012] PGNC 110.

1201 See *Berekame v DPP* [1985-1986] SILR 272.

1202 See *R v DESM* (1993) 80 CCC (3rd) 371; *Murphy* (1990) 12 Cr App R (S) 530; *U* (1992) 13 Cr App R (S) 530; *R v B* (1992) 8 CRNZ 176; *R v Edwards* (1994) 12 CRNZ 302 and *R v Stephens* (1991) 7 CRNZ 347.

1203 Refer also to the section titled 'Hearsay Evidence' in the chapter titled 'Evidence' in the text titled 'Injia on Criminal Practice and Procedure in Papua New Guinea and the Pacific'.

1204 See *The State (Stanbridge) v Mahon* [1979] IR 214 and *R v Marquis* (1951) 35 Cr App R 33, per Goddard LCJ.

As regards the law in relation to 'Hearsay Evidence', refer to the chapter titled 'Evidence' in the text titled 'Injia on Criminal Practice and Procedure in Papua New Guinea and the Pacific'.

MITIGATING FACTORS

[4.0] CRIMINAL HISTORY[1205]

It is a mitigating factor that an accused person has no previous convictions.[1206]

As a general principle of sentencing it takes a very serious offence to warrant a custodial sentence for a person with an unblemished record.[1207]

However, an offence committed by a first time offender may be taken as the result of a deliberate conscious choice made with full appreciation of the significance of his or her actions.[1208]

A Court may treat an accused person as being:

- rehabilitated; and
- of good character

when there has been a considerable lapse of time since the last conviction.[1209]

Whilst a previous conviction cannot be disregarded the lapse of considerable time since the last conviction may reduce the weight to given to it.

1205 Section 16(9) of the *Professional Conduct Rules 1989* states:

> 'If, in a case, the Court has been led by the prosecution to believe that the accused person has no previous convictions, the defending lawyer is under no duty to –
> (a) disclose facts to the contrary which are known to him; or
> (b) correct any information given by the prosecution, if such disclosure or correction would be to his client's detriment, provided that the lawyer shall not –
> (i) lend himself to any assertion that his client has no convictions; or
> (ii) ask a prosecution witness whether there are previous convictions against his client in the hope that he will receive a negative answer'.

1206 See *Sakarowa Koe v The State* (2004) SC739, [2004] PGSC 33; *Simon Kama v The State* (2004) SC740, [2004] PGSC 32; *The State v Nelson N Ngasele* (2003) SC731, [2003] PGSC 2 and *Kondon Kale v The State* (1983) SC250.

See however: *The State v John Telape* (2009) N3815 and *The State v Janos Berenyi and Irene Berenyi* (2009) N3813.

1207 See *Crawley v R* (1981) 36 ALR 241, (1981) 5 A Crim R 451.

1208 See *The State v Henry Opu* (1980) N250.

1209 See *R v Smith* (1983) 5 Cr App R (S) 61.

MITIGATING FACTORS

Whilst a Court should be hesitant to impose a term of imprisonment on a first time offender, the imposition of such a sentence also depends on the 'aggravating factors[1210,1211], including the seriousness of the offence[1212].

A previous conviction:

- must be proven in accordance with the law[1213], if it is disputed; and
- must not to be disclosed until after a conviction has been recorded[1214].

[5.0] CO-OPERATION WITH POLICE

The policy of the Courts to recognise useful assistance to the authorities in mitigation of sentence is based on the public interest.[1215]

No distinction is drawn between disclosure of information concerning:

- the offence for which the accused person is being sentenced[1216];

1210 Refer also to the chapter titled 'Aggravating Factors'.

1211 See *R v Saungao* [1997] SBHC 60.

1212 See *The State v Oa Seseka* (1990) N921.

Refer also to the section titled 'Seriousness Of An Offence Generally' in the chapter titled 'Aggravating Factors'.

1213 See *R v Finney* (1924) 18 Cr App R 41.

See also: *Ex parte Kelly; Re Teece* (1966) 85 WN (Pt. 1) NSW 151 at 153-156.

As regards the law in relation to a previous conviction, refer to the subsection titled 'Previous Convictions' in the section titled 'Wording Of Charges' in the chapter titled 'Charges' in the text titled 'Injia on Criminal Practice and Procedure in Papua New Guinea and the Pacific'.

1214 See *Gregory Kasen v The State* (2001) N2133.

1215 See *R v Cartwright* (1989) 17 NSWLR 243 at 252 and *MA v R* (2001) 125 A Crim R 349, [2001] WASCA 325.

1216 See *Z v HKSAR* [2007] HKCFA 22; *R v Sivan* (1988) 87 Cr App R 407 at 412; *R v Many* (1990) 51 A Crim R 54 at 68; *R v Accused* (1993) 10 CRNZ 397 at 402 and *R v Rostom* [1996] 2 VR 97 at 104.

- offences associated with the offence for which the accused person is being sentenced[1217]; or

- offences that are unconnected to the offence for which the accused person is being sentenced[1218].

The fact that an accused person co-operates with the police in the investigation of an offence, including voluntarily surrendering to the police,[1219] is a mitigating factor.[1220]

This is particularly so if such assistance is a demonstration of genuine remorse or contrition[1221].

Assisting in the investigation by either:

- turning oneself in; or

- assisting in the investigations of other offences,

 should help expedite the course of justice.[1222]

[1217] See *R v Sivan* (1988) 87 Cr App R 407 at 412; *R v Many* (1990) 51 A Crim R 54 at 68; *R v Accused* (1993) 10 CRNZ 397 at 402; *R v Rostom* [1996] 2 VR 97 at 104 and *Z v HKSAR* [2007] HKCFA 22.

[1218] See *R v Sivan* (1988) 87 Cr App R 407 at 412; *R v Many* (1990) 51 A Crim R 54 at 68; *R v Accused* (1993) 10 CRNZ 397 at 402; *R v Rostom* [1996] 2 VR 97 at 104 and *Z v HKSAR* [2007] HKCFA 22.

[1219] See *The State v Issau Parao* (2009) N3625, [2009] PGNC 38 and *The State v Tony Dom* (2012) N4767, [2012] PGNC 97.

[1220] See *R v McGrath* [1971-72] PNGLR 247, per Raine J at 253 and *Kali Mari v The State* (1980) SC175.

See also: *R v Cartwright* (1989) 17 NSWLR 243; *R v Gallagher* (1991) 23 NSWLR 220; *R v James and Sharman* (1913) 9 Cr App R 142; *R v Caust* [1936] SASR 170; *R v Shannon* (1979) 21 SASR 442 at 450; *Heferen v R* (1999) 106 A Crim R 89 at 92; *R v Accused* (1993) 10 CRNZ 397 at 402; *R v B* [2004] WASCA 1; *F v R* [2005] WASCA 135; *Adifaka v DPP* [1984] SILR 44 at 50; *James and Sharman* (1913) 9 Cr App R 142; *Z v HKSAR* [2007] HKCFA 22; *R v Sivan* (1988) 87 Cr App R 407 at 412; *R v Many* (1990) 51 A Crim R 54 at 68; *R v Rostom* [1996] 2 VR 97 at 104; *The People (DPP) v Moloney* 3 Frewen 267; *R v Lowe* (1977) 66 Cr App R 122; *R v Davies and Gorman* (1978) 66 Cr App R 319; *R v Rose and Sapiano* (1980) 2 Cr App R (S) 239; *R v Sinfield* (1981) 2 Cr App R (S) 258; *R v Thomas* (1985) 7 Cr App R (S) 95; *R v King* (1985) 7 Cr App R (S) 227, (1985) 82 Cr App R 120; *R v Preston and McAleny* (1987) 9 Cr App R (S) 155 and *R v Wood* (1987) Cr App R (S) 238.

[1221] See *MA v R* (2001) 125 A Crim R 349, [2001] WASCA 325.

[1222] See The Law Reform Commission of Ireland, 1993, 'Consultation Paper on Sentencing', paragraph 5.85.

> As a consequence witnesses and, in particular, victims, may be spared the trauma of a long wait before the matter comes before the courts.[1223]

Co-operation may encourage others to assist the police in the investigation of other offences.[1224]

The weight to be given to this mitigating factor depends on all the circumstances of the particular case.[1225]

A 'pragmatic case by case approach' should be adopted.[1226]

What is to be rewarded is genuine co-operation with the authorities.[1227]

Where genuine co-operation has been provided, a reduction in sentence will not be lost merely as a result of the authorities not acting on the information because, for example:

- more cogent evidence from another source has emerged; or
- the subject of the information has pleaded guilty.[1228]

However, the weight to be given to this mitigating factor will be reduced where the information is not acted upon in circumstances where the accused person has:

- deliberately delayed in providing information for a lengthy period of time; or
- destroyed some relevant evidence,

with the result that the information eventually supplied is of little effective value or benefit to the authorities.[1229]

[1223] See The Law Reform Commission of Ireland, 1993, 'Consultation Paper on Sentencing', paragraph 5.85.

[1224] See *Duffy* (1996) 85 A Crim R 456 and *Gallagher v R* (1991) 23 NSWLR 220.

[1225] See *MXP v The State of Western Australia* (2010) 41 WAR 149, [2010] WASCA 215; *Bazzi v The State of Western Australia* [2007] WASCA 195 and *R v Gallagher* (1991) 23 NSWLR 220 at 234.

[1226] See *Hayes v R* [1981] WAR 252 at 253.

[1227] See *R v Cartwright* (1989) 17 NSWLR 243 at 253 and *MA v R* (2001) 125 A Crim R 349, [2001] WASCA 325.

[1228] See *R v Cartwright* (1989) 17 NSWLR 243 at 253 and *MA v R* (2001) 125 A Crim R 349, [2001] WASCA 325.

[1229] See *Assafiri v R* [2007] NSWCCA 159.

However, the seriousness of the offence and 'aggravating factors' may render co-operation with police meaningless.[1230]

The reduction in sentence should be greater than that of a plea of guilty.[1231]

The factors to be taken into account include:

- the nature and extent of the assistance.[1232]

  There is a distinction to be drawn between:

  - an offer;
  - an intention to assist; and
  - actual assistance.[1233]

  Greater weight is given to the provision of actual assistance, rather than an intention to assist is not enough; actual assistance is necessary.[1234]

  However, irrespective a sentence should be reduced in relation to an accused person who has given or promised some material information or assistance.[1235]

  Where an accused person has given past or promised future co-operation, the focus of attention, in relation to sentencing, must be on:

  - the nature;
  - the extent; and

[1230] See *The State v Michael Kilau* (2006) N3107, [2006] PGNC 125 and *Gibson Lulip v The State* (2000) SC636.

[1231] See *R v Wood* [1997] 1 Cr App R (S) 347, [1996] Crim LR 916.

[1232] See *Z v HKSAR* [2007] *HKCFA 22 and MXP v The State of Western Australia* (2010) 41 WAR 149, [2010] WASCA 215.

[1233] See *Radebe v R* (2001) 162 FLR 313, (2001) 122 A Crim R 559, [2001] WASCA 254; *R v Sukkar* [2005] NSWCCA 55; *Alchikh v R* [2007] NSWCCA 345 and *Assafiri v R* [2007] NSWCCA 159.

[1234] See *Radebe v R* (2001) 162 FLR 313, (2001) 122 A Crim R 559, [2001] WASCA 254; *R v Sukkar* [2005] NSWCCA 55; *Alchikh v R* [2007] NSWCCA 345 and *Assafiri v R* [2007] NSWCCA 159.

[1235] See *Nannup v The State of Western Australia* [2011] WASCA 257.

   - the value

 of this co-operation[1236];

- the quality, quantity and accuracy of the information.[1237]

 Information that an accused person is an 'informer' should be written down, not read out and handed to the Court.[1238]

 The information or assistance does not have to have been effective in the law enforcement process.[1239]

 The provision of information is a reflection of an accused person's guilt and remorse, provided the information resulted in the prosecution of other accused persons[1240];

- the likely consequences of an accused person giving assistance, such as:
   - threats to his or her safety;
   - more burdensome conditions of his or her imprisonment as he or she may have to be placed in protective custody; and
   - the possibility of reprisals on the family of the accused person[1241];[1242]

1236 See *Nannup v The State of Western Australia* [2011] WASCA 257.

1237 See *R v King* (1985) 7 Cr App R (S) 227, (1985) 82 Cr App R 120 and *Nannup v The State of Western Australia* [2011] WASCA 257.

1238 See *R v Ealing Justices; ex parte Weafer* (1982) 74 Cr App R 204 at 206 and *X* [1999] 2 Cr App R 125, per Hughes J at 127-128.

1239 See *MXP v The State of Western Australia* (2010) 41 WAR 149, [2010] WASCA 215.

1240 See *R v Sinfield* (1981) 3 Cr App R (S) 258 and *R v Debbay and Izett* (1990-1991) 12 Cr App R (S) 733.

1241 See *R v King* (1985) 7 Cr App R (S) 227, (1985) 82 Cr App R 120.

See also: The Law Reform Commission of Ireland, 1993, 'Consultation Paper on Sentencing', paragraph 5.85.

1242 See *R v King* (1985) 7 Cr App R (S) 227, (1985) 82 Cr App R 120; *R v Sivan* (1988) 87 Cr App R 407 at 412; *R v Many* (1990) 51 A Crim R 54 at 68 and *Z v HKSAR* [2007] HKCFA 22.

- whether there has been voluntary disclosure of guilt and it is unlikely that guilt would otherwise have been discovered[1243];

- whether there has been 'full and frank disclosure' of everything that the accused person knows[1244]; and

- whether an accused person is willing to give evidence[1245].

The extent of the co-operation should be verified by the prosecution.[1246]

[6.0] YOUTHFULNESS

It is part of the Court's duty to protect the young accused person.[1247]

Youthfulness is generally considered as a strong 'mitigating factor'.[1248]

The law recognises the potential for the:

- cognitive;

- emotional; and/or

[1243] See *AB v R* (1999) 198 CLR 111, per Hayne J at 155, [1999] HCA 46; *Cameron v R* (2002) 209 CLR 339, (2002) 76 ALJR 382, [2002] HCA 6; *Ryan v R* (2001) 206 CLR 267, per McHugh J at 273, (2001) 75 ALJR 815, (2001) 179 ALR 193, [2001] HCA 21; *R v Ellis* (1986) 6 NSWLR 603, per Street CJ at 604; *R v Brazel* (2005) 153 A Crim R 152 at 159-160; *Schriever v The State of Western Australia* [2008] WASCA 133; *Karolides v The State of Western Australia* [2006] WASCA 240; *Casbolt v The State of Western Australia* [2005] WASCA 41; *Barr v R* [2003] WASCA 55; *Howorth v The State of Western Australia* [2007] WASCA 78; *Webb v R* [2003] WASCA 266; *H v The State of Western Australia* (2006) 163 A Crim R 151, [2006] WASCA 53; *R v Kelly* (1993) 113 ALR 535 at 541 and *R v PW* [2005] QCA 177.

[1244] See *R v Cartwright* (1989) 17 NSWLR 243 at 252-253; *MA v R* (2001) 125 A Crim R 349, [2001] WASCA 325 and the observations of Burt CJ in *Hayes v R* [1981] WAR 252 at 254.

[1245] See *R v King* (1985) 7 Cr App R (S) 227, (1985) 82 Cr App R 120.

[1246] See *Radebe v R* (2001) 162 FLR 313, (2001) 122 A Crim R 559, [2001] WASCA 254.

[1247] See *Acting Public Prosecutor v Joe Kovea Mailai* [1981] PNGLR 258.

[1248] See *The State v August David* (2008) N3612, [2008] PGNC 226 and *The State v John Erip Muge* [2006] PGNC 69.

- psychological immaturity

of a young person to contribute to their breach of the law.[1249]

Young people are in the main not too sophisticated in the ways of adults and are easily led astray.[1250]

Not too many young people are hardened criminals or have set on a determined path of a life of crime.[1251]

Where the Courts are able, they have a responsibility to ensure that young people do not offend again.[1252]

One way to do this is not to incarcerate them, but to give them a chance to mend their ways and become responsible citizens, unless it becomes apparent that the young person will not change no matter how many chances he or she is given.[1253]

However, not all children will be the same in terms of:

- their chronological age; or

- their level of intellectual and emotional maturity

[1249] See *KT v R* (2008) 182 A Crim R 571, [2008] NSWCCA 51.

[1250] As was said by Andrew, J in *Acting Public Prosecutor v Clement Maki and Tom Kasen* [1981] SC205.

See also: *The State v Garry Pokas* (2011) N4375, [2011] PGNC 106.

[1251] As was said by Andrew, J in *Acting Public Prosecutor v Clement Maki and Tom Kasen* [1981] SC205.

See also: *The State v Garry Pokas* (2011) N4375, [2011] PGNC 106.

[1252] As was said by Andrew, J in *Acting Public Prosecutor v Clement Maki and Tom Kasen* [1981] SC205.

See also: *The State v Garry Pokas* (2011) N4375, [2011] PGNC 106.

[1253] As was said by Andrew, J in *Acting Public Prosecutor v Clement Maki and Tom Kasen* [1981] SC205.

See also: *The State v Garry Pokas* (2011) N4375, [2011] PGNC 106.

when an offence is committed.[1254]

Accordingly, allowance should be made for an accused person's youthfulness, and not just their biological age.[1255]

Emotional maturity and impulse control develop progressively during adolescence and early adulthood, and may not be fully developed until the early to mid twenties.[1256]

The question is:

> Was the young accused person's judgement was impaired through lack of development?[1257]

Where the judgement of a young accused person is impaired then he or she may be viewed as less culpable, just as an adult accused person who suffers from a mental impairment[1258] would be regarded as less culpable than a younger accused person of full mental capacity.[1259]

Furthermore, the younger the accused person the greater the mitigation.[1260]

Although persons between the ages of 17 and 19 assume adult responsibilities[1261], an accused person 20 years and under may receive some leniency in view of their age[1262].

1254 See *DBW (a child) v The State of Western Australia* [2011] WASCA 206.

1255 See *R v Hearne* (2001) 124 A Crim R 451, [2001] NSWCCA 37.

1256 See *R v Slade* [2005] 2 NZLR 526 and *R v Elliott* (2006) 68 NSWLR 1, [2006] NSWCCA 305, per Kirby J.

1257 See The Law Reform Commission of Ireland, 1993, 'Consultation Paper on Sentencing', paragraph 5.61.

1258 Refer also to the subsection titled 'Mental Health' in the section titled 'Motive' in the chapter titled 'Extenuating Circumstances'.

1259 See The Law Reform Commission of Ireland, 1993, 'Consultation Paper on Sentencing', paragraph 5.61.

1260 See *R v Hoang* [2003] NSWCCA 380 and *R v Hearne* (2001) 124 A Crim R 451, [2001] NSWCCA 37.

1261 See *Peter Naibiri and Kutoi Soti Apia v The State* (1978) SC137.

However, a Court must sentence in accordance with section 30 of the *Juvenile Courts Act 1991* in relation to a juvenile, ie., a child under the age of 18 years.

1262 See *Wesley Nobudi, John Evoa and Frank Yalikiti v The State* (2009) SC999, [2009] PGSC 20 and *The State v Fidelis Kiatni* (2011) N4331, [2011] PGNC 67.

MITIGATING FACTORS

Where the immaturity of the accused person is a significant factor in the commission of an offence, the criminality involved will be less than if the same offence was committed by an adult.[1263]

The weight to be given to the fact of an accused person's youthfulness does not vary depending upon the seriousness of the offence.[1264]

Youthfulness does not *per se* mitigate seriousness:

> it is still a question of whether or not the culpability of the accused person should be reduced because of impaired judgement.[1265]

A Court should investigate alternatives to imprisonment when dealing with a youthful first offender and imprisonment should be used as the last resort[1266], depending on:

- the seriousness[1267];
- the gravity; and
- the prevalence[1268]

of the offence committed.[1269]

Usually, a first time young offender is treated more leniently.[1270]

[1263] See *R v Hearne* (2001) 124 A Crim R 451, [2001] NSWCCA 37 and *MS2 v R* (2005) 158 A Crim R 93, [2005] NSWCCA 397.

[1264] See *R v Hearne* (2001) 124 A Crim R 451, [2001] NSWCCA 37.

[1265] See The Law Reform Commission of Ireland, 1993, 'Consultation Paper on Sentencing', paragraph 5.61.

[1266] See *Passingan v Beaton* [1971-72] PNGLR 206, [1971] PGSC 37 and *Kuri Willie v The State* [1987] PNGLR 298, [1987] PGSC 19.

[1267] Refer also to the section titled 'Seriousness Of An Offence Generally' in the chapter titled 'Aggravating Factors'.

[1268] Refer also to the section titled 'Prevalence Of The Offence' in the chapter titled 'Aggravating Factors'.

[1269] See *The State v Juvenile 'D'* (2008) N3508, [2008] PGNC 153.

[1270] See *The State v Patrick Puppy Kaikara Loavi* (2006) N3384, [2006] PGNC 104.

This is because of:

- the belief that, imposing a more severe sentence may turn him or her into a worser offender whilst in prison; and

- the well accepted fact that most growing young people do not have the maturity to clearly differentiate and appreciate the effects of getting involved with criminal activities.[1271]

So once they are caught, opportunity must be given to them to appreciate their mistakes and rehabilitate.[1272]

A youthful first offender on a relatively minor charge should not be sentenced to a term of imprisonment, unless there are compelling reasons warranting such a sentence.[1273]

Whilst an accused person below the age of 18 years may be given lenient treatment on sentence by suspension of sentence for a serious offence, it is inappropriate to suspend a sentence for a serious offence in relation to a young accused person who is 18 years and above.[1274]

A long term of imprisonment for a young accused person may result in such an accused person becoming so institutionalised that he or she may not be able to fit back into society when released.[1275]

A term of imprisonment does not change a young accused person into a law-abiding citizen, but in effect destroys any chance they may have of becoming a law-abiding citizen.[1276]

[1271] See *The State v Patrick Puppy Kaikara Loavi* (2006) N3384, [2006] PGNC 104.

[1272] See *The State v Patrick Puppy Kaikara Loavi* (2006) N3384, [2006] PGNC 104.

[1273] See *Paia Lifi v Phillip Dege* (1981) N291(M).

[1274] See *Gimble v The State* [1988-89] PNGLR 272 at 275, (1988) SC369, [1988] PGSC 15.

[1275] See *R v Willie Abusae* [1999] SBHC 81.

[1276] See *Kuri Willie v The State* [1987] PNGLR 298, [1987] PGSC 19; *Paia Lifi v Phillip Dege* (1981) N291(M) and *The State v Buka Irai* (2003) N2448.

MITIGATING FACTORS

Whilst the sentence imposed should reflect the seriousness and gravity of the offence it should not being 'crushing' because of the youth of an accused person[1277] whilst taking into consideration the need for rehabilitation[1278] back into society.[1279]

For a young accused person rehabilitation is an important consideration.[1280]

However, rehabilitation must be carefully considered in every case within the context of:

- the other principles of sentencing[1281]; and
- the circumstances of each case[1282];

Rehabilitation is not the only objective or purpose of sentencing.[1283]

1277 See *Acting Public Prosecutor v Lalaiva and Ume* (1981) SC201; *Passingan v Beaton* [1971-72] PNGLR 206, [1971] PGSC 37; *The State v Juvenile 'D'* (2008) N3508, [2008] PGNC 153 and *The State v Anos Naime Maraga, Hariki Badi and Gaigo Arua* (2002) N2433.

1278 Refer also to the section titled 'The Need For Reformation And Rehabilitation' in the chapter titled 'Objectives And Purposes Of Sentencing'.

1279 See *R v K* (2003) 20 CRNZ 62.

1280 See *Wesley Nobudi, John Evoa and Frank Yalikiti v The State* (2009) SC999, [2009] PGSC 20; *The State v Anos Naime Maraga, Hariki Badi and Gaigo Arua* (2002) N2433; *Kuri Willie v The State* [1987] PNGLR 298, [1987] PGSC 19; *The State v Justin Vincent Nyama* [1991] PNGLR 127 and *The State v Morobet Awui Komia and Peter Kevin* [1987] PNGLR 262 at 266.

See also: *Lauritsen v R* (2000) 114 A Crim R 333, [2000] WASCA 203; *R v Accused* [1989] 1 NZLR 643; *R v Mahoni* (1998) 15 CRNZ 428 at 436-437; *R v GDP* (1991) 53 A Crim R 112 at 115-116; *R v E (a child)* (1993) 66 A Crim R 14 at 28; *R v Adamson* (2002) 132 A Crim R 511, [2002] NSWCCA 349 and *WO (A Child) v Western Australia* (2005) 153 A Crim R 352 at 362, [2005] WASCA 94.

1281 Refer also to the chapter titled 'Objectives And Purposes Of Sentencing'.

1282 See *Acting Public Prosecutor v Clement Maki and Tom Kasen* (1981) SC205.

1283 See *R v Tran* [2002] 4 VR 457, per Callaway JA.

Refer also to the chapter titled 'Objectives And Purposes Of Sentencing'.

The emphasis on rehabilitation is based on the long established understanding that the community is best protected by determined efforts to effect the rehabilitation of young accused persons. Although retribution, punishment and general deterrence are relevant sentencing objects and purposes in respect of children they are ordinarily given significantly reduced weight.[1284]

However, it is not the case that young accused persons, including those with no previous record and good personal circumstances, can never receive a sentence of detention. Regard must be had to:

- the circumstances of the offence; and
- the accused person's personal circumstances.[1285]

A young accused person must show real prospects of:

- rehabilitation; and
- an unlikelihood of re-offending[1286].

Therefore, youthfulness does not automatically justify leniency.[1287]

The emphasis given to rehabilitation, rather than general deterrence[1288] and retribution[1289], when sentencing young accused persons, may be moderated when the young person has:

- conducted himself or herself in the way an adult might conduct himself or herself; and

---

[1284] See *The State of Western Australia v A Child* (2007) 172 A Crim R 51, [2007] WASCA 115.

[1285] See *F (a child) v The State of Western Australia* [2004] WASCA 193.

[1286] *See R v Mako* [2000] 2 NZLR 170.

[1287] See *R v Rapira* [2003] NZCA 217; *R v Mahoni* (1998) 15 CRNZ 428 at 436 and *R v Accused* [1989] 1 NZLR 843 at 855.

[1288] Refer also to the section titled 'The Need For Deterrence' in the chapter titled 'Objectives And Purposes Of Sentencing'.

[1289] Refer also to the section titled 'The Need For Retribution' in the chapter titled 'Objectives And Purposes Of Sentencing'.

- committed a crime of violence or considerable gravity.[1290]

  In determining whether a young accused person has engaged in 'adult behaviour[1291]' the Court will look to various matters, including:

  - the use of weapons[1292];
  - planning or pre-meditation[1293];
  - the existence of an extensive criminal history[1294]; and
  - the nature and circumstances of the offence[1295];

- when deterrent sentences are required where the offence is prevalent[1296]; and

---

1290 See *R v Tran* [1999] NSWCCA 109; *R v TJP* [1999] NSWCCA 408; *R v LC* [2001] NSWCCA 175; *R v AEM Snr; R v KEM; R v MM* [2002] NSWCCA 58; *R v Adamson* (2002) 132 A Crim R 511, [2002] NSWCCA 349 and *R v Voss* [2003] NSWCCA 182.

1291 See *R v Voss* [2003] NSWCCA 182.

1292 Refer also to the section titled 'Carrying, Using Or Threatening To Use A Weapon' in the chapter titled 'Aggravating Factors'.

1293 Refer also to the section titled 'Pre-planning Or Pre-meditation' in the chapter titled 'Aggravating Factors'.

1294 Refer also to the section titled 'Character And Antecedents' in the chapter titled 'Aggravating Factors'.

1295 See *R v Adamson* (2002) 132 A Crim R 511, [2002] NSWCCA 349.

1296 See *Rakatani v The State* [1979] PNGLR 556, [1979] PGSC 21; *Paulus Mandatititip and another v The State* [1978] PNGLR 128, [1978] PGSC 5; *Peter Naibiri and Kutoi Soti Apia v The State* (1978) SC178 and *The State v Donald Angavia and others (Ch. 2)* (2004) N2590.

See also: *The State of Western Australia v Johnson* [2010] WASCA 187.

Refer also to the section titled 'Prevalence Of The Offence' in the chapter titled 'Aggravating Factors'.

MITIGATING FACTORS

- in serious cases[1297], including:
    - wilful murder;
    - murder;
    - rape[1298];
    - robbery[1299];
    - other crimes of violence[1300]; and
    - break and enter[1301].

[1297] See *JTP v The State of Western Australia* [2010] WASCA 191; *A Child v The State of Western Australia* [2007] WASCA 285 and *TL (a child) v The State of Western Australia* [2005] WASCA 173.

[1298] See *The State v Billy Turmur and Sou Mesak* (2011) N4349, [2011] PGNC 92.

[1299] See *Wesley Nobudi, John Evoa and Frank Yalikiti v The State* (2009) SC999, [2009] PGSC 20; *Joseph Nimagi, Tom Gurua Kerui And David Bawai Laiam v The State* (2004) SC741, [2004] PGSC 31; *Bokum Umba v The State* (1976) SC92; *Paulus Manadatitip and another v The State* [1978] PNGLR 128, [1978] PGSC 5; *Peter Naibiri and Kutoi Soti Apia v The State* (1978) SC137; *The State v Thomas Waim, Tala Gena and Alois Wanpis* [1995] PNGLR 187 at 192, (1995) N1356, [1995] PGNC 161; *The State v Richard Amuna Koupa* [1987] PNGLR208; *The State v Kevin Anis and Martin Ningigan* (2003) N2360; *The State v Donald Angavia and others (No. 2)* (2004) N2590; *The State v Charles Maniwa and Joseph Utura Maniwa* (2004) N2674 and *The State v Vincent Simbago* (2005) N2954, [2005] PGNC 3.

[1300] See *R v Tran* [1999] NSWCCA 109; *R v TJP* [1999] NSWCCA 408; *R v LC* [2001] NSWCCA 175; *R v AEM Snr; R v KEM; R v MM* [2002] NSWCCA 58; *R v Adamson* (2002) 132 A Crim R 511, [2002] NSWCCA 349; *R v Voss* [2003] NSWCCA 182; *R v Pham and Ly* (1991) 55 A Crim R 128 at 135; *KT v R* (2008) 182 A Crim R 571, [2008] NSWCCA 51; *Attorney-General's Reference No. 59 of 1996* [1997] 2 Cr App R (S) 250; *Attorney-General's Reference Nos. 30 and 31 of 1998* [1999] 1 Cr App R (S) 200; *Attorney-General's Reference No. 121 of 2002* [2003] EWCA Crim 684; *Attorney-General's Reference Nos. 59, 60 and 63 of 1998* [1999] 2 Cr App R (S) 128, per Bingham LCJ at 131; *R v Mahoni* (1998) 15 CRNZ 428 at 436; *R v MA* [2004] NSWCCA 92 and *R v Pham and Ly* (1991) 55 A Crim R 128, per Lee CJ at CL at 135.

[1301] See *Acting Public Prosecutor v Mailai* [1981] PNGLR 258, [1981] PGSC 7.

In such circumstances a youthful accused person should not receive special treatment, unless there are exceptional circumstances that call for leniency.[1302]

If an accused person is relying on being youthful as a mitigating factor then the accused person must provide evidence as to the proof of his or her age.[1303] However, a Court is entitled to come to its own conclusion as to the age of an accused person.[1304]

The weight to be given to considerations relevant to a person's youth diminishes the closer the accused person approaches the age of maturity.[1305]

[7.0] DELAY

It may be argued in Papua New Guinea that delay does constitute a powerful 'mitigatory factor'[1306], but it very much depends on the circumstances[1307].

But delay or the lapse of time between:

- the commission of an offence; and
- sentence

[1302] See *Wesley Nobudi, John Evoa and Frank Yalikiti v The State* (2009) SC999, [2009] PGSC 20; *Paulus Mandatititip and another v The State* [1978] PNGLR 128; *Peter Naibiri and Kutoi Soti Apia v The State* (1978) SC178; *Acting Public Prosecutor v Joe Kovea Mailai* [1981] PNGLR 258; *The State v Frank Kagai* [1987] PNGLR 320; *The State v Kalama Daniel* (2003) N2476; *The State v Donald Angavia and others (No. 2)* (2004) N2590 and *The State v Kevin Anis and Martin Ningigan* (2003) N2360.

[1303] See *Public Prosecutor v Don Hale* (1998) SC564 and *The State v Edward Toude and others (No. 2)* (2001) N2299.

[1304] See *Tau Jim Anis and others v the State* (2000) SC642, [2000] PGSC 12.

Section 63 of the *Evidence Act* (Ch. 48) states:

> In any legal proceedings, if the court does not consider that there is evidence or sufficient evidence to determine the age of a person the court, having seen the person, may itself determine the question.

[1305] See *R v Hoang* [2003] NSWCCA 380 and *DBW (a child) v The State of Western Australia* [2011] WASCA 206.

[1306] *See R v Liang and Li* (1995) 82 A Crim R 39 at 45 and *R v Cockerell* (2001) 126 A Crim R 444, per Chernov JA at 447.

[1307] See *R v Todd* (1982) 2 NSWLR 517 at 519; *R v Kay* [2004] NSWCCA 130 and *R v ECG* [2005] NSWCCA 392.

without more is not a mitigating factor.[1308]

The state of suspense or uncertainty that will be relevant as a consequence of the delay is any state of suspense or uncertainty experienced by an accused person:

- after he or she has been arrested; or
- after it has been indicated to him or her by some person in authority that he or she is likely to be prosecuted for the offence.[1309]

However, any suspense or uncertainty on the part of an accused person as to whether his or her commission of an offence will ever be detected is not to be taken into account.[1310]

The lapse of time must reveal unfairness to an accused person calling for the extension of leniency.[1311]

In order for delay to be a mitigating factor there are a number of factors to be considered, including:

- the reason for the delay.[1312]

  The impact of the delay must be due to:

  - the operation of the judicial system, such as the failure to prosecute an accused person within a reasonable time in accordance with section 37(3) of the *Constitution of the Independent State of Papua New Guinea*[1313]; and

---

[1308] See *Bell v R* [2001] WASCA 40 and *Sell v R* (1995) 15 WAR 240.

[1309] See *R v Shorten* [2005] NSWCCA 106.

[1310] See *R v Law* [1996] 2 Qd R 63, (1995) 84 A Crim R 142 at 145 and *R v Shorten* [2005] NSWCCA 106.

[1311] See *Wagenaar v R* [2000] WASCA 325 and *R v Law* [1996] 2 Qd R 63, (1995) 84 A Crim R 142.

[1312] See *R v V* (1998) 99 A Crim R 297.

[1313] See *R v Law* [1996] 2 Qd R 63, (1995) 84 A Crim R 142; *R v Duncan* (1983) 47 ALR 746, (1983) 9 A Crim R 354; *Crawley v R* (1981) 36 ALR 241, (1981) 5 A Crim R 451 at 458, *Jones and Harris* (1989) 41 A Crim R 1 at 19; *Kane* [1974] VR 750 at 767 and *R v Leggett* [2000] WASCA 327.

Refer also to the section titled 'Right To A Fair Hearing Within A Reasonable Time' in the chapter titled 'Rights Of An Accused Person'.

- not the actions of the accused person.[1314]

  Little leniency should be granted where the delay is a result of an accused person fleeing the jurisdiction[1315];

- whether the delay was 'unreasonable'[1316];

- the impact of the delay upon the accused person.[1317]

  A significant delay may enable an accused person to show that he or she has rehabilitated himself or herself[1318]; and

- whether as a consequence of the delay the offence can be considered to be 'stale'[1319].

However, delay in bringing the matter to trial should merit a reduction in sentence, except in the most extraordinary of circumstances, such as where an accused person is remanded in custody for a considerable length of time pending sentence, but receives only a fine.[1320]

1314 See *R v Barker, R v Gibson* [2006] NSWCCA 20; *R v Kay* [2004] NSWCCA 130; *R v Abusae* [1996] SBHC 9; *R v Todd* [1982] 2 NSWLR 517 at 519-520; *R v Tiburcy* [2006] VSCA 244; *Scook v R* (2008) 185 A Crim R 164, [2008] WASCA 114 and *Brecker v The State of Western Australia* [2010] WASCA 32.

1315 See *R v Shore* (1992) 66 A Crim R 37.

1316 See *R v Fakatonu* [1990] SILR 97 at 100; *Mills v Her Majesty's Advocate* [2002] 3 WLR 1597; *R v Bosley* (1992) 18 CR (4th) 347; *R v Leaver* (1996) 3 CR (5th) 138 and *R v Panousis* (2002) ABQB 1109, 329 AR 47.

1317 See *R v V* (1998) 99 A Crim R 297.

1318 See *R v King* [2000] WASCA 130; *Duncan v R* (1983) 47 ALR 746, (1983) 9 A Crim R 354 at 356-357; *R v Todd* [1982] 2 NSWLR 517, per Street CJ at 519-520; *Mill v R* (1988) 166 CLR 59 at 64, (1998) 83 ALR 1, [1988] HCA 70; *Bell* (1981) 5 A Crim R 347 at 351; *R v Leggett* [2000] WASCA 327 and *R v D'Arcy* [2001] QCA 325, per Chesterman J.

Refer also to the section titled 'The Need For Reformation Or Rehabilitation' in the chapter titled 'Objectives And Purposes Of Sentencing'.

1319 See *Mill v R* (1988) 166 CLR 59 at 64, (1998) 83 ALR 1, [1988] HCA 70.

1320 See The Law Reform Commission of Ireland, 1993, 'Consultation Paper on Sentencing', paragraph 5.108.

[8.0] ILL-HEALTH[1321]

Ill-health cannot be allowed to become a licence to commit an offence; nor can an accused person generally expect to escape punishment because of the condition of their health.[1322]

A medical condition of an accused person should not form any foundation for a lenient sentence unless, it is a case of life and death and no arrangements can made administratively by the Correction Services for a prisoner with a medical condition to access and receive appropriate medical attention and treatment.[1323]

Generally speaking ill-health will be a factor to mitigate punishment only when:

- it appears that imprisonment will be likely to cause a permanent disability to an accused person; or
- it appears that imprisonment will be dangerous to either the life of:
    - an accused person; or
    - other prisoners[1324],

and the provisions of sections 89 and 141 of the *Correctional Services Act 1995* cannot or are unlikely to be observed or will not be sufficient to protect the accused person or the other prisoners.[1325]

1321 See also: *R v Canavan and others* [1998] 1 Cr App R 79, [1998] 1 All ER 42, [1998] 1 WLR 604, [1997] Crim LR 766, [1998] 1 Cr App R (S) 243, [1997] EWCA Crim 1773, (1997) 161 JP 709.

Refer also to the subsection titled 'Mental Health' in the section titled 'Motive' in the chapter titled 'Extenuating Circumstances'.

1322 See *R v Smith* (1987) 44 SASR 587, per King CJ at 589.

1323 See *Thress Kumbamong v The State* (2008) SC1017, [2008] PGSC 51.

1324 See however: *The State v John Seregat* (2007) N3266, [2007] PGNC 133; *R v Smith* (1987) 44 SASR 587, per King CJ at 589; *R v Paparone* (2000) 112 A Crim R 190, [2000] WASCA 127; *Bailey v DPP* (1988) 62 ALJR 319; *R v Vachalec* [1981] 1 NSWLR 351; *R v Badanjak* [2004] NSWCCA 395; *R v Burrell* (2004) 114 A Crim R 207; *R v Azar* [2000] NSWCCA 26; *Morgan* (1997) 87 A Crim R 104 at 107; *Iskandar v R* (2001) 126 A Crim R 546, [2001] WASCA 409; *R v Cumberbatch* (2004) 8 VR 9, [2004] VSCA 37; *R v Van Boxtel* (2005) 11 VR 258, [2005] VSCA 175; *R v Pope and Attorney-General (Queensland)* [1996] QCA 318 and *Eliasen* (1991) 53 A Crim R 391.

1325 See *Ben Wafia and others v The State* (2006) SC851, [2006] PGSC 19.

It is relevant to the weight to be given to the ill-health of an accused person when the offence was committed while the accused person was suffering from the same condition for which he or she seeks sympathetic treatment on the sentencing.[1326]

Irrespective, in relation to a health issue there must be clear medical evidence.[1327]

[9.0] SOCIAL OR CULTURAL PRESSURES AND ISOLATION

In determining the duration of a custodial sentence, a Court should take into account features of:

- the offence; or
- the accused person

that will result in imprisonment bearing down more severely upon the accused person than upon the average prisoner.[1328]

Therefore, social and cultural isolation as a consequence of an accused person being imprisoned is a mitigating factor[1329], including a foreign national with limited support[1330].

However, it is a factor that should only be given minimum weight.[1331]

1326 See *R v Guthrie* [2002] QCA 509.

1327 See *Rojumana v R* [1990] SILR 132; *R v Irlam; ex parte Attorney-General* [2002] QCA 235; *R v Verschaffelt* [2002] 3 NZLR 772 and *R v Bernard* [1997] 1 Cr App R (S) 135.

1328 See *Deffley* [1972] Crim LR 123.

See also: *Neal v R* (1982) 149 CLR 305, per Brennan J at 326; *Astill (No. 2)* (1992) 64 A Crim R 289, per Kirby P at 293; *R v Todd* [1976] Qd R 21; *R v Vachalec* [1981] 1 NSWLR 351 at 353; *Everett v R* (1994) 181 CLR 295, (1994) 68 ALJR 875, (1994) 124 ALR 529, (1994) 73 A Crim R 550, per Ipp J at 564-565, [1994] HCA 49 and *Houghton v The State of Western Australia* (2006) 32 WAR 260, [2006] WASCA 143.

1329 See *Senda v The Republic of Nauru* [1969-1982] NLR 38, [1975] NRSC 7 and *R v Fate* (1988) 16 CRNZ 88.

1330 See *R v Huang* (2000) 113 A Crim R 386, [2000] NSWCCA 238; *Yang v R* [2007] NSWCCA 37 and *R v Ferrer-Esis* (1991) 55 A Crim R 231.

1331 See *R v Ferrer-Esis* (1991) 55 A Crim R 231 at 239.

MITIGATING FACTORS

[10.0] RISK OF REPETITION

The unlikelihood of repetition of an offence, ie., an offence that is spontaneous, unplanned and one-off, is a mitigating factor.[1332]

[11.0] FAMILY CIRCUMSTANCES

For the purpose of sentencing the welfare of the children of an accused person is a relevant factor.[1333]

However, as a general principle, a Court should not have regard to:

> the impact that a sentence of imprisonment will have upon the members of an accused person's family[1334],

---

[1332] See *The State v Tonai Kuse* (2011) N4304, [2011] PGNC 54.

See also: *Attorney-General's Reference No. 4 of 1989* [1990] 1 WLR 41, (1990) 90 Cr App R 366 at 370.

[1333] See *The State v Michael Rende* (2013) N5220, [2013] PGNC 44; *The State v Relvie Joe* (2005) N2832, [2005] PGNC 127 and *The State v Peter Jai* (2011) 4391.

See also: *R v Tilley* (1991) 53 A Crim R 1 at 3.

[1334] See *Allan Peter Utieng v The State* (2000) SCR No. 15 of 2000; *The Public Prosecutor v Vangu'u Ame* [1983] PNGLR 424 at 427, [1983] PGSC 23; *The State v Margaret John (No. 1)* [1995] PNGLR 446, (1995) N1326; *The State v Lucas Yovura* (2003) N2366; *The State v Isidor Kaream* (2004) N2610; *The State v Henry Mapi* (1998) N1936; *The State v Stanley Sabiu* (2005) N3659, [2005] PGNC 177; *The State v Kuk Kuli* (2006) CR No. 309 of 2004; *The State v Donald Angavia and others (No. 2)* (2004) N2590; *The State v Philip Iparu* (2005) N2995, [2005] PGNC 11; *The State v Raphael Kimba Aki (No. 2)* (2001) N2082; *The State v Ansong Ising* (2005) N2994, [2005] PGNC 14; *The State v Moki Lepi (No. 3)* (2004) N2734; *The State v Pablito P Miguel* (2002) N2338 and *The State v Donald Poni* (2004) N2663.

See also: *R v Edwards* (1996) 90 A Crim R 510, per Gleeson CJ at 515-516 and *R v Wirth* (1976) 14 SASR 291, per Wells J at 296.

although this is not an absolute principle and may be departed from in exceptional cases[1335].

An accused person should not use his or her family to try to avoid punishment.[1336]

Hardship to an accused person's family must be quite out of the ordinary before it can substantially mitigate penalty.[1337]

It is however a little too late to talk about an accused person's personal and family background after he or she has committed an offence.[1338]

The accused person ought to have thought about the consequences before committing the offence.[1339]

[1335] See *The State v John Peril; The State v Erika M Lucas* (2005) N2883, [2005] PGNC 85.

See also: *R v Yates* (1997) 99 A Crim R 483, per Charles JA at 486-487; *R v Holland* (2002) 134 A Crim R 451, per Batt JA at 452, Eames JA at 454 and O'Bryan AJA at 457; *R v Stewart* (1994) 72 A Crim R 17, per Franklyn J at 21; *R v Carmody* (1998) 100 A Crim R 41, per Tadgell JA at 45; *Gegeo v R* [1991] SBHC 8; *The State of Western Australia v Skaines* [2006] WASCA 160; *The State of Western Australia v Bruce* [2004] WASCA 226; *Dib* [2003] NSWCCA 117; *R v Togias* (2001) 127 A Crim R 23 at 25; *R v Matthews* (1996) 130 FLR 230 at 233; *R v Nagle* [2007] VSCA 8, per Chernov JA; *R v Boyle* (1987) 34 A Crim R 202; *R v Maslen* (1995) 79 A Crim R 199, per Hunt CJ at 209; *R v Wirth* (1976) 14 SASR 291, per Wells J at 295-296; *R v T* (1990) 47 A Crim R 29; *R v Adami* (1989) 51 SASR 229; *R v Thai* [2005] VSCA 283; *R v D'Arrigo; ex parte Attorney-General of Queensland* [2004] QCA 399; *R v Chong; ex parte Attorney-General (Queensland)* [2008] QCA 22; *R v MP* [2004] QCA 170; *Arnold v Trenerry* (1997) 118 NTR 1 and *R v Edwards* (1996) 90 A Crim R 510.

[1336] See *Public Prosecutor v Vangu'u Ame* [1983] PNGLR 424; *Ivoro Kaumin Lupu v The State* (SCRA No. 2 of 1997, Unreported & Unnumbered Judgement dated 13 June 1997, Kapi, DCJ, Los & Jalina JJ); *The State v Margaret John (No. 1)* [1995] PNGLR 446; *The State v Peter Yandi* (2010) N4064, [2010] PGNC 50 and *The State v Wamaong Robert* (2010) N4065, [2010] PGNC 100.

[1337] See *Hodder v R* (1995) 15 WAR 264 at 287.

[1338] See *Thress Kumbamong v The State* (2008) SC1017, [2008] PGSC 51; *Allan Peter Utieng v The State* (2000) SCR No. 15 of 2000; *The State v Toipo Dimasi* (2008) N3551, [2008] PGNC 193; *The State v Lucas Yovura* (2003) N2366; *The State v Luke Toyana Gisigesi and Joseph Mwaisiga* (2010) N4124, [2010] PGNC 126; *The State v Isidor Kaream* (2004) N2610; *The State v Henry Mapi* (1998) N1936; *The State v Gerald Kirafe* (2005) N3660, [2005] PGNC 175; *The State v Eric Papen (No. 2)* (2009) N3639, [2009] PGNC 58; *The State v Raphael Kimba Aki (No. 2)* (2001) N2082 and *The State v Ansong Ising* (2005) N2994, [2005] PGNC 14.

[1339] See The Law Reform Commission of Ireland, 1993, 'Consultation Paper on Sentencing', paragraph 5.113.

MITIGATING FACTORS

This mitigating factor may be given little or no weight when considering the:

- gravity[1340];
- seriousness[1341]; and
- prevalence[1342]

of the offence committed.[1343]

An accused person should bear in mind before he or she sets out to commit a serious crime such as murder or wilful murder using dangerous weapons against the victim as death of such person may lead to a long period of imprisonment if convicted. Welfare of wives, children and parents are becoming lame excuses and should be treated with caution.[1344]

The hardship and distress shared by the family of an accused person cannot be allowed to overwhelm factors, such as:

- retribution[1345]; and

1340 See *R v Stewart* (1994) 72 A Crim R 17 at 21 and *R v Chong; ex parte Attorney-General (Queensland)* [2008] QCA 22.

1341 See *Hodder v R* (1995) 15 WAR 264 at 287.

Refer also to the section titled 'Seriousness Of An Offence Generally' in the chapter titled 'Aggravating Factors'.

1342 Refer also to the section titled 'Prevalence Of The Offence' in the chapter titled 'Aggravating Factors'.

1343 See *The State v Collin Paino; The State v David Paino; The State v Michael Paino and The State v Rose Todi Paino* (2007) N3199, [2007] PGNC 88; *The State v Ansong Ising* (2005) N2994, [2005] PGNC 14; *The State v Moki Lepi (No. 3)* (2004) N2734; *The State v Lucas Yovura* (2003) N2366; *The State v Raphael Kimba Aki (No. 2)* (2001) N2082; *The State v Donald Poni* (2004) N2663 and *The State v Donald Angavia and others (Ch. 2)* (2004) N2590.

See also: *R v MP* [2004] QCA 170.

1344 See *Ivoro Kaumin Lupu v The State* (SCRA No.2 of 1997, Unreported & Unnumbered Judgement dated 13 June 1997).

1345 Refer also to the section titled 'The Need For Retribution' in the chapter titled 'Objectives And Purposes Of Sentencing'.

- deterrence[1346].[1347]

In any event, an offender should not use his or her children to escape punishment.[1348]

[12.0] ADVANCED AGE

If an accused person is aged more than 50 years then that fact may be taken into consideration as a mitigating factor[1349], but the weight to be given to this mitigating factor is not determined in isolation[1350].

The justification for the acceptance of such a mitigating factor is based on a number of factors, including:

- moral culpability is reduced by reason of advanced age.[1351]

  The question to be determined is:

  > Was the accused person's judgement impaired through senility?[1352]

  Where the judgement of an accused person is impaired then he or she may be viewed as less culpable.[1353]

[1346] Refer also to the section titled 'The Need For Deterrence' in the chapter titled 'Objectives And Purposes Of Sentencing'.

[1347] See *Le and Le v R* [1996] 2 Qd R 516, per Thomas J at 522.

[1348] See *The Public Prosecutor v Vangu'u Ame* [1983] PNGLR 424.

[1349] See *The State v Soeto Wembo* (2008) CR No. 229 of 2008; *The State v Michael Rende* (2013) N5220, [2013] PGNC 44; *The State v Ereman Kepas* (2007) N3192, [2007] PGNC 77; *The State v Tonny Kupin* (2009) N3641; *The State v Mahuva Jimmy and Uta Helisha* (2004) N2632; *The State v Jerry Kui* (2011) N4367, [2011] PGNC 85 and *The State v Tonai Kuse* (2011) N4304, [2011] PGNC 54.

[1350] See *Kaye v R* [2004] WASCA 227.

[1351] See *Gulyas v The State of Western Australia* (2007) 178 A Crim R 539, [2007] WASCA 263, per Steytler P.

[1352] See The Law Reform Commission of Ireland, 1993, 'Consultation Paper on Sentencing', paragraph 5.61.

[1353] See The Law Reform Commission of Ireland, 1993, 'Consultation Paper on Sentencing', paragraph 5.61.

Old age does not *per se* mitigate seriousness – it is still a question of whether or not the culpability of the accused person should be reduced because of impaired judgement[1354];

- the recognition that for an accused person of advanced age each year of a term of imprisonment represents a substantial proportion of the period of life that is left to him or her[1355];

- circumstances associated with advanced age, such as:

    - ill-health[1356]; or

    - ill-health coupled with physical or mental frailty[1357]

  will make imprisonment more arduous for such an accused person than is normal[1358]; and

- a lengthy sentence of imprisonment is likely to destroy any reasonable expectation of useful life after release.[1359]

[1354] See The Law Reform Commission of Ireland, 1993, 'Consultation Paper on Sentencing', paragraph 5.61.

[1355] See *R v Hunter* (1984) 36 SASR 101, per King CJ at 103; *R v Whyte* (2004) 7 VR 397, per Winneke P at 405-406, [2004] VSCA 5; *R v Liddy (No. 2)* (2002) 84 SASR 231, [2002] SASC 306; *Martino v The State of Western Australia* [2006] WASCA 78; *Braham v R* (1994) 116 FLR 38 at 51; *Gulyas v The State of Western Australia* (2007) 178 A Crim R 539, [2007] WASCA 263 and *R v Iles* [2009] VSCA 197.

[1356] Refer also to the section titled 'Ill-Health' in this chapter.

[1357] Refer also to the subsection titled 'Mental Health' in the section titled 'Motive' in the chapter titled 'Extenuating Circumstances'.

[1358] See *Gulyas v The State of Western Australia* (2007) 178 A Crim R 539, [2007] WASCA 263, per Steytler P; *Houghton v The State of Western Australia* (2006) 32 WAR 260, [2006] WASCA 143; *R v Eliasen* (1991) 53 A Crim R 391 at 395 and *R v Vachalec* [1981] 1 NSWLR 351, per Street CJ at 353.

[1359] See *Gulyas v The State of Western Australia* (2007) 178 A Crim R 539, [2007] WASCA 263, per Steytler P; *Martino v The State of Western Australia* [2006] WASCA 78 and *Bishop v R* [2003] WASCA 79.

Refer also to the subsection titled 'Totality Principle' in the section titled 'Imprisonment' in the chapter titled 'Sentencing Options'.

However, the punishment must still reflect the seriousness of the offence[1360].[1361]

An accused person of a very advanced age is a mitigating factor in a case of murder.[1362]

Advanced age may be significant to, but is not determinative of, the length of a period of imprisonment.[1363]

[13.0] EXTRA-CURIAL PUNISHMENT

The theory which underlies the relevance of extra-curial punishment to sentence is that it:

- deters an accused person from re-offending by providing a reminder of the unhappy consequence of criminal misconduct; or
- leaves the accused person with a disability or some other affliction that is a consequence of criminal activity.[1364]

1360 Refer also to the section titled 'Seriousness Of An Offence Generally' in the chapter titled 'Aggravating Factors'.

1361 See *Joe Giamur v The State* (2007) SC884, [2007] PGSC 7 and *The State v Mitige Neheya* [1988-89] PNGLR 174.

See also: *Gulyas v The State of Western Australia* (2007) 178 A Crim R 539, [2007] WASCA 263; *Collard v The State of Western Australia* [2004] WASCA 297; *Bishop v R* [2003] WASCA 79; *Crowley* (1991) 55 A Crim R 201, per Crockett J at 205-206; *Bazley* (1993) 65 A Crim R 154 at 158; *Holyoak* (1995) 82 A Crim R 502; *R v Cumberbatch* (2004) 8 VR 9, [2004] VSCA 37; *R v Miller* (2000) 76 SASR 151, [2000] SASC 16; *Kaye v R* [2004] WASCA 227; *R v Poh* (1981) 3 Cr App R (S) 304 and *Wheeler v The State of Western Australia* [2007] WASCA 109.

1362 See *Lawrence Simbe v The State* [1994] PNGLR 38 and *The State v Eddy Kava Laura (No. 2)* [1988-89] PNGLR 98 at 99.

See however: *Public Prosecutor v Apava Keru; Public Prosecutor v Aia Moroi* [1985] PNGLR 78, [1985] PGSC 7.

1363 See *DPP v Che Kien* (2000) 116 A Crim R 339 and *S v Tasmania* (2007) 16 Tas R 292.

1364 See *R v Hannigan* (2009) 193 A Crim R 399, per Chesterman JA.

MITIGATING FACTORS

A Court in determining what sentence it should impose, can properly take into account that an accused person has already suffered some serious loss or detriment as a result of having committed the offence[1365], including:

- injuries suffered as a consequence of the unlawful actions of a law enforcement officer[1366];

- injuries suffered as a consequence of the unlawful actions of members of the public.[1367]

  However, when the injuries are inflicted by the victim against whom the offence is being committed, a Court is entitled to take into account:

  - whether the act that caused the injuries was an unreasonable reaction by the victim to the behaviour of the accused person; and

  - the degree of the injury inflicted[1368];

- injuries suffered as a consequence of the commission of an offence[1369]; and

---

[1365] See *R v Daetz; R v Wilson* (2003) 139 A Crim R 398 at 411; *R v Allpass* (1993) 72 A Crim R 561; *R v Clampitt-Wotten* (2002) 37 MVR 340; *R v Webb* [1971] VR 147 at 150-151; *R v P* (1992) 64 A Crim R 381 at 384-385; *Siganto v R* (1998) 194 CLR 656 at 646-666, (1998) 105 A Crim R 184, [1998] HCA 74; *R v Noble and Verheyden* [1996] 1 Qd R 329; *R v Barci* (1994) 76 A Crim R 103; *R v Haddara* (1997) 95 A Crim R 108 and *R v Sharpe* [2006] NSWCCA 255.

[1366] See *Bafe Quati v The State* [1990] PNGLR 57; *The State v Kevin Karoa* (2001) N2151; *The State v Simon Sulu Uraken and Jack Charles Joku* (1990) N884 and *The State v Andy Koko* (2009) N3615, [2009] PGNC 31.

See also: *R v Nasogaluak* (2010) SCC 6, [2010] 1 SCR 206; *R v Noble and Verheyden* [1996] 1 Qd R 329 at 331; *R v Daetz; R v Wilson* (2003) 139 A Crim R 398; *Alameddine v R* [2006] NSWCCA 317; *R v Hook* [2006] QCA 458 and *Silvano v R* (2008) 184 A Crim R 593, [2008] NSWCCA 118.

[1367] See *The State v Smith Ondari* (1990) N867; *The State v Daniel Soma* [2006] PGNC 71 and *The State v Sam Pap* [2007] PGNC 10.

See also: *Silvano v R* (2008) 184 A Crim R 593, [2008] NSWCCA 118.

[1368] See *Sharpe v R* [2006] NSWCCA 255 and *Alameddine v R* [2006] NSWCCA 317.

[1369] See *Silvano v R* (2008) 184 A Crim R 593, [2008] NSWCCA 118; *Whybrow v R* [2008] NSWCCA 270; *R v Webb* [2004] NSWCCA 330 and *Alameddine v* R [2006] NSWCCA 317.

See however: *R v Noble and Verheyden* [1996] 1 Qd R 329 at 330-331.

- loss of property that was unlawfully destroyed as a consequence of the commission of the offence[1370].

How much weight a Court should give extra-curial punishment depends, of course, upon all the circumstances of the case[1371], including the seriousness of the offence[1372] when compared with:

- the punishment inflicted[1373]; and

- the nature of the injuries suffered[1374].

[14.0] PAYMENT OF COMPENSATION

Compensation for physical and non-physical injury to a person wrongfully inflicted by another person is widely practised in many Papua New Guinean traditional societies.[1375]

Compensation for injury or damage to personal property is also widely practised.[1376]

Indeed compensation for personal injury and injury to personal property is a universal principle.[1377]

1370 See *The State v Benjamin Towari and others* (2011) N4353, [2011] PGNC 79.

1371 See *R v Daetz; R v Wilson* (2003) 139 A Crim R 398 at 411.

1372 Refer also to the section titled 'Prevalence Of The Offence' in the chapter titled 'Aggravating Factors'.

1373 See *R v Davidson; ex parte Attorney-General (Queensland)* [2009] QCA 283.

1374 See *Sharpe v R* [2006] NSWCCA 255 and *R v Webb* [2004] NSWCCA 330.

1375 See *Manu Kovi v The State* (2005) SC789, [2005] PGSC 34.

1376 See *Manu Kovi v The State* (2005) SC789, [2005] PGSC 34.

1377 See *Manu Kovi v The State* (2005) SC789, [2005] PGSC 34.

However in *The State v William Muma*[1378] Injia J (as he then was) stated:

> 'Whilst it is true that compensation was paid to harmonise the differences between the accused and the victim's relatives caused by the offence, the victim was not really compensated for the wrong done to her. She was too young to recognise and appreciate the efforts made between the two sides to normalise their relationship'.[1379]

The payment of customary compensation is a sign of an accused person's acceptance of criminal responsibility.[1380]

No officer is to participate in or sanction in any way community compensation negotiations and payments designed to shield offenders of violent crimes from facing criminal prosecution. The payment of compensation as a form of punishment is the exclusive jurisdiction of the National Court and District Court as provided for by the *Criminal Law (Compensation) Act 1991*.[1381]

Compensation arises to be considered by the Court after conviction when sentence is considered.

When an accused person pays customary compensation it is a 'mitigating factor'.[1382]

It is not appropriate to deduct a specific period of imprisonment from the sentence imposed on account of the payment of customary compensation.[1383]

[1378] [1995] PNGLR 161, (1995) N1371, [1995] PGNC 76.

[1379] As regards the victim of a sexual offence, see also: *The State v Gidingeng Yaking (No. 2)* [2006] PGNC 98; *The State v Kenneth Peter* (2002) N2336 and *The State v Alexander Junior Nara (No. 2)* (2007) N3214, [2007] PGNC 86.

[1380] See *The Public Prosecutor v Panikuiaka Nopi* [1979] PNGLR 536.

[1381] Refer also to the section titled 'Compensation Order' in the chapter titled 'Sentencing Options'.

[1382] See *Manu Kovi v The State* (2005) SC789, [2005] PGSC 34; *Rex Lialu v The State* [1990] PNGLR 487; *Joe Giamur v The State* (2006) SC884, [2007] PGSC 7; *The State v Michael Tangip (*2012) N4782, [2012] PGNC 205; *The State v Neiman Dua* (2013) N4957, [2013] PGNC 8; *The State v Sali Kevin Mavuug* (2012) N4898, [2012] PGNC 255; *The State v Paul Potape Huliya* (2005) N2872, [2005] PGNC 77; *The State v Abel Airi* (2000) N2007; *The State v Sinzai Karawa* (2004) N2631; *The State v Ebes Tiun* (2001) N2129; *The State v Issau Parao* (2009) N3625, [2009] PGNC 38; *The State v Carol Alfred* (2009) N3602, [2009] PGNC 29; *Acting Public Prosecutor v Uaname Aumane and others* [1980] PNGLR 410; *The State v Emp Mek* [1993] PNGLR 330 and *The State v Jimmy Ketu (No. 2)* (2007) N3394, [2007] PGNC 153.

[1383] See *Acting Public Prosecutor v Nitak Mangilonde Taganis of Tambitanis* [1982] PNGLR 299, [1982] PGSC 6.

MITIGATING FACTORS

Where an accused person relies on the payment of customary compensation as a 'mitigating factor' on sentence he or she bears the onus of proving as a 'matter of fact' the existence of such a custom.[1384]

The payment of compensation:

- does not excuse an accused person from his or her criminal liability because under no circumstances should compensation be a substitute for a penalty[1385];
- can restore a victim to his or her position before the commission of an offence[1386]; and
- is a relevant 'mitigating factor'[1387] in the context of considering both already paid and future compensation[1388].

[1384] See *Acting Public Prosecutor v Nitak Mangilonde Taganis of Tambitanis* [1982] PNGLR 299, [1982] PGSC 6.

[1385] See *Joe Giamur v The State* (2007) SC884, [2007] PGSC 7; *Kepa Wanege v The State* (2004) SC742, [2004] PGSC 22; *Baune Bernard Olmi v The State* (2004) SC872, [2004] PGSC 43; *Sakarowa Koe v The State* (2004) SC739, [2004] PGSC 33; *The State v Rex Lialu* [1988-89] PNGLR 499; *Acting Public Prosecutor v Nitak Mangilonde Taganis of Tambitanis* [1982] PNGLR 299, [1982] PGSC 6; *The State v Paul Potape Huliya* (2005) N2872, [2005] PGNC 77; *The State v Alice Wilmot* (2005) N2857, [2005] PGNC 105; *The State v Darius Taulo* (2001) N2034; *The State v Abel Airi* (2000) N2007; *The State v Nickson Pari (No. 2)* (2001) N2033; *The State v Henry Idab* (2001) N2172; *The State v Jim Paupa* (1973) No. 765; *The State v Lossy Karapus* (2009) N3640, [2009] PGNC 59; *The State v Eddie John Naopa* (2003) N2411; *The State v Jimmy Ketu (No. 2)* (2007) N3394, [2007] PGNC 153; *The State v Martin Muru* [2007] PGNC 117; *The State v Moki Lepi (No. 3)* (2004) N2734 and *The State v Gibson Haulai* (2004) N2555.

[1386] See *The State v Oa Seseka* (1990) N921.

[1387] See *Baune Bernard Olmi v The State* (2004) SC872, [2004] PGSC 43; *Manu Kovi v The State* (2005) SC789, [2005] PGSC 34; *Sakarowa Koe v The State* (2004) SC739, [2004] PGSC 33; *Acting Public Prosecutor v Nitak Mangilonde Taganis of Tambitanis* [1982] PNGLR 299, [1982] PGSC 6; *R v Jim Kaupa* (1973) No. 765; *The State v Abel Airi* (2000) N2007; *The State v Nickson Pari (No. 2)* (2001) N2033; *The State v Henry Idab* (2001) N2172; *The State v Ebes Tiun* (2001) N2129 and *The State v Grace John (No. 3)* (2011) N4371, [2011] PGNC 104.

[1388] See *Sakarowa Koe v The State* (2004) SC739, [2004] PGSC 33 and *The State v Henry Idab* (2001) N2172.

MITIGATING FACTORS

But compensation can be taken into account as a 'mitigating factor' only when there is appropriate evidence confirming the payment of any compensation, including:

- the amount paid;
- when was the compensation paid;
- by whom was the compensation paid; and
- to whom was the compensation paid.[1389]

If an accused person plays no meaningful part in the organisation and payment of compensation it should not operate in his or her favour.[1390]

This is because:

- the whole basis of the criminal justice system and any penalty imposed is dependent on the accused person's culpability[1391]; and
- the accused person is the only one that is personally responsible for his or her actions.[1392]

Customary compensation is a matter that may be taken into account on sentencing in homicide cases where such payment is considered relevant to sentence.[1393]

[1389] See *Sakarowa Koe v The State* (2004) SC739, [2004] PGSC 33 and *The State v Steven Mul Mangi (No. 2)* (2005) N2993, [2005] PGNC 12.

[1390] See *Kepa Wanege v The State* (2004) SC742, [2004] PGSC 22; *The State v Darius Taulo* (2001) N2034; *The State v Eddie John Naopa* (2003) N2411 and *The State v Alice Wilmot* (2005) N2857, [2005] PGNC 105.

[1391] See *The State v Abel Airi* (2000) N2007.

[1392] See *The State v Nickson Pari (No. 2)* (2001) N2033.

As to the involvement of the family of an accused person in paying compensation, see *The State v Allan Nareti and Amstrong Kupe* (2004) N2582 and *The State v Dobi Ao (No. 2)* (2002) N2247.

[1393] See *Acting Public Prosecutor v Nitak Mangilonde Taganis of Tambitanis* [1982] PNGLR 299, [1982] PGSC 6; *The State v Billy Kauwa* [1994] PNGLR 503 at 508 and *The State v Dilu Kimam* (2011) N4323, [2011] PGNC 58.

MITIGATING FACTORS

Whilst the Courts acknowledge that:

- compensation should not be used to pay for the commissioner of a crime; and
- no amount of remorse or compensation will restore loss of life,

the payment of compensation is an important 'mitigating factor'.[1394]

The amount or value of compensation will vary depending on the special circumstances and values of each traditional society.[1395]

The weight to be given to compensation by the Court will also vary depending on different factors involved, including:

- the existence of custom of compensation for death wrongfully caused;
- whether there was a request or demand for compensation made by the deceased person's relatives and the response given by the deceased person's relatives;
- the amount or value offered and accepted[1396];
- the amount the accused person himself or herself has paid or contributed;
- the promptness of the response or payment;
- any expression of genuine remorse accompanying the payment[1397]; and

---

[1394] See *Manu Kovi v The State* (2005) SC789, [2005] PGSC 34 and *The State v Carol Alfred* (2009) N3602, [2009] PGNC 29.

[1395] See *Manu Kovi v The State* (2005) SC789, [2005] PGSC 34 and *The State v Carol Alfred* (2009) N3602, [2009] PGNC 29.

[1396] See *The State v Sali Kevin Mavuug* (2012) N4898, [2012] PGNC 255.

[1397] Refer also to:
- the section titled 'Plea Of Guilty' in the chapter titled 'Mitigating Factors'; and
- the section titled 'No Remorse' in the chapter titled 'Aggravating Factors'.

- the cessation of animosity and restoration of peace between the two sides of the conflict.[1398]

In order for compensation to be regarded as an ordinary or special 'mitigating factor', two important indicators are:

- the form.

  A payment in the form of money is almost indispensable in modern times. Valuable personal property such as pigs and foodstuff is common. Some societies use land[1399]; and

- amount or value of compensation paid.[1400]

  The amount or value of customary compensation often varies.[1401]

  In terms of money, it is difficult to fix any specific amount or figure for compensation, but some guidance may be obtained from the maximum amount of compensation prescribed under the *Criminal Law (Compensation) Act 1991* which is K5,000.[1402]

  Despite the limit fixed by the Act, compensation of amounts in excess of K10,000 are common in homicide cases.[1403]

  Compensation to the value of between K5,000 and K10,000 or over is a substantial payment which would take the payment out of the 'ordinary mitigating factor' category and place it in the 'special mitigating factor' category.[1404]

[1398] See *Manu Kovi v The State* (2005) SC789, [2005] PGSC 34 and *The State v Carol Alfred* (2009) N3602, [2009] PGNC 29.

[1399] See *Manu Kovi v The State* (2005) SC789, [2005] PGSC 34.

[1400] See *Manu Kovi v The State* (2005) SC789, [2005] PGSC 34.

[1401] See *Manu Kovi v The State* (2005) SC789, [2005] PGSC 34.

[1402] See *Manu Kovi v The State* (2005) SC789, [2005] PGSC 34.

[1403] See *Manu Kovi v The State* (2005) SC789, [2005] PGSC 34.

[1404] See *Manu Kovi v The State* (2005) SC789, [2005] PGSC 34.

COMPARATIVE SENTENCES

[1.0] GENERAL PRINCIPLES

Whilst the outcome of discretionary decision-making in sentencing can never be uniform, it ought to depend as little as possible upon the identity of the judge or magistrate who hears the case. Like cases should be treated in a like manner.[1405]

When considering the sentencing standards it is necessary to have regard to a range of comparable cases.[1406]

However, as to customary sentencing standards, caution is needed when trying to determine the level of severity of a particular sentence by comparison with those imposed in other cases.[1407]

This is because there will inevitably be differences in the circumstances of:

- accused persons; and
- offences.[1408]

Each case turns on its own particular facts and circumstances.[1409]

Sentencing is not a process that follows exact mathematical rules. Circumstances and people vary and a Court should not consider a comparative sentence as more than a very imprecise guide.[1410]

The sentencing process is not:

- mechanistic; and

1405 See *Wong and Leung v R* (2001) 207 CLR 584, per Gleeson CJ at 591, (2001) 76 ALJR 79, [2001] HCA 64.

1406 See *Penney v The State of Western Australia* [2011] WASCA 71.

1407 See *The State of Western Australia v Higgins* [2008] WASCA 157 and *Penney v The State of Western Australia* [2011] WASCA 71.

1408 See *The State of Western Australia v Higgins* [2008] WASCA 157; *Tulloh v R* [2004] WASCA 169; *Ziino v The State of Western Australia* [2007] WASCA 222 and *Penney v The State of Western Australia* [2011] WASCA 71.

1409 See *The State of Western Australia v Higgins* [2008] WASCA 157.

1410 See *Joel Likilua and Allen Kokolobu v R* [1988-1989] SILR 148 at 149 and *R v Timo* [2005] SBHC 51.

- directed towards ensuring the sentences imposed exhibit perfect proportionality with others.[1411]

A Court should take into consideration sentencing tariffs.[1412]

1411 See *R v Hart* [2012] QCA 38 and *Dowie v R* [1989] Tas R 167, [1989] TASSC 44, per Wright J.

1412 See *Richard Liri v The State* (2007) SC883, [2007] PGSC 3; *Joe Giamur v The State* (2007) SC884, [2007] PGSC 7; *James Pangnan and Patrick Ponat v The State* (2006) SCRA Nos. 39 and 54 of 2004 and *The State v Dobi Ao (No. 2)* (2002) N2247.

As regards the issuance of tariffs, see *Ura Francis Miriva v The State* (1981) SC197, per Miles J; Kondan *Kale v The State* (1983) SC250, per Andrew J; *Wellington Belawa v The State* [1988-89] PNGLR 496 at 505, [1988] PGSC 6; *Rex Lialu v The State* [1990] PNGLR 487 and *John Aubuku v The State* [1987] PNGLR 267.

It is an important aspect in sentencing that tariffs must be considered to determine sentences in future cases if subsequent sentences are to have any relevance to the interest of society to appropriately deal with accused persons, see *The State v Dobi Ao (No. 2)* (2002) N2247.

A standard sentence as specified in a tariff should be increased progressively, rather than by leaps and bounds, see *Tau Jim Anis and others v The State* (2000) SC642, [2000] PGSC 12.

Refer also to the section titled 'General Principles' in the chapter titled 'Introduction To Sentencing'.

As regards the disadvantages of the tariff system, see *Griffiths v R* (1977) 137 CLR 293, (1977) 51 ALJR 749 at 765, [1977] HCA 44.

Notwithstanding their limitations [see New Zealand Law Commission, 2005, 'Criminal Pre-Trial Processes: Justice Through Efficiency', Report 89, page 93], tariff or guideline judgements are used as a tool for directing judicial discretion:

- in the United Kingdom.

  The United Kingdom Sentencing Guidelines Council has published a compendium of guideline judgements which can be viewed at http://www.sentencing-guidelines.gov.uk/index.html;

- to a lesser extent in Australia.

  See for example *R v Jurisic* (1998) 45 NSWLR 209; *R v Henry* (1999) 46 NSWLR 346; *R v Wong and Leung* (1999) 48 NWSWLR 340; *R v Thomson* (2000) 49 NSWLR 383 and *R v Ponfield* (1999) 48 NSWLR 327; and

- in New Zealand.

  See *R v Taueki* [2005] 3 NZLR 372.

See also: New Zealand Law Commission, 2006, 'Reforms to the Sentencing and Parole Structure: Consultative Draft', Preliminary Paper 1, page 20.

COMPARATIVE SENTENCES

Previous sentences demonstrate principles or parameters of sentence; but such sentences should not be used as binding precedents to reach a sentence in a particular case.[1413]

Other cases can do no more than become part of a range for sentencing.[1414]

Sentencing ranges can provide only general guidance.[1415]

The guidance afforded by comparable cases is flexible, rather than rigid.[1416]

Sentencing patterns can be taken into account as a yardstick[1417], but a history of sentences does not necessarily:

- establish a range; or
- indicate the upper and lower limits of the range.[1418]

In any event, consistency is not a matter of numerical equivalence.[1419]

While the general principle of consistency of sentencing is achieved by a consideration of comparable cases which inform the range of sentences applicable[1420], such cases are not the litmus test of what is a sound exercise of sentencing discretion[1421].

[1413] See *Sau v R* [1982] SILR 65 at 69 and *Taoai v Police* [2002] WSSC 5.

[1414] See *R v George* (2004) 149 A Crim R 38, [2004] NSWCCA 247; *R v Araya* (2005) 155 A Crim R 555, [2005] NSWCCA 283 and *DPP (Commonwealth) v De La Rosa* [2010] NSWCCA 194.

[1415] See *Coleski v The State of Western Australia* [2008] WASCA 260.

[1416] See *Quach v R* [1999] WASCA 210.

[1417] See *McGregor v The State of Western Australia* [2011] WASCA 88.

[1418] See *Hili v R* (2010) 242 CLR 520, [2010] HCA 45.

[1419] See *Hili v R* (2010) 242 CLR 520, [2010] HCA 45.

[1420] See *Hudson v R* [2010] VSCA 332; *Farrugia v R* [2011] VSCA 24; *The State of Western Australia v Higgins* [2008] WASCA 157; *Bosworth v The State of Western Australia* (2007) 175 A Crim R 49, [2007] WASCA 144; *Ziino v The State of Western Australia* [2007] WASCA 222 and *Penney v The State of Western Australia* [2011] WASCA 71.

See however: *R v George* (2004) 149 A Crim R 38, [2004] NSWCCA 247; *R v Morgan* (1993) 70 A Crim R 368 and *R v Trevenna* [2004] NSWCCA 43, per Barr J.

[1421] See *Hili v R* (2010) 242 CLR 520, [2010] HCA 45.

COMPARATIVE SENTENCES

When considering other cases it is important for the Court to consider:

- the objective gravity of the particular offence; and
- the subjective circumstances of the particular accused person;

and not whether it is more severe or more lenient than some other sentences (other than a co-accused) which merely forms part of that range.[1422]

The mere fact that:

- a sentence is within the range of other sentences imposed for similar offences does not necessarily establish that there was an appropriate exercise of the sentencing discretion in the particular case; and
- a sentence that is outside the range of other sentences imposed for similar offences does not necessarily establish that the exercise of the sentencing discretion in the particular case miscarried.[1423]

The circumstances of each case are to be determined on their own facts and should reflect the views of the community, not only previous courts.[1424]

The reference to an appropriate sentence is apt to be misunderstood. Generally speaking, a sentence within a limited range of years is appropriate to:

- the circumstances in which the offence was committed; and
- the character, antecedents and conditions of the accused person.[1425]

However, the importance of comparative sentencing is that there should be less 'objectionable' disparity[1426] in sentencing, provided the sentences imposed are within the range provided by the comparative sentences.

[1422] See *R v Morgan* (1993) 70 A Crim R 368.

[1423] See *Ly v R* [2007] NSWCCA 28 and *R v Baldock* (2010) 243 FLR 120, [2010] WASCA 170.

[1424] See *R v Roland Timo* [2005] SBHC 51.

[1425] As Mason J commented in *Lowe v R* (1984) 154 CLR 606 at 612, [1984] HCA 46.

[1426] Refer also to:
- the chapter titled 'Inequality In Sentencing'; and
- the section titled 'Disparity In Sentencing' in the chapter titled 'Appeals Against Sentence'.

COMPARATIVE SENTENCES

Sentences imposed in other jurisdictions are, in general, of little assistance since sentencing policies and the quantum of any sentence in any country must relate to:

- the culture of the country;
- its degree of development;
- its penal policy; and
- the prevalence of crime therein.[1427]

Consequently, it is more appropriate for reference to be made to local decisions.[1428]

A Court should consider alternatives to a term of imprisonment for non-violent offences.[1429] However, that does not necessarily mean that there should be drastic reduction in the head sentences. Rather, it means that there be sterner head sentences and then have the sentences either wholly or partly suspended on strict terms. This is to show the seriousness of the offence and to serve both the purposes of deterrence and rehabilitation of accused persons. It would also give an accused person a reason to faithfully meet any conditions imposed for a suspended sentence. The absence of a sanction or conditions might give no reason to an accused person to appreciate his or her sentence and take meaningful steps to rehabilitate.[1430]

[1427] See *Lialu v The State* [1990] PNGLR 487, [1990] PGSC 16 and *John Aubuku v The State* [1987] PNGLR 267.

See also: *The State v Marcus Pitmete* (2007) N3229, [2007] PGNC 105 and *Harris v The DPP (Nauru)* [1998] NRSC 2.

[1428] See *Lialu v The State* [1990] PNGLR 487, [1990] PGSC 16 and *John Aubuku v The State* [1987] PNGLR 267.

See also: *The State v Marcus Pitmete* (2007) N3229, [2007] PGNC 105 and *Harris v The DPP (Nauru)* [1998] NRSC 2.

[1429] See *Doreen Liprin v The State* (2001) SC673, [2001] PGSC 11.

[1430] See *The State v Eric Emmanuel Vele* (2002) N2252.

COMPARATIVE SENTENCES

[2.0] ABDUCTION[1431]

See:

- *The State v Dekley Cornelius Kivung* (2008) N3519, [2008] PGNC 161
- *The State v Julius Ombi (No. 2)* (2004) N2552
- *The State v Eki Kondi and others* (2004) N2543
- *The State v Paul Wanda* (1997) N1600
- *The State v John Pep Pera* (1989) N758

The maximum sentence is for this offence is life imprisonment.

Sentences imposed have ranged from one to twenty-two years imprisonment.

[3.0] ABUSE OF OFFICE

See:

- *The State v Alphonse Aiwol* (2012) N4681, [2012] PGNC 68

The maximum sentence is two years imprisonment, but if the offence was committed for gain the maximum sentence is three years imprisonment.

In the case cited the sentence imposed was two years imprisonment and that was a case in which the offence was committed for gain.

[4.0] AIRCRAFT HIJACKING

See:

- *The State v John Michael Awa; The State v Eric Steven Gituthe; The State v Degemba Michael; The State v John Michael Awathe; The State v Eric Steven Gituthe; The State v Degemba Michael; The State v Harry Ewag* (2000) N2012
- *The State v Michael Kamipe* (1996) N1471

The maximum sentence for this offence is life imprisonment.

Sentences imposed have ranged from six to twelve years imprisonment.

[1431] Refer to the section titled 'Kidnappings' in the chapter titled 'Offences Against The Person' in the text titled 'Injia on Criminal Offences in Papua New Guinea and the Pacific'.

COMPARATIVE SENTENCES

[5.0] ARSON OFFENCES

[5.1] ARSON[1432]

[5.1.1] GENERAL PRINCIPLES

The offence of 'Arson' can be an extremely serious offence if there was a potential risk to life. A reckless and careless form of arson is less serious than if it was deliberate and planned.[1433]

The offence of 'Arson' is a prevalent offence.[1434]

The following categories apply[1435]:

- A dwelling house with people inside;
- A dwelling house without any occupants;
- Public institutions, such as schools, hospitals or offices, with occupants inside;
- Public institutions, such as schools, hospitals or offices, without occupants inside; and
- A house wing, garden house or run down and deteriorated or incomplete structure.

In order to determine an appropriate sentence the factors to be considered, include:

- did the accused person cause damage of a relatively low value?[1436];

1432 The law in relation to this offence is examined in the section titled 'Arson And Attempted Arson' in the chapter titled 'Offences Against Property' in the text titled 'Injia on Criminal Offences in Papua New Guinea and the Pacific'.

1433 See *R v Mason* (1981) 3 Cr App R (S) 182.

1434 Refer also to the section titled 'Prevalence Of The Offence' in the chapter titled 'Aggravating Factors'.

1435 See *Emil Kongian and others v The State* (2007) SC928, [2007] PGSC 45 and *Lemen Polau v The State* (2013) SC1231, [2013] PGSC 6.

1436 See *The State v Anton Towakra and others* (2009) N3845 and *The State v Bart Kiohin Mais and Henry Kevi* (2005) N2811, [2005] PGNC 142.

Refer also to the section titled 'Seriousness Of An Offence Generally' in the chapter titled 'Aggravating Factors'.

- the type and value of the house or building[1437];
- the value of the house or building to the occupants/owner, ie., whether the house or building was permanent, semi permanent or of bush materials, and its contents[1438];
- did the accused person deliberately or recklessly put lives at risk?[1439];
- was there a person or class of persons directly affected by the damage or destruction of the property?[1440];
- was there more than one offender?[1441];
- did the owner of the property or any other person provoke the accused person in 'the non-legal sense'?[1442];

1437 See *The State v Andrew Yeskulu* (2003) N2410.

Refer also to the section titled 'Seriousness Of An Offence Generally' in the chapter titled 'Aggravating Factors'.

1438 See *The State v Langalen Yandan (No. 2)* (2012) N4833, [2012] PGNC 158; *The State v Ipu Samuel Yomb* [1992] PNGLR 261; *The State v Matthew Balu and Bernard Kavanamur Balu* (2011) N4362, [2011] PGNC 97 and *The State v Andrew Yeskulu* (2003) N2410.

1439 See *The State v Ipu Samuel Yomb* [1992] PNGLR 261; *The State v Pricilla Piru* (2010) N4221, [2010] PGNC 188 and *The State v Matthew Balu and Bernard Kavanamur Balu* (2011) N4362, [2011] PGNC 97.

See also: *The State v Anton Towakra and others* (2009) N3845 and *The State v Bart Kiohin Mais and Henry Kevi* (2005) N2811, [2005] PGNC 142.

1440 See *The State v Bart Kiohin Mais* (2005) N2811; *The State v Samson Leila* (2012) N4770, [2012] PGNC 226; *The State v Mapi Mack* (2010) N4100 and *The State v Mono Kukiwa,* (Unreported CR No.1093 of 2008, David J, 22 March 2011).

1441 See *The State v Bart Kiohin Mais* (2005) N2811; *The State v Samson Leila* (2012) N4770, [2012] PGNC 226; *The State v Mapi Mack* (2010) N4100 and *The State v Mono Kukiwa,* (Unreported CR No.1093 of 2008, David J, 22 March 2011).

Refer also to the section titled 'Member Of A Gang' in the chapter titled 'Aggravating Factors'.

1442 See *The State v Bart Kiohin Mais* (2005) N2811; *The State v Samson Leila* (2012) N4770, [2012] PGNC 226; *The State v Mapi Mack* (2010) N4100 and *The State v Mono Kukiwa,* (Unreported CR No.1093 of 2008, David J, 22 March 2011).

Refer also to the section titled 'De-facto Provocation' in the chapter titled 'Extenuating Circumstances'.

- was it an isolated incident?[1443];

- did the accused person plan the offence in a deliberate and calculated manner?[1444], including whether there was the deliberate pouring of kerosene or any inflammable liquor and setting fire to the roof knowing that people were inside, the deliberate locking of the door so preventing escape by the occupants and the deliberate cold blooded planning of the offence[1445];

- did the accused person give himself or herself up after the incident?[1446];

- did the accused person co-operate with the police in their investigation?[1447];

[1443] See *The State v Bart Kiohin Mais* (2005) N2811; *The State v Samson Leila* (2012) N4770, [2012] PGNC 226; *The State v Mapi Mack* (2010) N4100 and *The State v Mono Kukiwa,* (Unreported CR No.1093 of 2008, David J, 22 March 2011).

[1444] See *The State v Langalen Yandan (No. 2)* (2012) N4833, [2012] PGNC 158; *The State v Anton Towakra and others* (2009) N3845 and *The State v Bart Kiohin Mais and Henry Kevi* (2005) N2811, [2005] PGNC 142.

Refer also to the section titled 'Pre-planning And Pre-meditation' in the chapter titled 'Aggravating Factors'.

[1445] See *The State v Ipu Samuel Yomb* [1992] PNGLR 261; *The State v Pricilla Piru* (2010) N4221, [2010] PGNC 188; *The State v Matthew Balu and Bernard Kavanamur Balu* (2011) N4362, [2011] PGNC 97 and *The State v Andrew Yeskulu* (2003) N2410.

[1446] See *The State v Bart Kiohin Mais* (2005) N2811; *The State v Samson Leila* (2012) N4770, [2012] PGNC 226; *The State v Mapi Mack* (2010) N4100 and *The State v Mono Kukiwa*, (Unreported CR No.1093 of 2008, David J, 22 March 2011).

Refer also to the section titled 'Co-operation With Police' in the chapter titled 'Mitigating Factors'.

[1447] See *The State v Bart Kiohin Mais* (2005) N2811; *The State v Samson Leila* (2012) N4770, [2012] PGNC 226; *The State v Mapi Mack* (2010) N4100 and *The State v Mono Kukiwa,* (Unreported CR No.1093 of 2008, David J, 22 March 2011).

Refer also to the section titled 'Co-operation With Police' in the chapter titled 'Mitigating Factors'.

- has the accused person done anything tangible towards repairing his or her wrong, eg., offering compensation[1448], engaging in a peace and reconciliation ceremony, personally or publicly apologising for what he or she did?;

- has the accused person caused further trouble since the incident?[1449];

- has the accused person pleaded guilty?[1450];

- has the accused person genuinely expressed remorse?[1451];

- is this the accused person's first offence?[1452];

[1448] See *The State v Bart Kiohin Mais* (2005) N2811; *The State v Samson Leila* (2012) N4770, [2012] PGNC 226; *The State v Mapi Mack* (2010) N4100 and *The State v Mono Kukiwa,* (Unreported CR No.1093 of 2008, David J, 22 March 2011).

Refer also to the section titled 'Payment Of Compensation' in the chapter titled 'Mitigating Factors'.

[1449] See *The State v Bart Kiohin Mais* (2005) N2811; *The State v Samson Leila* (2012) N4770, [2012] PGNC 226; *The State v Mapi Mack* (2010) N4100 and *The State v Mono Kukiwa,* (Unreported CR No.1093 of 2008, David J, 22 March 2011).

[1450] See *The State v Bart Kiohin Mais* (2005) N2811; *The State v Samson Leila* (2012) N4770, [2012] PGNC 226; *The State v Mapi Mack* (2010) N4100 and *The State v Mono Kukiwa,* (Unreported CR No.1093 of 2008, David J, 22 March 2011).

Refer also to the section titled 'Plea Of Guilty' in the chapter titled 'Mitigating Factors'.

[1451] See *The State v Bart Kiohin Mais* (2005) N2811; *The State v Samson Leila* (2012) N4770, [2012] PGNC 226; *The State v Mapi Mack* (2010) N4100 and *The State v Mono Kukiwa,* (Unreported CR No.1093 of 2008, David J, 22 March 2011).

Refer also to the section titled 'Plea Of Guilty' in the chapter titled 'Mitigating Factors' and the section titled 'No Remorse' in the chapter titled 'Aggravating Factors'.

[1452] See *The State v Bart Kiohin Mais* (2005) N2811; *The State v Samson Leila* (2012) N4770, [2012] PGNC 226; *The State v Mapi Mack* (2010) N4100 and *The State v Mono Kukiwa,* (Unreported CR No.1093 of 2008, David J, 22 March 2011).

Refer also to the section titled 'Criminal History' in the chapter titled 'Mitigating Factors'.

- can the accused person be regarded as a youthful offender?[1453]; and
- are there any other circumstances of the incident or the accused person that warrant mitigation of the head sentence?[1454]

[5.1.2] COMPARATIVE CASES

See:

- *Lemen Polau v The State* (2013) SC1231, [2013] PGSC 6
- *Emil Kongian and others v The State* (2007) SC928, [2007] PGSC 45
- *The State v Matthew Balu and Bernard Kavanamur Balu* (2011) N4362, [2011] PGNC 97
- *The State v Langalen Yandan (No. 2)* (2012) N4833, [2012] PGNC 158
- *The State v Samson Leila* (2012) N4770, [2012] PGNC 226
- *The State v Keith Kwelik* (2011) N4335, [2011] PGNC 71
- *The State v Mapi Mack* (2010) N4100, [2010] PGNC 123
- *The State v Pricilla Piru* (2010) N4221, [2010] PGNC 188
- *The State v James Wakis* (2008) N3426, [2008] PGNC 111
- *The State v Yunati Epa* (2008) N3309, [2008] PGNC 41
- *The State v Michael Keari and others* (2007) CR No. 868 of 2007
- *The State v Sylvester Heai Evore* (2006) N3236, [2006] PGNC 148
- *The State v Joe Sekin* [2006] PGNC 74
- *The State v Peni Bilak* (2005) N2866, [2005] PGNC 92
- *The State v Bart Kiohin Mais and Henry Kevi* (2005) N2811, [2005] PGNC 142
- *The State v Prodie Akoi and Steven Akoi* (2004) N2584
- *The State v Henny Wamahau Ilomo* (2003) N2420
- *The State v Robin Warren and others (No. 2)* (2003) N2418
- *The State v Andrew Yeskulu* (2003) N2410
- *The State v Gilman Mui* (2000) N1992

[1453] See *The State v Bart Kiohin Mais* (2005) N2811; *The State v Samson Leila* (2012) N4770, [2012] PGNC 226; *The State v Mapi Mack* (2010) N4100 and *The State v Mono Kukiwa,* (Unreported CR No.1093 of 2008, David J, 22 March 2011).

Refer also to the section titled 'Youthfulness' in the chapter titled 'Mitigating Factors'.

[1454] See *The State v Bart Kiohin Mais* (2005) N2811; *The State v Samson Leila* (2012) N4770, [2012] PGNC 226; *The State v Mapi Mack* (2010) N4100 and *The State v Mono Kukiwa,* (Unreported CR No.1093 of 2008, David J, 22 March 2011).

Refer also to the chapters titled 'Mitigating Factors' and 'Extenuating Circumstances'.

- *The State v Kai Kuhe* (1999) N1907
- *The State v Seye Wasea Bukere* (1999) N1848
- *The State v Akena Pawa* (1998) N1710
- *The State v Layman Homa* (1998) N1687

The maximum sentence for this offence is life imprisonment.

Sentences imposed have ranged from three to sixteen years imprisonment.

[5.2] ATTEMPTED ARSON[1455]

See:

- *The State v Scott Lalio* (2006) N2967, [2006] PGNC 27

The maximum sentence for this offence is fourteen years imprisonment.

The sentence imposed in the case cited was two years imprisonment, with part suspended on conditions.

[6.0] ASSAULT WITH INTENT TO STEAL[1456]

See:

- *The State v Newman Saimon Bonga* (2007) N3388, [2007] PGNC 154

The maximum sentence for this offence is three years imprisonment.

The sentence imposed in the case cited was one year and eight months imprisonment, wholly suspended on conditions.

[1455] The law in relation to this offence is examined in the section titled 'Arson And Attempted Arson' in the chapter titled 'Offences Against Property' in the text titled 'Injia on Criminal Offences in Papua New Guinea and the Pacific'.

[1456] The law in relation to this offence is examined in the section titled 'Assault With Intent' in the chapter titled 'Offeances Against The Person' in the text titled 'Injia on Criminal Offences in Papua New Guinea and the Pacific'.

COMPARATIVE SENTENCES

[7.0] ATTEMPT TO PERVERT THE COURSE OF JUSTICE[1457]

See:

- *The State v John Peril; The State v Erika M Lucas* (2005) N2883, [2005] PGNC 85

The maximum sentence for this offence is two years imprisonment.

Sentences imposed have involved accused persons being discharged on conditions.

[8.0] BODILY HARM[1458]

[8.1] GENERAL PRINCIPLES

In order to determine an appropriate sentence the factors to be considered, include[1459]:

- did the assault on the victim consist of a single blow?[1460];
- was there some other cause of bodily harm, ie., did the injury result directly from the assault committed by the accused person?;
- was the victim injured by only a fist?;
- did the accused person set out to hurt anyone?[1461];

1457 The law in relation to this offence is examined in the chapter titled 'Administration Of Justice Offences' in the text titled 'Injia on Criminal Offences in Papua New Guinea and the Pacific'.

1458 The law in relation to this offence is examined in the section titled 'Bodily Harm' in the chapter titled 'Offences Against The Person' in the text titled 'Injia on Criminal Offences in Papua New Guinea and the Pacific'.

1459 See *The State v Judah Lusan Piries* (2007) CR No. 886 of 2007.

1460 Refer also to the section titled 'Repeated Acts Causing Multiple Injuries Or Loss Of Property' in the chapter titled 'Aggravated Factors'.

1461 Refer also to:
- the section titled 'Pre-planning Or Pre-meditation' in the chapter titled 'Aggravating Factors';
- the section titled 'Viciuosness Or Deliberate Intention To Harm' in the chapter titled 'Aggravating Factors'; and
- the subsection titled 'Impulsiveness' in the section titled 'Motive' in the chapter titled 'Extenuating Circumstances'.

- did the victim have a pre-existing condition making him or her susceptible to injury by a moderate blow?; and

- can the assault on the victim be classed as 'not vicious'?[1462]

[8.2] COMPARATIVE CASES

See also:

- *The State v Peter Jai* (2011) 4391, [2011] PGNC 118
- *The State v Jerry Andrias* (2010) N4537, [2010] PGNC 212
- *The State v Caroline Aiwa* (2008) N3330
- *The State v Dick Meaea* (2006) N3163, [2006] PGNC 149
- *The State v Mathew Sabuin and others* [2006] PGNC 76
- *The State v Fredinand Naka Penge* (2002) N2244
- *The State v Albina Sinowi* (2001) N2175

The maximum sentence for this offence is three years imprisonment.

Sentences imposed have ranged from six months to three years imprisonment.

[9.0] BREAK AND ENTER[1463]

[9.1] GENERAL PRINCIPLE

The commission of a break and enter is a prevalent offence.[1464]

1462 Refer also to the section titled 'Viciuosness Or Deliberate Intention To Harm' in the chapter titled 'Aggravating Factors'.

1463 The law in relation to this offence is examined in the section titled 'Break And Enter And Related Offences' in the chapter titled text titled 'Injia on Criminal Offences in Papua New Guinea and the Pacific'.

1464 Refer to the section titled 'Prevalence Of The Offence' in the chapter titled 'Aggravating Factors'.

[9.2] BUILDING

See:

- *The State v Urika Iari* (2006) N3238, [2006] PGNC 152
- *The State v Dominic Kanga* (2005) N2953, [2005] PGNC 169
- *The State v Brendan Oll and Nathan Saisai* (2003) N2554
- *The State v Paeyan Sikar and Leonard Gawi* (2003) N2545
- *The State v Buka Irai* (2003) N2448
- *The State v Michael Kamban Mani* (2002) N2246
- *The State v Ted Dong and others* (2000) N1990
- *The State v Aiton Ipai* (1997) N1629
- *The State v Arijopa Levipaja* (1997) N1601

The maximum sentence for this offence is fourteen years imprisonment.

Sentences imposed have ranged from two to fourteen years imprisonment.

For imposition of the maximum sentence which involved a soldier breaking into an armoury and stealing firearms, see *The State v Dominic Kauga*[1465].

[9.3] DWELLING-HOUSE

[9.3.1] GENERAL PRINCIPLES

As would be apparent from the prescribed penalty, a break and enter of a dwelling-house is a serious offence. This recognises the importance of a dwelling house. Parliament has made the commission of the offence in the night much more serious by prescribing the penalty of life imprisonment[1466].[1467]

[1465] (2005) N2953, [2005] PGNC 169.

[1466] See section 395(2) of the *Criminal Code* (Ch. 262).

Refer also to:
- the section titled 'Circumstance Of Aggravation' in the chapter titled 'Aggravating Factors'; and
- the subsection titled 'Circumstances Of Aggravation' in the section titled 'Wording Of Charges' in the chapter titled 'Charges' in the text titled 'Injia on Criminal Practice and Procedure in Papua New Guinea and the Pacific'.

[1467] See *Ian Napoleon Setep v The State* (2001) SC666, [2001] PGSC 14; *The State v Brendan Oll and Nathan Saisai* (2004) N2554 and *The State v Jonah Yohang Monalen* (2004) N2677.

This is appropriately so because a dwelling house is a "man's castle". It does not matter whether it is of permanent and high-class level or one made out of bush material.[1468]

The distress caused to the householders should also be taken into consideration in sentencing.[1469]

[9.3.2] COMPARATIVE CASES

See also:

- *The State v Barnabas Janguan* (2008) N3363, [2008] PGNC 50
- *The State v Koi Poyep Posanau* (2004) N2642
- *The State v Peter Rasta Karl* (2000) N1978

The maximum sentence for this offence is life imprisonment.

Sentences imposed have ranged from eighteen months to four years imprisonment.

[10.0] BRIBERY[1470]

[10.1] GENERAL PRINCIPLES

An attempt to bribe a police officer is a serious offence because it strikes at the very heart of the system of justice in the country and should attract a severe penalty.[1471]

An accused person who is tempted to try to bribe a public officer must realise he or she will go to prison.[1472]

[1468] See *Ian Napoleon Setep v The State* (2001) SC666, [2001] PGSC 14; *The State v Brendan Oll and Nathan Saisai* (2004) N2554 and *The State v Jonah Yohang Monalen* (2004) N2677.

[1469] See *R v Luckhurst* (1972) 56 Cr App R 209.

[1470] The law in relation to the offence of 'Bribery Of A Member Of Parliament' is examined in the chapter titled 'Administration Of Justice Offences' in the text titled 'Injia on Criminal Offences in Papua New Guinea and the Pacific'.

[1471] See *Baura v DPP* (Solomon Islands Criminal Appeal Case No. 38 of 1986).

[1472] See *Baura v DPP* (Solomon Islands Criminal Appeal Case No. 38 of 1986).

[10.2] COMPARATIVE CASES

See:

- *Robert Yabara v The State* [1984] PNGLR 378
- *The State v Kiap Bonga* [1988-89] PNGLR 360
- *The State v Pablito P Miguel* (2002) N2338
- *The State v Peter Oh Piom Mo* (1998) N1704

The maximum sentence for this offence is seven years imprisonment.

Sentences imposed have ranged from a fine of K2,000 to four years imprisonment.

[11.0] CARRYING TOO MANY PASSENGERS[1473]

See:

- *Paul Ahopa v Noah Maibuko* (1999) N1838

The prescribed sentence for this offence is a fine of not less than K20 and not more than K100.

A sentence of a fine of K40 was imposed in the case cited.

[12.0] CAST AWAY VESSEL

See:

- *The State v Obert Poesan Pokanas* (2004) N2702

The maximum sentence for this offence is life imprisonment.

A sentence of ten years imprisonment was imposed in the case cited.

[1473] The law in relation to this offence is examined in the section titled 'Illegally Carrying Passengers' in the chapter titled 'Traffic Offences' in the text titled 'Injia on Criminal Offences in Papua New Guinea and the Pacific'.

[13.0] CHILD STEALING

See:

- *The State v Jacklyn Buka* (2007) N3179, [2007] PGNC 53

The maximum sentence for this offence is seven years imprisonment.

A sentence of three years imprisonment was imposed in the case cited.

[14.0] COMMON ASSAULT[1474]

[14.1] GENERAL PRINCIPLES

In order to determine an appropriate sentence the factors to be considered, include[1475]:

- did the accused person cause any physical injury to the victim?[1476];
- did the accused person use a threatening weapon?[1477];
- did the accused person use aggravated physical violence?;
- did the accused person cause the victim to be concerned about his or her safety?;
- was the assault of an aggravated nature due to the accused person's own actions?; and
- was it an isolated incident?

[1474] The law in relation to this offence is examined in the section titled 'Common Assault' in the chapter titled 'Offences Against The Person' in the text titled 'Injia on Criminal Offences in Papua New Guinea and the Pacific'.

[1475] See *The State v A Juvenile, 'M'* (2005) N2815, [2005] PGNC 141.

[1476] Refer also to the section titled 'Viciousness Or Deliberate Intention To Harm' in the chapter titled 'Aggravating Factors'.

[1477] Refer also to the section titled 'Carrying, Using Or Threatening To Use A Weapon' in the chapter titled 'Aggravating Factors'.

[14.2] COMPARATIVE CASES

See:

- *The State v A Juvenile, 'M'* (2005) N2815, [2005] PGNC 141
- *The State v James Benny Songo* (2004) N2659

The maximum sentence for this offence is three years imprisonment.

Sentences imposed have ranged from a fine of K2,000 to three months imprisonment.

[15.0] CONCEALING DEEDS, ETC

See

- *The State v Boma Bango* (2010) N4918, [2010] PGNC 226

The maximum penalty for this offence is a term of imprisonment for three years.

A sentence of eighteen months imprisonment, wholly suspended was imposed in the case cited.

[16.0] CONCEALING THE BIRTH OF A CHILD

See:

- *The State v Augusta Paai* (2012) N4592, [2012] PGNC 264
- *The State v Vuvu Frida Talim* (2010) N4041, [2010] PGNC 40
- *The State v Roselyne Namui Venzakie* (2008) N3678, [2008] PGNC 231
- *The State v Suwaire Mary Kua* (2000) N1976

The maximum sentence for this offence is two years imprisonment.

Sentences imposed have ranged from five months to one year eight months imprisonment.

[17.0] CONSPIRACY

[17.1] INTRODUCTION

Normally it is not right to pass a higher sentence for conspiracy than could be passed for the substantive offence: it can be justified only in very exceptional cases.[1478]

[17.2] CONSPIRACY TO COMMIT A CRIME[1479]

See:

- *The State v William Nanua Kapris and others* (2011) N4305, [2008] PGNC 51

The maximum sentence for this offence is seven years imprisonment.

Sentences in the range from four to seven years imprisonment were imposed in the case cited.

[17.3] CONSPIRACY TO DEFRAUD

The types of 'White Collar' offences like conspiracy to defraud are perpetrated by very smart and intelligent people. It may sometimes involve little or big planning depending on the size and the complexity of the unlawful activity to be undertaken by the accused person.[1480]

The offence of 'Conspiracy To Defraud' is a prevalent offence.[1481]

[1478] See *Verrier v DPP* [1966] 3 WLR 924, [1967] AC 195, [1966] 3 All ER 586, (1966) 50 Cr App R 315, per Lord Pearson at 326.

See also: *R v Smith* (1988) 87 Cr App R 393.

[1479] The law in relation to this offence is examined in the section titled 'Conspiracy' in the chapter titled 'Parties To Offences' in the text titled 'Injia on Criminal Offences in Papua New Guinea and the Pacific'.

[1480] See *The State v David Kang* (2009) N3603, [2009] PGNC 47 and *The State v Sipe Gohuse* (2012) N4751, [2012] PGNC 138.

[1481] Refer also to the section titled 'Prevalence Of The Offence' in the chapter titled 'Aggravating Factors'.

COMPARATIVE SENTENCES

See:

- *Public Prosecutor v Arthur Jawodimbari and Monty Derari* (2006) SC891, [2006] PGSC 28
- *The State v Martha Agua* (2011) N4499, [2011] PGNC 207
- *The State v David Kang* (2009) N3603, [2009] PGNC 47
- *The State v Henry Eliakim* (2007) N3190, [2007] PGNC 76
- *The State v Iori Veraga* (2005) N2921, [2005] PGNC 43

The maximum sentence for this offence is seven years imprisonment.

Sentences imposed have ranged from one to four years imprisonment.

[18.0] DANGEROUS DRUG OFFENCES

[18.1] CONSPIRACY TO EXPORT DANGEROUS DRUG

See:

- *The State v John Goea Kevandi* (1997) N1531

The prescribed penalty for this offence is a sentence of not less than three months and not exceeding two years imprisonment.

The maximum sentence was imposed in the case cited.

[18.2] CULTIVATING A DANGEROUS DRUG[1482]

See:

- *Gheong v Nemiel* [1981] PNGLR 472

The prescribed penalty for this offence is a sentence of not less than three months and not exceeding two years imprisonment.

An appeal against a sentence of three months imprisonment was dismissed by the Supreme Court in the case cited.

1482 The law in relation to this offence is examined in the section titled 'Cultivate' in the chapter titled 'Dangerous Drugs' in the text titled 'Injia on Criminal Offences in Papua New Guinea and the Pacific'.

[18.3] TRAFFICKING IN A DANGEROUS DRUG

See:

- *John Ten Komonga v Jowi Gruman* (1995) N1283

The sentence for this offence is a minimum of three months and maximum of three years imprisonment.

In the case cited a sentence of eight months imprisonment imposed by a Magistrate was upheld on appeal by the National Court.

[19.0] DANGEROUS DRIVING[1483]

[19.1] GENERAL PRINCIPLES

A sentence to a term of imprisonment appears to be in tune with what public conscience and community feeling demand in most cases of dangerous driving causing death.[1484]

The offence of 'Dangerous Driving Causing Death' is a prevalent offence.[1485]

A punitive and deterrent[1486] sentence in the form of custodial sentence may be considered necessary for serious cases of dangerous driving.[1487] However, there may exist circumstances in individual cases which may warrant other sentences.[1488]

1483 The law in relation to this offence is examined in the section titled 'Dangerous Driving' in the chapter titled 'Traffic Offences' in the text titled 'Injia on Criminal Offences in Papua New Guinea and the Pacific'.

1484 See *The State v Daniel Soma* [2006] PGNC 71 and *The Public Prosecutor v Willy Moke Soki* [1977] PNGLR 165, [1977] PGSC 16.

1485 Refer also to the section titled 'Prevalence Of The Offence' in the chapter titled 'Aggravating Factors'.

1486 Refer also to the section titled 'The Need For Detterence' in the chapter titled 'Objectives And Purposes Of Sentencing'.

1487 See *The Public Prosecutor v Sima Kone* [1979] PNGLR 294, [1979] PGSC 14.

1488 See *Karo Gamoga v The State* [1981] PNGLR 443, [1981] PGSC 11.

COMPARATIVE SENTENCES

In order to determine an appropriate sentence the factors to be considered, include[1489]:

- was the accused person under the influence of alcohol or a drug?;
- was the accused person speeding?;
- was there a problem with the vehicle that the accused person was aware of?;
- was the vehicle registered?[1490];
- was the vehicle insured?[1491];
- was there some other contributing cause of the accident or collision?;
- was the accident or collision due to heedlessness (an error of judgement or momentary negligence), rather than recklessness (careless risk taking)?;
- how many persons were killed?[1492];
- did the accused person give himself or herself up after the incident?[1493]; and
- was there any good reason for the accused person driving the vehicle the way he or she did, such as was there an emergency that he or she was dealing with?[1494]

1489 See *The State v Daniel Soma* [2006] PGNC 71.

1490 The law in relation to the offence of 'Driving An Unregistered Motor Vehicle' is examined in the chapter titled 'Traffic Offences' in the text titled 'Injia on Criminal Offences in Papua New Guinea and the Pacific'.

1491 The law in relation to the offence of 'Driving An Uninsured Motor Vehicle' is examined in the chapter titled 'Traffic Offences' in the text titled 'Injia on Criminal Offences in Papua New Guinea and the Pacific'.

1492 See *The Public Prosecutor v Willie Moke Soki* [1977] PNGLR 165, [1977] PGSC 16.

1493 Refer also to the section titled 'Co-operation With Police' in the chapter titled 'Mitigating Factors'.

1494 As regards the defence of 'Extraordinary Emergency', refer to:

- the chapter titled 'Criminal Responsibility' in the text titled 'Injia on Criminal Offences in Papua New Guinea and the Pacific'; and
- the section titled 'Dangerous Driving' in chapter titled 'Traffic Offences' in the text titled 'Injia on Criminal Offences in Papua New Guinea and the Pacific'.

Additional factors to consider are[1495]:

- was the accused person racing or competitively driving against another motorist?;
- was the accused person showing off?;
- did the accused person disregard warnings of passengers?;
- was there a prolonged, persistent and deliberate course of very bad driving?;
- were other traffic offences committed at the same time?;
- does the accused person have any previous convictions for motoring offences, particularly offences that involved bad driving or the consumption of alcohol?;
- was the dangerous driving in an attempt to avoid detection and apprehension?; and
- whether the victim is either a close relative or a friend when emotional shock will likely be great.

Further additional factors to consider are[1496]:

- extent and nature of the injuries inflicted;
- number of people put at risk or killed;
- length of the journey during which others were exposed to risk;
- ignoring of warnings; and
- degree of sleep deprivation.

[1495] See *R v Boswell and others* (1984) 79 Cr App R 277.

[1496] See *R v Whyte* (2002) 55 NSWLR 252, [2002] NSWCCA 343; *Shipton v R* [2003] TASSC 23, per Cox CJ at 5 and Blow J at 8; *DPP v Watson* [2004] TASSC 54, per Slicer J at 11 and *Gallagher v The State of Tasmania* [2009] TASSC 84.

COMPARATIVE SENTENCES

[19.2] COMPARATIVE CASES

See:

- *Alex Yembi v The State* (2003) SCR No. 45 of 2003
- *Karo Gamoga v The State* [1981] PNGLR 443, [1981] PGSC 11 [Death]
- *The Public Prosecutor v Sima Kone* [1979] PNGLR 294, [1979] PGSC 14 [Death]
- *The Public Prosecutor v Willy Moke Soke* [1977] PNGLR 165, [1977] PGSC 16 [Death]
- *Warep v The State* (2009) N3579, [2009] PGNC 6 [GBH]
- *The State v Eric Papen (No. 2)* (2009) N3639, [2009] PGNC 58 [Death and GBH]
- *The State v Daniel Soma* [2006] PGNC 71 [Death]
- *The State v Philip Iparu* (2005) N2995, [2005] PGNC 11 [Death]
- *The State v Alphonse Naulo Raphael* [1979] PNGLR 47 [Death]

The maximum sentence for this offence is five years imprisonment.

Sentences imposed have ranged from release on a good behaviour bond to four years imprisonment.

[20.0] DEPRIVATION OF LIBERTY[1497]

See:

- *Emil Kongian and others v The State* (2007) SC928, [2007] PGSC 45
- *The State v William Nanua Kapris and others* (2011) N4305, [2011] PGNC 51
- *The State v Junior Gano Bagitogu* [2007] PGNC 116
- *The State v Enni Mathew and others (No. 2)* (2004) N2563
- *The State v Buka Irai* (2003) N2448

The maximum sentence for this offence is three years imprisonment.[1498]

Sentences imposed have ranged from six months to three years imprisonment.

[1497] The law in relation to this offence is examined in the section titled 'Deprivation Of Liberty' in the chapter titled 'Offences Against The Person' in the text titled 'Injia on Criminal Offences in Papua New Guinea and the Pacific'.

[1498] See also: section 20 of the *Criminal Code* (Ch. 262).

[21.0] DOMESTIC VIOLENCE[1499]

Whilst the compelling circumstances under which the offence was committed is a relevant extenuating circumstance or mitigating factor on sentence, the fact that an incident occurs in a domestic relationship does not:

- justify; or
- minimise

its significance.[1500]

The courts have long recognised that personal and general deterrence[1501] have a heightened significance when sentencing for the offences involving domestic violence in order to protect the vulnerable.[1502]

[22.0] DRIVING UNDER THE INFLUENCE[1503]

A licence to drive a motor vehicle is a privilege that carries with it significant obligations.[1504]

Those obligations require a driver to:

- drive safely on the road; and

[1499] Refer also to the chapter titled 'Family Violence' in the text titled 'Injia on Investigatory Practice in Papua New Guinea and the Pacific'.

[1500] See *Kunia v R* [2005] SBHC 60.

[1501] Refer also to the section titled 'The Need For Deterrence' in the chapter titled 'Objectives And Purposes Of Sentencing'.

[1502] See *R v Lennon* (2003) 86 SASR 295, per Doyle CJ and *Hiron v R* [2007] NSWCCA 336.

[1503] The law in relation to this offence is examined in the section titled 'Under The Influence' in the chapter titled 'Traffic Offences' in the text titled 'Injia on Criminal Offences in Papua New Guinea and the Pacific'.

[1504] See *Gillett v R* [2006] NSWCCA 370.

- ensure that by reason of their physical health and capacity they do not endanger the lives of others.[1505]

It is trite to observe that, what is commonly referred to as 'drink-driving', amounts to socially irresponsible behaviour of a very significant degree having regard to the potential consequences of any driver on a public road being unable to properly manage and control a motor vehicle.[1506]

[23.0] DRIVING WHILST DISQUALIFIED[1507]

Driving whilst disqualified is a serious offence because it shows a flagrant disregard for a court order.[1508]

[24.0] ESCAPED PRISONER OFFENCES

[24.1] ESCAPING FROM LAWFUL CUSTODY[1509]

[24.1.1] GENERAL PRINCIPLES

The offence of 'Escaping From Lawful Custody' is an affront to the judicial system and law enforcement, and it must be met with an equally stern punishment.[1510]

[1505] See *Gillett v R* [2006] NSWCCA 370.

[1506] See *Re Attorney-General's Application under s 37 of the Crimes (Sentencing Procedure) Act 1999 (NSW) (No. 3 of 2002)* (2004) 147 A Crim R 546, (2004) 61 NSWLR 305, [2004] NSWCCA 303.

[1507] The law in relation to this offence is examined in the section titled 'Driving Whilst Disqualified Or Suspended' in the chapter titled 'Traffic Offences' in the text titled 'Injia on Criminal Offences in Papua New Guinea and the Pacific'.

[1508] See *R v Peter Baru* [1988-1989] SILR 132.

[1509] The law in relation to this offence is examined in the section titled 'Escape From Lawful Custody' in the chapter titled 'Miscellaneous Offences' in the text titled 'Injia on Criminal Offences in Papua New Guinea and the Pacific'.

[1510] See *Brian Laki v The State* (2005) SC783, [2005] PGSC 42 and *Edmund Gima v The State; Siune Arnold v The State* (2003) SC730, [2003] PGSC 3.

COMPARATIVE SENTENCES

Police, prison staff and resources are deployed at enormous cost to the Government to mount search operations when an accused person escapes from custody.[1511]

Where an accused person has:

- remained at large for a very lengthy period; or
- used the opportunity of being at large to commit further offences,

then the overall objective seriousness of his or her criminality is potentially increased.[1512]

In order to determine an appropriate sentence the factors to be considered, include[1513]:

- receipt of information by the escapee of a retaliatory killing of a close relative supported by a prison officer;
- any evidence of violent sexual attacks upon weaker and younger inmates by more aggressive inmates supported by prison officers;
- whether the escape was en mass;
- whether any weapon was used[1514];
- where a weapon was used whether any personal or property damage or injury had been occasioned;
- the expense to which the State has been put to in order to recapture the escapee;[1515]

[1511] See *The State v Toto* (2009) N3746, [2009] PGNC 127.

See however: *R v Bracefield* [1988] NZCA 320/87.

[1512] See *The State v Toto* (2009) N3746, [2009] PGNC 127.

See also: *R v Plummer* [2000] NSWCCA 363 and *R v Josef Regina* [2000] NSWCCA 100.

[1513] See *Edmund Gima v The State; Siune Arnold v The State* (2003) SC730, [2003] PGSC 3.

[1514] Refer also to the section titled 'Carrying, Using Or Threatening To Use A Weapon' in the chapter titled 'Aggravating Factors'.

[1515] See however: *R v Bracefield* [1988] NZCA 320/87.

- when and how the recapture occurred[1516]; and
- whether there is a guilty plea, but this has to be contrasted against the chances of a successful denial[1517].

[24.1.2] COMPARATIVE CASES

See also:

- *Jack Kumul v The State* (2006) SC839, [2006] PGSC 3
- *Brian Laki v The State* (2005) SC783, [2005] PGSC 42
- *Alphonse Dambui v The State* (2003) SC724, [2003] PGSC 20
- *Edmund Gima v The State; Siune Arnold v The State* (2003) SC730, [2003] PGSC 3
- *The State v Paul Maima* (2012) N4752, [2012] PGNC 193
- *The State v Haiveta* (2012) N4677, [2012] PGNC 71
- *The State v Kawa Koroiwe* (2010) N4154, [2010] PGNC 177
- *The State v Allan Nemo* (2010) N4098, [2010] PGNC 89
- *The State v Etane Toto* (2009) N3746, [2009] PGNC 127
- *The State v A Juvenile, 'CL'* (2008) N3432
- *The State v Richard Ranga Sora* (2008) N3428, [2008] PGNC 113
- *The State v Linus Rebo Dakoa* (2008) N3427, [2008] PGNC 112
- *The State v Ali Karis Wasiura* (2008) N3425, [2008] PGNC 110
- *The State v John Kanua Siune and Kenneth Kunda Siune* [2006] PGNC 112
- *The State v Danny Pirino* (2006) CR No. 251 of 2006
- *The State v William Akiri Francis* (2006) CR No. 473 of 2006
- *The State v Ass Medron Nangil and others* (2005) N2823
- *The State v Kerowa Kana* (2003) N2376
- *The State v Irox Winston* (2003) N2347
- *The State v James Tei Wana and Gend Yanisa Thomas* (2000) N2304
- *The State v Tui Kila Tairo* (1999) N1830
- *The State v Okuk Seke* (1999) N1826
- *The State v Inema Yawok* (1998) N1766
- *The State v Thomas Waim, Tala Gena and Alois Wanpis* [1998] PNGLR 360, (1998) N1750, [1998] PGNC 174

[1516] Refer also to the section titled 'Co-operation With Police' in the chapter titled 'Mitigating Factors'.

[1517] Refer also to the section titled 'Plea Of Guilty' in the chapter titled 'Mitigating Factors'.

COMPARATIVE SENTENCES

- *The State v Richard Olso Kumis* (1997) N1517
- *The State v Jack Moge* [1995] PNGLR 246, (1995) N1318

The minimum sentence for 'Escaping Lawful Custody' under section 139 of the *Criminal Code* (Ch. 262) is five years imprisonment.

However, the Court has a discretion to suspend the whole or part of the sentence, but only after imposing the minimum sentence.[1518]

The sentences imposed have ranged from a wholly suspended sentence to three years imprisonment and in several cases, the maximum sentence of five years imprisonment has been imposed.[1519]

[24.2] AIDING PRISONER TO ESCAPE[1520]

See:

- *Isaac Aua v The State* (1997) SC535, [1997] PGSC 17
- *The State v Robert Konny* (2012) N4691, [2012] PGNC 77

The minimum sentence for this offence is seven years imprisonment.

Sentences imposed have ranged from one to five years imprisonment.

1518 See *SCR No. 1 of 1994; The State v Aruve Waiba* (Unreported and Unnumbered judgement of the Supreme Court, 4 April 1996, Los and Salika JJ).

1519 See *Jack Kumul v The State* (2006) SC839, [2006] PGSC 3.

1520 The law in relation to this offence is examined in the section titled 'Excape From Lawful Custody' in the chapter titled 'Miscellaneous Offences' in the text titled 'Injia on Criminal Offences in Papua New Guinea and the Pacific'.

[24.3] HARBOURING ESCAPED PRISONER[1521]

The offence of 'Harbouring An Escaped Prisoner' is a prevalent offence.[1522]

See:

- *The State v Collin Paino; The State v David Paino; The State v Michael Paino and The State v Rose Todi Paino* (2007) N3199, [2007] PGNC 88

The maximum sentence for this offence is two years imprisonment.

Sentences imposed have been in the vicinity of six months imprisonment.

[24.4] PERMITTING A PRISONER TO ESCAPE[1523]

See:

- *The State v Koivi Ipai (No. 2)* (2010) N4173, [2010] PGNC 184

The maximum penalty is imprisonment for a term of three years.

In the case cited a term of imprisonment for ten months that was wholly suspended was imposed.

[25.0] EXTORTION

[25.1] DEMANDS FOR COMPENSATION OR OTHER PAYMENT

See:

- *The State v Titus Kep and others* (2004) N2616

[1521] The law in relation to this offence is examined in the section titled 'Escaped From Lawful Custody' in the chapter titled 'Miscellaneous Offences' in the text titled 'Injia on Criminal Offences in Papua New Guinea and the Pacific'.

[1522] See *The State v Collin Paino; The State v David Paino; The State v Michael Paino and The State v Rose Todi Paino* (2007) N3199, [2007] PGNC 88.

[1523] The law in relation to this offence is examined in the section titled 'Excape From Lawful Custody' in the chapter titled 'Miscellaneous Offences' in the text titled 'Injia on Criminal Offences in Papua New Guinea and the Pacific'.

COMPARATIVE SENTENCES

The maximum sentence for this offence is seven years imprisonment.

Sentences imposed have been in the vicinity of four to five years imprisonment.

[25.2] DEMANDING PROPERTY BY THREATS

See:

- *The State v George Pelly* (2011) N4392, [2011] PGNC 119

The maximum sentence for this offence is fourteen years imprisonment.

The sentence imposed in the case cited was five years imprisonment, wholly suspended on conditions.

[26.0] FALSE PRETENCES[1524]

The offence of 'False Pretences' is a prevalent offence.[1525]

See:

- *Wesley Embahe v The State* (1988) SC351, [1988] PGSC 1
- *The State v Joseph Sape* (2013) N5096, [2013] PGNC 36
- *The State v Trister Solien* (2012) N4665, [2012] PGNC 26
- *The State v John Bolkun* (2012) N4689, [2012] PGNC 75
- *The State v Angela Tokonai* (2012) N4679, [2012] PGNC 67
- *The State v Gaibole Dickson Larry* (2011) N4455, [2011] PGNC 166
- *The State v Dominic Kurai* (2008) N3435
- *The State v Jimmy Kendi (No. 2)* (2007) N3131, [2007] PGNC 32
- *The State v Thomas Wakai and others* (2006) N3360, [2006] PGNC 165
- *The State v Jack Ostekal Metz* (2005) N2824, [2005] PGNC 129
- *The State v John Kil* (2000) N1974
- *The State v Paulus Takesi* (1996) N1468

[1524] The law in relation to this offence is examined in the section titled 'False Pretences' in the chapter titled 'Fraud Related Offences' in the text titled 'Injia on Criminal Offences in Papua New Guinea and the Pacific'.

[1525] Refer also to the section titled 'Prevalence Of The Offence' in the chapter titled 'Aggravating Factors'.

COMPARATIVE SENTENCES

The maximum sentence for this offence is five years imprisonment.

Sentences imposed have ranged from eight months to four years imprisonment and in the case of *The State v John Bolkun*[1526] the sentence of three years imprisonment was wholly suspended.

[27.0] FORGERY[1527]

The offence of 'Forgery' is a prevalent offence.[1528]

See:

- *The State v Raka Benson* [2006] PGNC 68
- *The State v Andrew Aopo Lengade* (2012) N4690, [2012] PGNC 76
- *The State v Louise Paraka* (2002) N2317

The maximum sentence for this offence is five years imprisonment.

Sentences imposed have ranged from eighteen months to three years imprisonment.

[28.0] GRIEVOUS BODILY HARM[1529]

[28.1] GENERAL PRINCIPLES

This offence of 'Grievous Bodily Harm' is a prevalent offence.[1530]

1526 (2012) N4689, [2012] PGNC 75.

1527 The law in relation to this offence is examined in the section titled 'Forgery' in the chapter titled 'Fraud Related Offences'in the text titled 'Injia on Criminal Offences in Papua New Guinea and the Pacific'.

1528 Refer also to the section titled 'Prevalence Of The Offence' in the chapter titled 'Aggravating Factors'.

1529 The law in relation to this offence is examined in the section titled 'Grievous Bodily Harm' in the chapter titled 'Offences Against The Person' in the text titled 'Injia on Criminal Offences in Papua New Guinea and the Pacific'.

1530 Refer also to the section titled 'Prevalence Of The Offence' in the chapter titled 'Aggravating Factors'.

COMPARATIVE SENTENCES

In order to determine an appropriate sentence the factors to be considered, include[1531]:

- did the assault on the victim consist of a single blow?[1532];
- was there some other cause of bodily harm, ie., did the injury result directly from the assault committed by the accused person?;
- was the victim injured by only a fist?;
- did the victim have a pre-existing condition making his or her susceptible to injury by a moderate blow?; and
- can the assault on the victim be classed as 'not vicious'?[1533]

[28.2] COMPARATIVE CASES

See also:

- *Naroi v The State* [1987] PNGLR 293, [1987] PGSC 14
- *The State v Neiman Dua* (2013) N4957, [2013] PGNC 8
- *The State v Paul Jumbugu* (2012) N4627, [2012] PGNC 36
- *The State v Bill Kara* (2012) N4663, [2012] PGNC 19
- *The State v Rada Mau* (2012) N5081, [2012] PGNC 283
- *The State v Maggie Rumints* (2012) N4900, [2012] PGNC 275
- *The State v Hilary Lemia* (2012) N4817, [2012] PGNC 179
- *The State v Michael Tangip (*2012) N4782, [2012] PGNC 205
- *The State v Willie Boi and Ikupu Iru* (2012) N4781, [2012] PGNC 2
- *The State v Julius Minsipi* (2012) N4595, [2012] PGNC 271
- *The State v Grace John (No. 3)* (2011) N4371, [2011] PGNC 104
- *The State v Fidelis Kiatni* (2011) N4331, [2011] PGNC 67

[1531] See *The State v Ludwina Waiguma* (2007) N3188, [2007] PGNC 80 and *The State v Bertrand Hianu* [2006] PGNC 75.

[1532] Refer also to the section titled 'Repeated Acts Causing Multiple Injuries Or Loss Of Property' in the chapter titled 'Aggravating Factors'.

[1533] Refer also to the section titled 'Viciousness Or Deliberate Intention To Harm' in the chapter titled 'Aggravating Factors'.

COMPARATIVE SENTENCES

- *The State v Abel City Ya Kund and The State v Wali Pyakai* (2011) N4262, [2011] PGNC 42
- *The State v Tolly Saun and Stanley Saun* (2011) N4390
- *The State v Ray Sheekiot* (2011) N4454, [2011] PGNC 165
- *The State v Grace John (No. 3)* (2011) N4371, [2011] PGNC 104
- *The State v Thomson Titus* (2011) N4671, [2011] PGNC 232
- *The State v James Kaminja* (2011) N4329, [2011] PGNC 69
- *The State v Lucy Kar* (2011) N4719, [2011] PGNC 230
- *The State v W* (2010) N3889; [2010] PGNC 10
- *The State v Martin Konos* (2010) N4157, [2010] PGNC 179
- *The State v Miriam John* (2009) N4128, [2009] PGNC 237
- *The State v David Carol* (2009) N3762, [2009] PGNC 143
- *The State v Ben Robert* (2009) N3629, [2009] PGNC 42
- *The State v Elsie Wabi* (2009) N3662, [2009] PGNC 69
- *The State v Ben Robert* (2009) N3629, [2009] PGNC 42
- *The State v Sam Piapin* (2009) N3585
- *The State v Tovita Mann* (2009) N4028
- *The State v Samuel Paranis* (2009) N3761, [2009] PGNC 145
- *The State v Yatime Korogula (No. 2)* (2009) N3742, [2009] PGNC 129
- *The State v Wilson Wiramas* (2008) N3456, [2008] PGNC 209
- *The State v Justin Ipa* (2008) N3439
- *The State v Mathias Betai* (2008) N3417
- *The State v Ala Ali David* (2008) N3416
- *The State v Peter Mol* (2008) N3707, [2008] PGNC 239
- *The State v Paul Membup* (2008) N3679, [2008] PGNC 229
- *The State v Moli Mumugap and Jessica Wunol* (2008) N3546
- *The State v John Wagi* (2008) N3543, [2008] PGNC 184
- *The State v Exley Hala Heni* (2008) N3541, [2008] PGNC 206
- *The State v Lucy Rusa* (2008) N3510, [2008] PGNC 151
- *The State v Francis Kurufher* (2008) N3364, [2008] PGNC 60
- *The State v Ambe Tu* (2008) N3306, [2008] PGNC 37
- *The State v John Bola* (2008) N3297, [2008] PGNC 22
- *The State v Salle Sorowi* (2007) N3467
- *The State v Bomai Hesi (No. 2)* (2007) N3232, [2007] PGNC 102
- *The State v Iso Bamaru* (2006) N3390, [2006] PGNC 168
- *The State v Inge Gotama* (2006) N3156, [2006] PGNC 135
- *The State v Bertrand Hianu* [2006] PGNC 75

- *The State v Patrick Jul* (2005) N3167, [2005] PGNC 180
- *The State v Francis Ketoi* (2005) CR No. 1764 of 2005
- *The State v Patrick Kimat* (2005) N2947, [2005] PGNC 33
- *The State v Guise Jopping* (2004) N2678
- *The State v Redford Bubura* (2004) N2577
- *The State v Lucas Huliahwere* (2003) N2544
- *The State v Anton Vail* (2003) N2473
- *The State v Amos Kiap* (2003) N2452
- *The State v Eddie John Naopa* (2003) N2411
- *The State v David Saun* (2003) N2409
- *The State v Larsen Talian* (2003) N2382
- *The State v Kenny Reuben Irowen* (2002) N2239
- *The State v Darius Taulo* (2001) N2034
- *The State v Nickson Pari (No. 2)* (2001) N2033

The maximum sentence for this offence is seven years imprisonment.

Sentences imposed have ranged from one to seven years imprisonment.

[29.0] GRIEVOUS BODILY HARM WITH INTENT

The offence of 'Grievous Bodily Harm With Intent' is a prevalent offence.[1534]

The Court cannot treat lightly serious attackers who intentionally cause grievous bodily harm. They are far too prevalent, and call for an immediate custodial sentence.[1535]

See:

- *The State v Kai Joip Dipa* (2007) SC868
- *The State v Kapaka Roga and others* (2012) N4804, [2012] PGNC 223
- *The State v Peter Pendin* (2012) N4541, [2012] PGNC 292
- *The State v Nerious Pinda* (2012) N4872, [2012] PGNC 291
- *The State v Mason Kinjon Karato (No. 2)* (2012) N4832, [2012] PGNC 157
- *The State v Oliver Toluana and Penias Kivung* (2011) N4417, [2011] PGNC 138
- *The State v Peter Pepa* (2010) N4146, [2010] PGNC 148

[1534] Refer also to the section titled 'Prevalence Of The Offence' in the chapter titled 'Aggravating Factors'.

[1535] See *The State v Tamurei Lawrence, Koloata James and Tobias Thomas* [2006] N311.

COMPARATIVE SENTENCES

- *The State v Tamumei Lawrence and others* (2007) N3117, [2007] PGNC 17
- *The State v Martin Muru* (2007) PGNC 117
- *The State v Lionel Gawi* (2005) N2951, [2005] PGNC 170
- *The State v Makis Lunge Kraningi* (2005) N2934, [2005] PGNC 18
- *The State v Yale Sambrai* (2005) N2886, [2005] PGNC 48
- *The State v So'on Taroh* (2004) N2675
- *The State v Inapero Susure* (1999) N1880

The maximum sentence for this offence is life imprisonment.

Sentences imposed have ranged from two to sixteen years imprisonment.

[30.0] HOMICIDE OFFENCES[1536]

[30.1] INTRODUCTION

The Court must protect human life because there is only one life for each of us to live in this world.[1537]

The basic principle that the sanctity and value of a human life is more precious and valuable than wealth must be given very serious consideration by a Court. Neither wealth nor worldly business nor money paid in the form of compensation nor even any remorse would restore or revive a life that has been lost.[1538]

Unlawful killings are prevalent.[1539]

There are so many wanton killings happening in the country at will as though life is some form of commodity or replaceable item that can be borrowed or bought from the hardware shops in town. Killings in this country are becoming more daring without fear and there is no respect for the sanctity of life. Brutal, horrific and cold-blooded killings are becoming too frequent.[1540]

[1536] Refer also to the section titled 'Homicide Offences' in the chapter titled 'Offences Against The Person' in the text titled 'Injia on Criminal Offences in Papua New Guinea and the Pacific'.

[1537] See *The State v Yuanis Ipiri* (2008) N3512, [2008] PGNC 159.

[1538] *See The State v Ladimat Kilala and others* (2012) N5080, [2012] PGNC 282.

[1539] Refer to the section titled 'Prevalence Of The Offence' in the chapter titled 'Aggravating Factors'.

[1540] See *The State v Bernard Hagei* (2005) N2913, [2005] PGNC 60.

COMPARATIVE SENTENCES

Parliament made no mistake in prescribing life imprisonment for someone who takes away any other person's life without any lawful excuse.[1541]

The onus is therefore on an accused person to:

- show why he or she should not be given the prescribed sentence; and
- make a case for it.[1542]

The custom of killing an adulteress cannot be taken into account in mitigation of sentence.[1543]

Whilst the dumping or concealing the body of a victim has been regarded as an aggravating factor[1544], the failure by an accused person to advise as to the location of the body of a deceased person should not be[1545].

In *Manu Kovi v The State*[1546] the Supreme Court issued sentencing guidelines for the offences of 'Wilful Murder', 'Murder' and 'Manslaughter'. However, see *Thress Kumbamong v The State*[1547] which deviated from the tariff principle in Manu Kovi case. It is to be noted that the Supreme Court in the Manu Kovi case did not fix the tariff by prescribing minimum sentences for offences with certain mitigating or aggravating circumstances; rather it suggested a range of sentences for different categories of homicide offences according to the presence of common mitigating and aggravating circumstances. It is entirely a matter of discretion for the sentencing judge to consider the appropriate sentence for a particular offence in the light of the circumstances of each case, taking into account the sentencing tariff suggested in Manu Kovi case.

1541 See *The State v Joseph Ulakua* (2002) N2240.

1542 See *The State v Joseph Ulakua* (2002) N2240.

1543 See *Public Prosecutor v Kerua and Kerua* [1985] PNGLR 85, [1985] PGSC 8.

1544 See *R v Von Einem* (1985) 38 SASR 207 at 218 and *R v Cavkic (No. 2)* [2009] VSCA 43.

1545 See *R v Cavkic (No. 2)* [2009] VSCA 43; *R v Wilkinson (No. 5)* [2009] NSWSC 432 and *Neill-Fraser v Tasmania* [2012] TASCCA 2.

1546 (2005) SC789, [2005] PGSC 34.

1547 (2008) SC1017, [2008] PGSC 51.

[30.2] WILFUL MURDER

[30.2.1] GENERAL PRINCIPLES

The offence of 'Wilful Murder' is a prevalent offence.[1548]

The Supreme Court has issued sentencing guidelines.[1549]

The death penalty is not mandatory, but is the maximum sentence that can be imposed.[1550]

A Court has a considerable discretion whether or not to impose the maximum sentence when reading section 229(2) in conjunction with section 19(1)(aa) of the *Criminal Code* (Ch. 262).[1551]

The death penalty should be:

- reserved for the worst cases of the offence[1552]; and
- decided on the facts of each particular case.[1553]

[30.2.2] COMPARATIVE CASES

See also:

- *Alois Erebebe and Taros Togot v The State* (2013) SC1228, [2013] PGSC 9
- *Wesley Nobudi, John Evoa and Frank Yalikiti v The State* (2009) SC999, [2009] PGSC 20

[1548] Refer to the section titled 'Prevalence Of The Offence' in the chapter titled 'Aggravating Factors'.

[1549] See *Manu Kovi v The State* (2005) SC789, [2005] PGSC 34 and *Steven Loke Ume, Charles Patrick Kaona and Greg Wawa Kavoa v The State* (2006) SC836, [2006] PGSC 9.

[1550] See *Steven Loke Ume, Charles Patrick Kaona and Greg Wawa Kavoa v The State* (2006) SC836, [2006] PGSC 9.

[1551] See *Steven Loke Ume, Charles Patrick Kaona and Greg Wawa Kavoa v The State* (2006) SC836, [2006] PGSC 9.

[1552] Refer also to the chapter titled 'Maximum Sentence'.

[1553] See *Steven Loke Ume, Charles Patrick Kaona and Greg Wawa Kavoa v The State* (2006) SC836, [2006] PGSC 9.

Refer also to the section titled 'Sentence Of Death' in the chapter titled 'Sentencing Options'.

COMPARATIVE SENTENCES

- *Irai Thomas v The State* (2007) SC867, [2007] PGSC 26
- *Tony Morikawa v The State* (2000) SC656
- *The State v Selmon Amos and Misialsi Amos (No. 3)* (2012) N5073, [2012] PGNC 289
- *The State v Ladimat Kilala and others* (2012) N5080, [2012] PGNC 282
- *The State v Soti Mesuno and others* (2012) N4701, [2012] PGNC 80
- *The State v Mark Bongede* (2012) N4683, [2012] PGNC 69
- *The State v Francis Waka Sapu* (2012) N4533, [2012] PGNC 290
- *The State v Lotivi Mal and others* (2012) N4591, [2012] PGNC 219
- *The State v Stanley Kuma Kuru (No. 3)* (2011) N4352, [2011] PGNC 77
- *The State v Dilu Kimam* (2011) N4323, [2011] PGNC 58
- *The State v Joel Otariv* (2011) N4409, [2011] PGNC 143
- *The State v Famundi Badi Moibamo (No. 3)* (2011) N4372, [2011] PGNC 105
- *The State v Gregory Kiapkot and others* (2011) N4381, [2011] PGNC 108
- *The State v Pondros Laki (No. 2)* (2011) N4905, [2011] PGNC 238
- *The State v Mathew Misek* (2011) N4561, [2011] PGNC 244
- *The State v Boas Kapai and others* (2010) N4209, [2010] PGNC 222
- *The State v Seth Ujan Talil* (2010) N4159, [2010] PGNC 176
- *The State v Peter Wirundi* (2010) N3994, [2010] PGNC 34
- *The State v Mamanane Guri (No. 2)* (2009) N3771, [2009] PGNC 152
- *The State v Ambrose Lati (No. 2)* (2009) N3740, [2009] PGNC 121
- *The State v Isak Wapsi* (2009) N3695, [2009] PGNC 84
- *The State v Jessie Balu* (2008) N3492, [2008] PGNC 189
- *The State v Elizah Nguma Lapankiming and Warren Jeremaiah* (2008) N3459, [2008] PGNC 208
- *The State v Michael Waragu and Anton Marko (No. 3)* (2007) N3282, [2007] PGNC 139
- *The State v Clarence Tema Mongi* (2007) N3259, [2007] PGNC 135
- *The State v Sedoki Lota and Fred Abenko* (2007) N3183, [2007] PGNC 167
- *The State v Upano Manake (No. 2)* (2006) N3504, [2006] PGNC 174

The maximum sentence for this offence is a sentence of death.

Sentences imposed have ranged from fifteen years imprisonment to death.

In the cases cited the sentences range from seventeen years to thirty years imprisonment, life imprisonment and death.

Earlier cases show a starting point at fifteen years imprisonment.

COMPARATIVE SENTENCES

[30.3] MURDER

[30.3.1] GENERAL PRINCIPLES

Every death, whether intentional, accidental or due to other causes is always a very serious matter whenever it occurs. It is particularly repulsive and despicable when death resulted from unlawful killing. The right to life and the protection of the sanctity of life by the *Constitution of the Independent State of Papua New Guinea* are amongst the many considerations that make murder a very serious crime.[1554]

Resorting to physical violence to resolve one's anger is not the right behavior of decent and respectable men. Men who expect respect and support from their women must earn that respect by their conduct deserving of praise and dignity.[1555]

The offence of 'Murder' is a prevalent offence.[1556]

Each case of murder must be decided on a case-by-case basis, but always remembering that the sentence laid down by section 300 of the *Criminal Code* (Ch. 262) is life imprisonment and the term of years is by virtue of section 19 of that Code.[1557]

In order to determine an appropriate sentence the factors to be considered, include:

- what was the nature of the attack?[1558];
- did the accused person directly kill the deceased person?[1559];

1554 See *The State v Philip Ngaufu* (2011) N4554, [2011] PGNC 222.

1555 See *The State v Steven Kenny* (1991) N1881.

1556 Refer also to the section titled 'Prevalence Of The Offence' in the chapter titled 'Aggravating Factors'.

1557 See *Simbe v The State* [1994] PNGLR 38, [1994] PGSC 18.

1558 See *Public Prosecutor v Ake* [1978] PNGLR 469, [1978] PGSC 3.

Refer also to the section titled 'Repeated Acts Causing Multiple Injuries Or Loss Of Property' in the chapter titled 'Aggravating Factors'.

1559 See *The State v Kevin Wakore* (2007) N3222, [2007] PGNC 61; *The State v David Yakuye Daniel (No. 2)* (2005) N2890, [2005] PGNC 58 and *The State v Jacky Vutnamur and Kaki Kialo (No. 2)* (2005) N2868, [2005] PGNC 91.

- was there some intervening cause of death?[1560];
- did the deceased person have a pre-existing condition making him or her susceptible to serious or fatal injury by a moderate blow?[1561];
- can the attack on the deceased person be classed as 'not vicious'?[1562];
- can the death of the deceased person be regarded as an unforeseeable consequence of the activity that the accused person was involved in?[1563]; and
- was sorcery involved?[1564]

An accused person who commits a payback murder in accordance with his or her custom may be entitled to some reduction in sentence for 'de-facto provocation[1565]'.[1566]

1560 See *The State v Kevin Wakore* (2007) N3222, [2007] PGNC 61; *The State v David Yakuye Daniel (No. 2)* (2005) N2890, [2005] PGNC 58 and *The State v Jacky Vutnamur and Kaki Kialo (No. 2)* (2005) N2868, [2005] PGNC 91.

1561 See *The State v Kevin Wakore* (2007) N3222, [2007] PGNC 61; *The State v David Yakuye Daniel (No. 2)* (2005) N2890, [2005] PGNC 58 and *The State v Jacky Vutnamur and Kaki Kialo (No. 2)* (2005) N2868, [2005] PGNC 91.

1562 See *The State v Kevin Wakore* (2007) N3222, [2007] PGNC 61; *The State v David Yakuye Daniel (No. 2)* (2005) N2890, [2005] PGNC 58 and *The State v Jacky Vutnamur and Kaki Kialo (No. 2)* (2005) N2868, [2005] PGNC 91.

Refer also to the section titled 'Viciousness Or Deliberate Intention To Harm' in the chapter titled 'Aggravating Factors'.

1563 See *The State v Kevin Wakore* (2007) N3222, [2007] PGNC 61; *The State v David Yakuye Daniel (No. 2)* (2005) N2890, [2005] PGNC 58 and *The State v Jacky Vutnamur and Kaki Kialo (No. 2)* (2005) N2868, [2005] PGNC 91.

1564 See *John Baipu v The State* (2005) SC796, [2005] PGSC 19.

Refer also to the section titled 'Belief In Sorcery' in the chapter titled 'Extenuating Circumstances'.

As a consequence of an amendment to the *Criminal Code* (Ch. 262) there is to be the additional offence of 'Wilful Murder Of A Person On Account Of Sorcery', see *Criminal Code (Amendment) Act 2013*.

However, this textbook was published prior to the enactment of that Act.

1565 Refer also to the section titled 'De-facto Provocation' in the chapter titled 'Extenuating Circumstances'.

1566 See *Public Prosecutor v Apava Keru; Public Prosecutor v Aia Moroi* [1985] PNGLR 78, [1985] PGSC 7.

COMPARATIVE SENTENCES

[30.3.2] COMPARATIVE CASES

See:

- *John Kule v The State* (2011) SC1138, [2011] PGSC 47
- *John Vali v The State* (2007) SCRA No. 61 of 2004, [2007] PGSC 31
- *Jack Peni v The State* (2007) SC913, [2007] PGSC 41
- *Steven Mul Mangi v The State* (2006) SC880, [2006] PGSC 30
- *Pemu Muro v The State* (2006) SC842, [2006] PGSC 11
- *Andrew Palili v The State* (2006) SC848, [2006] PGSC 16
- *Manu Kovi v The State* (2005) SC789, [2005] PGSC 34
- *Baune Bernard Olmi v The State* (2004) SC872, [2004] PGSC 43
- *Kepa Wanege v The State* (2004) SC742, [2004] PGSC 22
- *The State v Michael Rende* (2013) N5220, [2013] PGNC 44
- *The State v Karl Niruk and Kurak Nurvue* (2012) N4821, [2012] PGNC 152
- *The State v Benjamin Wakupa* (2012) N4783, [2012] PGNC 229
- *The State v Douglas Mareva* (2012) N4805, [2012] PGNC 222
- *The State v Miriki Arato* (2012) N4764, [2012] PGNC 186
- *The State v Mupa Lom* (2012) N4725, [2012] PGNC 63
- *The State v Michael Bake* (2012) N4890, [2012] PGNC 246
- *The State v Marcus Woibun* (2012) N4631, [2012] PGNC 198
- *The State v Jacob Aku Matai* (2011) N4256, [2011] PGNC 26
- *The State v Two Juveniles, 'FSD' and 'SW'* (2011) N4456, [2011] PGNC 16
- *The State v Laurie Kemuel; The State v Paugari Kopol Kepao; The State v Raywill Parapen* (2011) N4438, [2011] PGNC 159
- *The State v Wilson Mari* (2011) N4419, [2011] PGNC 145
- *The State v Philip Ngaufu* (2011) N4554, [2011] PGNC 222
- *The State v Malachi Mathias and John Giamalu* (2011) N4670, [2011] PGNC 228 [sorcery killing]
- *The State v Alois Lagu* (2011) N4354, [2011] PGNC 80
- *The State v Margaret Topi* (2010) N4667, [2010] PGNC 221
- *The State v Agnes Baru Anton* (2010) N4117, [2010] PGNC 131
- *The State v Kabua Kove* (2010) N4063, [2010] PGNC 52
- *The State v John Laiam* (2010) N3995, [2010] PGNC 61
- *The State v Peter Wanam* (2010) N3981
- *The State v Tupis Tom; The State v Nathan Bobi (No. 2)* (2009) N3675, [2009] PGNC 65
- *The State v Issau Parao* (2009) N3625, [2009] PGNC 38
- *The State v Maria Tuu* (2008) N3706, [2008] PGNC 235

COMPARATIVE SENTENCES

- *The State v Steven Tabogani and others* (2008) N3559, [2008] PGNC 194
- *The State v Amos Young* (2008) N3548, [2008] PGNC 212
- *The State v Paul Semelkit* (2008) N3438
- *The State v Angeline Winara (No. 2)* (2008) N3352, [2008] PGNC 67
- *The State v Baika Martin and others* (2008) N3312, [2008] PGNC 29
- *The State v Gein Mari* (2008) N3516, [2008] PGNC 168
- *The State v Rudolf Reme Koki* (2007) CR No. 1967 of 2005
- *The State v Kevin Wakore* (2007) N3222, [2007] PGNC 61
- *The State v Philip Eki Vaki* (2007) N3464, [2007] PGNC 163
- *The State v Jonathan Joseph* (2007) CR No. 866 of 2007
- *The State v Tukal Waninara (No. 3)* (2007) N3280, [2007] PGNC 140
- *The State v Jimmy Ketu (No. 2)* (2007) N3394, [2007] PGNC 153
- *The State v Kevin Jeffo* (2007) CR No. 1303 of 2006
- *The State v Charles Rava Pake* (2007) CR No. 315 of 2007
- *The State v Alphonse Aia Mohavila* (2006) N3385, [2006] PGNC 106
- *The State v Maraka Jackson* (2006) N3237, [2006] PGNC 154
- *The State v Kiri Kirihau Harisu* (2006) N3168, [2006] PGNC 137
- *The State v Relvie Joe* (2005) N2832, [2005] PGNC 127
- *The State v John Wanimba and others* (2005) N2863, [2005] PGNC 108
- *The State v David Yakuye Daniel (No. 2)* (2005) N2890, [2005] PGNC 58
- *The State v Paul Potape Huliya* (2005) N2872, [2005] PGNC 77
- *The State v Steven Mul Mangi (No. 2)* (2005) N2993, [2005] PGNC 12
- *The State v Sebastian Justin Kelly* (2005) CR No. 75 of 2001
- *The State v Jacky Vutnamur and Kaki Kialo (No. 2)* (2005) N2868, [2005] PGNC 91

The maximum sentence for this offence is life imprisonment.

Sentences imposed have ranged from twelve years to thirty-five years imprisonment, and life imprisonment.[1567]

Sentences between fifteen years to twenty-five years imprisonment appear to be the median range since 2005 after the Supreme Court in *Manu Kovi v The State.*[1568]

[1567] See *The State v Alphonse Aia Mohavila* (2006) N3385, [2006] PGNC 106.

[1568] (2005) SC789, [2005] PGSC 34.

COMPARATIVE SENTENCES

In *The State v Okata Talangahin (No. 2)*[1569] the accused person, a male, killed an unborn ten month old baby by kicking the child's mother in the abdomen. He was charged, convicted and sentenced to life imprisonment for the offence of 'Murder' under section 300(1)(b) of the *Criminal Code* (Ch. 262). The conviction for 'Murder' is however questionable and the Supreme Court may be invited to review the conviction.[1570] Therefore, it is advisable that the sentence imposed in that case should not be used as a guide.

[30.4] ATTEMPTED MURDER

[30.4.1] INTRODUCTION

The offence of 'Attempted Murder' is an offence that is viewed with gravity by the legislature in that it carries a maximum sentence of life imprisonment.[1571]

The sentence to be imposed for such an offence may be appropriately beyond those imposed in Manslaughter cases because of an intention to kill in the case of an 'Attempted Murder'.[1572]

[30.4.2] COMPARATIVE CASES

See:

- *The State v Matthew Balu and Bernard Kavanamur Balu* (2011) N4362, [2011] PGNC 97
- *The State v Misin Kinapa* (2009) N3814, [2009] PGNC 183
- *The State v Michael Waragu* (2007) N3265, [2007] PGNC 134
- *The State v Frank Johnston, Murray William and Moses William (No. 2)* (2004) N2586
- *The State v Elizah Ute* (2004) N2550
- *The State v Joe Foe Leslie Leslie* (1996) N1496

The maximum sentence for this offence is life imprisonment.

[1569] (2004) N2671.

[1570] See *The State v Okata Talangahin (No. 1)* (2004) N2581.

[1571] See *The Pubic Prosecutor v Tumu Waria of Yogos* [1977] PNGLR 170, [1977] PGSC 18.

[1572] See *The State v Rex Lialu* [1988-89] PNGLR 449.

COMPARATIVE SENTENCES

Sentences imposed have ranged from five years to twenty-five years imprisonment and life imprisonment.[1573]

It appears that this offence is treated seriously and the sentences imposed are similar to some of the sentences imposed for the offences of 'Murder' and 'Manslaughter' and even 'Wilful Murder'.

[30.5] MANSLAUGHTER

[30.5.1] GENERAL PRINCIPLES

The offence of 'Manslaughter' is a prevalent offence.[1574]

The Supreme Court has set tariffs for this offence.[1575]

Sentences for the offence of 'Manslaughter' will normally be lower than sentences for 'Murder' and 'Wilful Murder', but there are those cases that will call for the imposition of a higher penalty up to the maximum prescribed.[1576]

A Court must have careful regard to:

- the circumstances of the death; and
- the way in which the death was actually caused

in determining the appropriate sentence.[1577]

[1573] See *The State v Joe Foe Leslie Leslie* (1996) N1496.

[1574] Refer also to the section titled 'Prevalence Of The Offence' in the chapter titled 'Aggravating Factors'.

[1575] See *The State v Wamaong Robert* (2010) N4065, [2010] PGNC 100.

[1576] See *Antap Yala v The State* (1996) SCRA No. 69/96 and *The State v Peter Noah* (2005) N2833, [2005] PGNC 123.

[1577] See *Rex Lialu v The State* [1990] PNGLR 487; *Norris v The State* [1979] PNGLR 605, [1979] PGSC 18; *The State v Peter Noah* (2005) N2833, [2005] PGNC 123; *The State v Misack Kilik* (2004) N2749 and *The State v Bali Tombe* (1998) N1708.

See also: *R v Phillips* (1985) 7 Cr App R (S) 235 at 237.

COMPARATIVE SENTENCES

In order to determine an appropriate sentence the factors to be considered, include:

- the circumstances of the death and the way in which death was actually caused[1578];
- can the assault on the deceased person be classed as 'not vicious'?[1579];
- whether there was deliberate intention to harm[1580];
- the nature and frequency of any attack or assault[1581];
- whether the injury which caused death arose directly from an attack or assault or was caused by, for example falling on an object[1582];
- whether the injury caused by the person or by a weapon[1583];
- was the deceased person injured by only a fist?[1584];

[1578] See *Rex Lialu v The State* [1990] PNGLR 487, [1990] PGSC 16.

Refer also to the section titled 'Repeated Acts Causing Multiple Injuries Or Loss Of Property' in the chapter titled 'Aggravating Factors'.

[1579] See *The State v Alphonse Kaparo and John Loangesa* (2007) N3189, [2007] PGNC 79 and *The State v Sebastian Sahoto Roho* [2006] PGNC 72.

Refer also to the section titled 'Viciousness Or Deliberate Intention To Harm' in the chapter titled 'Aggravating Factors'.

[1580] See *Rex Lialu v The State* [1990] PNGLR 487 and *The State v Peter Wanam* (2010) N3981, [2010] PGNC 31.

Refer also to the section titled 'Viciousness Or Deliberate Intention To Harm' in the chapter titled 'Aggravating Factors'.

[1581] See *Rex Lialu v The State* [1990] PNGLR 487 and *The State v Peter Wanam* (2010) N3981, [2010] PGNC 31.

[1582] See *Rex Lialu v The State* [1990] PNGLR 487 and *The State v Peter Wanam* (2010) N3981, [2010] PGNC 31.

[1583] See *Rex Lialu v The State* [1990] PNGLR 487 and *The State v Peter Wanam* (2010) N3981, [2010] PGNC 31.

[1584] See *The State v Alphonse Kaparo and John Loangesa* (2007) N3189, [2007] PGNC 79 and *The State v Sebastian Sahoto Roho* [2006] PGNC 72.

- was there some intervening cause of death, such as did the death result directly from the assault due to death being caused by an object when the deceased person fell down?[1585];
- did the deceased person have a pre-existing condition making him or her susceptible to serious or fatal injury by a moderate blow, such as did the deceased person have a thin skull or enlarged spleen?[1586]; and
- whether there was provocation in the non-legal sense[1587].

[30.5.2] COMPARATIVE CASES

See:

- *Thress Kumbamong v The State* (2008) SC1017, [2008] PGSC 51
- *Timothy Diwa v The State* (2007) SC892, [2007] PGSC 30
- *Gerald Kirafe v The State* (2007) SC893, [2007] PGSC 29
- *Irai Thomas v The State* (2007) SC867, [2007] PGSC 26
- *Joe Giamur v The State* (2007) SC884, [2007] PGSC 7
- *Manu Kovi v The State* (2005) SC789, [2005] PGSC 34
- *The State v Andrew Jessie* (2012) N4904, [2012] PGNC 239
- *The State v Jackson Peng* (2012) N4737, [2012] PGNC 110
- *The State v Tony Dom* (2012) N4767, [2012] PGNC 97
- *The State v Noelyn Anton* (2012) N4828, [2012] PGNC 120
- *The State v Daniel Kondonga* (2012) N4619, [2012] PGNC 24
- *The State v Elisha Mema* (2012) N4602, [2012] PGNC 21
- *The State v Esther Koite Nokup* (2012) N4787, [2012] PGNC 225; N4787
- *The State v Tony Dom* (2012) N4767, [2012] PGNC 97

[1585] See *Rex Lialu v The State* [1990] PNGLR 487, [1990] PGSC 16; *The State v Alphonse Kaparo and John Loangesa* (2007) N3189, [2007] PGNC 79 and *The State v Sebastian Sahoto Roho* [2006] PGNC 72.

[1586] See *Rex Lialu v The State* [1990] PNGLR 487, [1990] PGSC 16; *The State v Peter Wanam* (2010) N3981, [2010] PGNC 31; *The State v Alphonse Kaparo and John Loangesa* (2007) N3189, [2007] PGNC 79 and *The State v Sebastian Sahoto Roho* [2006] PGNC 72.

[1587] See *Rex Lialu v The State* [1990] PNGLR 487 and *The State v Peter Wanam* (2010) N3981, [2010] PGNC 31.

Refer also to the section titled 'De-facto Prococation' in the chapter titled 'Extenuating Circumstances'.

COMPARATIVE SENTENCES

- *The State v Jimmy Mogoi* (2012) N4680, [2012] PGNC 78
- *The State v Godfrey Watakasi* (2012) N4597, [2012] PGNC 266
- *The State v Serah Joe Wennis* (2011) N4661, [2011] PGNC 216
- *The State v Benjamin Towari and others* (2011) N4353, [2011] PGNC 79
- *The State v Roy Wani* (2011) N4328, [2011] PGNC 65
- *The State v Tolly Saun and Stanley Saun* (2011) N4390
- *The State v Jenny Dei* (2011) N4260, [2011] PGNC 29
- *The State v Amos Dickson* (2011) N4539, [2011] PGNC 199
- *The State v Two Juveniles, 'FSD' and 'SW'* (2011) N4456, [2011] PGNC 164
- *The State v Asi Piro* (2011) N4410, [2011] PGNC 144
- *The State v Josephine Las Ninjipa* (2010) N4135, [2010] PGNC 141
- *The State v Elis Nema Mara* (2010) N4133, [2010] PGNC 140
- *The State v Kunduk Nime John* (2010) N4116, [2010] PGNC 130
- *The State v Wamaong Robert* (2010) N4065, [2010] PGNC 100
- *The State v Regina Jako* (2010) N4110, [2010] PGNC 119
- *The State v Christopher Dubun* (2010) N4109, [2010] PGNC 118
- *The State v Albert Kududu* (2010) N4108, [2010] PGNC 117
- *The State v Peter Wanam* (2010) N3981, [2010] PGNC 31
- *The State v Melchior Kapus and others* (2010) N4114, [2010] PGNC 109
- *The State v James Kendiagl* (2009) N4212, [2009] PGNC 272
- *The State v Mamanane Guri (No. 2)* (2009) N3771, [2009] PGNC 152
- *The State v Lawrence Giobun* (2009) N3728, [2009] PGNC 119
- *The State v Lossy Karapus* (2009) N3640, [2009] PGNC 59
- *The State v Anita Kelly* (2009) N3624, [2009] PGNC 34
- *The State v Carol Alfred* (2009) N3602, [2009] PGNC 29
- *The State v Ilai Bate* (2008) N3556, [2008] PGNC 198
- *The State v Steven Lucas* (2008) N3540
- *The State v Yuanis Ipiri* (2008) N3512, [2008] PGNC 159
- *The State v Juvenile 'D'* (2008) N3508, [2008] PGNC 153
- *The State v Michael Langan Sapri* (2008) N3434
- *The State v Henson Poponil* (2008) N3433
- *The State v Abraham Nobi* (2008) N3412, [2008] PGNC 105
- *The State v Robert Potou* (2008) N3316, [2008] PGNC 35
- *The State v Tou Aitsi (No. 2)* (2008) N3296, [2008] PGNC 21
- *The State v Tony Pinuana* [2007] PGNC 119
- *The State v Michael Gitarukin Arimin* [2007] PGNC 129
- *The State v Japhet Marshall Ano* (2007) N3465, [2007] PGNC 162

- *The State v John Loangesa* (2007) N3187, [2007] PGNC 166
- *The State v Saweno Visari and Ragu Maioi* [2006] PGNC 61
- *The State v Timothy Job* (2006) CR No. 1028 of 2005
- *The State v John Uranau* [2006] PGNC 99
- *The State v Sebastian Sahoto Roho* [2006] PGNC 72
- *The State v Ronny Aike* (2006) N3455, [2006] PGNC 102
- *The State v Elias Peter Wano Miva* (2006) N3454, [2006] PGNC 103
- *The State v Lien Kaingi* [2006] PGNC 108
- *The State v Hiliong Gunaing* (2005) N2803, [2005] PGNC 146
- *The State v Daniel Ronald Walus* (2005) N2802, [2005] PGNC 147
- *The State v Mark Kanupio and others* (2005) N2800, [2005] PGNC 159
- *The State v Peter Noah* (2005) N2833, [2005] PGNC 123
- *The State v Timothy Diwa* (2005) N3381, [2005] PGNC 184

As with 'Wilful Murder' and 'Murder', the maximum sentence for this offence is also life imprisonment.

In *Manu Kovi v The State*[1588] the Supreme Court suggested sentences in the range of eight to twenty-five years imprisonment for this offence.

Sentences imposed since *Manu Kovi v The State*[1589] have been in the range from six to twenty years imprisonment.

In most cases the starting point appears to be eight to ten years imprisonment. The lowest is six years imprisonment which was imposed in *The State v Pinuana*[1590] and *The State v Daniel Kondonga*[1591].

The highest is twenty years imprisonment imposed in *The State v Ilai Bati*[1592] where the accused person changed his plea to guilty to this offence after a trial on 'Wilful Murder'.

[1588] (2005) SC789, [2005] PGSC 34.

[1589] (2005) SC789, [2005] PGSC 34.

[1590] [2007] PGNC 119.

[1591] (2012) N4619, [2012] PGNC 24.

[1592] (2008) N3556, [2008] PGNC 198.

COMPARATIVE SENTENCES

[30.6] KILLING UNBORN CHILD

See:

- *The State v Fambian Diofila Joseph* [1992] PNGLR 238

The maximum sentence for this offence (mother killing a child under the age of twelve months) is life imprisonment (the same maximum sentence for the offence of 'Manslaughter').[1593]

Sentences imposed have ranged from four to five years imprisonment.[1594]

[30.7] CONSPIRING TO KILL[1595]

See:

- *The State v Melba Posara* (2012) N4596, [2012] PGNC 267

The maximum sentence is fourteen years imprisonment.

In the case cited the accused person was sentenced to eight years imprisonment.

[30.8] FAILURE TO REPORT KILLING

See:

- *The State v Henry Gendari* (2011) N4545, [2011] PGNC 203

The maximum penalty on summary conviction is imprisonment for a term not exceeding six months; whereas the maximum penalty on conviction on indictment is imprisonment for a term not exceeding two years.

In the case cited a sentence of ten months imprisonment was imposed.

[1593] See section 301 of the *Criminal Code* (Ch. 262).

[1594] See *The State v Fambian Diofila Joseph* [1992] PNGLR 238.

[1595] The law in relation to this offence is examined in the chapter titled 'Offences Against The Person' in the text titled 'Injia on Criminal Offences in Papua New Guinea and the Pacific'.

[31.0] KIDNAPPING FOR RANSOM[1596]

See:

- *The State v William Nanua Kapris and others* (2011) N4305, [2011] PGNC 51

The maximum sentence for this offence is fourteen years imprisonment.

In the case cited the Court imposed a range of three to nine years imprisonment.

[32.0] MISAPPROPRIATION[1597]

[32.1] GENERAL PRINCIPLES

The offence of 'Misappropriation' is a prevalent offence.[1598]

The Supreme Court has issued sentencing guidelines.[1599]

In order to determine an appropriate sentence the factors to be considered, include[1600]:

- the amount of money involved[1601];
- the period of time it took to commit the offence[1602];

[1596] The law in relation to this offence is examined in the section titled 'Kidnapping' in the chapter titled 'Offences Against The Person' in the text titled 'Injia on Criminal Offences in Papua New Guinea and the Pacific'.

[1597] The law in relation to this offence is examined in the section titled 'Misappropriation' in the chapter titled 'Fraud Related Offences' in the text titled 'Injia on Criminal Offences in Papua New Guinea and the Pacific'.

[1598] Refer also to the section titled 'Prevalence Of The Offence' in the chapter titled 'Aggravating Factors'.

[1599] See *Wellington Belawa v The State* [1988-89] PNGLR 496, [1988] PGSC 6.

[1600] See *Wellington Belawa v The State* [1988-89] PNGLR 496, [1988] PGSC 6 *and The State v Morgan Bae* (2010) N4076, [2010] PGNC 152.

[1601] Refer also to the section titled 'Seriousness Of An Offence Generally' in the chapter titled 'Aggravating Factors'.

[1602] Refer also to the section titled 'Duration Of The Offence' in the chapter titled 'Aggravating Factors'.

- the use to which the money taken was applied;
- the effect on the complainant;
- the impact of the offence on the public;
- the effect on the accused person; and
- whether restitution had been effected[1603].

[32.2] COMPARATIVE CASES

See:

- *Dorren Liprin v The State* (2001) SC673, [2001] PGSC 11
- *Rokpa v The State* [1994] PNGLR 535, (1994) PGSC 16
- *Lawi v The State* [1987] PNGLR 183, [1987] PGSC 12
- *The State v Evelyn Rapola (No. 2)* [1990] PNGLR 91
- *The State v Peman Etami* (2012) N4769, [2012] PGNC 96
- *The State v Jacob Amonea* (2012) N4688, [2012] PGNC 74
- *The State v Alphonsa Magum* (2011) N4524, [2011] PGNC 202
- *The State v Morgan Bae* (2010) N4076, [2010] PGNC 152
- *The State v Francisca Iralu* (2008) N3710, [2008] PGNC 241
- *The State v Ruth Mamando* (2008) N3709, [2008] PGNC 242
- *The State v William Chilen* (2008) N3549, [2008] PGNC 200
- *The State v Ranu Karo* (2008) N3521, [2008] PGNC 160
- *The State v Elizabeth Teka* (2008) N3509, [2008] PGNC 154
- *The State v David Kaki* (2008) N3458, [2008] PGNC 210
- *The State v Siba Kua* (2007) N3230, [2007] PGNC 103
- *The State v Jimmy Kendi (No. 2)* (2007) N3131, [2007] PGNC 32
- *The State v Livingston Haurahaela* [2006] PGNC 100
- *The State v Robert Lorou Sevese* (2006) N3453, [2006] PGNC 101
- *The State v Seilala Ipai* (2006) N3169, [2006] PGNC 138
- *The State v Ansong Ising* (2005) N2994, [2005] PGNC 14
- *The State v Christian Korei* (2005) N2946, [2005] PGNC 32

[1603] Refer also to the section titled 'Payment Of Compensation' in the chapter titled 'Mitigating Factors'.

COMPARATIVE SENTENCES

- *The State v Iori Veraga* (2005) N2921, [2005] PGNC 43
- *The State v Alice Wilmot* (2005) N2857, [2005] PGNC 105
- *The State v Bill Saun Daniel* (2005) N3502, [2005] PGNC 187
- *The State v Derrick Sakatea Niso* (2005) N2930
- *The State v Daniel Mapiria* (2004) Unreported National Court judgement CR No. 1118 of 2000
- *The State v Imoi Maino* (2004) N2773
- *The State v Lukeson Olewale* (2004) N2758
- *The State v Scholar Zuvani* (2004) N2641
- *The State v Mahuva Jimmy and Uta Helisha* (2004) N2632
- *The State v Andrew Ludwig Posai* (2004) N2624
- *The State v Margaret Donny* (2004) N2609
- *The State v Nerrius Boas* (2004) N2608
- *The State v Sam Pipi* (2004) N2574
- *The State v Gibson Haulai* (2003) N2555
- *The State v Benson Likius* (2004) N2518
- *The State v Eric Emmanuel Vele* (2002) N2252
- *The State v Dobi Ao (No. 2)* (2002) N2247
- *The State v Makeu Kig* (2001) N2177
- *The State v Simon Paul Vurmete* (2000) N2008
- *The State v Fano Kuromu* (1999) N1942
- *The State v Tony Baik* (1999) N1930
- *The State v Bluey Hanua* (1997) N1625
- *The State v Kepi Vala* (1997) N1527
- *The State v Sukope Tova* (1997) N1522
- *The State v Micky Kauri* (1996) N1501
- *The State v Bygonnes Tuse Nae* (1996) N1474
- *The State v Ako Arua* (1995) N1315
- *The State v Napilye Kuri* (1994) N1269
- *The State v Auto Kamuta* (1990) N952

The maximum sentence for this offence is ten years imprisonment.

In *Wellington Belawa v The State* ('the Belawa case')[1604] the Supreme Court set out gaol terms ranging from one to five years for amounts misappropriated between K1 and K150,000.

Since the Belawa case, amounts misappropriated have surpassed K150,000.

[1604] [1988-89] PNGLR 496, [1988] PGSC 6.

COMPARATIVE SENTENCES

The highest amount involved is in the millions of kina.[1605]

The sentences imposed in cases since the Belawa case range from a fine to nine years imprisonment.

In 90% of those cases the sentences have been either wholly or partially suspended.

[33.0] MONEY LAUNDERING[1606]

In the context of a money laundering offence, the most important consideration will be what the accused person did; there may be little or no evidence before the Court as to:

- the organisation behind the offence;
- the source of the funds; or
- the ultimate use to be made of the funds.[1607]

An accused person's belief as to the source of the funds is a relevant sentencing consideration.[1608]

However, if there is no evidence as to the accused person's state of knowledge as to:

- the source of the funds;
- the purpose of dealing with the funds; or
- their ultimate destination,

1605 See *The State v Jimmy Kendi (No. 2)* (2007) N3131, [2007] PGNC 32 [K4.29 million] and *The State v Daniel Mapiria* (2004) Unreported National Court judgement CR No. 1118 of 2000 [K3.18 million].

1606 The law in relation to this offence is examined in the section titled 'Money-Laundering' in the chapter titled 'Fraud Related Offences' in the text titled 'Injia on Criminal Offences in Papua New Guinea and the Pacific'.

1607 See *R v Olbrich* (1999) 199 CLR 270, [1999] HCA 54 and *Ansari v R* (2007) 70 NSWLR 89, [2007] NSWCCA 204.

1608 See *R v Huang* (2007) 174 A Crim R 370, [2007] NSWCCA 259.

then the Court must simply deal with the matter on the objective facts as proved by the evidence.[1609]

[34.0] MUTINY OFFENCES

[34.1] INCITING TO MUTINY[1610]

See:

- *Ben Wafia and others v The State* (2006) SC851, [2006] PGSC 19.

The maximum sentence for this offence is life imprisonment.

In the case cited the Supreme Court dismissed an appeal against sentence of twenty years imprisonment.

[34.2] MUTINY

See:

- *The State v 87929, Captain Bola Renagi of Kemabolo Village, Kwikila, Central Province and others* (2000) N1955
- *The State v Major Walter Enuma and others* (1998) N1724

The maximum sentences for this offence range from three to ten years imprisonment.

In the cases cited sentences imposed have ranged from five to eight years imprisonment.

1609 See *Ansari v R* (2007) 70 NSWLR 89, [2007] NSWCCA 204.

1610 The law in relation to this offence is examined in the chapter titled 'Administration Of Justice Offences' in the text titled 'Injia on Criminal Offences in Papua New Guinea and the Pacific'.

COMPARATIVE SENTENCES

[35.0] OFFICIAL CORRUPTION[1611]

[35.1] GENERAL PRINCIPLES

The offence of 'Official Corruption' was created by Parliament to deter public officials from using their positions for personal gain or advantage because holding a position of power or authority may often than not be abused or misused.[1612]

The offence of 'Official Corruption' is difficult to prove as it relies on the honesty of the person who is offered the bribe or encouraged to engage in corrupt practices. There are rarely independent witnesses to the event. For these reasons when a case has been successfully proved the National Court has a duty to treat the matter seriously.[1613]

Once detected, tried and proved the need to impose a punitive and deterrent sentence[1614] to deter others, becomes crucial.[1615]

[35.2] COMPARATIVE CASES

See:

- *Danny Mako v The State* (2006) SC889, [2006] PGSC 29
- *The State v Robert Konny* (2012) N4691, [2012] PGNC 77
- *The State v Jimmy Naime* (2005) N2873, [2005] PGNC 76
- *The State v Kiap Bonga* [1988-89] PNGLR 360

The maximum sentence for this offence is seven years imprisonment.

[1611] The law in relation to this offence is examined in the section titled 'Corruption' in the chapter titled 'Administration Of Justice Offences' in the text titled 'Injia on Criminal Offences in Papua New Guinea and the Pacific'.

[1612] See *The State v Robert Konny* (2012) N4691, [2012] PGNC 77.

[1613] See *Robert Yabara v The State* (1984) PNGLR 378.

See also: *The State v Pablito P. Miguel* (2002) N2338, [2002] PGNC 25.

[1614] Refer also to the chapter titled 'Objectives And Purposes Of Sentencing'.

[1615] See *Robert Yabara v The State* (1984) PNGLR 378.

See also: *The State v Pablito P. Miguel* (2002) N2338, [2002] PGNC 25.

COMPARATIVE SENTENCES

Sentences imposed have ranged from four months to five years imprisonment.

In *Danny Makao v The State*[1616] the Supreme Court reduced a sentence of seven years imprisonment imposed on a police officer who corruptly received K150.

[36.0] PERJURY[1617]

Perjury is a very serious offence and should attract a severe penalty.[1618]

[37.0] PLAYING UNLAWFUL GAME

See:

- *Apa Kokoti and others v Kaori Iri* (1997) N1597

The maximum sentence for this offence is a fine of K40 or one month imprisonment.

In the case cited a sentence of nine days imprisonment was considered adequate punishment.

[38.0] PORNOGRAPHIC MATERIAL

[38.1] PRODUCTION

See:

- *The State v Ron Suma* (2012) N4622, [2012] PGNC 27

The maximum sentence for this offence is a term of imprisonment for two years.

This case involved consented adults and the accused person was sentenced to a term of imprisonment for one year.

[1616] (2006) SC889, [2006] PGSC 29.

[1617] The law in relation to this offence is examined in the section titled 'Perjury' in the chapter titled 'Administration Of Justice Offences' in the text titled 'Injia on Criminal Offences in Papua New Guinea and the Pacific'.

[1618] *See R v Simmonds* (1969) 53 Cr App R 488.

[38.2] POSSESSION

See:

- *Glenn Lucena v The State* (2008) N3460, [2008] PGNC 211
- *The State v Gregory Kasen* (2001) N2133

The maximum sentence for this offence is a fine of K2,000 or one years imprisonment.

Custodial sentences ranging from three to four months imprisonment imposed by the District Courts have been quashed on appeal and sentences reduced to a fine or a few days in jail.

[39.0] POSSESSION OF FORGED BANK NOTES

See:

- *The State v Cornellius Po'owa and Ismael Bawah* (2003) CR No. 156 of 2003 and CR No. 214 of 2003

The maximum sentence for this offence is four years imprisonment.

[40.0] POSSESSION OF PROPERTY SUSPECTED STOLEN OR UNLAWFULLY OBTAINED[1619]

The offence of 'Possession Of Property Suspected Stolen Or Unlawfully Obtained' must be treated seriously as the person who buys or acquires goods knowing or suspecting that they were illegally acquired gives an outlet to others who commit crimes, such as theft or break, enter and steal, to dispose of the goods they have taken.[1620]

[1619] The law in relation to this offence is examined in the subsection titled 'Convey Property Suspected Of Being Stolen Or Unlawfully Obtained' in the section titled 'Unlawfully Obtained Property' in the chapter titled 'Offences Against Property' in the text titled 'Injia on Criminal Offences in Papua New Guinea and the Pacific'.

[1620] See *Albert Marum v Pitu Lapai* (1993) N1147.

[41.0] RECEIVED FORGED BANK NOTE

See:

- *The State v Ivan Kikimaro* (2008) N3529, [2008] PGNC 173

The maximum sentence for this offence is seven years imprisonment.

In the case cited in which involved an amount of K48,975 a sentence of four years imprisonment was imposed.

[42.0] RECEIVING[1621]

[42.1] GENERAL PRINCIPLES

The offence of 'Receiving' is a prevalent offence.[1622]

In order to determine an appropriate sentence the factors to be considered, include[1623]:

- the closeness of the receiver to the primary offence (geographical or temporal);
- the particular seriousness of the primary offence;
- the value of property, including sentimental value;
- whether the property was the proceeds of a domestic burglary;
- the level of sophistication in relation to the receiving;
- the provision by the receiver as a regular outlet for stolen property;
- the level of profit made or expected by the receiver; and

[1621] The law in relation to this offence is examined in the subsection titled 'Receiving' in the section titled 'Unlawfully Obtained Property' in the chapter titled 'Offences Against Property' in the text titled 'Injia on Criminal Offences in Papua New Guinea and the Pacific'.

[1622] Refer also to the section titled 'Prevalence Of The Offence' in the chapter titled 'Aggravating Factors'.

[1623] See *R v Webbe, The Times*, June 13, 2001.

- any threats of violence or abuse of power by the receiver.

[42.2] COMPARATIVE CASES

See:

- *Acting Public Prosecutor v Yonnga* [1981] PNGLR 314, [1981] PGSC 8
- *The State v Jelio Yawi* (2009) N3631, [2009] PGNC 44
- *The State v Tony Mwayawa* (2008) N3557, [2008] PGNC 199
- *The State v Anton Dima* (2007) N3119, [2007] PGNC 16
- *The State v Henry Kenori* (2007) CR No. 572 of 2007
- *The State v Levo Miha and Cecil Kehara* (2006) N3157, [2006] PGNC 136
- *The State v Aisi Eki and others* (2005) N3387, [2005] PGNC 185
- *The State v James Hilux Palu* (2004) N2585, [2004] PGNC 182

The maximum sentence for this offence is seven years imprisonment.

Sentences imposed have ranged from one to five years imprisonment for amounts of money or property valued between K100 and K5,800.

[43.0] ROBBERY OFFENCES

[43.1] ROBBERY[1624]

[43.1.1] GENERAL PRINCIPLES

In general, armed robbery has become the most prevalent offence[1625] and feared crime of violence confronting our people today. It is a very serious crime as it attacks the very essence of constitutional guarantees for every man, woman and children in this country to have the freedom to live, move around and go about his or her lawful business anywhere and at any time of the day, without fear or apprehension of unwarranted attacks.[1626]

[1624] The law in relation to this offence is examined in the section titled 'Robbery And Attempted Robbery' in the chapter titled 'Offences Against The Person' in the text titled 'Injia on Criminal Offences in Papua New Guinea and the Pacific'.

[1625] Refer also to the section titled 'Prevalence Of The Offence' in the chapter titled 'Aggravating Factors'.

[1626] See *The State v Tai Magani* (2011) N4555, [2011] PGNC 210.

COMPARATIVE SENTENCES

People should feel safe in their homes, at their work places, on the streets and roads, without fear as many do, of prowling armed robbers threatening and stealing from them.[1627]

Armed robbery has become a very common occurrence in our cities, towns, along the roads, highways and spreading into rural areas. It is an unfortunate reality that hardly a day goes by without a report of such crimes in the print as well as the electronic media. Consequently, our people and the image of our country suffer through adverse publicity. Armed robberies damage our people and the image of this country.[1628]

Armed Robbery a very serious crime because it is a crime committed against another fellow human being. For any victim of the crime of armed robbery, it is a terrifying experience, both physical and emotional and even death. In a case of highway armed robbery, it is even more terrifying experience because the victims are held up in an unfamiliar and isolated location where it is difficult to seek help.[1629]

People should feel safe throughout Papua New Guinea when and wherever they are going about their lawful duties or at their leisure time. They should be able to move around freely and should not have to live in fear as many do, of armed robbers prowling the cities, towns and rural areas to steal from the unwary on the road or streets, business houses, clubs, vehicles on the road, factories, banks and homes.[1630]

The Courts must be tough with their decisions when it comes to sentencing an accused person in a robbery case.[1631]

The Supreme Court has issued sentencing guidelines.[1632]

[1627] See *The State v Tai Magani* (2011) N4555, [2011] PGNC 210.

[1628] See *The State v Clinton Tikambari* (2011) N4553, [2011] PGNC 224.

[1629] See *The State v Petrus Abai* (2010) N4132, [2010] PGNC 137.

[1630] See *The State v Clinton Tikambari* (2011) N4553, [2011] PGNC 224.

[1631] See *The State v Paul Kumkumbun* (2009) N3645, [2009] PGNC 60.

See also: *Richard Liri v The State* (2007) SC883, [2007] PGSC 3; *The State v Patrick Puppy Kaikara Loavi* (2006) N3384, [2006] PGNC 104; *The State v Jackson Nimai* (2008) N3355, [2008] PGNC 72; *The State v Andrew Nane John (No. 2)* (2007) N3197, [2007] PGNC 84; *The State v Philip Eki Vaki* (2007) N3464, [2007] PGNC 163; *The State v Nipi Beo Bayu* [2006] PGNC 96; *The State v Vincent Malara* (2002) N2188 and *The State v Paul Maima Yogol and Dama Teiye* (2004) N2583.

[1632] See *Gimble v The State* [1988-89] PNGLR 271, (1988) SC369, [1988] PGSC 15; *Hawai John v The State* (1998) SCR No. 9 of 1995; *Public Prosecutor v Don Hale* (1998) SC564; *Tau Jim Anis and others v The State* (2000) SC642, [2000] PGSC 12 and *Dadly Henry Gorop v The State* (2003) SC732.

COMPARATIVE SENTENCES

The current starting points for terms of imprisonment are as follows:

- Robbery of a house – ten years
- Robbery of a bank – nine years
- Robbery of a store, hotel, club, vehicle on the road etc – eight years
- Robbery of a person on the street – six years[1633]

It is within the discretion of a Court to increase or decrease from the suggested starting point depending on the facts of each case.[1634]

The maximum sentence for 'Simple Robbery' is fourteen years imprisonment and for 'Aggravated Robbery' is life imprisonment.

Most cases dealt with by the Courts however involve 'Aggravated Robbery'.

Since 1989 when the Supreme Court[1635] suggested a range of sentences for different categories of 'Robbery' sentences imposed by the Courts have increased and surpassed those range of sentences. This is evident from the range of sentences set out under the various categories of robberies.

The increase in sentences is the result of continuing prevalence and significant increase in the offence.

A Court may however exercise its discretion under section 19 of the *Criminal Code* (Ch. 262).[1636]

[1633] See *The State v John Carl Endekra and others* (2007) N3185, [2007] PGNC 82.

[1634] See *John Arua Peter v The State* (2000) SC638; *Phillip Kassman v The State* (2004) SC759, [2004] PGSC 9; *Bobolan Mebu Peter v The State* (2007) SC894, [2007] PGSC 28 and *Alex Pori v The State* (2007) SC912, [2007] PGSC 39.

[1635] See *Gimble v The State* [1988-89] PNGLR 271, (1988) SC369, [1988] PGSC 15.

[1636] See *The State v Steward Pariwan* (1999) N1834 and *The State v Gilbert James* (2009) N3752, [2009] PGNC 134.

COMPARATIVE SENTENCES

In order to determine an appropriate sentence the factors to be considered, include[1637]:

- did the accused person [or other members of their gang[1638]] commit actual violence during the course of the robbery?;
- did the accused person [or other members of their gang] threaten the victims of the robbery with violence?;
- did the accused person [or other members of their gang] put the victims or innocent bystanders in real danger of being injured or killed?;
- did the accused person [or other members of their gang] ensure that especially vulnerable victims, such as children, women or older people, were not threatened or treated badly?; and
- did the accused person [or other members of their gang] steal money or property of a relatively small value?[1639]

[43.1.2] COMPARATIVE CASES

HOUSE

See:

- *The State v Nelson N Ngasele* (2003) SC731, [2003] PGSC 2
- *Jimmy Ono v The State* (2002) SC698, [2002] PGSC 10
- *Public Prosecutor v Don Hale* (1998) SC564
- *The State v Philip Saku and others* (2011) N4355, [2011] PGNC 78
- *The State v Thompson Kevin and Edwin Saki Morris* (2011) N4675, [2011] PGNC 214
- *The State v Gilbert James* (2009) N3752, [2009] PGNC 134

[1637] See *The State v John Carl Endekra and others* (2007) N3185, [2007] PGNC 82 and *The State v Aaron Lahu* (2005) N2798, [2005] PGNC 161.

[1638] Refer also to the sections titled 'Member Of A Gang' and 'Leadership In A Gang' in the chapter titled 'Aggravating Factors'.

[1639] Refer also to the section titled 'Seriousness Of An Offence Generally' in the chapter titled 'Aggravating Factors'.

COMPARATIVE SENTENCES

- *The State v David Tovaboda and others* (2008) N3554, [2008] PGNC 196
- *The State v Charlie Kevin and others* (2007) N3191, [2007] PGNC 78
- *The State v Dick John Moi* [2006] PGNC 12
- *The State v Allan Esri Waluta* (2005) N2911, [2005] PGNC 52
- *The State v James Negol* (2005) N2801, [2005] PGNC 148
- *The State v Austin Upena and others* (2002) N2222
- *The State v Benjamin Nabate and Jeffery Jajata* (2002) N2216
- *The State v Billy Bimaru* (2000) N2025

The maximum sentence for this offence is life imprisonment.

The sentences imposed have ranged from five to eleven years imprisonment.

BANK

See:

- *Philip Kassman v The State* (2004) SC759, [2004] PGSC 9
- *The State v William Nanua Kapris and others* (2011) N4305, [2008] PGNC 51

The maximum sentence for this offence is life imprisonment.

The sentences imposed have been in the vicinity of ten years imprisonment.

However, in the case of *The State v William Nanua Kapris and others*[1640] the Court imposed sentences that ranged from eight to twenty-five years imprisonment.

STORE, HOTEL, CLUB, VEHICLE ON A ROAD, ETC

See:

- *The State v Nelson N Ngasele* (2003) SC731, [2003] PGSC 2 [House and Vehicle]
- *Bobolan Mebu Peter v The State* (2007) SC894, [2007] PGSC 28 [Vehicle]
- *The State v Masol Ailya* [2007] PGSC 32 [Business]
- *Richard Liri v The State* (2007) SC883, [2007] PGSC 3 [Club]

[1640] (2011) N4305, [2008] PGNC 51.

COMPARATIVE SENTENCES

- *Ramsey Lester Pitaro v The State* (2006) SC842, [2006] PGSC 11 [Vehicle]
- *Richard Sebastian v The State (*2003) SCRA No. 43 of 2002 [Vehicle]
- *Tau Jim Anis and others v The State* (2000) SC642, [2000] PGSC 12 [Factory]
- *John Arua Peter v The State* (2000) SC638 [Vehicle]
- *The State v Clinton Tikambari* (2011) N4553, [2011] PGNC 224 [Factory]
- *The State v Tai Magani* (2011) N4555, [2011] PGNC 210 [Vehicle]
- *The State v Titus Manai* (2011) N4556, [2011] PGNC 218 [Vehicle]
- *The State v Petrus Abai* (2010) N4132, [2010] PGNC 137 [Vehicle]
- *The State v Alphonse Asarombo and Timothy Asarombo* (2010) N4121, [2010] PGNC 132 [Store]
- *The State v Peter Yandi* (2010) N4064, [2010] PGNC 50 [Vehicle]
- *The State v Mila Renof* (2009) N4027 [Store]
- *The State v Jonathan Sengi* (2009) N3692, [2009] PGNC 91 [Vehicle]
- *The State v Waiyape Kuromu and others* (2009) N3743, [2009] PGNC 130 [Vehicle]
- *The State v Paul Kumkumbun* (2009) N3645, [2009] PGNC 60 [Vehicle]
- *The State v John Pais Kawage* (2009) N3626, [2009] PGNC 37 [Prison]
- *The State v Peter Sarufa* (2009) N3595, [2009] PGNC 22 [Vehicle]
- *The State v Bani Basil* (2008) N3671, [2008] PGNC 228 [Vehicle]
- *The State v Chan Alois and Augustine Tutut* (2008) N3668, [2008] PGNC 180 [Vehicle]
- *The State v Toipo Dimasi* (2008) N3551, [2008] PGNC 193
- *The State v Kevin Aku Knox and Alex Ambi* (2008) N3339, [2008] PGNC 79
- *The State v Manuel Harry Mauta and Michael Sani* (2008) N3530, [2008] PGNC 176 [Yacht]
- *The State v Jackson Nimai* (2008) N3355, [2008] PGNC 72 [Vehicle]
- *The State v Alus Tamagi and Paija Teke* (2008) N3310, [2008] PGNC 42 [Store]
- *The State v Sam Pap* [2007] PGNC 10 [Club]
- *The State v Andrew Nane John (No. 2)* (2007) N3197, [2007] PGNC 30 [Store]
- *The State v John Carl Endekra and others* (2007) N3185, [2007] PGNC 82 [Vehicle]
- *The State v Patrick Puppy Kaikara Loavi* (2006) N3384, [2006] PGNC 104 [Store]
- *The State v Alphonse Polpolio and Jeffrey Baru* [2006] PGNC 16 [2 x Stores]
- *The State v Nipi Beo Bayu* [2006] PGNC 96 [Vehicle]
- *The State v Kingsley Sovek and Andrew Kedani* [2006] PGNC 13 [Store]
- *The State v Leslie Warim Cletus Malo* [2006] PGNC 111 [Vehicle]
- *The State v Tomkuk Herman Itagau* [2006] PGNC 105 [Hotel]
- *The State v Ismael Pavo Wrakuhau (No. 2)* (2005) N2955, [2005] PGNC 4 [Vehicle]
- *The State v Aaron Lahu* (2005) N2798, [2005] PGNC 161 [Store]
- *The State v Honenu Kinzong* (2005) N2942, [2005] PGNC 22 [Vehicle]

COMPARATIVE SENTENCES

- *The State v Justin Komboli* (2005) N2891, [2005] PGNC 61 [Store]
- *The State v Kevin Anish and Banik Kaiman* (2005) N2887, [2005] PGNC 49 [Store]
- *The State v Warip Mondol and others* (2004) N2707, [2004] PGNC 72 [Vehicle]
- *The State v Chris Banban and Nare Steri Banban* (2004) N2645 [Vehicle]
- *The State v Wesley Aldu* (2004) N2640 [Club]
- *The State v Gilbert Monai* (2004) N2617 [Vehicle]
- *The State v Robin Richard Ingia* (2004) N2615 [Vehicle]
- *The State v Robson Joseph* (2004) N2613 [Store]
- *The State v Paul Maima Yogol and Dama Teiye* (2004) N2583 [Vehicle]
- *The State v Graham Chris and others* (2004) N2575 [Vehicle]
- *The State v Kalama Daniel* (2003) N2476 [Vehicle (x2), Office and Store]
- *The State v Timothy Thomas Moriloma (No. 2)* (2003) N2395 [Factory]
- *The State v Lucas Yovura* (2003) N2366 [Vehicle]
- *The State v Jamie Campbell Fereka* (2003) N2359 [Warehouse]
- *The State v Fabian Kenny* (2002) N2237 [Vehicle]
- *The State v Damien Anis* (2002) N2236 [Vehicle]
- *The State v Kenken Kindou* (2002) N2215 [Vehicle]
- *The State v Collin Amoko* (2002) N2214 [Hotel]
- *The State v Vincent Malara* (2002) N2188 [Store]
- *The State v Max Charles and others* (2002) N2187 [Hotel]
- *The State v Edward Toude and others (No. 2)* (2001) N2299 [Boat]
- *The State v Danny Pakai* (2001) N2174 [Office]
- *The State v Kevin Karoa* (2001) N2151 [Vehicle]
- *The State v James Gatana and others* (2001) N2127 [Vehicle]
- *The State v Kennedy Arus* (2001) N2081 [Vehicle]
- *The State v Gore Yogal* (2001) N2080 [Store]
- *The State v Abel Airi* (2000) N2007 [Vehicle]
- *The State v Gilbert Peter Diga* (2000) N1991 [Vehicle]

The maximum sentence for this offence is life imprisonment.

The sentences imposed have ranged from three to seventeen years imprisonment.

COMPARATIVE SENTENCES

Cases with special mitigating factors such as:

- youthfulness[1641]; and
- lack of actual participation in the robbery[1642]

attract sentences in the lower end of this range, see *The State v Wesley Aldu*[1643].

Cases with special aggravating features such as:

- robbery involving theft of substantial amount of money[1644];
- robbery of innocent and helpless persons; and
- accidental killing of a person in the course of the robbery

attract sentences in the top end of this range, see *The State v Alus Tamagi and Paija Teke*[1645], *The State v Ismael Pavo Wrakuhau (No. 2)*[1646] and *The State v Aaron Lahu*[1647] where sentences in the range of thirteen to seventeen years imprisonment were imposed.

STREET

See:

- *Alex Pori v The State* (2007) SC912, [2007] PGSC 39
- *Kennedy Kara v The State* [2006] PGSC 14
- *Dadly Henry Gorop v The State* (2003) SC732

[1641] Refer also to the section titled 'Youthfulness' in the chapter titled 'Mitigating Factors'.

[1642] Refer also to the section titled 'Role Played In The Commission Of An Offence' in the chapter titled 'Extenuating Circumstances'.

[1643] (2004) N2640.

[1644] Refer also to the section titled 'Seriousness Of An Offence Generally' in the chapter titled 'Aggravating Factors'.

[1645] (2008) N3310, [2008] PGNC 42.

[1646] (2005) N2955, [2005] PGNC 4.

[1647] (2005) N2798, [2005] PGNC 161.

COMPARATIVE SENTENCES

- *McKenzie Bonny v The State* (2003) SCRA No. 78 of 2002
- *The State v Nigel Kopper Kingsley* (2011) N4465, [2011] PGNC 187
- *The State v Desmond Gobe* (2011) N4547, [2011] PGNC 205
- *The State v Nelson Sakias* (2009) N3777, [2009] PGNC 137
- *The State v Maxon Nanguan* (2009) N3689, [2009] PGNC 82
- *The State v Andy Koko* (2009) N3615, [2009] PGNC 31
- *The State v Terence Yabok Hiafrie (No. 2)* (2008) N3366, [2008] PGNC 56
- *The State v Richard Saku and others* (2006) N3284, [2006] PGNC 162
- *The State v Vere Vanua and others* [2006] PGNC 11
- *The State v Odei Boromake* (2006) N3159, [2006] PGNC 142
- *The State v Luke Mera Yauwe; The State v David Marcus* (2006) N3158, [2006] PGNC 140
- *The State v Moses Tingin and Kennedy Kara* (2005) N2956, [2005] PGNC 5
- *The State v Cherobim Kani Peso* (2003) N2412
- *The State v Frank Suwari* (2001) N2173
- *The State v Sul Kora* (2001) N2092
- *The State v Micky John Lausi* (2001) N2073
- *The State v Billy Nawe* (2001) N2030
- *The State v John Michael Awa; The State v Eric Steven Gituthe; The State v Degemba Michael; The State v John Michael Awathe; The State v Eric Steven Gituthe; The State v Degemba Michael; The State v Harry Ewag* (2000) N2012

The maximum sentence for this offence is life imprisonment.

The sentences imposed have ranged from three to twenty years imprisonment.

Cases with special mitigating factors such as:

- youthfulness[1648]; and
- lack of actual participation in the robbery[1649]

attract sentences in the lower end of this range.

[1648] Refer also to the section titled 'Youthfulness' in the chapter titled 'Mitigating Factors'.

[1649] Refer also to the section titled 'Role Played In The Commission Of An Offence' in the chapter titled 'Extenuating Circumstances'.

COMPARATIVE SENTENCES

Cases with special aggravating features such as:

- robbery involving theft of substantial amount of money[1650]; and
- robbery of innocent and helpless persons and inflicting injuiries on them such as foreign tourists

attract sentences in the top end of this range, see *The State v Edward Toude and others (No. 2)*[1651] and *Dadly Henry Gorop v The State*[1652] where sentences of seventeen to twenty years imprisonment were imposed.

[43.2] ATTEMPTED ROBBERY[1653]

See:

- *Gibson Lulip v The State* (2000) SC636
- *The State v Raphael Walimini* (2004) N2628
- *The State v Terence Kumai (No. 2)* (2004) N2699
- *The State v Tarere Mamu* (2002) N2228
- *The State v Chris Daniel Levatoro* (1997) N1547
- *The State v Joe Rex Steven Basu* (1997) N1537

The maximum sentence for this offence is seven years, and fourteen years and life imprisonment if committed with aggravating circumstances[1654].

1650 Refer also to the section titled 'Seriousness Of An Offence Generally' in the chapter titled 'Aggravating Factors'.

1651 (2001) N2299.

1652 (2003) SC732.

1653 The law in relation to this offence is examined in the section titled 'Robbery And Attempted Robbery' in the chapter titled 'Offences Against The Person' in the text titled 'Injia on Criminal Offences in Papua New Guinea and the Pacific'.

1654 See section 387(2) and (3) of the *Criminal Code* (Ch. 262).

Refer also to:

- the section titled 'Circumstance Of Aggravation' in the chapter titled 'Aggravating Factors'; and
- the subsection titled 'Circumstances Of Aggravation' in the section titled 'Wording Of Charges' in the chapter titled 'Charges' in the text titled 'Injia on Criminal Practice and Procedure in Papua New Guinea and the Pacific'.

COMPARATIVE SENTENCES

Sentences imposed have ranged from three years to life imprisonment.

[44.0] SERIOUS ASSAULT[1655]

See:

- *The State v Martin Herman and others* (1998) N1656

The maximum sentence for this offence is three years imprisonment.

In the case cited a two years suspended sentence was imposed.

[45.0] SEXUAL OFFENCES GENERALLY

[45.1] GENERAL PRINCIPLES

The function of the criminal law in the field of sexual offences is to:

- preserve public order and decency;
- protect the citizens from what is offensive and injurious; and
- provide sufficient safeguards against exploitation and corruption of others, particularly those who are specially vulnerable because they are:
    - young;
    - weak in body or mind;
    - inexperienced; or
    - in a state of special physical, official or economic dependence.[1656]

[1655] Refer also to:

- the section titled 'Assault With Intent' in the chapter titled 'Offences Against The Person' in the text titled 'Injia on Criminal Offences in Papua New Guinea and the Pacific'; and
- the section titled 'Assault With Intent To Steal' in this chapter.

[1656] As commented by Lane LCJ in *Attorney General's Reference (No. 1 of 1989)* [1989] 3 All ER 571 at 573.

COMPARATIVE SENTENCES

Offences of a sexual nature are prevalent.[1657]

To punish accused persons by imposing very light sentence or to punish an accused person by imposing a fully suspended sentence is to seriously undermine the gravity and seriousness of sexual crimes.[1658]

Crimes of sexual violence warrant severe custodial sentences to:

- punish the accused person; and
- act as a deterrent (both personal and public).[1659]

[45.2] RAPE[1660]

[45.2.1] GENERAL PRINCIPLES

The offence of 'Rape' is a prevalent offence.[1661]

The offence of rape is always serious because it offends against humanity's standard of decency and analogous to the crime of robbery. In armed robbery cases, a robber steals from someone who helplessly watches what is going on and he or she is robbed of whatever property they may have. Likewise, in a rape case, sexual intercourse is forced upon the victim against her wish. When sex which is the intimate relationship is had without consent, there is no love.[1662]

1657 Refer also to the section titled 'Prevalence Of The Offence' in the chapter titled 'Aggravating Factors'.

1658 See *The State v Joe Leli and Philip Mato* (2011) N4527, [2011] PGNC 206.

1659 See *The State v Clarence Tema Mongi* (2011) N4364, [2011] PGNC 88.

1660 Refer also to the section titled 'Rape And Attempted Rape' in the chapter titled 'Sexual Offences' in the text titled 'Injia on Criminal Offences in Papua New Guinea and the Pacific'.

1661 Refer also to the section titled 'Prevalence Of The Offence' in the chapter titled 'Aggravating Factors'.

1662 See *The State v Sou Mesak and others* (2009) N3907, [2009] PGNC 214.

COMPARATIVE SENTENCES

Rape constitutes an invasion of privacy of the most intimate part of a woman's body. Women become objects of sex, and sex alone, to men who prey upon them and rape them. But women are, after all, human beings just like men.[1663]

It is not only a violent offence against women and girls, but it is also a serious offence against the community and the nation as it goes against the good conscience of normal law-abiding people.[1664]

Rape of a child is the most despicable act, ever. Sentences imposed by the Courts in this country have not changed the attitude of men who are determined to sexually molest or assault infants, toddlers, teenagers and adults, be it female or male.[1665]

Rape committed by more than one person or pack rape as it is known in Papua New Guinea is unthinkable and is:

- unbearable; and
- inhuman

to the victim, victim's parents and relatives.[1666]

The agony undergone by the victim is also unforgettable. It is a scar of her life time because there was never consent given by the victim of a rape.[1667]

All women:

- have rights and opportunities equal to men, as guaranteed to them under the *Constitution of the Independent State of Papua New Guinea*;
- are entitled to be respected and fairly treated; and

[1663] See *The State v Kenneth Penias* [1994] PNGLR 48; *James Mora Meaoa v The State* [1996] PNGLR 280 and *Grace Lome by Her Next Friend Jack Lome v Allan Kundi, Western Highlands Provincial Police Commander and The State* (2009) N3791.

See also: *The State v Clarence Tema Mongi* (2011) N4364, [2011] PGNC 88.

The offence of 'Rape' now also applies to males.

[1664] See *The State v Pais Steven Sow* (2004) N2588.

[1665] See *The State v Jerome Deila* (2009) N3804.

[1666] See *The State v Billy Turmur and Sou Mesak* (2011) N4349, [2011] PGNC 92.

[1667] See *The State v Billy Turmur and Sou Mesak* (2011) N4349, [2011] PGNC 92.

- have the right to travel freely alone or in groups, in any place they choose to be and at any time of the day.[1668]

Rape involves a severe degree of emotional and psychological trauma; it may be described as a violation which in fact obliterates the personality of the victim. Its psychological consequences equally are severe. Notwithstanding the actual physical harm occasioned by an act of intercourse involving violence or force and in some cases degradation, there is also the victim's:

- continuing insecurity; and
- fear of venereal diseases and pregnancy

to consider.[1669]

Rape is particularly unpleasant if it involves sexual intercourse because it involves:

- such intimate proximity between an accused person and the victim; and
- an act to which society attaches considerable value.[1670]

The prescribed penalty is a reflection of how serious the Parliament thought these crimes are. It is trite law that each case must be considered in the light of the different and peculiar circumstances under which they were committed. On this head, the Court will look at circumstances under which a crime is committed. Whether it was committed with aggravation or not and if there was what where those aggravations?[1671]

[1668] See *The State v Kenneth Penias* [1994] PNGLR 48; *James Mora Meaoa v The State* [1996] PNGLR 280 and *Grace Lome by Her Next Friend Jack Lome v Allan Kundi, Western Highlands Provincial Police Commander and The State* (2009) N3791.

See also: *The State v Clarence Tema Mongi* (2011) N4364, [2011] PGNC 88.

[1669] See *The State v Peter Kaudik* [1987] PNGLR 201 and *Grace Lome by Her Next Friend Jack Lome v Allan Kundi, Western Highlands Provincial Police Commander and The State* (2009) N3791.

[1670] See *The State v Peter Kaudik* [1987] PNGLR 201 and *Grace Lome by Her Next Friend Jack Lome v Allan Kundi, Western Highlands Provincial Police Commander and The State* (2009) N3791.

[1671] See *The State v Sou Mesak and others* (2009) N3907, [2009] PGNC 214.

COMPARATIVE SENTENCES

The sentence should reflect the society's utter revulsion at this kind of violation of females, however old and of whatever race or nationality. They have the same rights as do men in relation to their private persons.[1672]

The sentence should:

- mark the gravity of the offence;
- emphasise public disapproval;
- serve as a warning to others; and
- punish the accused person and to protect women.[1673]

The effect upon the victim, whether physical or mental, is of special seriousness.[1674]

Rape is a very serious crime warranting an immediate and strong custodial sentence.[1675]

In order to determine an appropriate sentence the factors to be considered, include:

- is the victim well over the age of 16 years?[1676];
- is the victim an old person?[1677];

[1672] See *The State v Peter Kaudik* [1987] PNGLR 201 at 207.

See also: *The State v Nick Teptep and Kindis Mis* (2004) N2612.

[1673] See *R v Roberts* [1982] 2 All ER 609.

[1674] See *Public Prosecutor v Ali August* [2000] VUSC 72.

[1675] See *Tony Mai v The State* (2008) SC903, [2008] PGSC 2; *John Aubuku v The State* [1987] PNGLR 267 and *The State v Tobby Tani* (1994) N2063.

[1676] See *The State v Jeffery Wangi* (2006) N3016, [2006] PGNC 48 and *The State v Joe Sime* [2006] PGNC 73.

[1677] See *The State v Jeffery Wangi* (2006) N3016, [2006] PGNC 48 and *The State v Joe Sime* [2006] PGNC 73.

- was the victim pregnant at the time of the offence?[1678];
- was the accused person in the company of another person or other persons?[1679];
- did the accused person at the time of, immediately before or immediately after the commission of the offence use or threaten to use a weapon?[1680];
- did the accused person at the time of, immediately before or immediately after the commission of the offence torture or cause grievous bodily harm to the victim?[1681];

[1678] This is a circumstance of aggravation, see sections 347(2) and 349A(h) of the *Criminal Code* (Ch. 262).

However, if the prosecution intends to rely on a circumstance of aggravation it should be specified in the wording of the charge, other than in relation to a previous conviction.

Refer also to:
- the section titled 'Circumstance Of Aggravation' in the chapter titled 'Aggravating Factors'; and
- the subsection titled 'Circumstances Of Aggravation' in the section titled 'Wording Of Charges' in the chapter titled 'Charges' in the text titled 'Injia on Criminal Practice and Procedure in Papua New Guinea and the Pacific'.

[1679] This is also a circumstance of aggravation, see sections 347(2) and 349A(a) of the *Criminal Code* (Ch. 262).

Refer also to the sections titled 'Member Of A Gang' and 'Leadership In A Gang' in the chapter titled 'Aggravating Factors'.

[1680] This is also a circumstance of aggravation, see sections 347(2) and 349A(b) of the *Criminal Code* (Ch. 262).

Refer also to the section titled 'Carrying, Using Or Threatening To Use A Weapon' in the chapter titled 'Aggravating Factors'.

[1681] See *The State v Jeffery Wangi* (2006) N3016, [2006] PGNC 48 and *The State v Joe Sime* [2006] PGNC 73.

This is also a circumstance of aggravation, see sections 347(2) and 349A(c) of the *Criminal Code* (Ch. 262).

Refer also to the section titled 'Viciousness Or Deliberate Intention To Harm' in the chapter titled 'Aggravating Factors'.

- did the accused person confine or restrain the victim before or after the commission of the offence?[1682];
- is the accused person a member of the same family or clan as the victim?[1683];
- did the accused person in committing the offence abuse a position of trust, authority or dependency?[1684];
- did the victim suffer from a serious physical or mental disability?;
- did the accused person suffer from HIV or AIDS?;
- did the accused person pass on a sexually transmitted disease to the victim?;
- did the accused person know that he or she was suffering from HIV or AIDS or a sexually transmitted disease?[1685];

[1682] See *The State v Jeffery Wangi* (2006) N3016, [2006] PGNC 48 and *The State v Joe Sime* [2006] PGNC 73.

This is also a circumstance of aggravation, see sections 347(2) and 349A(d) of the *Criminal Code* (Ch. 262).

[1683] See *The State v Jeffery Wangi* (2006) N3016, [2006] PGNC 48 and *The State v Joe Sime* [2006] PGNC 73.

This is also a circumstance of aggravation, see sections 347(2) and 349A(f) of the *Criminal Code* (Ch. 262).

[1684] This is also a circumstance of aggravation, see sections 347(2) and 349A(e) of the *Criminal Code* (Ch. 262).

Refer also to the section titled 'Breach Of Trust' in the chapter titled 'Aggravating Factors'.

[1685] See *The State v Jeffery Wangi* (2006) N3016, [2006] PGNC 48 and *The State v Joe Sime* [2006] PGNC 73.

This is also a circumstance of aggravation, see sections 347(2) and 349A(i) of the *Criminal Code* (Ch. 262).

- was the offence unplanned, ie., was it a spontaneous incident?[1686];
- was the victim subjected to further sexual indignities or perversions, in addition to the act of rape?[1687]; and
- did the accused person treat the victim with dignity immediately after committing the offence?[1688]

Bearing in mind the psychological trauma and the degradation she had to go through and the fear, continuing insecurity, the fear of pregnancy and contact of AIDS are serious consequences that a sentencing Court must consider.[1689]

[45.2.2] COMPARATIVE CASES

See also:

- *Paul Palma v The State* (2008) SC1214, [2008] PGSC 56
- *Robert Solomon v The State* (2007) SC871, [2007] PGSC 9
- *The State v KT (No. 2)* (2012) N4831, [2012] PGNC 154
- *The State v Michael Dulung Biket (*2012) N4789, [2012] PGNC 220
- *The State v Bibi Frank (No. 2)* (2012) N4700, [2012] PGNC 88
- *The State v Seke Kapieng* (2012) N4695, [2012] PGNC 102
- *The State v Billy Turmur and Sou Mesak* (2011) N4349, [2011] PGNC 92
- *The State v Clarence Tema Mongi* (2011) N4364, [2011] PGNC 88

1686 See *The State v Jeffery Wangi* (2006) N3016, [2006] PGNC 48 and *The State v Joe Sime* [2006] PGNC 73.

Refer also to:
- the section titled 'Pre-planning Or Pre-meditation' in the chapter titled 'Aggravating Factors; and
- the subsection titled 'Impulsiveness' in the section titled 'Motive' in the chapter titled 'Extenuating Circumstances'.

1687 See *The State v Jeffery Wangi* (2006) N3016, [2006] PGNC 48 and *The State v Joe Sime* [2006] PGNC 73.

1688 See *The State v Jeffery Wangi* (2006) N3016, [2006] PGNC 48 and *The State v Joe Sime* [2006] PGNC 73.

1689 See *The State v Sou Mesak and others* (2009) N3907, [2009] PGNC 214.

COMPARATIVE SENTENCES

- *The State v Jerry Kui* (2011) N4367, [2011] PGNC 85
- *The State v Joel Otariv* (2011) N4466, [2011] PGNC 188
- *The State v Kenneth Minja (No. 2)* (2011) N4332, [2011] PGNC 70
- *The State v Taulaola Pakai and others* (2010) N4125, [2010] PGNC 127
- *The State v Robert Yochie* (2010) N4113, [2010] PGNC 108
- *The State v Sou Mesak and others* (2009) N3907, [2009] PGNC 214
- *The State v Felix Minja* (2010) N4156, [2010] PGNC 174
- *The State v Steven Tari Nangimon Garasai* (2010) N4155, [2010] PGNC 173
- *The State v Joe Moore* (2010) N3980; [2010] PGNC 30
- *The State v David Panake* (2010) CR No. 86 of 2009
- *The State v Jerome Deila* (2009) N3804, [2009] PGNC 188
- *The State v Amos Jonathan (No. 2)* (2009) N3840
- *The State v Philip Kombo* (2009) N3816, [2009] PGNC 180
- *The State v Ludwig Camilus* (2009) N3760, [2009] PGNC 144
- *The State v Jacob Ori* (2008) N3522
- *The State v Vanabule Solomon* (2008) N3419
- *The State v Noel Kukupeu* (2008) N3414, [2008] PGNC 107
- *The State v Ludwick Jokar (No. 2)* (2008) N3362, [2008] PGNC 62
- *The State v Emmanuel George* (2008) N3358, [2008] PGNC 52
- *The State v Joe Kanau Tomitom* (2008) N3301, [2008] PGNC 26
- *The State v Ruap Gemung (No. 2)* (2007) N3136, [2007] PGNC 31
- *The State v Gene Urika* [2006] PGNC 95
- *The State v Ilam Peter* (2006) N3090, [2006] PGNC 80
- *The State v James Yali* (2006) N2989, [2006] PGNC 26
- *The State v Lucas Dabo and Alista Gele* [2006] PGNC 97
- *The State v Moses Jafisa Winga (No. 2)* (2005) N2958, [2005] PGNC 7
- *The State v Bernard Nanau Porai* (2005) N2944, [2005] PGNC 30
- *The State v Mufe Gabing* (2005) N2943
- *The State v Seyo Aroko* (2005) N2822, [2005] PGNC 130
- *The State v Komai Balal (No. 2)* (2005) N2821, [2005] PGNC 132
- *The State v Dibol Petrus Kopal* (2004) N2778
- *The State v Henry Nandiro (No. 2)* (2004) N2668
- *The State v Thomas Madi* (2004) N2625
- *The State v Nick Teptep and Kindis Mis* (2004) N2612
- *The State v Donald Angavia and others* (2004) N2590

COMPARATIVE SENTENCES

- *The State v Garry Sasoropa, John Aremeiko and Mathew Melton (No. 2)* (2004) N2569
- *The State v Junior Apen Sibu (No. 2)* (2004) N2567
- *The State v Luke Sitban (No. 2)* (2004) N2566
- *The State v Ezra Hiviki* (2004) N2548
- *The State v Eki Kondi and others* (2004) N2543
- *The State v Flotyme Sina (No. 2)* (2004) N2541

The maximum sentence for this offence is life imprisonment.

In *John Aubuku v The State*[1690] the Supreme Court set out a range of sentences for this offence. The Supreme Court suggested sentences in the range of five to fifteen years imprisonment as starting points and more where additional aggravating factors were present.

In subsequent cases the National Court and the Supreme Court in numerous cases called for heavier punishment given the prevalence of the offence.

Sentences imposed for this offence in recent years have significantly increased.

Sentences imposed for aggravated 'Rape' have ranged from five to twenty-seven years imprisonment with sentences between thirteen and eighteen years imprisonment as the median sentence.

Cases with special aggravating factors such as:

- the very young age of the victim; and
- a breach of trust[1691]

have attracted sentences in the top range (eighteen to twenty-seven years imprisonment).[1692]

1690 [1987] PNGLR 267.

1691 This is also a circumstance of aggravation, see section 347(2) of the *Criminal Code* (Ch. 262).

1692 See *The State v Philip Kombo* (2009) N3816; *The State v Ruap Gemung (No. 2)* (2007) N3136, [2007] PGNC 31; *The State v Lucas Dabo and Alista Gele* [2006] PGNC 97; *The State v Henry Nandiro (No. 2)* (2004) N2668; *The State v Garry Sasoropa, John Aremeiko and Mathew Melton (No. 2)* (2004) N2569 and *The State v Eki Kondi and others* (2004) N2543.

[45.3] ATTEMPTED RAPE[1693]

[45.3.1] GENERAL PRINCIPLES

Generally speaking, an attempt is to be punished with a lesser sentence than that for the completed offence, but there may be some circumstances in which an attempt will be more severely punished.[1694] Furthermore, there may be circumstances when an attempt is almost as serious as the complete rape would be.[1695]

In order to determine an appropriate sentence the factors to be considered, include:

- is the victim well over the age of 16 years?;
- is the victim an old person?;
- was the attempted act not completed due to the accused person's actions?[1696];
- did the accused person cause a physical injury to the victim?[1697];
- did the accused person pass on a sexually transmitted disease to the victim?[1698];

1693 Refer also to the section titled 'Rape And Attempted Rape' in the chapter titled 'Sexual Offences' in the text titled 'Injia on Criminal Offences in Papua New Guinea and the Pacific'.

1694 See *Koraua and Kaitira v R* [1988-1989] SILR 4 at 5.

1695 See *Koraua and Kaitira v R* [1988-1989] SILR 4 at 5.

1696 See *The State v Pascal Maya Omi* (2005) N2808, [2005] PGNC 151 and *The State v John Erip Muge* [2006] PGNC 69.

1697 See *The State v Pascal Maya Omi* (2005) N2808, [2005] PGNC 151 and *The State v John Erip Muge* [2006] PGNC 69.

Refer also to the section titled 'Viciousness Or Deliberate Intention To Harm' in the chapter titled 'Aggravating Factors'.

1698 See *The State v Pascal Maya Omi* (2005) N2808, [2005] PGNC 151 and *The State v John Erip Muge* [2006] PGNC 69.

- was it an isolated incident?[1699];
- was the offence unplanned, ie., was it a spontaneous incident?[1700];
- was the victim subjected to further sexual indignities or perversions, in addition to the act of attempted rape?;
- did the accused person suffer from HIV or AIDS?; and
- did the accused person treat the victim with dignity immediately after committing the offence?

Furthermore, the following factors are circumstances of aggravation[1701], and therefore should be considered:

[1699] See *The State v Pascal Maya Omi* (2005) N2808, [2005] PGNC 151 and *The State v John Erip Muge* [2006] PGNC 69.

[1700] See *The State v Jeffery Wangi* (2006) N3016, [2006] PGNC 48 and *The State v Joe Sime* [2006] PGNC 73.

Refer also to:
- the section titled 'Pre-planning Or Pre-meditation' in the chapter titled 'Aggravating Factors; and
- the subsection titled 'Impulsiveness' in the section titled 'Motive' in the chapter titled 'Extenuating Circumstances'.

[1701] See section 349A of the *Criminal Code* (Ch. 262).

However, if the prosecution intends to rely on a circumstance of aggravation it should be specified in the wording of the charge, other than in relation to a previous conviction.

It should however be noted that section 348 of the *Criminal Code* (Ch. 262) does not provide for an increased maximum penalty as a consequence of the offence being committed with a circumstance of aggravation.

Refer also to:
- the section titled 'Circumstance Of Aggravation' in the chapter titled 'Aggravating Factors'; and
- the subsection titled 'Circumstances Of Aggravation' in the section titled 'Wording Of Charges' in the chapter titled 'Charges' in the text titled 'Injia on Criminal Practice and Procedure in Papua New Guinea and the Pacific'.

- was the accused person in the company of another person or other persons?[1702];

- did the accused person at the time of, immediately before or immediately after the commission of the offence use or threaten to use a weapon?[1703];

- did the accused person confine or restrain the victim before or after the commission of the offence?;

- is the accused person a member of the same family or clan as the victim?;

- did the accused person in committing the offence abuse a position of trust, authority or dependency?[1704];

- did the victim suffer from a serious physical or mental disability?;

- was the victim pregnant at the time of the offence?; and

- did the accused person know that he or she was suffering from HIV or AID?

[45.3.2] COMPARATIVE CASES

See:

- *Daniel Kemi Mebil v The State* (2004) SC749, [2004] PGSC 24
- *Ruddy Yekat v The State* [2000] PNGLR 225, (2000) SC665
- *The State v Martin Bruno* (2008) N3461
- *The State v Israel Kout* (2008) N3413, [2008] PGNC 106
- *The State v John Erip Muge* [2006] PGNC 69
- *The State v John Seregat* (2007) N3266, [2007] PGNC 133

[1702] This is also a circumstance of aggravation, see sections 347(2) and 349A(a) of the *Criminal Code* (Ch. 262).

Refer also to the sections titled 'Member Of A Gang' and 'Leadership In A Gang' in the chapter titled 'Aggravating Factors'.

[1703] Refer also to the section titled 'Carrying, Using Or Threatening To Use A Weapon' in the chapter titled 'Aggravating Factors'.

[1704] Refer also to the section titled 'Breach Of Trust' in the chapter titled 'Aggravating Factors'.

- *The State v Kakou Pilai* (2005) N2945, [2005] PGNC 31
- *The State v Pascal Maya Omi* (2005) N2808, [2005] PGNC 151
- *The State v Julius Ombi (No. 2)* (2004) N2552
- *The State v Otto Paulus* (2002) N2241
- *The State v Otom Masa* (2000) N2021

The maximum sentence for this offence is fourteen years imprisonment.

Sentences imposed have ranged from one to nine years imprisonment.

[45.4] SEXUAL ASSAULT[1705]

[45.4.1] GENERAL PRINCIPLES

In order to determine an appropriate sentence the factors to be considered, include:

- is the victim well over the age of 16 years?;
- is the victim an old person?;
- did the sexual assault progress further due to the accused person's actions?[1706];
- did the accused person cause a physical injury to the victim?[1707];
- was the offence unplanned, ie., was it a spontaneous incident?[1708];

[1705] Refer also to the section titled 'Sexual Assault' in the chapter titled 'Sexual Offences' in the text titled 'Injia on Criminal Offences in Papua New Guinea and the Pacific'.

[1706] See *The State v Mark Samuel Haupas* (2007) N3186, [2007] PGNC 81.

[1707] Refer also to the section titled 'Viciousness Or Deliberate Intention To Harm' in the chapter titled 'Aggravating Factors'.

[1708] See *The State v Jeffery Wangi* (2006) N3016, [2006] PGNC 48 and *The State v Joe Sime* [2006] PGNC 73.

Refer also to:

- the section titled 'Pre-planning Or Pre-meditation' in the chapter titled 'Aggravating Factors; and
- the subsection titled 'Impulsiveness' in the section titled 'Motive' in the chapter titled 'Extenuating Circumstances'.

- was the victim subjected to further sexual indignities or perversions, in addition to the act of sexual assault?;
- did the accused person suffer from HIV or AIDS?;
- was it an isolated incident?[1709];
- did the accused person treat the victim with dignity immediately after committing the offence?; and
- did the accused person pass on a sexually transmitted disease to the victim?[1710];

The following factors are circumstances of aggravation[1711], and therefore such factors should be considered:

- was the accused person in the company of another person or other persons?[1712];

[1709] See *The State v Mark Samuel Haupas* (2007) N3186, [2007] PGNC 81.

[1710] See *The State v Mark Samuel Haupas* (2007) N3186, [2007] PGNC 81.

The passing on of a sexually transmitted disease is a circumstance of aggravation, see sections 349(4) and 349A(a) of the *Criminal Code* (Ch. 262).

However, if the prosecution intends to rely on a circumstance of aggravation it should be specified in the wording of the charge, other than in relation to a previous conviction.

Refer also to:
- the section titled 'Circumstance Of Aggravation' in the chapter titled 'Aggravating Factors'; and
- the subsection titled 'Circumstances Of Aggravation' in the section titled 'Wording Of Charges' in the chapter titled 'Charges' in the text titled 'Injia on Criminal Practice and Procedure in Papua New Guinea and the Pacific'.

[1711] See sections 349(4) and 349A of the *Criminal Code* (Ch. 262).

[1712] This is also a circumstance of aggravation, see sections 347(2) and 349A(a) of the *Criminal Code* (Ch. 262).

Refer also to the sections titled 'Member Of A Gang' and 'Leadership In A Gang' in the chapter titled 'Aggravating Factors'.

- did the accused person at the time of, immediately before or immediately after the commission of the offence use or threaten to use a weapon?[1713];

- did the accused person at the time of, immediately before or immediately after the commission of the offence torture or cause grievous bodily harm?;

- did the accused person confine or restrain the victim before or after the commission of the offence?;

- is the accused person a member of the same family or clan as the victim?;

- did the accused person in committing the offence abuse a position of trust, authority or dependency?[1714];

- did the victim suffer from a serious physical or mental disability?;

- was the victim pregnant at the time of the offence?; and

- did the accused person know that he or she was suffering from HIV or AIDS?

[45.4.2] COMPARATIVE CASES

See:

- *The State v Joe Leli and Philip Mato* (2011) N4527, [2011] PGNC 206
- *The State v Marcus Yame* (2010) N4131, [2010] PGNC 161
- *The State v Hilary Laris* (2009) N3724, [2009] PGNC 104
- *The State v Ima Esiko* (2009) N3607, [2009] PGNC 54
- *The State v Mark Samuel Haupas* (2007) N3186, [2007] PGNC 81

The maximum sentence for this offence is five years imprisonment without a circumstances of aggravation.

[1713] This is also a circumstance of aggravation, see sections 347(2) and 349A(b) of the *Criminal Code* (Ch. 262).

Refer also to the section titled 'Carrying, Using Or Threatening To Use A Weapon' in the chapter titled 'Aggravating Factors'.

[1714] Refer also to the section titled 'Breach Of Trust' in the chapter titled 'Aggravating Factors'.

COMPARATIVE SENTENCES

If this offence is committed with a circumstance of aggravation the maximum penalty is ten years imprisonment.

Sentences imposed have ranged from one to nine years imprisonment.

[45.5] INCEST[1715]

[45.5.1] GENERAL PRINCIPLES

The offence of 'Incest' is a prevalent offence.[1716]

There is a diversity of considerations (religious, moral, eugenic, psychological and physical) that should be taken into account in assessing the nature of a particular incestuous relationship for the purpose of punishment.[1717]

An incestuous act or relationship adversely impacts the family.[1718]

The crime of incest is evil.[1719]

Incest is an offence even between willing participants. The main reason for this prohibition, apart from scientific reasons, is to maintain the security, love, respect, honour, trust, happiness, peace and joy of the family unit and blood relations for a better and stronger family, community and a nation.[1720]

An incestuous act with a child is an aggravating factor of the most severe kind. When young girls are the victims, it is difficult to imagine that such girls will not be scarred emotionally, perhaps for life.[1721]

[1715] Refer also to the section titled 'Incest' in the chapter titled 'Sexual Offences' in the text titled 'Injia on Criminal Offences in Papua New Guinea and the Pacific'.

[1716] Refer also to the section titled 'Prevalence Of The Offence' in the chapter titled 'Aggravating Factors'.

[1717] See *R v J* (1982-1983) 45 ALR 331 and *R v Scc* [1989] ACTSC 53.

[1718] See *The State v James Donald Keimou* (2001) N2295 and *The State v Samuel Kawar* (2011) N4234, [2011] PGNC 22.

[1719] See *The State v Waninara Judas Liligau* (2007) N3195, [2007] PGNC 87.

[1720] See *The State v Donald Keimou* (2001) N2295.

[1721] See *The State v Mitige Neheya* [1988-89] PNGLR 174 at 177.

There is no doubt that the offence of 'Incest':

- destroys:
    - trust; and
    - the security of the home; and
- leaves for ever:
    - lifetime scars for the victim; and
    - a bad stigma for the victim and his or her family and relations.[1722]

Love gets replaced by hate and trust with distrust. Insecurity replaces security and fear replaces confidence in the family unit and the immediate community. Happiness, peace and joy are replaced with shame, ridicule and unhappiness in the family unit and in the wider community. If the victim gets infected with a sexually transmitted disease his or her health is replaced by sickness.[1723]

Incest is a violation of the most fundamental principle of the 'sacred trust' that a child has in his or her father or mother.[1724] The offence infringes and violates the fundamental duty of the father and mother to:

- care for their children; and
- rear them up in the manner expected by the *Constitution of the Independent State of Papua New Guinea* and the law.[1725]

[1722] See *The State v James Donald Keimou* (2001) N2295 and *The State v Samuel Kawar* (2011) N4234, [2011] PGNC 22.

[1723] See *The State v James Donald Keimou* (2001) N2295 and *The State v Samuel Kawar* (2011) N4234, [2011] PGNC 22.

[1724] See *Mitige Neheye v The State; Martin Gawi v The State* [1994] PNGLR 71, [1994] PGSC 13.

[1725] See *The State v Waninara Judas Liligau* (2007) N3195, [2007] PGNC 87.

That breach of trust is:

- a betrayal of the most severe kind; and
- a form of 'personal treason'.[1726]

In order to determine an appropriate sentence the factors to be considered, include[1727]:

- the relationship of the parties;
- whether force, threats or intimidation were involved and, if so, the degree of such force, threats or intimidation[1728];
- whether it was consensual between adults[1729];
- the number of times;
- over what period of time the incidents occurred (if more than one)[1730];
- whether pregnancy ensued by reason of the accused person failing to take contraceptive measures; and
- the comparative ages.

1726 See *The State v Sottie Apusa* [1988-89] PNGLR 172.

1727 See *The State v Mitige Neheya* [1988-89] PNGLR 174 at 177 and *The State v Tikiria Amos* (2004) N2614.

1728 Refer also to the section titled 'Carrying, Using Or Threatening To Use A Weapon' in the chapter titled 'Aggravating Factors'.

1729 If there was no consent then a charge of 'Rape', as provided for by section 347 of the *Criminal Code* (Ch. 262), should also be preferred.

1730 See *Mitige Neheye v The State; Martin Gawi v The State* [1994] PNGLR 71, [1994] PGSC 13 and *The State v Tikiria Amos* (2004) N2614.

Refer also to the section titled 'Duration Of An Offence' in the chapter titled 'Aggravated Factors'.

COMPARATIVE SENTENCES

The following are additional factors that should be considered[1731]:

- is there a small age difference between the accused person and the victim?;
- was the victim of a mature age at the time of the offence?;
- what was the form of penetration, other than penile penetration?;
- did the accused person cause a physical injury to the victim?[1732]; and
- did the accused person pass on a sexually transmitted disease to the victim?

The following are other aggravating factors, regardless of age of the victim, to consider[1733]:

- has the victim suffered physically or psychologically from the offence?[1734];
- was the offence accompanied by perversions abhorrent to the victim?; and
- has the accused person committed similar offences against more than one girl?

If the act of incest is committed without consent or by force then it is appropriate to apply the tariff for the offence of 'Rape'.[1735]

[45.5.2] COMPARATIVE CASES

See also:

- *Dori Inara v The State* (2002) SC688, [2002] PGSC 6 [father and daughter]
- *Grayson Andowa v The State* (1998) SC576, [1998] PGSC 33 [father and daughter]

1731 See *The State v Raphael Torona* (2007) CR No. 875 of 2007.

1732 Refer also to the section titled 'Viciousness Or Deliberate Intention To Harm' in the chapter titled 'Aggravating Factors'.

1733 See *Mitige Neheye v The State; Martin Gawi v The State* [1994] PNGLR 71, [1994] PGSC 13 and *The State v Tikiria Amos* (2004) N2614.

1734 See also: *The State v Raphael Torona* (2007) CR No. 875 of 2007.

1735 See *Mitige Neheye v The State; Martin Gawi v The State* [1994] PNGLR 71, [1994] PGSC 13.

COMPARATIVE SENTENCES

- *Joel Samson v The State* (1998) SC575, [1998] PGSC 34 [brother and sister]
- *The State v Willie Mas Sangep* (2012) N4684, [2012] PGNC 70 [uncle and niece]
- *The State v Jackson Yaul* (2011) N330, [2011] PGNC 66 [father and daughter]
- *The State v Samuel Kawar* (2011) N4234, [2011] PGNC 22 [father and daughter]
- *The State v Junias Tolom and Dorish Voa* (2009) N3620 [uncle and niece]
- *The State v Nicholas Issam* (2008) N3418 [father and daughter]
- *The State v Tom Feri* (2008) N3305, [2008] PGNC 30 [father and daughter]
- *The State v Henry Matatenge* (2007) N3218, [2007] PGNC 59 [father and daughter]
- *The State v Marcus Pitmete* (2007) N3229, [2007] PGNC 105 [father and daughter]
- *The State v Peter Mandari* (2007) CR No. 872 of 2007 [father and daughter]
- *The State v Waninara Judas Liligau* (2007) N3195, [2007] PGNC 87 [father and daughter]
- *The State v Raphael Torona* (2007) CR No. 875 of 2007 [father and daughter]
- *The State v Sevi Kwetok* (2006) N3389, [2006] PGNC 167 [cousin brother and cousin sister]
- *The State v Michael Siwiri* (2006) N3382, [2006] PGNC 172 [uncle and neice]
- *The State v Gidingeng Yaking (No. 2)* [2006] PGNC 98 [father and daughter]
- *The State v Tewa Kolwin Towin* (2006) N3053, [2006] PGNC 52 [father and daughter]
- *The State v Michael Saitus* (2004) N2705 [father and daugther]
- *The State v Tikiria Amos* (2005) N2614 [father and daughter]
- *The State v Francis Angosiwen (No. 2)* (2004) N2670 [father and daughter]

The maximum sentence for this offence is seven years imprisonment.

Sentences imposed have ranged from three to seven years imprisonment.

The Courts have treated the offence of 'Incest' seriously and in many cases have recommended that the maximum sentence be increased.

In a number of cases, the Courts have imposed a punishment close to or the maximum sentence.[1736]

[1736] See *The State v Mitige Neheya* [1988-89] PNGLR 174 at 177; *Grayson Andowa v The State* (1998) SC576, [1998] PGSC 33; *The State v Michael Siwiri* (2006) N3382, [2006] PGNC 172; *The State v Gidingeng Yaking (No. 2)* [2006] PGNC 98; *The State v Henry Matatenge* (2007) N3218, [2007] PGNC 59; *The State v Tewa Kolwin Towin* (2006) N3053, [2006] PGNC 52 and *The State v Francis Angosiwen (No. 2)* (2004) N2670.

[45.6] UNNATURAL OFFENCE

See:

- *The State v John Kinaliu* (2006) N3025, [2006] PGNC 44

The maximum sentence for this offence is fourteen years imprisonment.

In the case cited three years imprisonment was imposed.

[45.7] SEXUAL PENETRATION AGAINST THE ORDER OF NATURE

See:

- *The State v Ron Suma* (2012) 4622, [2012] PGNC 27
- *The State v Siaro Unde* [1999] PNGLR 24, [1999] PGNC 164

The maximum sentence for this offence is fourteen years imprisonment.

In the case cited six months imprisonment was imposed.

[45.8] ATTEMPTED SEXUAL PENETRATION AGAINST THE ORDER OF NATURE

See:

- *The State v Pius Menhun* (2008) N3415

The maximum sentence for this offence is seven years imprisonment.

Sentences imposed have been in the vicinity of five years imprisonment.

[46.0] SEXUAL OFFENCES AGAINST CHILDREN[1737]

[46.1] INTRODUCTION[1738]

Children are not born out of holes in the trees or from stone holes or caves so that they can be treated the way perpetrators of sexual abuse treat them. They are born from human beings and rightly deserve to be treated with care and all human courtesy due to them just like adult human beings. They have all the basic right to the protection of the law enshrined in the *Constitution*.[1739]

The People of Papua New Guinea decided through their duly elected representatives in the National Parliament to change the law and express their abhorrence to sexual offences committed against children. The People of Papua New Guinea have indicated that they will not tolerate children being abused, particularly by those in a position of trust. This is in recognition of the central role that children play in all societies and cultures in Papua New Guinea. In Papua New Guinea children are treated like kings and queens. They are the future of Papua New Guinea and the People depend on them and their upbringing.[1740]

Today's children are the country's future leaders of tomorrow.[1741]

Parliament considers that sexual exploitation and abuse of young children are very serious offences.[1742]

1737 Refer also to the section titled 'Sexual Offences Involving Children' in the chapter titled 'Sexual Offences' in the text titled 'Injia on Criminal Offences in Papua New Guinea and the Pacific'.

1738 As regards general comments on the sentencing of paedophiles, see *Ryan v R* (2001) 206 CLR 267, (2001) 75 ALJR 815, (2001) 179 ALR 193, [2001] HCA 21, per McHugh J.

1739 See *The State v Thomas Tukaliu* (2006) N3026.

1740 See *The State v Paul Nelson* (2005) N2844, [2005] PGNC 113 and *The State v Pennias Mokei (No. 2)* (2004) N2635.

1741 See *The State v Brady Meki* (2006) N3391, [2006] PGNC 169.

1742 See *The State v Damien Mangawi* (2003) N2419.

COMPARATIVE SENTENCES

Parliament passed the *Criminal Code (Sexual Offences and Crimes Against Children) Act 2002* amidst growing concerns over the need to protect women, girls and young children in our country. Parliament then was of the view that this category of our population were rather defenceless[1743] and more prone and vulnerable to sexual exploitation and sexual abuse at the whims and desires of sexual predators such as the prisoner here. Furthermore, it was concerned that penalties being imposed on offenders by the courts were rather too lenient. It wanted the Courts to impose heavier penalties upon offenders who prey upon defenceless females and commit various sexual crimes upon women and children. Parliament has now confirmed just how serious it is to abuse a position of trust, authority or dependency.[1744]

Modern medicine and science confirm that, whatever happens to a person's earlier life, remains long in their memories. Even though there might be no evidence of any physical harm, numerous sexual and other violent offence cases clearly show that victims of such offences continue to suffer ongoing psychological problems.[1745]

In countries like Australia and elsewhere, there are readily available appropriate medical services to assist victims to overcome such problems. But the situation is not the same in Papua New Guinea. Such specialist medical services are almost non-existent. This means, victims of such offences in Papua New Guinea are left with no assistance at all. Therefore, the need to protect young children is far more urgent and important than it is the case in other countries.[1746]

Pedophiles must be appropriately punished.[1747]

The Courts and especially the National Court being the trial Court is given an enormous responsibility to ensure that:

- child abuse and exploitation is eliminated; and
- children are protected from predators.[1748]

[1743] See *The State v Brady Meki* (2006) N3391, [2006] PGNC 169.

[1744] See *The State v Esorom Asupa* (2011) N4540, [2011] PGNC 197.

[1745] See *The State v Peter Yawoma* (2001) N2032.

[1746] See *The State v Brady Meki* (2006) N3391, [2006] PGNC 169.

[1747] See *The State v Isaac Kuila (No. 2)* (2009) N3736, [2009] PGNC 110 and *The State v Simam July Melly (No. 2)* (2009) N3779, [2009] PGNC 138.

[1748] See *The State v Simam July Melly (No. 2)* (2009) N3779, [2009] PGNC 138.

This means that perpetrators of these offences must be severely punished so that a strong message is sent out to the community that the Court will do everything within its power to punish those committing these offences against children. Furthermore, it will be a lesson to the perpetrators so that they too will change their way of behaving and thinking.[1749]

Sentences must involve recognition of:

- the kind of personal damage that is occasioned by sexual abuse of children; and
- the reality that the rehabilitation of the victim may be far more difficult to accomplish than that of the perpetrator.[1750]

The Courts must, in order to protect future possible victims against such damage, endeavour to deter those who may be so inclined from engaging in such activities.[1751]

The primary sentencing considerations for these offences are:

- punishment of the accused person, specific and general deterrence[1752]; and
- the protection of vulnerable children.[1753]

Offences involving the penetration of a young child in circumstances involving an abuse of trust are so serious that less weight should be given to mitigating factors and extenuating circumstances than would otherwise have been the case.[1754]

1749 See *The State v Simam July Melly (No. 2)* (2009) N3779, [2009] PGNC 138.

1750 See *DPP v DJK* [2003] VSCA 109.

1751 See *DPP v DJK* [2003] VSCA 109.

1752 Refer also to the section titled 'The Need For Deterrence' in the chapter titled 'Objectives And Purposes Of Sentencing'.

1753 See *Woods v R* (1994) 14 WAR 341 at 345-346; *PP v The State of Western Australia* [2004] WASCA 144 and *M v The State of Western Australia* [2006] WASCA 256.

1754 See *R v Leggett* [2000] WASCA 327 and *State of Western Australia v Rock* [2007] WASCA 121.

COMPARATIVE SENTENCES

The younger the child, the more serious the offence.[1755]

In order to determine an appropriate sentence the factors to be considered, include:

- what was the age difference between the accused person and the victim?[1756];
- was there consent?[1757];
- did the accused person use a threatening weapon?[1758];
- did the accused person use aggravated physical violence?[1759];
- did the accused person pass on a sexually transmitted disease to the victim?[1760];
- was it an isolated incident?[1761];

[1755] See *The State v Pennias Mokei (No. 2)* (2004) N2635.

See also: *R v T* (1990) 47 A Crim R 29; *R v AJP* (2004) 150 A Crim R 575, [2004] NSWCCA 434; *Shannon v R* [2006] NSWCCA 39; *MLP v R* (2006) 164 A Crim R 93, [2006] NSWCCA 271; *FV v R* [2006] NSWCCA 237 and *R v PGM* (2008) 187 A Crim R 152, [2008] NSWCCA 172.

[1756] See *Sabiu v The State* (2007) SC866, [2007] PGSC 24; *The State v Titus Soumi* (2005) N2809, [2005] PGNC 150 and *The State v John Ritsi Kutetoa* (2005) N2814, [2005] PGNC 137.

Refer also to the section titled 'Age Difference' in the chapter titled 'Aggravating Factors'.

[1757] See *Sabiu v The State* (2007) SC866, [2007] PGSC 24; *The State v Titus Soumi* (2005) N2809, [2005] PGNC 150 and *The State v John Ritsi Kutetoa* (2005) N2814, [2005] PGNC 137.

[1758] See *Sabiu v The State* (2007) SC866, [2007] PGSC 24; *The State v Titus Soumi* (2005) N2809, [2005] PGNC 150 and *The State v John Ritsi Kutetoa* (2005) N2814, [2005] PGNC 137.

Refer also to the section titled 'Carrying, Using Or Threatening To Use A Weapon' in the chapter titled 'Aggravating Factors'.

[1759] See *Sabiu v The State* (2007) SC866, [2007] PGSC 24; *The State v Titus Soumi* (2005) N2809, [2005] PGNC 150 and *The State v John Ritsi Kutetoa* (2005) N2814, [2005] PGNC 137.

[1760] See *Sabiu v The State* (2007) SC866, [2007] PGSC 24; *The State v Titus Soumi* (2005) N2809, [2005] PGNC 150 and *The State v John Ritsi Kutetoa* (2005) N2814, [2005] PGNC 137.

[1761] See *Sabiu v The State* (2007) SC866, [2007] PGSC 24; *The State v Titus Soumi* (2005) N2809, [2005] PGNC 150 and *The State v John Ritsi Kutetoa* (2005) N2814, [2005] PGNC 137.

- was the victim far under the age of 16 years?[1762];
- did the accused person cause a physical injury to the victim?[1763];
- has the accused person caused further trouble to the victim or the victim's family since the incident?[1764]; and
- was there an existing relationship of trust, authority or dependency between the accused person and the child?[1765]

[1762] See *Sabiu v The State* (2007) SC866, [2007] PGSC 24; *The State v Titus Soumi* (2005) N2809, [2005] PGNC 150 and *The State v John Ritsi Kutetoa* (2005) N2814, [2005] PGNC 137.

By virtue of sections 229A(2), 229B(4) and 229C(2) of the *Criminal Code* (Ch. 262), if the age of the child was under the age of 12 years then the prosecution should allege a circumstance of aggravation in the wording of the charge.

Refer also to:
- the section titled 'Circumstance Of Aggravation' in the chapter titled 'Aggravating Factors'; and
- the subsection titled 'Circumstances Of Aggravation' in the section titled 'Wording Of Charges' in the chapter titled 'Charges' in the text titled 'Injia on Criminal Practice and Procedure in Papua New Guinea and the Pacific'.

[1763] See *Sabiu v The State* (2007) SC866, [2007] PGSC 24; *The State v Titus Soumi* (2005) N2809, [2005] PGNC 150 and *The State v John Ritsi Kutetoa* (2005) N2814, [2005] PGNC 137.

Refer also to the section titled 'Viciousness Or Deliberate Intent To Harm' in the chapter titled 'Aggravating Factors.

[1764] See *Sabiu v The State* (2007) SC866, [2007] PGSC 24; *The State v Titus Soumi* (2005) N2809, [2005] PGNC 150 and *The State v John Ritsi Kutetoa* (2005) N2814, [2005] PGNC 137.

[1765] By virtue of sections 229A(3), 229B(5) and 229C(3) of the *Criminal Code* (Ch. 262), if the age of the child was under the age of 12 years then the prosecution should allege a circumstance of aggravation in the charge.

Refer also to:
- the section titled 'Circumstance Of Aggravation' in the chapter titled 'Aggravating Factors'; and
- the subsection titled 'Circumstances Of Aggravation' in the section titled 'Wording Of Charges' in the chapter titled 'Charges' in the text titled 'Injia on Criminal Practice and Procedure in Papua New Guinea and the Pacific'.

Refer also to the section titled 'Abuse Of Trust' in the chapter titled 'Aggravating Factors'.

[46.2] SEXUAL PENETRATION OF A CHILD

[46.2.1] GENERAL PRINCIPLES

In 2002, the elected representatives in the National Parliament in their wisdom made substantial amendments to the *Criminal Code* (Ch. 262) with a view to protecting the children of this country against sexual exploitation and abuse. Under section 229A of the *Criminal Code* (Ch. 262), a person who sexually penetrates a child under the age of twelve (12) years commits a crime and the maximum penalty for the crime is life imprisonment. This clearly shows the intention of Parliament that the court treats sexual exploitation and abuse of children, the most vulnerable members of the society, seriously. The Court is required to take into account the underlying purpose of the legislation in sentencing.[1766]

The offence of 'Sexual Penetration of a Child' is a prevalent offence.[1767]

In order to determine an appropriate sentence the factors to be considered, include:

- what was the age difference between the accused person and the victim?[1768];
- was the victim far under the age of 16 years?[1769];
- was there consent?[1770];
- what was the form of penetration, other than penile penetration?[1771];

[1766] See *The State v Oj Pohangat Palou* (2010) N4666, [2010] PGNC 215.

[1767] Refer also to the section titled 'Prevalence Of The Offence' in the chapter titled 'Aggravating Factors'.

[1768] See *The State v Sawan Raumo* (2007) CR No. 876 of 2007.

Refer also to the section titled 'Age Difference' in the chapter titled 'Aggravating Factors'.

[1769] See *Stanley Sabiu v The State* (2007) SC866, [2007] PGSC 24; *The State v Biason Benson Samson* (2005) N2799; *The State v Pennias Mokei (No. 2)* (2004) N2635; *The State v Ndrakum Pu-Uh* (2005) N2949; *The State v Luke Toyana Gisigesi and Joseph Mwaisiga* (2010) N4124, [2010] PGNC 126 and *The State v Sawan Raumo* (2007) CR No. 876 of 2007.

[1770] See *Stanley Sabiu v The State* (2007) SC866, [2007] PGSC 24; *The State v Biason Benson Samson* (2005) N2799; *The State v Pennias Mokei (No. 2)* (2004) N2635; *The State v Ndrakum Pu-Uh* (2005) N2949; *The State v Luke Toyana Gisigesi and Joseph Mwaisiga* (2010) N4124, [2010] PGNC 126 and *The State v Sawan Raumo* (2007) CR No. 876 of 2007.

[1771] See *The State v Sawan Raumo* (2007) CR No. 876 of 2007.

- did the accused person use a threatening weapon?[1772];
- did the accused person use aggravated physical violence?[1773];
- did the accused person cause a physical injury to the victim?[1774];
- did the accused person pass on a sexually transmitted disease to the victim?[1775];
- what was the degree of impact on the victim?[1776];

[1772] See *Stanley Sabiu v The State* (2007) SC866, [2007] PGSC 24; *The State v Biason Benson Samson* (2005) N2799; *The State v Pennias Mokei (No. 2)* (2004) N2635; *The State v Ndrakum Pu-Uh* (2005) N2949; *The State v Titus Soumi* (2005) N2809, [2005] PGNC 150; *The State v John Ritsi Kutetoa* (2005) N2814, [2005] PGNC 137; *The State v Luke Toyana Gisigesi and Joseph Mwaisiga* (2010) N4124, [2010] PGNC 126 and *The State v Sawan Raumo* (2007) CR No. 876 of 2007.

Refer also to the section titled 'Carrying, Using Or Threatening To Use A Weapon' in the chapter titled 'Aggravating Factors'.

[1773] See *Stanley Sabiu v The State* (2007) SC866, [2007] PGSC 24; *The State v Biason Benson Samson* (2005) N2799; *The State v Pennias Mokei (No. 2)* (2004) N2635; *The State v Ndrakum Pu-Uh* (2005) N2949; *The State v Luke Toyana Gisigesi and Joseph Mwaisiga* (2010) N4124, [2010] PGNC 126 and *The State v Sawan Raumo* (2007) CR No. 876 of 2007.

[1774] See *Stanley Sabiu v The State* (2007) SC866, [2007] PGSC 24; *The State v Biason Benson Samson* (2005) N2799; *The State v Pennias Mokei (No. 2)* (2004) N2635; *The State v Ndrakum Pu-Uh* (2005) N2949; *The State v Titus Soumi* (2005) N2809, [2005] PGNC 150; *The State v John Ritsi Kutetoa* (2005) N2814, [2005] PGNC 137; *The State v Luke Toyana Gisigesi and Joseph Mwaisiga* (2010) N4124, [2010] PGNC 126 and *The State v Sawan Raumo* (2007) CR No. 876 of 2007.

Refer also to the section titled 'Viciousness Or Deliberate Intent To Harm' in the chapter titled 'Aggravating Factors.

[1775] See *Stanley Sabiu v The State* (2007) SC866, [2007] PGSC 24; *The State v Biason Benson Samson* (2005) N2799; *The State v Pennias Mokei (No. 2)* (2004) N2635; *The State v Ndrakum Pu-Uh* (2005) N2949; *The State v Luke Toyana Gisigesi and Joseph Mwaisiga* (2010) N4124, [2010] PGNC 126 and *The State v Sawan Raumo* (2007) CR No. 876 of 2007.

[1776] See *The State v Sawan Raumo* (2007) CR No. 876 of 2007.

- was it an isolated incident?[1777];
- has the accused person caused further trouble to the victim or the victim's family since the incident?[1778];
- is there a small age difference between the accused person and the victim?[1779];
- was there one offender?[1780];

1777 See *Stanley Sabiu v The State* (2007) SC866, [2007] PGSC 24; *The State v Biason Benson Samson* (2005) N2799; *The State v Pennias Mokei (No. 2)* (2004) N2635; *The State v Ndrakum Pu-Uh* (2005) N2949; *The State v Luke Toyana Gisigesi and Joseph Mwaisiga* (2010) N4124, [2010] PGNC 126 and *The State v Sawan Raumo* (2007) CR No. 876 of 2007.

Refer also to subsection titled 'Impulsiveness' in the section titled 'Motive' in the chapter titled 'Extenuating Circumstances'.

1778 See *Stanley Sabiu v The State* (2007) SC866, [2007] PGSC 24; *The State v Biason Benson Samson* (2005) N2799; *The State v Pennias Mokei (No. 2)* (2004) N2635; *The State v Ndrakum Pu-Uh* (2005) N2949; *The State v Luke Toyana Gisigesi and Joseph Mwaisiga* (2010) N4124, [2010] PGNC 126 and *The State v Sawan Raumo* (2007) CR No. 876 of 2007.

1779 See *Stanley Sabiu v The State* (2007) SC866, [2007] PGSC 24; *The State v Biason Benson Samson* (2005) N2799; *The State v Pennias Mokei (No. 2)* (2004) N2635; *The State v Ndrakum Pu-Uh* (2005) N2949; *The State v Luke Toyana Gisigesi and Joseph Mwaisiga* (2010) N4124, [2010] PGNC 126 and *The State v Arthur Tangi (No. 3)* (2012) N5075, [2012] PGNC 280.

Refer also to the section titled 'Age Difference' in the chapter titled 'Aggravating Factors'.

1780 See *Stanley Sabiu v The State* (2007) SC866, [2007] PGSC 24; *The State v Biason Benson Samson* (2005) N2799; *The State v Pennias Mokei (No. 2)* (2004) N2635; *The State v Ndrakum Pu-Uh* (2005) N2949; *The State v Luke Toyana Gisigesi and Joseph Mwaisiga* (2010) N4124, [2010] PGNC 126 and *The State v Arthur Tangi (No. 3)* (2012) N5075, [2012] PGNC 280.

Refer also to the sections titled 'Membership Of A Gang' and 'Leadership In A Gang' in the chapter titled 'Aggravating Factors'

- was there a relationship of trust, dependency or authority between the accused person[1781] and the victim or, if there was such relationship, was it a distant one?[1782];
- did the accused person give himself or herself up after the incident?[1783];
- did the accused person co-operate with the police in their investigations?[1784];
- has the accused person done anything tangible towards repairing his or her wrong such as offering compensation[1785], engaging in a peace and reconciliation ceremony, personally or publicly apologising for what he or she did?[1786];

[1781] This is a circumstance of aggravation as provided for by section 229A(3) of the *Criminal Code* (Ch. 262).

Refer also to:

- the section titled 'Circumstance Of Aggravation' in the chapter titled 'Aggravating Factors'; and
- the subsection titled 'Circumstances Of Aggravation' in the section titled 'Wording Of Charges' in the chapter titled 'Charges' in the text titled 'Injia on Criminal Practice and Procedure in Papua New Guinea and the Pacific'.

[1782] See *Stanley Sabiu v The State* (2007) SC866, [2007] PGSC 24; *The State v Biason Benson Samson* (2005) N2799; *The State v Pennias Mokei (No. 2)* (2004) N2635; *The State v Ndrakum Pu-Uh* (2005) N2949; *The State v Luke Toyana Gisigesi and Joseph Mwaisiga* (2010) N4124, [2010] PGNC 126 and *The State v Arthur Tangi (No. 3)* (2012) N5075, [2012] PGNC 280.

[1783] See *Stanley Sabiu v The State* (2007) SC866, [2007] PGSC 24; *The State v Biason Benson Samson* (2005) N2799; *The State v Pennias Mokei (No. 2)* (2004) N2635; *The State v Ndrakum Pu-Uh* (2005) N2949; *The State v Luke Toyana Gisigesi and Joseph Mwaisiga* (2010) N4124, [2010] PGNC 126 and *The State v Arthur Tangi (No. 3)* (2012) N5075, [2012] PGNC 280.

Refer also to the section titled 'Co-operation With Police' in the chapter titled 'Mitigating Factors'.

[1784] See *Stanley Sabiu v The State* (2007) SC866, [2007] PGSC 24; *The State v Biason Benson Samson* (2005) N2799; *The State v Pennias Mokei (No. 2)* (2004) N2635; *The State v Ndrakum Pu-Uh* (2005) N2949; *The State v Luke Toyana Gisigesi and Joseph Mwaisiga* (2010) N4124, [2010] PGNC 126 and *The State v Arthur Tangi (No. 3)* (2012) N5075, [2012] PGNC 280.

Refer also to the section titled 'Co-operation With Police' in the chapter titled 'Mitigating Factors'.

[1785] Refer also to the section titled 'Payment Of Compensation' in the chapter titled 'Mitigating Factors'.

[1786] See *Stanley Sabiu v The State* (2007) SC866, [2007] PGSC 24; *The State v Biason Benson Samson* (2005) N2799; *The State v Pennias Mokei (No. 2)* (2004) N2635; *The State v Ndrakum Pu-Uh* (2005) N2949; *The State v Luke Toyana Gisigesi and Joseph Mwaisiga* (2010) N4124, [2010] PGNC 126 and *The State v Arthur Tangi (No. 3)* (2012) N5075, [2012] PGNC 280.

- has the accused person pleaded guilty?[1787];
- has the accused person genuinely expressed remorse?[1788];
- is this the accused person's first offence?[1789];
- can the accused person be regarded as a youthful offender[1790] or are his or her personal circumstances such that they should mitigate the sentence?[1791]; and
- are there any other circumstances of the incident or the accused person that warrant mitigation of the head sentence?[1792]

[1787] See *Stanley Sabiu v The State* (2007) SC866, [2007] PGSC 24; *The State v Biason Benson Samson* (2005) N2799; *The State v Pennias Mokei (No. 2)* (2004) N2635; *The State v Ndrakum Pu-Uh* (2005) N2949; *The State v Luke Toyana Gisigesi and Joseph Mwaisiga* (2010) N4124, [2010] PGNC 126 and *The State v Arthur Tangi (No. 3)* (2012) N5075, [2012] PGNC 280.

Refer also to the section titled 'Plea Of Guilty' in the chapter titled 'Mitigating Factors'.

[1788] See *Stanley Sabiu v The State* (2007) SC866, [2007] PGSC 24; *The State v Biason Benson Samson* (2005) N2799; *The State v Pennias Mokei (No. 2)* (2004) N2635; *The State v Ndrakum Pu-Uh* (2005) N2949; *The State v Luke Toyana Gisigesi and Joseph Mwaisiga* (2010) N4124, [2010] PGNC 126 and *The State v Arthur Tangi (No. 3)* (2012) N5075, [2012] PGNC 280.

Refer also to the section titled 'Plea Of Guilty' in the chapter titled 'Mitigating Factors' and the section titled 'No Remorse' in the chapter titled 'Aggravating Factors'.

[1789] See *Stanley Sabiu v The State* (2007) SC866, [2007] PGSC 24; *The State v Biason Benson Samson* (2005) N2799; *The State v Pennias Mokei (No. 2)* (2004) N2635; *The State v Ndrakum Pu-Uh* (2005) N2949; *The State v Luke Toyana Gisigesi and Joseph Mwaisiga* (2010) N4124, [2010] PGNC 126 and *The State v Arthur Tangi (No. 3)* (2012) N5075, [2012] PGNC 280.

Refer also to the section titled 'Criminal History' in the chapter titled 'Mitigating Factors'.

[1790] Refer also to the section titled 'Youthfulness' in the chapter titled 'Mitigating Factors'.

[1791] See *Stanley Sabiu v The State* (2007) SC866, [2007] PGSC 24; *The State v Biason Benson Samson* (2005) N2799; *The State v Pennias Mokei (No. 2)* (2004) N2635; *The State v Ndrakum Pu-Uh* (2005) N2949; *The State v Luke Toyana Gisigesi and Joseph Mwaisiga* (2010) N4124, [2010] PGNC 126 and *The State v Arthur Tangi (No. 3)* (2012) N5075, [2012] PGNC 280.

Refer also to the chapters titled 'Mitigating Factors' and 'Extenuating Circumstances'.

[1792] See *Stanley Sabiu v The State* (2007) SC866, [2007] PGSC 24; *The State v Biason Benson Samson* (2005) N2799; *The State v Pennias Mokei (No. 2)* (2004) N2635; *The State v Ndrakum Pu-Uh* (2005) N2949; *The State v Luke Toyana Gisigesi and Joseph Mwaisiga* (2010) N4124, [2010] PGNC 126 and *The State v Arthur Tangi (No. 3)* (2012) N5075, [2012] PGNC 280.

[46.2.2] COMPARATIVE CASES

See:

- *Chris Awin v The State* (2008) SC926 [7 years; breach of trust] [digital]
- *Stanley Sabiu v The State* (2007) SC866, [2007] PGSC 24 [6 years; breach of trust]
- *Jack Mari v The State* (2007) SC1147, [2007] PGSC 49 [14 years]
- *Joe Nawa v The State* (2007) SC 1148, [2007] PGSC 50 [8 years; breach of trust]
- *Robert Solomon v The State* (2007) SC871, [2007] PGSC 9 [>16 years; breach of trust]
- *Saperus Yalibakut v The State* (2006) SC890, [2006] PGSC 27 [11 years]
- *The State v Olwin Noel* (2012) N4664, [2012] PGNC 20 [9 years; breach of trust]
- *The State v David Matanu* (2012) N4891, [2012] PGNC 249 [12 years]
- *The State v Bernard Soeka Hela* (2012) N4788, [2012] PGNC 228 [12 years; breach of trust]
- *The State v Arthur Tangi (No. 3)* (2012) N5075, [2012] PGNC 280 [9 years; breach of trust]
- *The State v Francis Molean* (2012) N4697, [2012] PGNC 81 [11 years; breach of trust]
- *The State v Luke Toyana Gisigesi and Joseph Mwaisiga* (2010) N4124, [2010] PGNC 126 [14 years]
- *The State v Oj Pohangat Palou* (2010) N4666, [2010] PGNC 215 [7 years]
- *The State v Henry David* (2010) 4544, [2010] PGNC 210 [8 years]
- *The State v Philip Peter* (2010) N4011, [2010] PGNC 48 [15 years]
- *The State v Simam July Melly (No. 2)* (2009) N3779, [2009] PGNC 138 [15 years]
- *The State v Elly Malpa (No. 2)* (2009) N3734, [2009] PGNC 113 [12 years; breach of trust]
- *The State v Chris Nawa (No. 2)* (2009) N3732, [2009] PGNC 115 [14 years; breach of trust]
- *The State v John Okupa* (2009) N3726, [2009] PGNC 117 [15 years]
- *The State v Brown Kawage* (2009) N3696, [2009] PGNC 87 [14 years; breach of trust]
- *The State v Tonny Kupin* (2009) N3641 [9 years; breach of trust]
- *The State v Timothy Bipi* (2009) N3608, [2009] PGNC 55 [9 years]
- *The State v Philip Soni and Tony Ilong* (2008) N3694, [2008] PGNC 237 [14 years]
- *The State v August David* (2008) N3612, [2008] PGNC 226 [15 years]
- *The State v Mas Kaipo* (2008) N3462 [>16 years; breach of trust]
- *The State v Ben Berry Tukuben* (2008) N3457 [between 16 and 18 years; breach of trust]
- *The State v Epesie Dabu* (2008) N3313, [2008] PGNC 76 [13 years]
- *The State v Siro Waida* (2008) N3311, [2008] PGNC 38 [14 years; breach of trust]

COMPARATIVE SENTENCES

- *The State v Manewa Suliga* (2008) N3307, [2008] PGNC 33 [13 years]
- *The State v Charlie Pupuka* (2007) N3184, [2007] PGNC 168 [7 years]
- *The State v Ruap Gemung (No. 2)* (2007) N3136, [2007] PGNC 31 [14 years; breach of trust]
- *The State v Johnson Roman* (2007) CR No. 1924 of 2005 [15 years]
- *The State v Charles Rome* (2007) CR No. 502 of 2007 [10 years; breach of trust]
- *The State v Paul Gule* (2007) CR No. 686 of 2006 [11 years]
- *The State v Sawan Raumo* (2007) CR No. 876 of 2007 [6 years; breach of trust]
- *The State v Joshua Makata* (2006) N3076, [2006] PGNC 59 [15 years; breach of trust]
- *The State v Tiama Esrom* (2006) N3054, [2006] PGNC 53 [9 years; breach of trust]
- *The State v Jeffery Toapas* (2006) CR No. 1924 of 2005 [14 years; breach of trust]
- *The State v Kaminiel Okole* (2006) N3052, [2006] PGNC 54 [>12 years; breach of trust]
- *The State v Joe Putubu* [2006] PGNC 93 [14 years; breach of trust]
- *The State v Rudy Solo* (2005) N3165, [2005] PGNC 179 [15 years]
- *The State v Anere Ota* (2005) N2939, [2005] PGNC 20 [15 years; breach of trust]
- *The State v Willie Dominic* (2005) N2938, [2005] PGNC 35 [14 years]
- *The State v Ian Unawing* (2005) CR No. 392 of 2005 [13 years]
- *The State v John Ura* (2005) N2862, [2005] PGNC 106 [13 years; breach of trust]
- *The State v Thomas Angup* (2005) N2830 [>12 years; breach of trust]
- *The State v Binga Thomas* (2005) N2828, [2005] PGNC 189 [15 years]
- *The State v Gomong Kauckesa* [2005] PGNC 182 [15 years]
- *The State v Titus Soumi* (2005) N2809, [2005] PGNC 150 [14-15 years; breach of trust]
- *The State v George Taunde* (2005) N2807, [2005] PGNC 152 [13 years; breach of trust]
- *The State v Biason Benson Samson* (2005) N2799, [2005] PGNC 160 [13 years]
- *The State v John Ritsi Kutetoa* (2005) N2814, [2005] PGNC 137 [10 years; breach of trust]
- *The State v Pennias Mokei (No. 2)* (2004) N2635 [13 years; breach of trust]
- *The State v Kemai Lumou* (2004) N2684 [14 years; breach of trust]
- *The State v Eddie Trosty* (2004) N2681 [>12 years; breach of trust]
- *The State v Peter Lare* (2004) N2557 [10 years; breach of trust]

The maximum sentence for this offence when a victim is under the age of twelve years is life imprisonment and a child under the age of sixteen years is twenty-five years imprisonment. Sentences imposed have ranged from two to seventeen years imprisonment and in the case of *The State v Francis Molean*[1793] a sentence of five years imprisonment was wholly suspended.

[1793] (2012) N4697, [2012] PGNC 81.

COMPARATIVE SENTENCES

Cases in which:

- the victim is young[1794]; and
- there has been:
  - a breach of trust[1795]; or
  - the infliction of injuries[1796]

have attracted sentences in the top end of the range.

For discussion on range of sentences, see *Sabiu v The State*[1797].

[46.3] SEXUAL TOUCHING

[46.3.1] GENERAL PRINCIPLE

Sexual touching offences are committed with or without violence and are prevalent in the community[1798] and are on the rise.[1799]

[1794] By virtue of section 229A(2) of the *Criminal Code* (Ch. 262), if the age of the child was under the age of 12 years then the prosecution should allege a circumstance of aggravation in the wording of the charge.

[1795] This is also a circumstance of aggravation, see section 229A(3) of the *Criminal Code* (Ch. 262), that should be alleged in the wording of the charge.

Refer also to the section titled 'Breach Of Trust' in the chapter titled 'Aggravating Factors'.

[1796] Refer also to the section titled 'Viciousness Or Deliberate Intention To Harm' in the chapter titled 'Aggravating Factors'.

[1797] (2007) SC866, [2007] PGSC 24.

[1798] Refer also to the section titled 'Prevalence Of The Offence' in the chapter titled 'Aggravating Factors'.

[1799] See *The State v Jack Andy* (2012) N4779, [2012] PGNC 227.

[46.3.2] COMPARATIVE CASES

See:

- *The State v Jacky Moses* (2012) N4886, [2012] PGNC 213 [2 years]
- *The State v George Philip* (2012) N4829, [2012] PGNC 165 [6 years]
- *The State v A Juvenile, 'JF'* (2012) N4827, [2012] PGNC 119 [11 years]
- *The State v Jack Andy* (2012) N4779, [2012] PGNC 227 [15 years; breach of trust
- *The State v Tala John* (2012) N4630, [2012] PGNC 197 [10 years; breach of trust]
- *The State v Gibson Kukurena* (2012) N4594, [2012] PGNC 268 [15 years]
- *The State v Garry Pokas* (2011) N4375, [2011] PGNC 106 [8 years; breach of trust]
- *The State v Tonai Kuse* (2011) N4304, [2011] PGNC 54 [10 years]
- *The State v Ledi Sogasog* (2011) N4471, [2011] PGNC 192 [9 years; breach of trust]
- *The State v Peter Tewi Poksen* (2011) N4668, [2011] PGNC 227 [3.5 years]
- *The State v Patrick Peter Mova* (2011) N4523, [2011] PGNC 201 [4 years; breach of trust]
- *The State v Stafford Hambo* (2010) N4120, [2010] PGNC 125 [8, 8 and 12 years; breach of trust]
- *The State v Levi Ateika* (2010) N3962, [2010] PGNC 25 [9 years; breach of trust]
- *The State v Jack Manuel Narakavi* (2009) N3737, [2009] PGNC 109 [14 years; breach of trust]
- *The State v Isaac Kuila (No. 2)* (2009) N3736, [2009] PGNC 110 [9 years; breach of trust]
- *The State v Elly Malpa (No. 2)* (2009) N3734, [2009] PGNC 113 [12 years; breach of trust]
- *The State v Chris Nawa (No. 2)* (2009) N3732, [2009] PGNC 115 [14 years; breach of trust]
- *The State v Steven Archie* (2009) N3727, [2009] PGNC 118 [13 years]
- *The State v Timothy Bipi* (2009) N3608, [2009] PGNC 55 [5 years; breach of trust]
- *The State v Peter Tulemanil* (2008) N3685, [2008] PGNC 233 [10 and 11 years; breach of trust]
- *The State v Wasa David Warifa* (2008) N3308, [2008] PGNC 32 [6 years; breach of trust]
- *The State v Alexander Junior Nara (No. 2)* (2007) N3214, [2007] PGNC 86 [9 years; breach of trust]
- *The State v Francis Keta* (2007) CR No. 548 of 2007
- *The State v Alois Dick* (2007) N3220, [2007] PGNC 58 [>13 years, breach of trust]
- *The State v Sailor Peter Tatanu* (2006) N3392, [2006] PGNC 170 [8 years; breach of trust]

COMPARATIVE SENTENCES

- *The State v Brady Meki* (2006) N3391, [2006] PGNC 169 [6 years]
- *The State v William Patangala* (2006) N3027, [2006] PGNC 43 [breach of trust]
- *The State v Thomas Tukaliu* (2006) N3026, [2006] PGNC 42 [10 years; breach of trust]
- *The State v Tony Towoit* (2005) N3164 [5 years]
- *The State v Kagewa Tanang* (2005) N2941, [2005] PGNC 21 [10 years; breach of trust]
- *The State v Paul Nelson* (2005) N2844, [2005] PGNC 113 [12 years]

The maximum sentence of this offence is seven years imprisonment in ordinary cases where the victim is under sixteen years; and twelve years imprisonment for an offence with circumstances of aggravation such as breach of position of authority and trust[1800].

Sentences imposed have ranged from eighteen months to six years imprisonment in ordinary cases and three years to eight years imprisonment for offences with circumstances of aggravation.

[46.4] ABUSE OF TRUST, AUTHORITY OR DEPENDENCY

See:

- *The State v Esorom Asupa* (2011) N4540, [2011] PGNC 197 [15 years; breach of trust]
- *The State v Peter Bobo (No. 3)* (2007) N3264, [2007] PGNC 131
- *The State v Daniel Latu Bun* (2007) CR No. 580 of 2007
- *The State v Michael Kilau* (2006) N3107, [2006] PGNC 125
- *The State v Kaminiel Okole* (2006) N3052, [2006] PGNC 54
- *The State v Raphael Dala* [2006] PGNC 110

The maximum sentence for this offence ranges from fifteen to twenty-five years and life imprisonment depending on the presence of circumstances of aggravation.

Sentences imposed have ranged from five to thirteen years imprisonment.

1800 Refer also to the section titled 'Breach Of Trust' in the chapter titled 'Aggravating Factors'.

[46.5] PERSISTENT SEXUAL ABUSE

[46.5.1] GENERAL PRINCIPLES

The offence of 'Persistent Sexual Abuse Of A Child' is a prevalent offence.[1801]

A general proposition in sentencing under section 229D of the *Criminal Code* (Ch. 262) is as follows:

- To make a general assessment of the frequency of the offending; and

- To make an assessment of the likely sentence if the accused person was sentenced for a series of offences involving the Division 2A offence/s particularised in the indictment pursuant to section 229D(4), keeping in mind that the maximum penalty is still available for the worst case.[1802]

In order to determine an appropriate sentence the factors to be considered, include[1803]:

- what was the age difference between the accused person and the victim?[1804];

- is the victim not far under the age of 16 years?;

- was there consent?;

- did the accused person use a threatening weapon?[1805];

- did the accused person use aggravated physical violence?[1806];

- did the accused person cause physical injury to the victim?[1807];

1801 Refer also to the section titled 'Prevalence Of The Offence' in the chapter titled 'Aggravating Factors'.

1802 See *The State v JB* (2007) N3224.

1803 See *The State v Danny Tutuvo* (2011) N4400.

1804 Refer also to the section titled 'Age Difference' in the chapter titled 'Aggravating Factors'.

1805 Refer also to the section titled 'Carrying, Using Or Threatening To Use A Weapon' in the chapter titled 'Aggravating Factors'.

1806 Refer also to the section titled 'Viciousness Or Deliberate Intention To Harm' in the chapter titled 'Aggravting Factors'.

1807 Refer also to the section titled 'Viciousness Or Deliberate Intention To Harm' in the chapter titled 'Aggravting Factors'.

- did the accused person pass on a sexually transmitted disease to the victim?;
- was it an isolated incident?; and
- has the accused person caused further trouble to the victim or the victim's family since the incident?

[46.5.2] COMPARATIVE CASES

See:

- *The State v Sali Kevin Mavuug* (2012) N4898, [2012] PGNC 255 [2 victims aged 11-13 years; breach of trust]
- *The State v Alphonse Makis* (2012) N4888, [2012] PGNC 243 [17 and 18 years; breach of trust]
- *The State v Danny Tutuvo* (2011) N4400 [9 years; breach of trust]
- *The State v Danny Aparti* (2011) N4326, [2011] PGNC 68 [17 years; breach of trust]
- *The State v Ben Sakias* (2011) N4238, [2011] PGNC 37 [13 years; breach of trust]
- *The State v Steven Makai* (2010) N3914, [2010] PGNC 107 [9-10 years; breach of trust]
- *The State v Steven Siname* (2009) N3908, [2009] PGNC 213 [15 years; breach of trust]
- *The State v Kuyaps Toki Jonathan* (2008) N3315, [2008] PGNC 31 [13 years; breach of trust]
- *The State v JB* (2007) N3224, [2007] PGNC 66 [6 weeks and 22 months; breach of trust]
- *The State v Ereman Kepas* (2007) N3192, [2007] PGNC 77 [10 years; breach of trust]
- *The State v Thomas Angup* (2005) N2830 [12 years; breach of trust]

The maximum sentence for this offence is fifteen years imprisonment for ordinary cases and life imprisonment for an offence with circumstances of aggravation such as breach of position of authority and trust[1808].

Sentences imposed have ranged from ten to twenty years imprisonment.

[1808] Refer also to the section titled 'Breach Of Trust' in the chapter titled 'Aggravating Factors'.

[46.6] CHILD PORNOGRAPHY[1809]

Ordinarily, a sentence of immediate imprisonment would be imposed where an accused person is found:

- in possession of child pornography; or
- importing child pornography.[1810]

This is because such offences are not victimless crimes. Those who are prepared to possess or import it help fuel the demand for it, and in that way encourage the corruption and exploitation of children.[1811]

In order to protect children, deterrence is the paramount sentencing consideration.[1812]

1809 See also: *R v Golligher* [2010] NICC 2; and *R v John Dunbar Fowler* [2007] ACTCA 4.

1810 See *R v Liddington* (1997) 18 WAR 394; *R v Jones* (1999) 108 A Crim R 50, [1999] WASCA 24; *Assheton v R* (2002) 132 A Crim R 237, [2002] WASCA 209; *Furber v R* [2008] WASCA 233, [2008] WASCA 233; *Hill v The State of Western Australia* [2009] WASCA 4; *Ponniah v R* [2011] WASCA 105; *Smit v The State of Western Australia* [2011] WASCA 124; *R v Cook; ex parte DPP (Commonwealth)* [2004] QCA 469; *Holland v R* (2005) 30 WAR 231, [2005] WASCA 140 and *R v Gent* (2005) 162 A Crim R 29, [2005] NSWCCA 370.

1811 See *R v Liddington* (1997) 18 WAR 394; *R v Jones* (1999) 108 A Crim R 50, [1999] WASCA 24; *Assheton v R* (2002) 132 A Crim R 237, [2002] WASCA 209; *Furber v R* [2008] WASCA 233, [2008] WASCA 233; *Hill v The State of Western Australia* [2009] WASCA 4; *Ponniah v R* [2011] WASCA 105; *Smit v The State of Western Australia* [2011] WASCA 124; *R v Cook; ex parte DPP (Commonwealth)* [2004] QCA 469; *Holland v R* (2005) 30 WAR 231, [2005] WASCA 140 and *R v Gent* (2005) 162 A Crim R 29, [2005] NSWCCA 370.

1812 See *R v Liddington* (1997) 18 WAR 394; *R v Jones* (1999) 108 A Crim R 50, [1999] WASCA 24; *Assheton v R* (2002) 132 A Crim R 237, [2002] WASCA 209; *Furber v R* [2008] WASCA 233, [2008] WASCA 233; *Hill v The State of Western Australia* [2009] WASCA 4; *Ponniah v R* [2011] WASCA 105; *Smit v The State of Western Australia* [2011] WASCA 124; *R v Cook; ex parte DPP (Commonwealth)* [2004] QCA 469; *Holland v R* (2005) 30 WAR 231, [2005] WASCA 140 and *R v Gent* (2005) 162 A Crim R 29, [2005] NSWCCA 370.

Refer also to the section titled 'The Need For Deterence' in the chapter titled 'Objectives And Purposes Of Sentencing'.

COMPARATIVE SENTENCES

The generation and existence of demand for possession of child pornography stimulates the supply side to the incalculable harm to the children involved. The creation and satisfaction of demand for child pornography is exponentially facilitated by the internet and there are significant difficulties in detecting the offences. These factors result in significant weight being given to general deterrence[1813] and correspondingly less weight being given to matters personal to the accused person. Indeed, positive personal antecedents and a reduced or absent need for personal deterrence[1814] are relatively commonplace amongst accused persons in possession of child pornography.[1815]

The Court of Appeal of England and Wales[1816] has adopted the following categorisation levels for child pornography:

1. Images depicting erotic posing with no sexual activity;
2. Sexual activity between children, or solo masturbation by a child;
3. Non-penetrative sexual activity between adults and children;
4. Penetrative sexual activity between children and adults; and
5. Sadism or bestiality.

[1813] See *R v Liddington* (1997) 18 WAR 394; *R v Jones* (1999) 108 A Crim R 50, [1999] WASCA 24; *Assheton v R* (2002) 132 A Crim R 237, [2002] WASCA 209; *Furber v R* [2008] WASCA 233, [2008] WASCA 233; *Hill v The State of Western Australia* [2009] WASCA 4; *Ponniah v R* [2011] WASCA 105; *Smit v The State of Western Australia* [2011] WASCA 124; *R v Cook; ex parte DPP (Commonwealth)* [2004] QCA 469; *Holland v R* (2005) 30 WAR 231, [2005] WASCA 140 and *R v Gent* (2005) 162 A Crim R 29, [2005] NSWCCA 370.

Refer also to the section titled 'The Need For Deterence' in the chapter titled 'Objectives And Purposes Of Sentencing'.

[1814] See *R v Liddington* (1997) 18 WAR 394; *R v Jones* (1999) 108 A Crim R 50, [1999] WASCA 24; *Assheton v R* (2002) 132 A Crim R 237, [2002] WASCA 209; *Furber v R* [2008] WASCA 233, [2008] WASCA 233; *Hill v The State of Western Australia* [2009] WASCA 4; *Ponniah v R* [2011] WASCA 105; *Smit v The State of Western Australia* [2011] WASCA 124; *R v Cook; ex parte DPP (Commonwealth)* [2004] QCA 469; *Holland v R* (2005) 30 WAR 231, [2005] WASCA 140 and *R v Gent* (2005) 162 A Crim R 29, [2005] NSWCCA 370.

Refer also to the section titled 'The Need For Deterence' in the chapter titled 'Objectives And Purposes Of Sentencing'.

[1815] See *Hill v The State of Western Australia* [2009] WASCA 4.

[1816] See *R v Oliver* (2003) 1 Cr App R 28, [2003] 2 Cr App R (S) 15.

This categorisation is intended to reflect levels of increasing seriousness.[1817]

Such a classification list is not intended to be a substitute for the sentencing judge viewing the pornographic material the subject of the conviction. The relative perversion and debauchery of the pornographic material is a relevant sentencing factor. Viewing a representative sample (as identified or agreed by the parties) of the material will ordinarily be necessary for the proper performance of the sentencing judge's duties.[1818]

When an accused person:

- views child pornography material on the internet;
- downloads it; and
- retains possession of it for the purposes of personal gratification,

keeping possession of the downloaded material is generally regarded as more serious criminal conduct than accessing it.[1819]

The criminality involved in the material that does not depict real children is of a different nature to that involving real children. This is not to say that material of this type is harmless; it:

- has the tendency to 'normalise' exploitative sexual activity involving children; and
- may stimulate a susceptible recipient to engage in sexual activity involving real children.[1820]

[1817] See *Smit v The State of Western Australia* [2011] WASCA 124.

[1818] See *Smit v The State of Western Australia* [2011] WASCA 124.

[1819] See *R v Oliver* (2003) 1 Cr App R 28, [2003] 2 Cr App R (S) 15; *Colbourn v R* [2009] TASSC 108 and *R v Talbot* [2009] TASSC 107.

[1820] See *Dodge v R* (2002) 134 A Crim R 435, [2002] WASCA 286 and *Hutchins v The State of Western Australia* [2006] WASCA 258.

[47.0] STEALING[1821]

[47.1] GENERAL PRINCIPLES

The offences of 'Stealing' and 'Stealing as a Servant' are prevalent offences. [1822]

The offence of 'Stealing as a Servant' is a very serious crime.[1823]

This is because there is a breach of trust which is entrusted to the accused person.[1824]

In order to determine an appropriate sentence the factors to be considered, include[1825]:

- the amount of money involved?[1826];
- was the money or property applied to a good use?;
- did the accused person's actions have a small adverse effect on other persons, such as the owner of the property?

[1821] The law in relation to this offence is examined in the chapter titled 'Stealing' in the chapter titled 'Offences Against Property' in the text titled 'Injia on Criminal Offences in Papua New Guinea and the Pacific'.

[1822] Refer also to the section titled 'Prevalence Of The Offence' in the chapter titled 'Aggravating Factors'.

[1823] See *The State v Keputong Nagong* (1980) N225.

[1824] See *The State v Keputong Nagong* (1980) N225.

Refer also to the section titled 'Breach Of Trust' in the chapter titled 'Aggravating Factors'.

[1825] See *The State v Henry Eliakim* (2007) N3190, [2007] PGNC 76.

The prosecution should also allege in the wording of the charge the circumstances of aggravation as specified in section 372 of the *Criminal Code* (Ch. 262).

Refer also to:

- the section titled 'Circumstance Of Aggravation' in the chapter titled 'Aggravating Factors'; and
- the subsection titled 'Circumstances Of Aggravation' in the section titled 'Wording Of Charges' in the chapter titled 'Charges' in the text titled 'Injia on Criminal Practice and Procedure in Papua New Guinea and the Pacific'.

[1826] Refer also to the section titled 'Seriousness Of An Offence Generally' in the chapter titled 'Aggravating Factors'.

- was the victim in a position to carry the losses caused by the accused person?;
- did the accused person's actions have a small adverse effect on public confidence in the integrity of the industry?; and
- has the accused person repaired his or her wrong, such as repaying the money?[1827]

[47.2] COMPARATIVE CASES

See:

- *Seo Ross v The State* (1999) SC605, [1999] PGSC 10 [breach of trust]
- *The State v Neville Miria* (2013) N5102, [2013] PGNC 37 [breach of trust]
- *The State v David Wilfred Yahresase* (2012) N4803, [2012] PGNC 233 [breach of trust]
- *The State v Bitaoko Bobo* (2011) N4416, [2011] PGNC 139
- *The State v Steven Luva* (2010) N3909, [2010] PGNC 19 [breach of trust]
- *The State v Edward Giragu Koima* (2010) N4115, [2010] PGNC 129
- *The State v Asi Taba* (2010) N3939, [2010] PGNC 178
- *The State v Simon Paul Korai* (2009) N3820, [2009] PGNC 23 [breach of trust]
- *Andrew Perea v The State* (2009) N3575, [2009] PGNC 5
- *The State v Johnson Maurani* (2008) N3560, [2008] PGNC 191
- *The State v Roselyn Waiembi* (2008) N3708, [2008] PGNC 240 [breach of trust]
- *The State v Geo Rayner Laina* (2008) N3344, [2008] PGNC 63 [breach of trust]
- *The State v Jack Maite and Tamring Nio* (2007) N3269, [2007] PGNC 132
- *The State v Thomas Malaisa* (2006) N3239, [2006] PGNC 150
- *The State v Aisi Eki and others* (2005) N3387, [2005] PGNC 185
- *The State v Janet Morgan* (2004) N2704 [breach of trust]
- *The State v Obert Poesan Pokanas* (2004) N2702
- *The State v Tobby Alekun* (2004) N2636
- *The State v Johnson Bale* (2004) N2626 [breach of trust]
- *The State v David Danny Mani* (2004) N2623
- *The State v Allan Nareti and Amstrong Kupe* (2004) N2582 [breach of de-facto trust]
- *The State v Romney Naptelai Simonopa* (2004) N2551

[1827] Refer also to the section titled 'Payment Of Compensation' in the chapter titled 'Mitigating Factors'.

COMPARATIVE SENTENCES

- *The State v Rocky Walesa Peraki* (2003) N2463
- *The State v Richard Dusal Bix and Siprian Sipi Karo* (2003) N2415
- *The State v Timothy Tio* (2002) N2265 [breach of trust]
- *The State v Robert Kawin* (2001) N2167 [breach of trust]
- *The State v John Akoko* (2000) N2061 [breach of trust]
- *The State v James Barmen* (1999) N1943
- *Patrick Maith v Thomas Pundu* (1997) N1592 [breach of trust]
- *The State v Bill Baru* (1997) N1546 [breach of trust]

The maximum sentence for this offence is three years imprisonment, seven years imprisonment for stealing specific items of property and life imprisonment for stealing testamentary instruments.

Sentences imposed have ranged from a fine of K200 to six years and six months imprisonment.

[48.0] UNLAWFUL USE OF A MOTOR VEHICLE[1828]

[48.1] GENERAL PRINCIPLES

The offence of 'Unlawful Use Of A Motor Vehicle' is a prevalent offence.[1829]

In order to determine an appropriate sentence the factors to be considered, include[1830]:

- whether the offence was committed under serious aggravating circumstances, such as:
    - a serious injury to the owner of the vehicle[1831]; or
    - serious damage to the vehicle itself or other property[1832];

[1828] The law in relation to this offence is examined in the section titled 'Unlawful Use' in the chapter titled 'Traffic Offences' in the text titled 'Injia on Criminal Offences in Papua New Guinea and the Pacific'.

[1829] Refer also to the section titled 'Prevalence Of The Offence' in the chapter titled 'Aggravating Factors'.

[1830] See *The State v James Gurave Guba* (2000) N2020.

[1831] Refer also to the section titled 'Viciousness Or Deliberate Intention To Harm' in the chapter titled 'Aggravating Factors'.

[1832] Refer also to the section titled 'Seriousness Of An Offence Generally' in the chapter titled 'Aggravating Factors'.

- whether the offence was committed in the course of or in the furtherance of a serious crime, such as a robbery;

- whether the offence was committed under some of the abovementioned serious aggravating circumstances, such as the vehicle being taken by force, but without injuring the owner or its lawful driver and recovered with minor damage to the vehicle or any other property;

- whether the offence was committed under one of the abovementioned serious aggravating circumstances, such the owner or legal driver leaving the vehicle unlocked and the accused person gaining entry, driving off and damaging the vehicle; and

- whether an owner or employer authorized his or her employee to use a vehicle for a specified purpose within a specified period, but he or she simply exceeds the authorized purpose and time for the employee's own purpose or interest without advancing his or her employer's interest in any way.

[48.2] COMPARATIVE CASES

See:

- *The State v Eric Papen (No. 2)* (2009) N3639, [2009] PGNC 58
- *The State v Patrick Sogi* (2008) N3437
- *The State v Thomas Wakai and others* (2006) N3360, [2006] PGNC 165
- *The State v Jackson Anias Ananias* (2006) N3161, [2006] PGNC 132
- *The State v Jimmy Banes Ere* (2002) N2254
- *The State v Micky John Lausi* (2001) N2073
- *The State v Jason Dongoma* (2001) N2038
- *The State v James Gurave Guba* (2000) N2020

The maximum sentence for this offence is five years imprisonment.

Sentences imposed have ranged from one to three years and six months imprisonment.

[49.0] UNLAWFUL WOUNDING[1833]

See:

- *The State v Julius Minsipi* (2012) N4595, [2012] PGNC 271
- *The State v Aine Petrus* (2011) N4257, [2011] PGNC 27
- *The State v Joe Sekin* [2006] PGNC 74
- *The State v Rubert Kassman* (2004) N2682
- *The State v Marshall Western Pangih* (2004) N2676
- *The State v Joseph Pingu* (2001) N2169

The maximum sentence for this offence is three years imprisonment.

In the cases cited sentences imposed range from one to three years imprisonment either wholely or partly suspended on conditions.

[50.0] UTTERING[1834]

See:

- *The State v Andrew Aopo Lengade* (2012) N4690, [2012] PGNC 76
- *The State v Janos Berenyi and Irene Berenyi* (2009) N3813, [2009] PGNC 179
- *The State v Raka Benson* [2006] PGNC 68
- *The State v Lukeson Olewale* (2004) N2758
- *The State v Louise Paraka* (2002) N2317

[1833] The law in relation to this offence is examined in the section titled 'Unlawful Wounding' in the chapter titled 'Offences Against The Person' in the text titled 'Injia on Criminal Offences in Papua New Guinea and the Pacific'.

[1834] The law in relation to this offence is examined in the section titled 'Utter' in the chapter titled 'Fraud Related Offences' in the text titled 'Injia on Criminal Offences in Papua New Guinea and the Pacific'.

COMPARATIVE SENTENCES

The maximum sentence for this offence is fourteen years imprisonment for uttering bank notes and three years imprisonment for other documents.[1835]

Sentences imposed have ranged from one to three years imprisonment.

[51.0] WILFUL DAMAGE/DESTRUCTION[1836]

[51.1] GENERAL PRINCIPLES

In order to determine an appropriate sentence the factors to be considered, include[1837]:

- the value of damage or destruction?[1838];
- was there any person or class of persons directly affected by the damage or destruction of the property?;
- did the accused person breach the peace or cause alarm or affront to other people when the property was damaged or destroyed?;
- did the accused person use a threatening weapon against any person?[1839];

1835 The prosecution should also allege in the wording of the charge the circumstances of aggravation as specified in section 462 of the *Criminal Code* (Ch. 262).

Refer also to:
- the section titled 'Circumstance Of Aggravation' in the chapter titled 'Aggravating Factors'; and
- the subsection titled 'Circumstances Of Aggravation' in the section titled 'Wording Of Charges' in the chapter titled 'Charges' in the text titled 'Injia on Criminal Practice and Procedure in Papua New Guinea and the Pacific'.

1836 The law in relation to this offence is examined in the section titled 'Wilful Damge' in the chapter titled 'Offences Against Property' in the text titled 'Injia on Criminal Offences in Papua New Guinea and the Pacific'.

1837 See *The State v Martin Sahin Terea* (2005) N2816, [2005] PGNC 136.

1838 Refer also to the section titled 'Seriousness Of An Offence Generally' in the chapter titled 'Aggravating Factors'.

1839 Refer also to the section titled 'Carrying, Using Or Threatening To Use A Weapon' in the chapter titled 'Aggravating Factors'.

- did the accused person threaten physical violence against any person?[1840];
- was there any risk of injury to any person as a result of the accused person's actions?;
- was it an isolated incident?[1841]; and
- has the accused person caused further trouble since the incident?

[59.2] COMPARATIVE CASES

See:

- *The State v Matthew Balu and Bernard Kavanamur Balu* (2011) N4362, [2011] PGNC 97
- *The State v Roger Meckpi* (2010) N4079, [2010] PGNC 99
- *The State v John Telape* (2009) N3815, [2009] PGNC 181
- *The State v Steven Molu Minji and others; The State v Didi Gelwak Sakol (No. 2)* (2009) N3794, [2009] PGNC 177
- *The State v Martin Sahin Terea* (2005) N2816, [2005] PGNC 136

The maximum sentence for this offence is two years imprisonment and seven years imprisonment for offences with circumstances of aggravation[1842].

Sentences imposed have ranged from ten months to seven years imprisonment.

[1840] Refer also to the section titled 'Viciousness Or Deliberate Intention To Harm' in the chapter titled 'Aggravating Factors'.

[1841] Refer also to the subsection titled 'Impulsiveness' in the section titled 'Motive' in the chapter titled 'Extenuating Circumstances'.

[1842] The prosecution should also allege in the wording of the charge the circumstances of aggravation as specified in section 444 of the *Criminal Code* (Ch. 262).

Refer also to:
- the section titled 'Circumstance Of Aggravation' in the chapter titled 'Aggravating Factors'; and
- the subsection titled 'Circumstances Of Aggravation' in the section titled 'Wording Of Charges' in the chapter titled 'Charges' in the text titled 'Injia on Criminal Practice and Procedure in Papua New Guinea and the Pacific'.

COMPARATIVE SENTENCES

The maximum sentence was imposed in *The State v John Telape*[1843] in a case involving felling of power poles that disrupted electricity supply to the gold mine.

[52.0] WILFUL FALSE PROMISE[1844]

See:

- *The State v Morris Yepin* (2005) N3503, [2005] PGNC 186

The maximum penalty for this offence is three years imprisonment.

In the case cited two years imprisonment (fully suspended on conditions) was imposed and it involved a false promise to pay a sum of K500.

[1843] (2009) N3815.

[1844] The law in relation to this offence is examined in the section titled 'False Pretences' in the chapter titled 'Fraud Related Offences' in the text titled 'Injia on Criminal Offences in Papua New Guinea and the Pacific'.

APPEALS AGAINST SENTENCE

[1.0] GENERAL PRINCIPLES[1845]

An appellate Court should not substitute its own opinion merely because it would have exercised its discretion differently.[1846]

A sentence should not be altered, unless the appellate Court is clearly satisfied that it should be altered.[1847]

Sentencing by its nature is an exercise that allows a range of possibly correct answers.[1848]

The question is:

> Has there has been an error in the exercise of the discretion?[1849]

The opinion of the victim about the appropriate level of sentence does not provide any sound basis for re-assessing a sentence.[1850]

An appellate Court is not bound by concessions made by the Public Prosecutor on behalf of the State.[1851]

1845 Refer also to the chapter titled 'Appeals' in the text titled 'Injia on Criminal Practice and Procedure in Papua New Guinea and the Pacific'.

1846 See *Government of Papua New Guinea v McLeary* [1976] PNGLR 321 at 322-333; *Public Prosecutor v Tardrew* [1986] PNGLR 91, [1986] PGSC 10 and *Paul Timiti v John Aubuku* (1983) N412(M).

See also: *Cranssen v R* (1936) 55 CLR 509 at 519-520; *Lowndes v R* (1999) 195 CLR 665, [1999] HCA 29; *Griffiths* (1977) 137 CLR 293 at 310; *House v R* (1936) 55 CLR 499; *Dinsdale v R* (2000) 202 CLR 321, [2000] HCA 54; *R v Wall* [2002] NSWCCA 42 and *Markarian v R* (2005) 228 CLR 357, [2005] HCA 25.

1847 See *Public Prosecutor v Terrence Kaveku* [1977] PNGLR 110.

1848 See *El Rakhawy v R* [2011] WASCA 209.

1849 See *El Rakhawy v R* [2011] WASCA 209.

1850 See *R v Nunn* [1996] 2 Cr App R (S) 136, per Judge J at 140.

See also: *R v Roche* [1999] 2 Cr App R (S) 105, per Bingham LCJ at 109 and *R v Matthews* [2003] 1 Cr App R (S) 26.

1851 See *Wood v R* (2002) 130 A Crim R 518, [2002] WASCA 95.

The fact that a co-accused has not been brought to trial and may not be brought to trial is not a relevant matter going to mitigation.[1852]

An appellant must show that the sentencing Court:

- fell into some demonstrable error:
    - in law[1853]; or
    - in fact[1854]

  in the exercise of its discretion[1855] which has the effect of vitiating the Court's discretion on sentence[1856]; or

---

[1852] See *Public Prosecutor v Ngudomp* [1982] PNGLR 357, [1982] PGSC 13.

[1853] See *Gabriel Laki v The State* [1981] PNGLR 350 and *William Norris v The State* [1979] PNGLR 605.

[1854] See *Wilkeson, Stephen and Michalov v Grant* [1967-68] PNGLR 112.

See also: *Readhead v The State of Western Australia* [2005] WASCA 191 and *Lowndes v R* (1999) 195 CLR 665 at 671-672.

[1855] See *The Public Prosecutor v Vangu'u Ame* [1983] PNGLR 424, per Kidu CJ at 425; *Mauwe Antape v The State* [1981] PNGLR 68 and *Tony Imunu Apu v The State* (2001) SC684, [2001] PGSC 2.

[1856] See *Acting Public Prosecutor v Konis Haha* [1981] PNGLR 205; *Public Prosecutor v Tardrew* [1986] PNGLR 91, [1986] PGSC 10; *Wanosa and others v R* [1971-72] PNGLR 90, [1971] PGSC 47; *William Norris v The State* [1979] PNGLR 605; *Robert Solomon v The State* (2007) SC871; *Simon Kama v The State* (2004) SC740, [2004] PGSC 32; *Denden Tom, Daniel Wilson and Samuel Tom v The State* (2008) SC967; *Joseph Nimagi, Tom Gurua Kerui and David Bawai Laiam v The State* (2004) SC741, [2004] PGSC 31; *Kepa Wanege v The State* (2004) SC742, [2004] PGSC 22; *Masolyau Piakali v The State* (2004) SC771, [2004] PGSC 20; *Ben Wafia and others v The State* (2006) SC851, [2006] PGSC 19; *Ian Napolean Setep v The State* (2001) SC666; *Baune Bernard Olmi v The State* (2004) SC872, [2004] PGSC 43; *Edmund Gima v The State; Siune Arnold v The State* (2003) SC730, [2003] PGSC 3; *Dadly Henry Gorop v The State* (2003) SC732; *Mary Bomai Michael v The State* (2004) SC737, [2004] PGSC 37; *Joseph Enn v The State* (2004) SC738; *Wesley Nobudi, John Evoa and Frank Yalikiti v The State* (2009) SC999, [2009] PGSC 20; *Richard Liri v The State* (2007) SC883, [2007] PGSC 3; *Kongian and others v The State* (2007) SC928, [2007] PGSC 45; *Joe Giamur v The State* (2007) SC884, [2007] PGSC 7; *James Pangnan and Patrick Ponat v The State* (2006) SCRA Nos. 39 and 54 of 2004 and *Glenn Lucena v The State* (2008) N3460.

- if an error of law cannot be identified, that there has been a manifest miscarriage of justice[1857].

An appellate Court is limited to:

- what was said at the time of sentence; and

- any omitted factors that the appellate Court considers to be important to sentence.[1858]

Although there may be no identifiable error, if the sentence is out of all reasonable proportion to the offence, and therefore plainly unjust[1859], there is an unidentifiable implied[1860] error.[1861]

A sentence may be excessive because the wrong type of sentence has been imposed.[1862]

1857 See *Gabriel Laku v The State* [1981] PNGLR 350.

See however: *Tremellan v R* [1973] PNGLR 116.

1858 See *Ura Francis Miriva v The State* (1981) SC197.

1859 See also: *House v R* (1936) 55 CLR 499 at 504-505 and *Markarian v R* (2005) 228 CLR 357 at 370-371.

1860 See *Young v The State of Western Australia* [2011] WASCA 13.

1861 See *Public Prosecutor v Tardrew* [1986] PNGLR 91, [1986] PGSC 10; *Mauwe Antape v The State* [1981] PNGLR 68; *William Norris v The State* [1979] PNGLR 605; *Gimble v The State* [1988-89] PNGLR 271 at 272; *The State v Ailya* [2007] PGSC 32; *Robert Solomon v The State* (2007) SC871; *Ben Wafia and others v The State* (2006) SC851, [2006] PGSC 19 and *Wesley Nobudi, John Evoa and Frank Yalikiti v The State* (2009) SC999, [2009] PGSC 20.

See also: *House v R* (1936) 55 CLR 499 at 504-505; *Markarian v R* (2005) 228 CLR 357 at 370-371; *Carroll v R* [2009] HCA 13 and *Dinsdale v R* (2000) 202 CLR 321, [2000] HCA 54.

1862 See *Dinsdale v R* (2000) 202 CLR 321 at 325, [2000] HCA 54.

APPEALS AGAINST SENTENCE

In order for an appellant to prove that a sentence was:

- manifestly excessive[1863], ie., the sentence imposed was so clearly beyond the range of discretionary sentences available as to show that some error must have been made although it cannot be identified[1864]; or

- manifestly inadequate[1865]

it must be shown that the sentencing Court:

- made a mistake as to the facts.[1866]

  It is necessary to establish that:

  - there is no evidence to support the finding;

  - the evidence is 'all one way'; or

  - the sentencing Court has misdirected itself.[1867]

[1863] See *Wanosa and others v R* [1971-72] PNGLR 90, [1971] PGSC 47; *Edmund Gima v The State; Siune Arnold v The State* (2003) SC730, [2003] PGSC 3; *Mary Bomai Michael v The State* (2004) SC737, [2004] PGSC 37; *Pemu Muro v The State* (2006) SC842, [2006] PGSC 11; *Paulus Mandatititip and another v The State* [1978] PNGLR 128 at 129, [1978] PGSC 5 and *Wilkeson, Stephens and Michalov v The State* [1967-68] PNGLR 112.

[1864] See *Vagh v The State of Western Australia* [2007] WASCA 17.

[1865] See *Kali Mari v The State* (1980) SC175; *Wanosa and others v R* [1971-72] PNGLR 90, [1971] PGSC 47; *Edmund Gima v The State; Siune Arnold v The State* (2003) SC730, [2003] PGSC 3; *Mary Bomai Michael v The State* (2004) SC737, [2004] PGSC 37; *Pemu Muro v The State* (2006) SC842, [2006] PGSC 11; *Paulus Mandatititip and another v The State* [1978] PNGLR 128 at 129, [1978] PGSC 5 and *Wilkeson, Stephens and Michalov v The State* [1967-68] PNGLR 112.

[1866] See *Masol Ailya v The State* [2007] PGSC 32; *William Norris v The State* [1979] PNGLR 605; *Wesley Nobudi, John Evoa and Frank Yalikiti v The State* (2009) SC999, [2009] PGSC 20 and *Wilkeson, Stephens and Michalov v The State* [1967-68] PNGLR 112.

See also: *House v R* (1936) 55 CLR 499 at 504-505; *Markarian v R* (2005) 228 CLR 357 at 370-371 and *R v Merritt* (2004) 59 NSWLR 557 at 573, [2004] NSWCCA 19.

[1867] See *R v O'Donoghue* (1988) 34 A Crim R 397 at 401 and *McBeth v R* [2009] NSWSCCA 235.

However, an appellate Court has no power to substitute its own findings for those of the sentencing Court[1868];

- allowed extraneous or irrelevant matters to guide or affect it[1869];
- did not take into account some material consideration or relevant matters.[1870]

A failure by a sentencing Court to expressly refer to all relevant factors in its sentencing remarks does not necessarily establish a failure to consider those factors[1871];

- did fail to give any or adequate weight or gave excessive weight to a relevant sentencing consideration.

An alleged failure by the sentencing Court to give any or adequate weight, or a complaint that the sentencing Court gave excessive weight, to a relevant sentencing consideration will only constitute an express appealable error if it amounts to a failure to exercise the discretion conferred on the Court.[1872]

It is very difficult to prove that a sentencing Court placed undue weight on, or failed adequately to take account of, relevant considerations.[1873]

[1868] See *R v O'Donoghue* (1988) 34 A Crim R 397 at 401.

[1869] See *Masol Ailya v The State* [2007] PGSC 32; *William Norris v The State* [1979] PNGLR 605 and *Wesley Nobudi, John Evoa and Frank Yalikiti v The State* (2009) SC999, [2009] PGSC 20.

See also: *House v R* (1936) 55 CLR 499 at 505 and *Markarian v R* (2005) 228 CLR 357 at 370-371.

[1870] See *Masol Ailya v The State* [2007] PGSC 32; *William Norris v The State* [1979] PNGLR 605; *Wesley Nobudi, John Evoa and Frank Yalikiti v The State* (2009) SC999, [2009] PGSC 20; *Muro v The State* (2006) SC842, [2006] PGSC 11; *Government of Papua New Guinea v McLeary* [1976] PNGLR 321 at 322-333 and *Paul Timiti v John Aubuku* (1983) N412(M).

See also: *House v R* (1936) 55 CLR 499 at 504-505 and *Markarian v R* (2005) 228 CLR 357 at 370-371.

[1871] See *Keating v The State of Western Australia* (2007) 35 WAR 1, [2007] WASCA 98.

[1872] See *Mallet v Mallet* (1984) 156 CLR 605 at 614, [1984] HCA 21; *Dinsdale v R* (2000) 202 CLR 321, [2000] HCA 54 and *Pedersen v The State of Western Australia* [2010] WASCA 175.

[1873] See *McKey v The State of Western Australia* [2010] WASCA 210.

Sentencing is a discretionary exercise and a failure of that kind will not give rise to an express appealable error, unless it was so significant as to lead to the conclusion that the sentencing Court failed to exercise the discretion entrusted to it[1874];

- acted on a wrong principle of law[1875];
- overlooked, undervalued or over-estimated some of the salient features of the evidence.[1876]

1874 See *Dinsdale v R* (2000) 202 CLR 321, [2000] HCA 54; *Mallet v Mallet* (1984) 156 CLR 605, per Gibbs CJ at 614; *Vagh v The State of Western Australia* [2007] WASCA 17; *Scook v R* [2008] WASCA 114; *Ponnusamy v The State of Western Australia* [2008] WASCA 224; *Speering v The State of Western Australia* [2008] WASCA 266 and *Keating v The State of Western Australia* [2007] WASCA 98.

1875 See *Wanosa and others v R* [1971-72] PNGLR 90, [1971] PGSC 47; *William Norris v The State* [1979] PNGLR 605; *Kali Mari v The State* (1980) SC175; *Ura Francis Miriva v The State* (1981) SC197; *The State v Ian Setep Napoleon* (2001) SC666; *Muro v The State* (2006) SC842, [2006] PGSC 11; *Simon Kama v The State* (2004) SC740, [2004] PGSC 32; *Denden Tom, Daniel Wilson and Samuel Tom v The State* (2008) SC967; *Edmund Gima v The State; Siune Arnold v The State* (2003) SC730, [2003] PGSC 3; *Mary Bomai Michael v The State* (2004) SC737, [2004] PGSC 37; *Wesley Nobudi, John Evoa and Frank Yalikiti v The State* (2009) SC999, [2009] PGSC 20; *Government of Papua New Guinea v McLeary* [1976] PNGLR 321 at 322-333; *Paul Timiti v John Aubuku* (1983) N412(M); *Public Prosecutor v Tardrew* [1986] PNGLR 91, [1986] PGSC 10; *Acting Public Prosecutor v Konis Haha* [1981] PNGLR 205; *The Public Prosecutor v Vangu'u Ame* [1983] PNGLR 424; *Pemu Muro v The State* (2006) SC842, [2006] PGSC 11; *Wilkeson, Stephens and Michalov v Grant* [1967-68] PNGLR 112 and *Masol Ailya v The State* [2007] PGSC 32.

See also: *R v Ball* (1951) 35 Cr App R 164; *Skinner v R* (1913) 16 CLR 336; *House v R* (1936) 55 CLR 499 at 504-505; *Markarian v R* (2005) 228 CLR 357 at 370-371 and *DPP v Fritz* [1969-1982] NLR 107, [1981] NRSC 1.

1876 See *Wanosa and others v R* [1971-72] PNGLR 90, [1971] PGSC 47; *William Norris v The State* [1979] PNGLR 605; *The State v Ian Setep Napoleon* (2001) SC666; *Muro v The State* (2006) SC842, [2006] PGSC 11; *Simon Kama v The State* (2004) SC740, [2004] PGSC 32; *Acting Public Prosecutor v Uname Aumane* [1980] PNGLR 510; *Denden Tom, Daniel Wilson and Samuel Tom v The State* (2008) SC967; *Edmund Gima v The State; Siune Arnold v The State* (2003) SC730, [2003] PGSC 3; *Mary Bomai Michael v The State* (2004) SC737, [2004] PGSC 37; *Wesley Nobudi, John Evoa and Frank Yalikiti v The State* (2009) SC999, [2009] PGSC 20; *Government of Papua New Guinea v McLeary* [1976] PNGLR 321 at 322-333; *Paul Timiti v John Aubuku* (1983) N412(M); *Masol Ailya v The State* [2007] PGSC 32; *Pemu Muro v The State* (2006) SC842, [2006] PGSC 11; *Public Prosecutor v Tardrew* [1986] PNGLR 91, [1986] PGSC 10; *The Public Prosecutor v Vangu'u Ame* [1983] PNGLR 424; *Acting Public Prosecutor v Konis Haha* [1981] PNGLR 205 and *Kali Mari v The State* (1980) SC175.

See also: *House v R* (1936) 55 CLR 499 at 504-505; *Markarian v R* (2005) 228 CLR 357 at 370-371 and *Skinner v R* (1913) 16 CLR 336.

A failure by a sentencing Court to expressly refer to all relevant factors in its sentencing remarks does not necessarily establish a failure to consider those factors[1877]; or

- misunderstood some salient features of the evidence[1878].

In order to determine whether there was a demonstrable error the following procedure should be applied[1879]:

- Were there any identifiable errors of law made by the sentencing Court?
- If yes, do the errors vitiate (ie., invalidate) the exercise of the sentencing Court's discretion?
- If it is a vitiating error, the sentence may be quashed and a substitute sentence passed.
- If there were no identifiable errors, is the sentence nonetheless obviously excessive (or inadequate)?
- If yes, the sentence may be quashed and a substitute sentence passed.
- If there were no identifiable errors and the sentence is not obviously excessive (or inadequate), the appellate Court will not form the opinion that some other sentence is warranted and the sentence should not be disturbed.

1877 See *Keating v The State of Western Australia* (2007) 35 WAR 1, [2007] WASCA 98.

1878 See *Acting Public Prosecutor v Uname Aumane* [1980] PNGLR 510.

See also: *Skinner v R* (1913) 16 CLR 336 at 340.

1879 See *Tony Mai v The State* (2008) SC903; *Joe Nawa v The State* (2007) SC1148, [2007] PGSC 50 and *Jack Mari v The State* (2007) SC1147, [2007] PGSC 49.

The discretion to increase a sentence:

- should be sparingly exercised; and
- only in cases where the sentence imposed by the sentencing Court was manifestly inadequate[1880];

  In determining whether a sentence is manifestly inadequate it is necessary to consider the following factors:

  - the maximum sentence prescribed by law for the offence;
  - the standards of sentencing customarily observed with respect to the offence;
  - the place that the criminal conduct occupies on the scale of seriousness of offences of that type; and
  - the personal circumstances of the accused person[1881];
- may be exercised either:
  - on the appellate Court's own initiative[1882]; or
  - upon an application by the State Prosecutor at the hearing of the appellant's appeal against sentence[1883]; and

---

[1880] See *Kailaysur v The State of Mauritius* [2004] 1 WLR 2316, [2004] UKPC 23.

[1881] See *Chan v R* (1989) 38 A Crim R 337 at 342 and *Scook v R* (2008) 185 A Crim R 164, [2008] WASCA 114.

[1882] See *Sakarowa Koe v The State* (2004) SC739, [2004] PGSC 33; *Joseph Nimagi, Tom Gurua Kerui and David Bawai Laiam v The State* (2004) SC741, [2004] PGSC 31; *Kepa Wanege v The State* (2004) SC742, [2004] PGSC 22; *Masolyau Piakali v The State* (2004) SC771, [2004] PGSC 20; *Irai Thomas v The State* (2007) SC867; *Richard Liri v The State* (2007) SC883, [2007] PGSC 3; *Joe Giamur v The State* (2007) SC884, [2007] PGSC 7; *James Pangnan and Patrick Ponat v The State* (2006) SCRA Nos. 39 & 54 of 2004 and *Lawrence Hindemba v The State* (1998) SC593, [1999] PGSC 48.

[1883] See *Lawrence Hindemba v The State* (1998) SC593, [1999] PGSC 48.

- should not be exercised, unless the appellant is given an opportunity to be heard on the option[1884].

If it is an appeal by an accused person then he or she should be given an opportunity to seek leave of the appellate Court to withdraw his or her application, rather than being sentenced to an increased penalty.[1885]

Irrespective in all cases the reasons for exercising this power should be explained.[1886]

A Court resentencing an accused person after an appeal should consider the following factors:

- any guidelines or suggestions of the appellate Court accompanying the remittance[1887];

- the usual sentencing guidelines for sentencing in the particular kind of offence under consideration, but within the guidelines or suggestions of the appellate Court[1888];

- subject to any guidelines, directions or suggestions of the appellate Court, the factors prevailing at the time of the earlier sentence[1889];

- unless the accused person shows good cause in terms of the factors for and against him or her, warranting a decision other than the one previously arrived at, the second sentencing Court should be careful not to readily and substantially differ from its earlier sentence[1890]; and

---

1884 See *Lawrence Hindemba v The State* (1998) SC593, [1999] PGSC 48.

See also: *Williams v The State* [2005] 1 WLR 1948, [2005] UKPC 11 and *Skeete v The State* [2003] UKPC 82.

1885 See *Williams v The State* [2005] 1 WLR 1948, [2005] UKPC 11 and *Skeete v The State* [2003] UKPC 82.

1886 See *Kailaysur v The State of Mauritius* [2004] 1 WLR 2316, [2004] UKPC 23.

1887 See *The State v Moki Lepi (No. 3)* (2004) N2734.

1888 See *The State v Moki Lepi (No. 3)* (2004) N2734.

1889 See *The State v Moki Lepi (No. 3)* (2004) N2734.

1890 See *The State v Moki Lepi (No. 3)* (2004) N2734.

- the second sentencing Court should start with the proposition that the accused person should not ordinarily receive a harsher sentence than initially imposed[1891].

The delay in hearing an appeal is a relevant factor in determining whether a sentence should be increased.[1892]

[2.0] DISPARITY IN SENTENCING

Equal justice requires that, as between co-accused, there should not be a marked disparity in sentencing to the extent that is possible with all things being more or less equal between co-accused[1893].

Otherwise, there may be a justifiable sense of grievance[1894]:

- in the sense that a co-accused has a justifiable feeling of dissatisfaction and injustice[1895]; and
- the appearance in the mind of an objective observer that justice has not been done[1896].

1891 See *R v Peterson* [1999] 2 Qd R 85; *R v Miers* (1994) 11 CRNZ 307 at 313; *R v Gilmore* (1979) 1 A Crim R 416, per Street CJ at 419; *R v Bedford* [1986] 5 NSWLR 711, per Street CJ at 714; *R v Moore* [1999] NZCA 274 and *Stoves v R* [2005] NZCA 119.

1892 See *Acting Public Prosecutor v Mailai [*1981] PNGLR 258, [1981] PGSC 7.

1893 See *Pemu Muro v The State* (2006) SC842, [2006] PGSC 11; *Secretary for Law v Binengim* [1975] PNGLR 172, [1975] PGSC 30 and *The State v Gurua* (2002) N2312, [2002] PGNC 41.

See also: *Lowe v R* (1984) 154 CLR 606 at 617-618, [1984] HCA 46; *Postiglione v R* (1997) 189 CLR 295, (1998) 71 ALJR 875, [1997] HCA 26; *R v Kollas and Mitchell* [2002] NSWCCA 491, per Wood CJ at CL and *R v Fawcett* (1983) 5 Cr App R (S) 158.

1894 See *Lowe v R* (1984) 154 CLR 606, per Brennan J at 617-618, [1984] HCA 46 and *Postiglione v R* (1997) 189 CLR 295, (1998) 71 ALJR 875, [1997] HCA 26.

1895 See *Andrew Uramani and others v The State* [1996] PNGLR 287 at 290-291, [1996] PGSC 33; *Winugini Urugitaru v R* [1974] PNGLR 283 at 286-287, [1974] PGSC 38 and *Ian Napoleon Setep v The State* (2001) SC666, [2001] PGSC 14.

1896 See *Postiglione v R* (1997) 189 CLR 295, per Dawson and Gaudron JJ at 301-303 and Kirby J at 338, (1998) 71 ALJR 875, [1997] HCA 26; *R v Kollas and Mitchell* [2002] NSWCCA 491; *Lowe v R* (1984) 154 CLR 606, [1984] HCA 46; *R v Taudevin* [1996] 2 VR 402 at 404, [1996] VICSC 7 and *England v R; Phanith v R* [2009] NSWCCA 274.

Whether there is a justifiable sense of grievance it has to be determined:

- 'objectively'; and
- by reference to the application and effect of other relevant sentencing principles, including the 'totality principle'.[1897]

However, disparity between sentences is not of itself a basis of appellate intervention, but a factor to be weighed when the appellate Court considers:

- whether the sentencing process has been attended by error; and, if so
- whether the appellate Court should intervene.[1898]

For a sense of grievance to be justifiable, the difference between the sentences must be manifestly excessive.[1899]

Notwithstanding that equal justice requires that like co-accused should be treated alike if there are relevant differences due allowance should be made for them.[1900]

The application and effect of relevant sentencing principles must be taken into account in determining whether there is a legitimate or justifiable sense of grievance.[1901]

There are justifiable grounds or reasons for disparity in sentences as long as this is clearly explained by the sentencing Court.[1902]

If there are factors that support different sentences being imposed on co-accused then there can be no justifiable sense of grievance on the part of an appellant who receives the heavier sentence[1903], provided that the sentences are imposed in accordance with the relevant sentencing principles.

[1897] See *Nguyen v The State of Western Australia* [2009] WASCA 8.

[1898] See *R v Li* [2005] NSWCCA 154.

[1899] See *Lowe v R* (1984) 154 CLR 606, per Dawson J at 624, [1984] HCA 46.

[1900] See *Postiglione v R* (1997) 189 CLR 295, per Dawson and Gaudron JJ at 301, (1998) 71 ALJR 875, [1997] HCA 26.

[1901] See *Jardim v The State of Western Australia* [2011] WASCA 83.

[1902] See *Max Sanawi v The State* (2010) SC1076.

[1903] See *R v Cox* (1996) 66 SASR 152, per Doyle CJ at 159.

A proper relationship should be established between the sentences passed on each co-accused[1904] whilst taking into consideration any relevant differences in circumstances[1905], including:

- the degree of culpability of each co-accused in the commission of the offence[1906].

  A sentencing Court should consider the overall criminality involved and then consider the part played by each accused person in that overall criminality[1907];

- whether the sentence imposed on a co-accused was wholly inadequate[1908];

[1904] See *Adifaka v DPP* [1984] SILR 44 at 50 and *Jardim v The State of Western Australia* [2011] WASCA 83.

[1905] See *R v Coe* [1969] 1 All ER 65, (1969) 53 Cr App R 66, [1968] 1 WLR 1950.

See also: *Postiglione v R* (1997) 189 CLR 295 at 301-303 and 342-343, (1998) 71 ALJR 875, [1997] HCA 26; *Lowe v R* (1984) 154 CLR 606 at 610, 613 and 623, [1984] HCA 46; *Van der Worp v R* [2000] WASCA 154; *McPherson v R* [2002] WACA 287; *Ilam v Dando* [1999] WASCA 129, (1999) 109 A Crim R 47; *R v Reaves* [2004] WASCA 106, (2004) 147 A Crim R 26; *Melgar Sevilla v R* [2007] WASCA 116; *Goddard v R* [1999] WASCA 281 and *R v Cox* (1996) 66 SASR 152.

[1906] See *Ian Napoleon Setep v The State* (2001) SC666, [2001] PGSC 14; *The State v Tony Pandau Hahuahoru (No. 2)* (2002) N2186; *The State v Gurua* (2002) N2312, [2002] PGNC 41, *Andrew Uramani and others v The State* [1996] PNGLR 287, [1996] PGSC 33 and *Winugini Urugitaru v R* [1974] PNGLR 283 at 286, [1974] PGSC 38.

See also: *Lowe v R* (1984) 154 CLR 606, [1984] HCA 46; *Postiglione v R* (1997) 189 CLR 295, (1998) 71 ALJR 875, [1997] HCA 26; *R v Kollas and Mitchell* [2002] NSWCCA 491, per Wood CJ at CL; *R v MacGowan* (1986) 42 SASR 580, per King CJ at 582-583; *R v Olbrich* (1999) 199 CLR 270, [1999] HCA 54; *R v Coe* [1969] 1 All ER 65, (1969) 53 Cr App R 66, [1969] 1 All ER 65, [1968] 1 WLR 1950; *Van der Worp v R* [2000] WASCA 154 and *McPherson v R* [2002] WACA 287.

Refer also to the section titled 'Role Played In The Commission Of The Offence' in the chapter titled 'Extenuating Circumstances'.

[1907] See *R v Wright* (1991) 7 CRNZ 624.

[1908] See *R v Coe* (1969) 53 Cr App R 66, [1969] 1 All ER 65, per Parker LCJ at 68-69.

See also: *Postiglione v R* (1997) 189 CLR 295, (1998) 71 ALJR 875, [1997] HCA 26; *Lowe v R* (1984) 154 CLR 606 at 617, [1984] HCA 46 and *R v Chamings* [2009] SASC 82.

Refer also to the chapter titled 'Inequality In Sentencing'.

- whether there are differences in the character and antecedents of the co-accused[1909], including whether a co-accused:
    - has a prior conviction[1910]; or
    - is otherwise of good character[1911];
- the age of each co-accused[1912], including whether a co-accused is:

[1909] See *Ian Napoleon Setep v The State* (2001) SC666, [2001] PGSC 14; *Winugini Urugitaru v R* [1974] PNGLR 283 at 286, [1974] PGSC 38 and *Andrew Uramani and others v The State* [1996] PNGLR 287, [1996] PGSC 33.

See also: *Lowe v R* (1984) 154 CLR 606, per Brennan J at 617, [1984] HCA 46 and *Postiglione v R* (1997) 189 CLR 295, per Kirby J at 338, (1998) 71 ALJR 875, [1997] HCA 26.

Refer also to:
- the section titled 'Character And Antecedents' in the chapter titled 'Aggravating Factors'; and
- the section titled 'Good Character Generally' in the chapter titled 'Mitigating Factors'.

[1910] See *The State v Tony Pandau Hahuahoru (No. 2)* (2002) N2186; *The State v Gurua* (2002) N2312, [2002] PGNC 41 and *The State v Frank Suwari* (2001) N2173.

See also: *Lowe v R* (1984) 154 CLR 606, [1984] HCA 46; *Postiglione v R* (1997) 189 CLR 295, (1998) 71 ALJR 875, [1997] HCA 26 and *R v Kollas and Mitchell* [2002] NSWCCA 491, per Wood CJ at CL.

Refer also to the section titled 'Criminal History' in the chapter titled 'Mitigating Factors'.

[1911] See *Andrew Uramani and others v The State* [1996] PNGLR 287, [1996] PGSC 33.

See also: *Diema v The Republic of Nauru* [1969-1982] NLR 50, [1976] NRSC 4.

[1912] See *The State v Yuanis Ipiri* (2008) N3512, [2008] PGNC 159; *The State v Juvenile "D"* (2008) N3508, [2008] PGNC 153 and *The State v Tupis Tom; The State v Nathan Bobi (No. 2)* (2009) N3675, [2009] PGNC 65.

See also: *Lowe v R* (1984) 154 CLR 606, [1984] HCA 46; *Postiglione v R* (1997) 189 CLR 295, (1998) 71 ALJR 875, [1997] HCA 26 and *R v Kollas and Mitchell* [2002] NSWCCA 491, per Wood CJ at CL.

  - a juvenile[1913]; or
  - of advanced age[1914];
- whether a co-accused has shown genuine remorse[1915];
- the rehabilitation prospects of each co-accused[1916];
- any other 'aggravating factors'[1917];
- any 'extenuating circumstances'[1918].

[1913] See *R v C (A Child)* (1995) 83 A Crim R 561.

A sentence imposed in a Juvenile Court should be taken into consideration, see *R v Boney* [2001] NSWCCA 432.

A grievance will not be justifiable where the disparity arises solely or primarily because adult co-accused persons and juvenile co-accused persons are sentenced under different legislative schemes, see *R v WT; ex parte Attorney-General (Queensland)* [2007] QCA 310; *R v Tuki* [2004] QCA 482; *R v Crossley* (1999) 106 A Crim R 80; [1999] QCA 223; *R v Harris (No. 2)* (1971) 2 SASR 255; *R v Homer* (1976) 13 SASR 377; *R v C (A Child)* (1995) 83 A Crim R 561 and *Penny v R* [1999] WASCA 1059.

Refer also to the section titled 'Youthfulness' in the chapter titled 'Mitigating Factors'.

[1914] Refer also to the section titled 'Advanced Age' in the chapter titled 'Mitigating Factors'.

[1915] See *Lowe v R* (1984) 154 CLR 606, [1984] HCA 46; *Postiglione v R* (1997) 189 CLR 295, (1998) 71 ALJR 875, [1997] HCA 26 and *R v Kollas and Mitchell* [2002] NSWCCA 491, per Wood CJ at CL.

Refer also to the section titled 'Plea Of Guilty' in the chapter titled 'Mitigating Factors' and the section titled 'No Remorse' in the chapter titled 'Aggravating Factors'.

[1916] See *Lowe v R* (1984) 154 CLR 606, [1984] HCA 46; *Postiglione v R* (1997) 189 CLR 295, (1998) 71 ALJR 875, [1997] HCA 26 and *R v Kollas and Mitchell* [2002] NSWCCA 491, per Wood CJ at CL.

Refer also to the section titled 'The Need For Reformation And Rehabilitation' in the chapter titled 'Objectives And Purposes Of Sentencing'.

[1917] See *The State v Frank Suwari* (2001) N2173.

See also: *R v MacGowan* (1986) 42 SASR 580, per King CJ at 582-583.

Refer also to the chapter titled 'Aggravating Factors'.

[1918] Refer also to the chapter titled 'Extenuating Circumstances'.

However, the benefit of an 'extenuating circumstance' is only to be applied to the accused person who is entitled to such a benefit in sentencing; and

- any other 'mitigating factors'.[1919]

  However, the benefit of a 'mitigating factor' is only to be applied to the accused person who is entitled to such a benefit in sentencing.[1920]

Furthermore, material in favour of or against a co-accused should not be used to the disadvantage of another co-accused, unless it is properly admissible in the proceedings against that co-accused.[1921]

A sentencing Court should:

- identify any relevant differences between the circumstances of each of the co-accused; and
- give reasons explaining any disparity between:
  - the sentence which it imposes; and
  - the earlier sentence imposed on a co-accused.[1922]

It is the failure to explain the disparity that often smacks of injustice and unfairness when two people or groups of people charged with the same offence and appearing at the same time or at different times, but are punished differently from each other that give rise to justifiable grievance that an appellate Court must rectify upon being satisfied that there was a clear error.[1923]

[1919] See *The State v Frank Suwari* (2001) N2173.

See also: *R v MacGowan* (1986) 42 SASR 580, per King CJ at 582-583.

Refer also to the chapter titled 'Mitigating Factors'.

[1920] See *R v Coffey* (1982) 74 Cr App R 168; *Attorney-General's References Nos. 62, 63 and 64 of 1995; R v O'Halloran and others* [1996] 2 Cr App R (S) 233 and *Attorney-General's Reference No. 73 of 1999; R v Charles* [2000] 2 Cr App R (S) 210.

[1921] See *R v Noffke* [1999] QCA 340.

[1922] See *Max Sanawi v The State* (2010) SC1076, [2010] PGSC 31.

See also: *R v MacGowan* (1986) 42 SASR 580, per King CJ at 583.

[1923] See *Max Sanawi v The State* (2010) SC1076.

The fact that a co-accused person feels a sense of grievance is not determinative.[1924]

The test to be applied is 'objective', and not 'subjective'.[1925]

In considering whether there is 'objectionable' disparity the question to be asked is:

- 'Would right-thinking members of the public, with full knowledge of the relevant facts and circumstances, learning of the sentence consider that something had gone wrong with the administration of justice?'[1926]; or

- 'Whether a reasonable person looking at the circumstances of the case would regard the grievance of the accused person as being justified?'[1927]

It is immaterial that proceedings have not been instituted against all co-accused.[1928]

Furthermore, the 'parity principle' does not apply to sentences imposed on a co-accused with similar characteristics who have committed similar offences.[1929]

1924 See *Postiglione v R* (1997) 189 CLR 295, per Kirby J at 338, (1998) 71 ALJR 875, [1997] HCA 26 and *MGM v The State of Western Australia* [2012] WASCA 24.

1925 See *Postiglione v R* (1997) 189 CLR 295, per Kirby J at 338, (1998) 71 ALJR 875, [1997] HCA 26; *R v Kollas and Mitchell* [2002] NSWCCA 491, per Wood CJ at CL; *R v Ilbay* [2000] NSWCCA 251; *R v Wei Pan* [2005] NSWCCA 114; *Lewins v R* [2007] NSWCCA 189; *Nguyen v R* [2008] NSWCCA 308; *Gurney v R; Willetts v R* [2011] NSWCCA 48; *Pavicevic v R* [2010] ACTCA 25; *Dwayhi v R; Bechara v R* [2011] NSWCCA 67 and *R v Pan* [2005] NSWCCA 114.

1926 See *R v Pitson* (1972) 56 Cr App R 391.

See also: *R v Fawcett* (1983) 5 Cr App R (S) 158.

1927 See *Postiglione v R* (1997) 189 CLR 295, per Dawson and Gaudron JJ at 301, (1998) 71 ALJR 875, [1997] HCA 26; *R v Ilbay* [2000] NSWCCA 251; *R v Kollas and Mitchell* [2002] NSWCCA 491, per Wood CJ at CL and *R v Pan* [2005] NSWCCA 114, per Johnson J.

1928 See *R v Caird* (1970) 54 Cr App R 499.

See also: *Igi v R* [1997] SBHC 39.

1929 See *R v Ellis* (1993) 68 A Crim R 449, per Hunt CJ at CL at 461.

See also: *R v Morgan* (1993) 70 A Crim R 368 at 371; *R v F* (2002) 132 A Crim R 308 at 315, [2002] NSWCCA 320; *R v George* (2004) 149 A Crim R 38 at 47, [2004] NSWCCA 247; *R v Singh* [2001] NSWCCA 424 and *R v Araya* [2005] NSWCCA 283.

The fact that one co-accused received too short a sentence is not a ground to lead an appellate Court to necessarily interfere with a longer sentence passed on another co-accused.[1930]

An appellate Court's power to intervene to redress disparity is discretionary and it will not necessarily act where the sentence of a co-accused is inadequate.[1931]

The 'parity principle' may be applied to reduce the sentence of a co-accused by reference to the sentence imposed on another co-accused where the co-accused have been participants in a common criminal enterprise, even though they have not been charged or found guilty of committing precisely the same offence or offences.[1932]

Where there is a degree of disparity so as to invite a reduction in the sentence imposed, it is not necessary for an appellate Court to intervene if the result of doing so is to produce a sentence disproportionate to the objective and subjective criminality involved. A stage can be reached at which the inadequacy of the sentence imposed upon the co-accused is so great that the sense of grievance engendered can no longer be regarded as a legitimate one.[1933]

The 'parity principle' does not compel a Court to:

- impose the same inadequate sentence; or
- impose an even more lenient sentence, if the circumstances of the accused person are less serious.[1934]

[1930] See *Winugini Urugitaru v R* [1974] PNGLR 283 and *Pemu Muro v The State* (2006) SC842, [2006] PGSC 11.

[1931] See *Lewins v R* [2007] NSWCCA 189.

[1932] See *Jimmy v R* (2010) 240 FLR 27, [2010] NSWCCA 60; *Dwayhi v R* (2011) 205 A Crim R 274, [2011] NSWCCA 67; *Farrugia v R* [2011] VSCA 24; *DPP (Commonwealth) v Gregory* (2011) 250 FLR 169, [2011] VSCA 145 and *Tomov v R* [2011] WASCA 189.

[1933] See *R v Boney* [2001] NSWCCA 432; *Lewins v R* [2007] NSWCCA 189; *Nguyen v R* [2008] NSWCCA 308; *Gurney v R; Willetts v R* [2011] NSWCCA 48; *Pavicevic v R* [2010] ACTCA 25; *R v Wei Pan* [2005] NSWCCA 114 and *Dwayhi v R; Bechara v R* [2011] NSWCCA 67.

[1934] See *Green v R; Quinn v R* [2011] HCA 49; *R v MacGowan* (1986) 42 SASR 580 at 583; *I (a child) v The State of Western Australia* [2006] WASCA 9; *Billing v The State of Western Australia [No. 2]* [2008] WASCA 11; *Hassan v The State of Western Australia* [2006] WASCA 139 and *MGM v The State of Western Australia* [2012] WASCA 24.

To do either of these things may result in the imposition of a sentence on an accused person that is:

- unacceptable to the public conscience; or
- a shock to the public conscience.[1935]

[3.0] SUPREME COURT OF JUSTICE

An accused person may, with leave of the Court[1936], appeal his or her sentence in the National Court to the Supreme Court.[1937]

An appellant must always bear in mind the risk that the sentence may be increased on appeal.[1938]

The prosecution may appeal to the Supreme Court a sentence imposed in the National Court whether in its appellate or original jurisdiction[1939], provided that the sentence is manifestly inadequate[1940].

[1935] See *Green v R; Quinn v R* [2011] HCA 49; *R v MacGowan* (1986) 42 SASR 580 at 583; *I (a child) v The State of Western Australia* [2006] WASCA 9; *Billing v The State of Western Australia [No. 2]* [2008] WASCA 11; *Hassan v The State of Western Australia* [2006] WASCA 139 and *MGM v The State of Western Australia* [2012] WASCA 24.

[1936] See section 29 of the *Supreme Court Act* (Ch. 37) ['Time For Appealing Under Division 3'].

See also: *Jim Kas, Frank Faibison, Michael Jim and Rodney Tongau v The State* (1999) SC772, [1999] PGSC 32; *Masol Ailya v The State* [2007] PGSC 32 and *Porewa Wani v The State* [1979] PNGLR 593, [1979] PGSC 30.

[1937] See section 22(d) of the *Supreme Court Act* (Ch. 37) ['Criminal Appeals'].

[1938] See *Saki v The State* [1980] PNGLR 33.

[1939] See section 24(2) of the *Supreme Court Act* (Ch. 37) ['Appeal By Public Prosecutor Against Sentence'].

[1940] See *Lawrence Hindemba v The State* (1998) SC593, [1999] PGSC 48.

See also: *Kailaysur v The State of Mauritius* [2004] 1 WLR 2316, [2004] UKPC 23.

APPEALS AGAINST SENTENCE

The *Supreme Court Act* (Ch. 37) does not impose a time limit on the Public Prosecutor's right to appeal provided by section 24(2) of that Act. It is only necessary that the Public Prosecutor file their appeal with all convenient speed.[1941]

Upon an appeal the Supreme Court may:

- increase; or
- decrease

the initial sentence of an accused person[1942], whether:

- upon a not guilty plea; or
- after a guilty plea[1943],

provided that it is:

- manifestly inadequate; or
- manifestly excessive[1944].

The Supreme Court does not have to consider whether a miscarriage of justice has actually occurred.[1945]

[1941] See *Alois Erebebe and Taros Togot v The State* (2013) SC1228, [2013] PGSC 9.

[1942] See section 23(4) of the *Supreme Court Act* (Ch. 37) ['Determination Of Appeals In Ordinary Cases'].

[1943] See *Lawrence Hindemba v The State* (1998) SC593, [1999] PGSC 48.

See also: *Rex v Ettridge* [1909] 2 KB 24 at 29.

[1944] See *Lawrence Hindemba v The State* (1998) SC593, [1999] PGSC 48.

See also: *Griffiths v R* (1977) 137 CLR 293 at 310, 327 and 329-330; *Everett v R* (1994) 181 CLR 295 at 300, (1994) 68 ALJR 875, (1994) 124 ALR 529 and *R v Melano; ex parte Attorney-General* [1995] 2 Qd R 186 at 189.

[1945] See *Tremellan v R* [1973] PNGLR 116.

The Supreme Court may:

- review the exercise of the sentencing discretion within the context of the circumstances of the particular case; and
- fix guidelines or tariff for sentence for a particular kind or category of offences.[1946]

[4.0] NATIONAL COURT OF JUSTICE

An accused person may appeal his or her sentence in the District Court to the National Court.[1947]

The prosecution may appeal to the National Court against any decision of the District Court as to sentence in respect of any indictable offence triable summarily under section 420 of the *Criminal Code* (Ch. 262).[1948]

Upon an appeal against sentence the National Court may:

- increase; or
- decrease

the initial sentence of an accused person[1949], whether:

- upon a not guilty plea; or
- after a guilty plea[1950].

[1946] See *Lialu v The State* [1990] PNGLR 487, [1990] PGSC 16.

Refer also to the chapter titled 'Comparative Sentences'.

[1947] See section 219(1) of the *District Courts Act* (Ch. 40) ['Appeal To National Court'].

[1948] See section 219(4) of the *District Courts Act* (Ch. 40) ['Appeal To National Court'].

[1949] See section 210(1)(b) of the *District Courts Act* (Ch. 40) ['Information Praying For Surety To Be Of Good Behaviour'].

[1950] See *Lawrence Hindemba v The State* (1998) SC593, [1999] PGSC 48.

See also: *Rex v Ettridge* [1909] 2 KB 24 at 29.

APPEALS AGAINST SENTENCE

An appeal shall be allowed only if it appears to the National Court that there has been a substantial miscarriage of justice[1951], ie., the sentence was either:

- manifestly inadequate[1952]; or
- manifestly excessive[1953].

The written report[1954] of the presiding magistrate should be as comprehensive as possible[1955], thereby enabling the National Court to know what occurred in the District Court[1956].

The general rule is that where there is a dispute as to what occurred in the District Court the National Court will accept the written report of the presiding magistrate.[1957]

1951 See section 230(2) of the *District Courts Act* (Ch. 40) ['Power Of National Court On Appeal'].

See also: *Pius Embari v Senior Constable Wangiwa* (1973) No. 751 and *Vagi Gau v Kenkone Eava* (1976) No. 67.

1952 See *Lawrence Hindemba v The State* (1998) SC593, [1999] PGSC 48 and *Pius Embari v Senior Constable Wangivoa* (1973) No. 751.

See also: *Kailaysur v The State of Mauritius* [2004] 1 WLR 2316, [2004] UKPC 23.

1953 See *Lawrence Hindemba v The State* (1998) SC593, [1999] PGSC 48; *Paulus Mandatititip and another v The State* [1978] PNGLR 128 at 129, [1978] PGSC 5 and *Enga Kilu v John Moroby* (1980) N246.

As regards a sentence in excess of the maximum penalty, see *Apa Kokoti and others* (1997) N1597 and *Joseph Kembu v Eko, Mason* [1971-72] PNGLR 407 at 413.

1954 See also: section 225 of the *District Courts Act* (Ch. 40) ['Report By Magistrate'].

1955 See *Appeal of McCallum* [1975] PNGLR 439 at 444.

1956 See *Benson Bareto v Donatus Kilimito* [1990] PNGLR 125.

1957 See *Leonard Eliza v Mandina* [1971-72] PNGLR 422 at 424 and *Yamore Memera v Matthew Bisang* [1976] PNGLR 419.

APPEALS AGAINST SENTENCE

[5.0] PROSECUTION[1958]

The following special considerations apply in relation to appeals against sentence by the prosecution:

- the prosecution is concerned with establishing matters of principle, including manifest inadequacy or inconsistency in sentencing trends[1959], for the governance and guidance of Courts[1960];

[1958] See also: *Lacey v Attorney-General of Queensland* [2011] HCA 10; *Peel v R* (1971) 125 CLR 447 at 452; *Griffiths v R* (1977) 137 CLR 293 at 310; *Whitaker v R* (1928) 41 CLR 230 at 248; *Malvaso v R* (1989) 168 CLR 227 at 234; *R v Grein* [1989] WAR 178 at 180; *R v Peterson* [1984] WAR 329 at 330-331; *R v Clarke* [1996] 2 VR 520 at 522-523; *Police v Etelagi* [2001] WSCA 2; *R v Tait* (1979) 24 ALR 473 at 477, (1979) 46 FLR 386 at 388-389; *R v Wilson* (1981) 28 SASR 362; *R v Allpass* (1993) 72 A Crim R 561 at 562-563 and 565; *R v Osenkowski* (1982) 30 SASR 212 at 212-213; *R v Jermyn* [1985] 2 NSWLR 194, (1985) 16 A Crim R 269; *R v Qi* (1998) 102 A Crim R 172; *R v Fletcher-Jones* (1994) 75 A Crim R 381; *Attorney-General v Roy* (1972) 18 CRNS 89; *Sutherland* (1974) 10 NRB (2d) 221; *R v MacArthur* (1978) 39 CCC (2d) 158; *R v Agozzino* [1970] 1 CCC 380; *R v Tipene* [2000] NZCA 358; *The State of Western Australia v Cameron* [2004] WASCA 299; *The State of Western Australia v Marchese* [2006] WASCA 153; *The State of Western Australia v Houston* [2005] WASCA 167; *Liddington v The State of Western Australia* [2005] WASCA 60 and *R v Dowie* [1989] Tas R 167 at 180.

Refer also to:
- section 17 of the Office of the Public Prosecutor, Prosecution Policy (2006); and
- The Law Reform Commission of Ireland, 1993, 'Consultation Paper on Sentencing', Chapter 14.

[1959] See *Everett v R* (1994) 181 CLR 295 at 300, [1994] HCA 49.

[1960] See *Griffiths v R* (1977) 137 CLR 293, per Barwick CJ at 308 and Jacobs J at 326-327 and *R v Wall* [2002] NSWCCA 42.

- such appeals should generally only be brought in a rare and exceptional case[1961], such as where there has been a clear error of principle identified[1962] and including those sentences that are manifestly inadequate[1963], but not in borderline cases[1964]; and
- the notion of 'double jeopardy[1965]' in the sense that the sentence imposed may be increased[1966].

The conduct of the prosecution at the original sentencing proceedings is a matter of significance that the appellate Court may consider.[1967]

1961 See *The State of Western Australia v Houston* [2005] WASCA 167 and *GAS v R* (2004) 217 CLR 198, [2004] HCA 22.

1962 See *Acting Public Prosecutor v Konis Haha* [1981] PNGLR 205.

See also: *R v Baker* [2000] NSWCCA 85 and *R v Wall* [2002] NSWCCA 42.

1963 See *Public Prosecutor v Willy Moke Soki* [1977] PNGLR 165.

See also: *Everett v R* (1994) 181 CLR 295 at 299, (1994) 68 ALJR 875, (1994) 124 ALR 529; *Dinsdale v R* (2000) 202 CLR 321 at 340, [2000] HCA 54 and *R v Wall* [2002] NSWCCA 42.

1964 See *R v Cargill* [1990] 2 NZLR 138 at 140.

1965 Refer also to the chapter titled 'Double Jeopardy' in the text titled 'Injia on Criminal Practice and Procedure in Papua New Guinea and the Pacific'.

1966 See *R v Peterson* [1984] WAR 329.

See however: *R v Holder and Johnston* [1983] 3 NSWLR 245 at 256, *Dinsdale v R* (2000) 202 CLR 321 at 340, [2000] HCA 54 and *R v Wall* [2002] NSWCCA 42.

1967 See *GAS v R* (2004] 217 CLR 198, [2004] HCA 22; *Allpass* (1993) 72 A Crim R 561 at 562-563 and *R v Clarke* [1996] 2 VR 520 at 522, [1996] VicSC 30.

INDEX

Page

A

INDEX

Page

A

B

C

INDEX

Page

C

D

E

INDEX

Page

E

F

G

H

INDEX

Page

INDEX

INDEX

INDEX

Page

S

INDEX

Page

T

U

V

W

Y

www.ingramcontent.com/pod-product-compliance
Lightning Source LLC
Jackson TN
JSHW062338160926
108328JS00012B/23
9789980879004